SOCIAL SKILLS TRAINING

SOCIAL
SKILLS TRAINING

*A Practical Handbook for Assessment
and Treatment*

Edited by

JAMES P. CURRAN / PETER M. MONTI

Veterans Administration Medical Center/
Brown University Medical School

THE GUILFORD PRESS
New York   London

©1982 The Guilford Press, New York
A Division of Guilford Publications, Inc.
200 Park Avenue South, New York, N.Y. 10003

Printed in the United States of America

LIBRARY OF CONGRESS CATALOGING IN PUBLICATION DATA
Main entry under title:
Social skills training.
"Based in part on papers delivered at a symposium on social competence and psychiatric disorders . . . in May of 1980 in Providence, Rhode Island."—Pref.
Bibliography: p.
Includes indexes.
Contents: pt. 1. Social skills training with schizophrenics: Social skills training and the nature of schizophrenia / Robert Paul Liberman, Keith Nuechterlein and Charles J. Wallace—The social skills training project of the Mental Health Clinical Research Center for the Study of Schizophrenia / Charles J. Wallace—Maintenance and generalization issues in skills training . . . / Murray Brown—[etc.]
1. Social skills—Psychological aspects—Congresses. 2. Mentally ill—Rehabilitation—Congresses. 3. Schizophrenics—Rehabilitation—Congresses. 4. Family psychotherapy—Congresses. I. Curran, James P. II. Monti, Peter M. [DNLM: 1.Interpersonal relations—Congresses. 2. Mental disorders—Rehabilitation—Congresses. HM 132 S679 1980]
RC489.S63S63   616.89'1   81-6374
ISBN 0-89862-610-2

CONTRIBUTORS

ALAN S. BELLACK, PhD, Clinical Psychology Center, University of Pittsburgh, Pittsburgh, Pennsylvania

ROBERT BOICE, PhD, Department of Psychology, State University of New York at Albany, Albany, New York

JEFFREY L. BOYD, PhD, Department of Psychiatry and the Behavioral Sciences, University of Southern California School of Medicine, Los Angeles, California

MURRAY BROWN, MD, Mental Health and Behavioral Sciences Education, Sepulveda Veterans Administration Medical Center, Sepulveda, California, and Department of Psychiatry, UCLA School of Medicine, Los Angeles, California

ANTHONY J. CONGER, PhD, Department of Psychological Sciences, Purdue University, West Lafayette, Indiana

JUDITH C. CONGER, PhD, Department of Psychological Sciences, Purdue University, West Lafayette, Indiana

DONALD P. CORRIVEAU, PhD, Veterans Administration Medical Center/Brown University Medical School, Providence, Rhode Island

JAMES P. CURRAN, PhD, Veterans Administration Medical Center/Brown University Medical School, Providence, Rhode Island

IAN R. H. FALLOON, MB, CHB, MRCPSYCH, Department of Psychiatry and the Behavioral Sciences, University of Southern California School of Medicine, Los Angeles, California

DORAN C. FRENCH, PhD, Department of Educational Psychology, University of Wisconsin, Madison, Wisconsin

MICHEL HERSEN, PhD, Western Psychiatric Institute and Clinic, University of Pittsburgh School of Medicine, Pittsburgh, Pennsylvania

JONATHAN M. HIMMELHOCH, MD, Western Psychiatric Institute and Clinic, University of Pittsburgh School of Medicine, Pittsburgh, Pennsylvania

NEIL S. JACOBSON, PhD, Department of Psychology, University of Washington, Seattle, Washington

ROBERT PAUL LIBERMAN, MD, Mental Health Clinical Research Center for the Study of Schizophrenia, Rehabilitation Research and Training Center for Mental Illness, Brentwood Veterans Administration Medical Center–UCLA Department of Psychiatry–Camarillo State Hospital, Camarillo, California

MARIAN L. MACDONALD, PhD, Department of Psychology, University of Massachusetts, Amherst, Massachusetts

CHRISTINE W. MCGILL, MSW, Department of Psychiatry and the Behavioral Sciences, University of Southern California School of Medicine, Los Angeles, California

PETER M. MONTI, PHD, Veterans Administration Medical Center/Brown University Medical School, Providence, Rhode Island

KEITH H. NUECHTERLEIN, PHD, Mental Health Clinical Research Center for the Study of Schizophrenia, Rehabilitation Research and Training Center for Mental Illness, Brentwood Veterans Administration Medical Center–UCLA Department of Psychiatry–Camarillo State Hospital, Camarillo, California

PETER TROWER, MSC, ABPSS, Department of Psychology, Hollymoor Hospital, Northfield, Birmingham, England

THOMAS F. TYNE, PHD, Department of Psychology, University of Rhode Island, Kingston, Rhode Island

CHARLES J. WALLACE, PHD, Mental Health Clinical Research Center for the Study of Schizophrenia, Rehabilitation Research and Training Center for Mental Illness, Brentwood Veterans Administration Medical Center–UCLA Department of Psychiatry–Camarillo State Hospital, Camarillo, California

PREFACE

Over the last decade social skills training has gained acceptance as a viable treatment alternative for a wide variety of disordered behaviors. While we feel that social skills training is a promising therapeutic strategy, we do not regard it as a panacea. We are somewhat distressed by the overly exuberant claims made in behalf of social skills training by individuals who view it as a cure-all for whatever afflicts the human condition. While recognizing the real limitations of social skills training, we are cautiously optimistic regarding its future. Although social skills training is a rather recent development, we feel that the chapters in this book reflect its increasing maturity. If we properly address the issues raised in this volume and heed the advice of its contributors, then the utility of social skills training will continue to grow.

We have tried to strike a balance in this volume between the applied aspects of social skills assessment and treatment and more basic research and philosophical issues. This book is divided into four parts. The first two parts deal with social skills training, with the first concentrating on schizophrenics and the second dealing with other populations. The third part focuses upon the assessment of social skills, with an emphasis on the issues involved in assessment and the development of assessment strategies. The fourth part is oriented toward a philosophy of science and indicates potential future directions for social skills training.

Most of the chapters in this volume are based in part on papers delivered at a symposium on Social Competence and Psychiatric Disorders, which we cohosted in May of 1980 in Providence, Rhode Island. Speaking for ourselves (although we believe our sentiment was shared by the other participants) we felt that the two-day symposium was one of the most pleasant professional interactions we had ever experienced. We were struck by the sincerity and dedication each participant brought to his or her work and the genuine desire to assist distressed individuals evidenced. We hope that this volume in a small way provides a testimonial to that dedication. Also, we would like to sincerely thank all the members of our own Behavior Training Clinic who have contributed so much to our research program over the years.

JAMES P. CURRAN
PETER M. MONTI

CONTENTS

CHAPTER 12. AN ETHOLOGICAL PERSPECTIVE ON SOCIAL SKILLS RESEARCH

ROBERT BOICE

PART IV. A GENERATIVE MODEL OF SOCIAL SKILLS, 397

CHAPTER 13. TOWARD A GENERATIVE MODEL OF SOCIAL SKILLS: A CRITIQUE AND SYNTHESIS

PETER TROWER

SOCIAL SKILLS TRAINING

I

SOCIAL SKILLS TRAINING WITH SCHIZOPHRENICS

The four chapters in this part are grouped together because they all deal exclusively with schizophrenic patients. Schizophrenia has been most refractory to treatment, with many patients requiring rehospitalization after a short period of time. Social skills training appears to hold some potential for the treatment of schizophrenia, but if this potential is to be realized, careful attention must be paid to the issues raised in these chapters. In Chapter 1, Liberman, Nuechterlein, and Wallace admonish social skills researchers for "making claims that are ahead of our data," and further state that we are "endangering the potential fruitfulness of training approaches by failing to design our treatment and assessment methods for the special and unique needs of our schizophrenic patients" (p. 6). Liberman *et al.* then go on to review five research areas within the domain of experimental psychopathology that they feel have especially important implications for social skills training with schizophrenics. These areas include family factors, social and community stressors, psychopathology, motivational deficits, and cognitive deficits. The authors conclude that in order for social skills training programs to prove maximally effective, some consideration of these factors must occur. The authors provide a model depicting possible interrelationships among environmental, cognitive, psychophysiological, and behavioral variables in the course of schizophrenic disorders. They go on to discuss the role of social skills training and how such programs may "cushion the full impact of social stressors on the vulnerable individual or enable the individual to better cope and resolve problems" (p. 51). The one inescapable conclusion that can be drawn from this chapter is that if social skills training is to have a significant clinical impact on the treatment of schizophrenia, it must be delivered in a more intensive fashion than is generally found in the literature. That is, given all the factors involved in schizophrenia disorders, it is unrealistic to expect that a brief regimen of social skills training will have any major impact. The authors feel that

1

in most cases a prolonged and extensive treatment protocol coupled with a long-term relationship between a schizophrenic patient and a therapist is probably necessary to promote a significant clinical treatment effect.

In each of the remaining three chapters of this part, broadly based intensive social skills training programs are described. All three programs include the usual response acquisition training procedures found in social skills training: instructions, prompts, modeling, behavioral rehearsal, feedback, and homework assignments. Although all three programs are intensive social skills training programs employing similar training procedures, major differential emphases exist within each program. For example, one program is an intensive program with inpatients, another program concentrates on instrumental behaviors and survival skills for community living, and the intervention in the third program occurs exclusively in the patient's home, with a focus on altering the skills levels of members of the family of the indexed patient. All three programs are explicitly described in these chapters, and each of the authors report some preliminary data that are encouraging with respect to the effectiveness of such an approach with schizophrenic patients.

The program described by Wallace in Chapter 2 was developed at the Mental Health Clinical Research Center at Camarillo State Hospital. The program is both intensive in concentration and extensive in scope. Treatment occurs 5 days a week, 2 to 6 hours daily, for a 9-week period. Unlike most programs, which heavily emphasize motoric responses, the social skills program described by Wallace is based on a model giving equal emphasis to receiving, processing, and sending functions. "Accurate reception" is defined as correct recognition of the interpersonal partner's status, emotions, and messages. "Flexible processing" is defined as the generation of possible responses and the evaluation of each in terms of its consequences. "Effective sending" is defined in terms of behavior such as appropriate eye contact, voice volume, etc. Two types of problematic situations are rehearsed—instrumental and interpersonal situations. Therapists stress goal attainment in each situation. An attempt is made to involve patients in problematic and realistic role plays in order to capture their interest.

In the study described in Chapter 2, Wallace compared the Camarillo social skills training program to holistic health training. The hypothesis tested was that increases in problem-solving skills would likely forestall relapses and/or rehospitalizations. The patients were well-defined schizophrenics, living with relatives who were judged to be overly critical and hostile toward the patient. The preliminary results were encouraging, with fewer patients in the social skills training group having relapsed or having been rehospitalized than patients in the holistic training group.

In Chapter 3, Brown describes his Life Skills Program, developed at the Sepulveda Veterans Administration Medical Center. This program was developed to assist patients to function in the community and to provide posthospitalization aftercare. Brown's program emphasizes instrumental skills to a greater extent than do most social skills training programs. The Life Skills Program began as a 7-week inpatient program operating 5 days a week for 4 hours a day. Each 7-week program is divided into modules comprising (1) interpersonal skills, (2) nutrition and meal planning, (3) health and hygiene, (4) money management, (5) nutrition, part two, (6) prevocational, and (7) community resources and social networks. For some of the patients, this inpatient phase is followed by a phase where they live with other patients in a halfway house for 2 months. Here they can further develop and improve their skills and be phased into the community at a slower pace. Brown reports some preliminary data on his program and concludes with suggestions for promoting generalization of treatment effects to the community.

Falloon's program, as described in Chapter 4, is an attempt to reduce family patterns that have been implicated as factors contributing to schizophrenic relapse. More specifically, his program is aimed at changing patterns of negative criticism and hostility toward the patients evidenced by members of their family. Another goal is to reduce the overdependent bonding between relatives and patients. This program is conducted almost in its entirety in the homes of the patients. The program, as described in the study, consists of weekly family therapy sessions for the first 3 months of the program, which are gradually faded to less intensive monthly follow-up visits after a 9-month period, for a total of 40 sessions over 2 years. Two major treatment strategies are employed: communication training and structured problem solving. As part of the communications training, procedures are employed to shape effective expression of positive and negative feelings, reflective listening, making requests, and reciprocity of conversation. In problem solving, family members are taught to (1) come to an agreement on a specific definition of the problem, (2) generate at least five possible solutions or alternatives to the problem without judging their relative merits, (3) evaluate the positive and negative aspects of each alternative, (4) agree upon the best solution or combination of several, (5) plan and carry out the agreed-upon solution, and (6) review and praise efforts at implementing the solution. Along with these two major components, Falloon's program involves educating the family members about schizophrenia, the careful monitoring of neuroleptic medication, and crisis intervention. The goal of the Falloon program is not only to increase the social competency of the patient but the competency of all family members. Data of a preliminary nature are reported, indicating that such a family approach may diminish schizophrenia relapse.

While the social skills training programs described in this section are in many ways model programs, several concerns should be mentioned. It should be noted that there exist scant empirical data that indicate that the behaviors being taught in these programs are those that are reinforced in the patient's natural environment. Conger and Conger, in Chapter 10, emphasize this issue and discuss strategies to obtain data that would empirically validate the content of social skills training programs. Another question revolves around realistic time expectations. For example, is it realistic to teach all the instrumental skills in Brown's program in a 7-week period? This is obviously a question that must be answered on an empirical basis. While arguing on the one hand that the time frame for some of these programs may have to be expanded, there exists the realistic concern that many clinical settings might not possess the resources to implement programs like those described in this section. However, to return to the point made by Liberman *et al.*, such intensive treatment may be necessary to produce a significant clinical effect. Another concern of ours is that the reader is left with the impression that each of the programs is inflexible and must be followed in lockstep fashion. It should be kept in mind that the authors are describing programs that were being evaluated in carefully controlled research studies and consequently were implemented in a rather standardized fashion. Practicing clinicians can be more flexible and tailor programs to meet the needs of individual patients. Such tailoring might mean spending more or less time on certain component skills, depending upon the strengths and limitations of each patient. Of course, a thorough assessment of each patient is necessary if one is to tailor an individualized treatment program.

1

SOCIAL SKILLS TRAINING
AND THE NATURE OF SCHIZOPHRENIA

ROBERT PAUL LIBERMAN
KEITH H. NUECHTERLEIN
CHARLES J. WALLACE

Social skills training for schizophrenics has developed rapidly in the past 10 years as social learning techniques have been "packaged" by behavior therapists for improving the social competence and emotional expressiveness of patients with a wide variety of psychiatric disorders (Goldstein, 1973; Hersen & Bellack, 1976; Liberman, King, DeRisi, & McCann, 1975; Trower, Bryant, & Argyle, 1978). Because of the well-documented correlation between premorbid social adjustment and course of schizophrenic illnesses, the face validity of therapeutic approaches aiming to strengthen the social competence of schizophrenics has attracted numerous clinicians and researchers. The early work using assertive or social skills training with schizophrenics yielded mixed results. Some investigators reported no benefit to schizophrenics accruing from social skills training while others reported positive outcomes (Wallace, Nelson, Liberman, Lukoff, & Aitchison, 1980). The accumulated findings, from the vantage point of early 1980, appear to confirm the effectiveness of social skills training during the training period, but to question the generality and durability of these short-term improvements in social functioning (Falloon, Lindley, McDonald, & Marks, 1977; Liberman, Lillie, Falloon, Hutchinson, & Harpin, 1980).

Robert Paul Liberman, Keith H. Nuechterlein, and Charles J. Wallace. Mental Health Clinical Research Center for the Study of Schizophrenia, Rehabilitation Research and Training Center for Mental Illness, Brentwood Veterans Administration Medical Center–UCLA Department of Psychiatry–Camarillo State Hospital, Camarillo, California.

While the exact training techniques and assessment methods vary somewhat among clinical research centers, there are more similarities than differences. Most social skills trainers working with schizophrenics use highly structured methods, including instructions, prompts, modeling, role playing, positive feedback, and homework assignments. Most training takes place in hospital or clinic settings. Training usually is given intensively from two to six sessions per week over a relatively brief period of up to 12 weeks. The goals of training are generally chosen *ad hoc* from among interpersonal situations that are viewed as being important for effective hospital, community, and family adjustment. Assessment of training has, by and large, flowed from stylized role-playing tests, confederate tests, global ratings, and self-reports from patients themselves. There is no doubt that progress is being made in this still-young field, propelled by the optimism and hopes held by many psychiatrists, psychologists, patients, and families that an effective psychosocial treatment for schizophrenia can be developed. However, as early proponents of social skills training for schizophrenics, we are concerned that the field is moving too fast. We have been guilty of making claims that are ahead of our data, and are endangering the potential fruitfulness of training approaches by failing to design our treatment and assessment methods for the special and unique needs of our schizophrenic patients.

While there is a vast literature on the multimodal deficits in the behavioral and psychological functioning of schizophrenics, workers applying social skills training appear to be scarcely aware of its existence. It is as though the behavior therapists using social skills training and the experimentalists and psychopathologists studying the nature of schizophrenia live in two separate worlds. This chapter, representing a foray into the domains of experimental psychopathology, aims to build a bridge between social skills training and what we know about the family, social, symptomatic, attentional, cognitive, motivational, and learning disturbances in schizophrenia.

In bridging the gap between the nature and course of schizophrenia on one side and social skills training on the other side, five areas of experimental inquiry will be reviewed—family factors, social situations, psychopathology, motivation, and cognitive/attentional factors. As each of these research areas are summarized for their contributions to an understanding of the schizophrenic process, implications will be drawn for the design of social skills training procedures.

FAMILY FACTORS

A series of studies over the past two decades, begun at the Medical Research Council's Social Psychiatry Unit at the Institute of Psychiatry in London and now continuing in studies supported by the World Health Organization and the National Institute of Mental Health in Denmark, India, and the United States, have highlighted the importance of the emotional climate in the family on the course of schizophrenic illness in a family member. Evidence has accumulated that points to the interpersonal processes within the family as one of the most powerful predictors of relapse in a person having an established schizophrenic illness.

The English studies were begun in response to the changing patterns of mental health care for schizophrenics in the 1950s, which were accompanied by increasing rates of discharges matched by increasing rates of readmissions. George Brown and his colleagues studied the possible influence of family relationships on the course of schizophrenia, stimulated by the early finding that schizophrenic patients who returned to parents or spouses relapsed more often than those discharged to hostels or apartments. Several years were spent devising a standardized method for assessing the quality of the emotional relationship between a schizophrenic patient and his or her key relatives. The successful development of a reliable interview format—the Camberwell Family Interview—led to a series of three replicated studies that concluded that the best single predictor of symptomatic relapse in the 9 months after discharge from the hospital was the level of emotion expressed by a relative toward the patient at the time of the patient's hospitalization (Brown, Birley, & Wing, 1972; Vaughn & Leff, 1976).

EVALUATING EXPRESSED EMOTION

The Camberwell Family Interview is conducted by a trained interviewer/rater with a single family member in a comfortable setting, usually the family home. It is semistructured and lasts about 1½ hours. The interview elicits the relative's report of interactions between the patient and family members as well as commentary on the patient's behavior during the 3 months prior to admission. Circumstances surrounding the decision to hospitalize, acting out, frequency of quarrels, social isolation, and symptoms shown by the patient are covered. Of even greater importance for the subsequent ratings of expressed emotion (EE) are the feelings and attitudes of the relative toward the patient and the patient's relationships with others in the family. Feelings are expressed spontaneously during the detailed questioning about family activities and the development of the patient's disorder. In measuring the relative's EE, the interviewer/rater evaluates nonverbal elements as well as the semantic verbal content of the relative's responses. Emphasis is placed on vocal aspects of speech—tone, pitch, intensity, rapidity, and fluency—in rating the various scales reflecting emotional qualities.

Five scales were developed by Brown and his colleagues, including warmth, hostility, positive comments, critical comments, and emotional overinvolvement. Each scale is operationalized with detailed referents and many examples. With sufficient training and supervision, interviewer/raters can reach acceptably high levels of reliability in scoring these scales. It should be noted, however, that training requires a 2-week, full-time workshop followed by 2 to 3 months of reliability checks on ratings of tape-recorded interviews.

The two scales that have turned out to be most predictive of relapse are critical comments and emotional overinvolvement. The number of critical comments made by the relative about the patient are rated on content and how the relative speaks of the patient. Tone of voice or clear and unambiguous statements of resentment, disapproval, or dislike of something the patient has said or done contribute to the identification of a critical comment. For example, if a relative reported that the patient, just prior to admission, "spent all of his time lying around the house," a critical comment would be rated only if the relative's tone of voice was disapproving, sarcastic, or angry. On the other hand, if the relative added, "He spent all of his time lying around the house because he's just plain lazy," the accusation of laziness, even without a disapproving tone of voice, would qualify the comment as a criticism.

Emotional overinvolvement is rated for the relative's expressions of overconcern, overprotectiveness, and excessive solicitude. Extreme worry or anxiety by the relative about the patient is also coded as overinvolvement. This category reflects the kind of relationship often referred to as symbiotic or schizophrenogenic by American psychiatrists. It is important to point out that most relatives who show excessive criticism or marked emotional overinvolvement do not appear abnormal or strikingly deviant in light of the extremely asocial, impaired, and symptomatic nature of their ill family member.

EXPRESSED EMOTION AND RELAPSE

The replicated results from three separate studies conducted in London over a 15-year period reveal that patients returning to families that are high on expressing criticism and emotional overinvolvement relapse four times as often as those returning to families that are low in these categories of EE. A family member qualifies for the designation of high on EE if he or she makes six or more critical comments during the interview or is rated at 4 or higher on a 6-point scale of emotional overinvolvement. Of patients returning to homes where a family member was high on EE, 51% relapsed during the 9 months after discharge, whereas only 13% relapsed who returned to low-EE families (Vaughn & Leff, 1976). The diagnosis of schizophrenia and clinical determinations of relapse were made on the basis of the Present State Examination (Wing, Cooper, & Sartorius, 1974), and not on the basis of rehospitalization data.

High EE did not explain all of the variance, since almost 50% of those from high-EE homes did not relapse. Thus, secondary analyses were conducted to determine which other factors were contributing to clinical outcome. No correlations with relapse could be found for syndromes or types and severity of symptoms (except a modest positive correlation between grandiose delusions and relapse), features of the psychiatric history (e.g., gradual or sudden onset, first or multiple admissions), or even severity of the behavioral disturbance. What did correlate with relapse were maintenance on antipsychotic drugs and amount of face-to-face contact between the patient and relative during the postdischarge period. Figure 1-1 shows the way in which (1) the use of antipsychotic medication, and (2) less than 35 hours per week of face-to-face contact protect schizophrenic individuals from relapse in families high, but not low, on EE. Patients living with family members high on EE who spend much time with their relatives and are not protected by maintenance drug therapy have a very poor prognosis, with 92% of them relapsing. Relapse rates drop if one of the two protective factors is operating. Prognosis is best of all—and is equivalent to that of patients returning to low-EE households—for those who have both protective factors operating.

Replications of these English studies are ongoing at the Mental Health Clinical Research Center (MHCRC) for the Study of Schizophrenia at Camarillo/UCLA; the University of Rochester; the University of Pittsburgh; and at research centers in India, Denmark, Hawaii, and

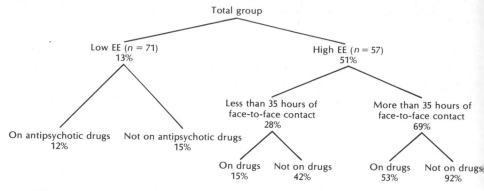

FIGURE 1-1. Nine-month relapse rates of 128 schizophrenic patients who were living with relatives rated high and low on expressed emotion (EE). Data are drawn from two separate studies carried out a decade apart in London (Brown, Birley, & Wing, 1972; Vaughn & Leff, 1976).

Chicago. Preliminary findings at Camarillo/UCLA suggest that patients returning to high-EE families do indeed frequently relapse; in fact, the proportion of patients from high-EE families who relapse is almost exactly the same as in the English studies. However, there is a much greater proportion of families high on EE in California than in England. In London, 45% of the families were high on EE, while at Camarillo/ UCLA 67% of the families were high on EE. Disproportionately larger numbers of high-EE families of schizophrenics also were found in the Rochester and Pittsburgh studies, while in India almost all of the families are low on EE. These international studies suggest that cultural factors may determine the proportion of families high on EE, but that, once present, high EE predisposes toward schizophrenic relapse regardless of culture.

COMMUNICATION DEVIANCE

Another line of research has implicated dysfunctional communication patterns in families as potential etiological influences on the development of schizophrenia. Measured in a variety of ways—responses to the Thematic Apperception Test (TAT), Rorschach tests; direct coding of interaction; coding of speech samples—communication deviance has been operationalized as vague amorphous statements; contradictory statements; disqualifications of others' comments; intrusiveness; failure to specify problems or perceptions; statements tangential to the issue at hand; and failure to resolve a problem. In both cross-sectional and prospective studies, measures of parental communication deviance have correlated highly with the psychopathology of offspring. For example, in a prospective, longitudinal study of families of nonpsychotically disturbed adolescents, communication deviance significantly predicted the appearance of schizophrenia spectrum disorders in the offspring 5 years later (Goldstein, Rodnick, Jones, McPherson, & West, 1978).

A number of attributes reflected in the EE concept are similar to familial communication patterns believed etiologically significant in the development of schizophrenia. Certain patterns of parental affective communication, obtained in a direct interaction situation involving family members discussing differences of opinion, have been found to be significantly predictive of subsequent psychiatric breakdown in vulnerable adolescents (Doane, West, Goldstein, Rodnick, & Jones, 1980). Factors such as parental criticism, intrusiveness, and guilt inducement—especially in the context of low emotional supportiveness—were the key predictive indices. Doane's negative interaction index, coded from audiotapes of face-to-face problem-solving interactions with offspring, suggests that critical and hostile parental behaviors result in deterioration of psychiatric status in young adulthood. Furthermore, using both communication deviance and negative interaction indices, accurate predictions of psychiatric status were made in virtually every case at the time of 5-year follow-up. Only families with both high communication deviance and negative interactional style had their young adult offspring show signs of schizophrenia spectrum disorders at the time of follow-up. These studies and those cited above on EE suggest that reliably measured indices of affective style and communication deviance may have important links to both the etiology and course of schizophrenia.

IMPLICATIONS FOR CLINICAL INTERVENTION
AND SOCIAL SKILLS TRAINING

Of significance in the studies on EE is the fact that a vulnerable target group of schizophrenics can now be identified as at high risk for relapse. The group at highest risk are individuals with schizophrenia living at home with parents who are high on EE and communication deviance. More importantly, independent of chronicity, this vulnerable group can be identified at the time of hospital admission through the administration of standardized interviews. What types of clinical interventions, then, can be utilized with this highly vulnerable group? The evidence from moderating variables on relapse rates suggests that clinicians should aim to provide maintenance antipsychotic drugs for these patients and to reduce the amount of fact-to-face contact between them and their relatives after discharge.

While special procedures, such as long-acting antipsychotic drug preparations and reinforcement methods (Liberman & Davis, 1975), may improve the sustained use of medication, side effects and noncompliance limit the success of this therapeutic avenue. Reducing the amount of face-to-face contact is easier said than done. Many of the high-EE families and their schizophrenic member are glued together through years of mutual dependency and gratifications. One approach developed by the Program for Assertive Community Training (PACT) project in Madison, Wisconsin (Stein & Test, 1978), employs constructive separation between patient and family. This community-based program, as a condition of acceptance, requires adherence to specific guidelines that regulate interactions between patients and families via phone, visits, and correspondence. However, as compensation for the loss of the family ties, the PACT staff provide 24-hour, round-the-clock personal support and crisis intervention. Few agencies working with schizophrenics can offer that degree of support and contact (Mendel, 1975).

Two other approaches, which are being evaluated at the Camarillo/ UCLA MHCRC for the Study of Schizophrenia and the University of Pittsburgh, involve (1) reducing EE and communication deviance in relatives through family therapy, and (2) strengthening the social and communication skills of the schizophrenic patient through a training program aimed at enabling the patient to better cope with high EE from family members or to leave the family and become more autonomous.

Clinicians employing behavioral therapies with schizophrenics can no longer ignore the areas of familial communication, affective expression, and problem solving. Even with patients who do not intend to return home after hospitalization, a focus on family themes and problems is important, since family influence and contacts tend to persist across time and geographical distance. The strategies used in family therapy—consisting of education, abreaction, communication skills training, modification of dependent relationships, and problem solving— are described in detail by Falloon (Chapter 4, this volume). With regard to social skills training offered to the patient outside of family therapy, family conflicts and problems need to be highlighted through role playing as a major goal and theme of training. In Chapter 2, this volume, Wallace outlines the use of problem situations elicited through the Camberwell Family Interview in social skills training carried out with small groups of schizophrenic patients.

SOCIAL AND COMMUNITY FACTORS

While in many cases, the family provides the most proximal and emotionally arousing of social stimuli to schizophrenic patients, there are other life events that influence the onset and course of this illness. Aside from family factors, much theoretical and experimental evidence has pointed toward other interpersonal and socioeconomic features of the environment that serve as antecedents or precipitants of acute schizophrenic reactions.

The best work in the field has been carried out in England, where investigators ascertained the frequency of life events in schizophrenics during a 3-month period preceding a psychotic breakdown that required hospitalization (Birley & Brown, 1970; Brown & Birley, 1968). Life events were determined by having the patient and significant other describe disappointments, losses, damages, and fulfillments that could be specifically dated. Life events were both agreeable (e.g., getting married, finding a new job, moving to a better residence) and noxious (e.g., losing a friend, suffering a drop in income, experiencing a theft) and included events that were outside the control of the patient as well as those linked with the patient's behavior. Comparisons were made for the same 3-month interval with a sample of normal people. During the 3-month reporting period, the proportion of normals having life events remained constant; however, the proportion of schizophrenics experiencing a life event increased markedly in the 3 weeks before the onset of their symptoms. Of the schizophrenic sample 60% had an abrupt change in their social environment during this 3-week prebreakdown period, compared to only 14% of the normal controls. Birley and Brown (1970) found that this concentration of life events occurred just prior to the first psychotic episode in young schizophrenics as well as prior to exacerbations and repeated relapses in more chronic schizophrenics.

While most of the inventories used in recording life events focus on major changes, it is very possible that schizophrenics, because of their perceptual and cognitive impairments, and increased psychological vulnerability, are stressed by mundane, small-scale, and everyday life events that would not be upsetting to normals. The accumulation of minor but unexpected or confusing changes in a schizophrenic's life space could conceivably tip the balance toward decompensation. A clinical anecdote attributed to Werner Mendel (1979) regarding a schizophrenic breakdown illustrates this phenomenon. A middle-aged schizophrenic man had lived continuously, albeit marginally, in the community for many years. He held a regular job to which he commuted every day by bus from his apartment in the city. His social life was constricted to brief conversations with the checkout clerks in the local supermarket and a friendly nod and "Good day" exchanged with the genial woman manager of his apartment house twice daily upon leaving for and returning from work. One day he noted that the manager's door was uncharacteristically shut and on his return from work discovered a new manager, who happened to be a large, burly man. Within hours, the patient's delusions and hallucinations had returned, he ran naked through the streets, and required hospitalization.

In a further investigation of the relationship of stressful events with relapse, psychiatrists at London's Social Psychiatry Research Unit found that patients who relapsed while taking neuroleptic medication were more likely to have experienced major life events in the period immediately preceding the flare-up of symptoms than other relapsing schizophrenics who were not taking medication (Hirsch, Gaind, Rohde, Stevens, & Wing, 1973; Leff & Wing, 1971). These investigators concluded that medication may protect vulnerable schizophrenic patients from the demands of daily living but not from stressful, large changes in their environments.

At a more macroeconomic level of analyzing social antecedents to schizophrenic psychopathology, Brenner (1973) studied the relationship between unemployment rate and admissions to New York State public and private mental hospitals from 1914 to 1967. There was a substantial correlation between poor economic conditions and hospital admissions, many of whom were schizophrenic. There are several explanations for this correlation, one of which is that poor economic conditions precipitate the onset or exacerbation of symptoms by increasing the number of noxious life events (e.g., loss of job, reduced income, changing jobs, losing unemployment or welfare benefits) to which an individual must adapt.

The social environment and the support it offers determines to a large extent the final common pathway and impact of life stressors and economic problems on the individual vulnerable to schizophrenia. It was found that patients experiencing close social relationships were more likely to remain in the community irrespective of the type of their living environment (Miller, 1967). Others have reported that the quality of hospital and posthospital environments was significantly related to outcome (Kayton, Beck, & Koh, 1976; Wing, 1978; Zubin, Sutton, Salzinger, Burdock, & Peretz, 1961). In particular, socially isolated, unstimulating, deprived and custodial living environments tend regularly to produce the social breakdown syndrome or institutionalism—apathy, social withdrawal, loss of self-care skills, and other negative symptoms of schizophrenia. The nature of the schizophrenic person's social network will modulate the impact of over- or understimulating environments on psychiatric symptoms and behavioral functioning.

The concept of social network encapsulates the reciprocal relationship between a patient and his or her interpersonal resources. The quality of this reciprocity can determine whether the social network has a salutary or damaging effect on the patient. In one of the rare empirical studies of social networks and their effects on psychiatric outcome, Tolsdorf (1976) intensively interviewed 10 recently hospitalized schizophrenic patients and 10 patients hospitalized for medical reasons. The two groups of patients were hospitalized in a Veterans Administration (VA) hospital and were matched on the basis of age, marital status, education, and socioeconomic level. Quantitative and qualitative information about the social network was gathered during a lengthy intervew and validated by telephone calls to two members of each patient's designated network. Results indicated that while both groups had similar numbers of social contacts, the psychiatric patient reported fewer intimate relationships, fewer but more powerful figures in the network, and fewer relationships with individuals other than family members. Qualitatively, the schizophrenic patients had a much more pessimistic and negative view of the ability and interest of their social networks to assist them in times of need, a view that reportedly developed long before the onset of the schizophrenic symptoms. A corollary of the negative attitudes held by the patients toward their social networks was the greater number of life stressors perceived by the patients as stemming from an excessively high set of expectations and demands for instrumental role functioning coming from the figures in the network.

Life events and stressors thus can be mitigated or amplified by the patient's social environment and, in addition, often vary greatly from patient to patient. For one patient living in a quiet and unstimulating board-and-care home, a major life event might be loss of the television set for 2 weeks or the arrival of a new, energetic staff member; on the other hand, a patient living independently in the middle of New York City would more likely suffer a life event if someone broke into his apartment or if a stranger offered him a seat on the subway. Changes in a patient's interpersonal life space will be experienced as stressful if they are relevant to the individual's level of functioning, that is, if they place an adaptational demand or challenge on the person.

A major weakness of most stress research has been its limitation to a two-step process—a life event occurs and then symptoms of schizophrenia are observed. While such simplistic and retrospective studies have highlighted the impact of stressors on the schizophrenic process, they are not taking enough of the stress–response phenomenon into account to lead us to higher levels of understanding. Psychopathological end states are not solely a function of the type and magnitude of environmental stressors, but are also affected by the responses of the individual to the stressors. Responses to stressors include perceptual filtering, cognitive labeling and processing, defensive reactions, coping style, and problem-solving efforts. At the interpersonal level, the adaptive capacity of the individual is strengthened by the supportiveness, encouragement, and reinforcement provided by primary relationships and figures in one's social network. A comprehensive view of the schizophrenic process requires us to evaluate the many levels on which human life proceeds. Interactions of schizophrenics with their environments have biological, intrapersonal, interpersonal, and sociocultural implications. The specific variables in this multimodal scheme of adaptation to stressors interact in complex ways to determine onset, exacerbation, and remission of schizophrenic symptoms.

IMPLICATIONS FOR CLINICAL INTERVENTION AND SOCIAL SKILLS TRAINING

An increase or reappearance of symptoms in a person vulnerable to schizophrenia is an outcome of the balance or interaction between the amount of life stressors and the problem-solving skills of the individual (Zubin & Spring, 1977). Either too much environmental change or stressor—such as an economic slump and loss of a job—or too few coping and problem-solving skills—such as a person who always responds to new situations with social withdrawal—can lead to symptomatic flare-ups. The significance of this two-way model of symptom formation lies in the emphasis given to the active role of the patient's coping skills in modulating vulnerability to relapse. But, at present, we lack specific knowledge of the truly crucial life stressors and events with which the patient must cope.

Social skills trainers have tended to assume, without empirical justification, that certain situations and events were critical to a schizophrenic's adjustment to and survival in the community. Thus, we have seen the familiar litany of situational typologies inserted into behavioral rehearsals—positive and negative assertion, starting conversations, making an appointment with a clinician, dating, and saying no to unreasonable requests. With rare exceptions (Goldsmith & McFall, 1975), scenes have been chosen for social skills training that have had only face validity.

Because of our failure to test the ecological validity of our choice of target goals in social skills training, it is important to do a better job in selecting interpersonal situations that can be documented as critical to a schizophrenic's functioning and survival in the community. At the Camarillo/UCLA Clinical Research Center, Wallace (1977–1979) conducted a pilot project to assess situations relevant to successful living in residential care facilities in the community. Five residential care operators and two social workers who were liaisons between the state hospital and these community facilities were interviewed at length to solicit those behaviors and social situations that were viewed as crucial in either the return of patients to the state hospital and/or in the production of discomfort and displeasure in the operators with their patients. A content analysis of the situations generated by this interview led to two commonly cited problems: a patient believes that his rights have been violated by another patient or by the operator; a patient is accused of violating the rights of another patient or the operator. Based on the content analysis of the interviews, 26 interpersonal situations were constructed.

The five operators and two social workers were again contacted and asked to indicate the best and worst responses that a hypothetical patient might make to each of the 26 situations. From the numerous possibilities mentioned, five alternatives were developed for each of the 26 situations, classified from "best" to "worst" in terms of the amount of aggression displayed in each response.

The situations and response alternatives were then formulated as a multiple-choice questionnaire that was mailed to a random sample of 50 residential care operators in Los Angeles and Ventura Counties who were asked to indicate for each situation the rank order from "best" to "worst" of the five response alternatives. Questionnaires were returned by 37 operators. Kendall's tau and the mean rank of each alternative were calculated for each situation. Four of the 26 situations were discarded either because their tau was less than .70 or because their alternatives were separated by less than a .75 difference in the mean ranks. Thus, situations were constructed that had been specified by the residential care operators themselves as being important for successful living in their facilities. In addition, the operators had suggested the response alternatives and had provided consensual validation of the adequacy of each alternative for dealing with the stressful situation.

The next step was integrating these potentially stressful scenes and their response alternatives into a social skills training framework. Ten situations from the questionnaire were randomly selected and used with 18 patients in a role-playing assessment/training program. The context of each situation was presented by the trainer and a role model delivered a prompt to open the scene. The patient was then expected to respond spontaneously to the prompt and attempt to deal with the stressful situation. After the behavior rehearsal was completed, the patient was asked to (1) identify his rights, duties, and goals prescribed by the situation; (2) generate response alternatives (including the response actually rehearsed); (3) predict the likely consequences of each alternative; and (4) evaluate each alternative as a means of achieving his identified goals.

Results indicated that the assessment/training program was reliable. Across the 10 scenes, scores for individual patients in selecting the best to worst alternatives were highly correlated ($r = +.89$), as were the total number of correct answers to the questions administered following the behavior rehearsal. The 10 situations did not differ in their difficulty level. Of course, patients differed significantly in their scores for the spontaneous rehearsal ($F = 3.47$, $p < .001$), and for their responses to the postrehearsal questions ($F = 10.78$, $p < .001$).

The goal of this project was to develop an individual problem-solving profile—which could be extrapolated to many dimensions of life outside of situations in residential care homes—that would be directly relevant to training. It was hypothesized that an individual might give an unskilled response because he either (1) did not accurately perceive the situation; (2) did not generate a reasonably good alternative; or (3) did not have the behavioral repertoire to effectively deliver the response alternative chosen. Wallace, in Chapter 2, this volume, describes the elaboration of this schema to a comprehensive social skills assessment/ training program for young adult schizophrenics.

At the Camarillo/UCLA Clinical Research Center, a further step has been planned for individualizing the social skills assessment/training program for schizophrenics. The focus will be on skill attainment at criterion levels for each patient, based upon the specific interpersonal problems facing each patient in the various settings of everyday life. Patients will enter the training sequence at a level commensurate with his or her skills, with some requiring basic skills acquisition, while others may begin at higher levels of skills training. Each patient progresses at his or her own pace through a four-level hierarchy of skills development—shown in Table 1-1—in areas such as peer and family relations, community living, vocations, and symptom management. The proposed assessment/training program, a personalized system of instruction, is designed to allow a person to progress at a different rate in each of these four areas of skill development. Thus, some individuals will possess adequate independent skills for community life (e.g., purchasing and preparing food, transportation, and obtaining an apartment), but will lack skills for socializing with peers and for obtaining a job. Alternatively, a person may have adequate employment skills, but lack the know-how for coping with distracting and distressing symptoms (e.g., how to obtain psychiatric consultation, how to request changes in medication or antidotes for side effects). The advantage of focusing separately on these various areas of skill development is that a person may reach a plateau in his or her progress in one area while continuing to advance to higher levels in another area. By the end of training, patients should have an opportunity to maximize their assets, and move capably into the least restrictive environment consistent with their level of skills.

PSYCHOPATHOLOGY

Schizophrenia means many different things to different clinicians and it is vital, should advances in social skills training occur, to clarify our understanding of the diagnosis and course of schizophrenic psychopathology. In the first place, the interpretation and generality of outcomes accruing from social skills training are seriously impeded by vagueness, unspecified criteria, and unreliability in the diagnosis of

TABLE 1-1. Areas of Functioning and Hierarchies of Clinical Intervention for the Community Living/Social Skills Training Program

Level of training	Social	Independent community living	Vocational	Symptom management
I	Basic social skills training	Sheltered living with specific training in grooming, house-cleaning, budgeting, and shopping	Prevocational training in MHCRC program	Supervision of symptoms and administration of medication by caretaker plus education in MHCRC program
II	Instrumental skills training	Community living with supportive roommate (daily staff visits)	Sheltered workshop/volunteer assignment	Training staff supervision
III	Conversational skills training	Community living with supportive roommate (some teaching and advanced training)	Community employment with staff supervision	Peer/family supervision
IV	Generalizing skills to special problem situations and enhancing social etiquette; continuation group	Community living with supportive roommate ("buddy") and continuation group	Independent community employment	Independent

schizophrenia. In the past 10 years, clinicians and researchers have brought unprecedented rigor and specificity to bear on the diagnostic process. While this chapter is not the place to describe advances in the diagnosis of schizophrenia, a comparison between the diagnostic criteria present in the second and third editions of the *Diagnostic and Statistical Manual* of the American Psychiatric Association—shown in Table 1-2—will immediately reveal the vast improvement in the precision of the diagnostic enterprise. There are now excellent, standardized mental status interviews—the Present State Examination and the Schedule for Affective Disorders and Schizophrenia—which adequately trained clinicians can use to effectively elicit the well-specified characteristic symptom criteria for schizophrenia. Research on social skills training with schizophrenics should not be acceptable for publication unless the investigators have described their care in eliciting and rating the characteristic symptoms and other criteria for the diagnosis. Requiring this diagnostic rigor will also have the beneficial effect of drawing together in useful collaboration psychologists, who generally carry out the social skills training, and psychiatrists, who generally conduct the diagnostic assessments.

Beyond the diagnosis of schizophrenia, individuals found at one point in time to suffer from the characteristic symptoms may have highly variable outcomes and courses as time goes on. One person, having had an acute and florid onset of symptoms precipitated by definite stressors and with good premorbid adjustment, may have a complete remission and never experience another psychotic episode again, or may experience long periods of remission between brief episodes of psychosis. Another individual, having had a slow, insidious onset of symptoms with no clear precipitants and a poor premorbid adjustment, may continue to experience severe symptoms and become socially and vocationally disabled for the remainder of his or her life. In Figure 1-2 are depicted five prototypical courses of schizophrenic illness, chosen somewhat arbitrarily, but revealing the diversity in outcomes to be found in schizophrenia.

Symptoms and social functioning experienced during the early years of a person's schizophrenic illness are likely to predict future symptoms and social functioning. For example, the same symptoms present during an initial acute episode of schizophrenia often reappear in subsequent psychotic episodes. The individual who has been socially withdrawn and friendless during the prepsychotic and initial periods of schizophrenia is likely to remain socially isolated and constricted for years to come. It

TABLE 1-2. Diagnosis of Schizophrenia: Comparison of DSM-II and DSM-III Criteria

---

DSM-II

Characteristic disturbances of thinking, mood, and behavior.

Disturbances in thinking are marked by alterations of concept formation, which may lead to misinterpretation of reality and sometimes to delusions and hallucinations, which appear psychologically self-protective.

Mood changes include ambivalent, constricted, and inappropriate emotional responsiveness and loss of empathy with others.

Behavior may be withdrawn, regressive, and bizarre.

The *schizophrenias*, in which the mental status is attributable primarily to a *thought disorder*, are to be distinguished from the *major affective illnesses*, which are dominated by a *mood disorder*. The *paranoid states* are distinguished from schizophrenia by the narrowness of their distortions of reality and by the absence of other psychotic symptoms.

DSM-III

A. *Characteristic schizophrenic symptoms*: At least one symptom from any of the following 10:
  1. Delusions of being controlled
  2. Thought broadcasting
  3. Thought insertion
  4. Thought withdrawal
  5. Other bizarre delusions
  6. Somatic, grandiose, religious, nihilistic, or other delusions without persecutory or jealous content
  7. Delusions of any type if accompanied by hallucinations
  8. Auditory hallucinations in which either a voice keeps up a running commentary on the individual's behavior or thoughts as they occur, or two or more voices converse with each other
  9. Auditory hallucinations on several occasions with content having no apparent relation to depression or elation, and not limited to one or two words
  10. Either incoherence, derailment, marked illogicality, or marked poverty of speech if accompanied by either blunted, flat, or inappropriate affect, delusions or hallucinations, or behavior that is grossly disorganized or catatonic

B. *Functional impairment*: During the active phase of the illness, the symptoms in A have been associated with significant impairment in two or more areas of daily functioning (e.g., work, social relations, self-care).

C. *Chronicity*: Signs of the illness have lasted continuously for at least 6 months at some time during the person's life and the individual now has some signs the illness. The 6-month period must include an active phase, during which there were symptoms from A with or without a prodromal or residual phase, as defined below.

Prodromal phase: A clear deterioration in functioning not due to a primary disturbance in mood or to substance abuse, and involving at least *two* of the symptoms noted below.

Residual phase: Following the active phase of the illness, at least *two* of the symptoms noted below, not due to a primary disturbance in mood or to substance abuse.

Prodromal or residual symptoms:
  1. Social isolation or withdrawal
  2. Marked impairment in role functioning as a wage earner, student, homemaker
  3. Markedly eccentric, odd, or peculiar behavior (e.g., collecting garbage, talking to self in cornfield or subway, hoarding food)

TABLE 1-2. (*Continued*)

DSM-III

4. Impairment in personal hygiene and grooming
5. Blunted, flat, or inappropriate affect
6. Speech that is tangential, digressive, vague, overelaborate, circumstantial, or metaphorical
7. Odd or bizarre ideation, or magical thinking (e.g., superstitiousness, clairvoyance, telepathy, "sixth sense," "others can feel my feelings", overvalued ideas, ideas of reference, or suspected delusions)
8. Unusual perceptual experiences (e.g., recurrent illusions, sensing the presence of a force or person not actually present, suspected hallucinations)

D. *Exclusive of affective disorder*: The full depressive or manic syndrome is either not present, or if present, developed after any psychotic symptoms.
E. *Exclusive of any organic mental disorder*

should be pointed out, however, that the first rank, characteristic symptoms of schizophrenia do not predict social and vocational outcome, or vice versa. Minor neuroticlike symptoms, such as depression, anxiety, and worry, are very common throughout the course of schizophrenia and, in some cases, have been found to be even better predictors of drug responsiveness than the major psychotic symptoms. Some individuals are more disabled and hampered by these neurotic symptoms than by psychotic symptoms, while for others the reverse is true.

Thus, there is no single "natural history" of schizophrenia. Even within a single individual who is in the midst of experiencing characteristic symptoms and the syndrome we label as schizophrenia, the symptom patterns and secondary deficits of the illness are not present 24 hours a day. Thus, some individuals are "more schizophrenic" than others, and within individuals schizophrenia is not a constant. There has been great controversy over whether schizophrenia is an illness, a group of illnesses, or a syndrome with manifold etiologies since Kraepelin's concept of dementia praecox was altered by Bleuler (1911/ 1950) to the group of schizophrenias. Even the much maligned and misquoted Kraepelin described the variation in courses and types of schizophrenia.

The vast majority of reports in the social skills training literature are based on heterogeneous groups of psychiatric patients, much less carefully diagnosed schizophrenics. This clumping of apples with oranges places a liability on social skills training outcomes, such that possibly

1. Episodic: periods of illness alternate with asymptomatic periods when behavior is normal or returned to premorbid behavior.

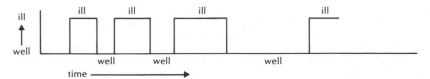

2. Acute exacerbations superimposed on either a residual illness or defect state; residual or defect state remains stable. Defect state refers to remaining disturbance of psychosocial functioning.

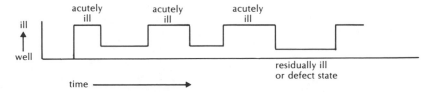

3. Acute exacerbations superimposed on either a residual illness or defect state; residual or defect state worsens after each acute exacerbation.

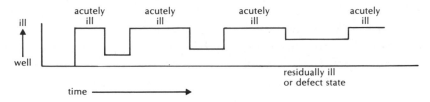

4. Continuous illness: some fluctuations in severity are common.

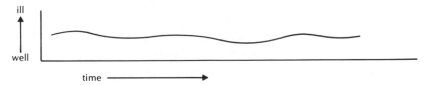

5. Continuous illness with deterioration.

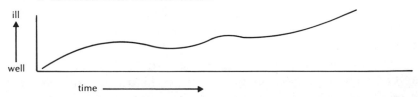

FIGURE 1-2. Examples of various courses of symptoms and social adjustment in schizophrenia. The course of illness has been somewhat arbitrarily divided into five main types (Luria & Meltzer, 1977).

important findings may be diluted or missed altogether. To the extent that variables affecting response to social skills training may be differentially applicable to the patients being trained, the impact of the training may be washed out when the data are grouped and averaged.

The living environments in which the person with schizophrenia exists have a profound impact on the course of illness and also on the person's responsiveness to biological and psychosocial treatments. There is evidence that improvements in the quality of hospital and community treatment during the past 70 years had led to corresponding improvements in symptoms, social functioning, and quality of life for schizophrenic individuals (Wing, 1978). For example, Kraepelin (cited in Wing, 1978) reported that 17% of dementia praecox patients were socially adjusted about 5 years later, while a study of 111 patients first admitted to three British psychiatric hospitals in 1956 revealed 56% of them socially recovered 5 years later (Brown, Bone, Dalison, & Wing, 1966).

The setting in which social skills training takes place may interact with variables within the patient and with the training methods to affect responsiveness and outcome. This interaction effect was clearly documented by Gordon Paul and his colleagues (Paul, Tobias, & Holly, 1972), who showed that neuroleptic drug therapy slowed improvements in long-stay, chronic schizophrenics who were receiving psychosocial therapy in an intensive treatment ward, but did not produce this deleterious effect in patients who were randomly assigned to a custodial, back ward. The same interaction among setting, patient, and treatment variables can impinge upon the endeavors to apply social skills training. For example, among chronically institutionalized schizophrenics who view release into the community with a mixture of fear and confusion, the implementation of social skills training with implicit goals for discharge will call into play unstated contingencies of reinforcement that may very well limit the effectiveness of the training program.

IMPLICATIONS FOR CLINICAL INTERVENTION AND
SOCIAL SKILLS TRAINING

There is tremendous importance in carefully diagnosing patients who are to participate in social skills training. With clear definition of characteristic symptoms, social adaptation, duration of illness, and course of illness, results emanating from social skills training can be linked to specific types of patients and can be generalized and replicated. Inadequate or improperly utilized diagnostic criteria and interview formats and an almost total absence of serious, scholarly interest in psychiatric description, phenomenology, and classification by American mental health professionals during the past 40 years has wreaked havoc with schizophrenia research by calling into question the verity of the subjects' diagnoses. With the availability of reliable means for diagnosing schizophrenia, there can be no further excuse for failure to specify the nature of the patients undergoing social skills training.

As our experience accumulates, we also must describe the severity, duration, and course of symptomatic and functional adjustment in our social skills trainees. The major differences among acute, relapsing, and chronic schizophrenics need to be taken into account when interpreting outcomes of social skills training. There is very compelling evidence that schizophrenic patients with acute-onset, brief psychotic episodes who have good premorbid adjustments are different from patients with chronic, sustained symptoms and social dysfunctions. Genetic studies from Denmark suggest that the chronic, but not the acute, reactive schizophrenias may have a hereditary loading. If chronically ill, poor premorbid schizophrenics have an illness more biologically determined than the acute and intermittently relapsing patients, then it stands to reason that they may benefit from different patterns of somatic and socioenvironmental therapies (Chodoff & Carpenter, 1975).

The multifarious course of schizophrenia should point us to optimal timing for making psychosocial and social skills training interventions. We need to become alert to the "when" to intervene as well as to the "how" and "what." Obviously, social skills trainers will not make much headway if they attempt their procedures while the patient is still flagrantly psychotic. On the other hand, with continuing psychotic symptoms and mild thought disorder, patients may improve, given the structure and positiveness of the social skills approach. The degree of psychoticism may determine whether or not a schizophrenic can benefit from social skills training. For patients with long histories of relapses or exacerbations superimposed upon periods of remission or periods of moderate impairment, social skills training would be best timed when the patients are in their good periods.

It will be necessary to take a longer view when working with schizophrenic patients—conducting brief, time-limited social skills training may be fine for helping college students improve their dating skills, but it falls flat when trying to assist schizophrenics in learning to deal with community life. For example, one multiclinic study found that only after 18 months of weekly and biweekly sessions did sociotherapy lead to significant improvements in the social functioning of schizophrenic patients—and after 24 months of therapy, the results were even better (Hogarty, Goldberg, & Schooler, 1974).

If we assume the realistic responsibility of continuing care of schizophrenics, it will be feasible to intervene with social skills training when the time is ripe—for example, when symptoms are in remission and when a patient is about to take a step forward in rehabilitation or independence. We will also have to learn how to integrate social skills training with optimal doses of neuroleptic drugs—using sufficient medication to suppress symptoms but not so much that the patient is "snowed" and unable to learn from the training. Research has begun to show which schizophrenic patients improve without the use of drugs—in most schizophrenic samples, 15%–25% do as well on placebo or on no drug whatsoever. Patients who are likely to benefit from social skills training without the addition of medication have had their onset of illness at a later age, have had briefer psychotic episodes, shorter hospitalizations, and better premorbid levels of adjustment (Marder, Van-Kammen, Docherty, Rayner, & Bunney, 1979).

An important part of psychosocial therapy will be teaching symptom management to patients so they become better able to self-monitor their symptoms—especially incipient signs of exacerbation—and seek early professional intervention. Knowing more about the beneficial effects and deleterious side effects of medication will make patients more cooperative and informed consumers of drugs. To facilitate medication adherence, we need to educate patients about their illness, the drugs they are taking, and ways for them to arrange their environments to increase the regularity of pill ingestion.

Certain elements of the psychopathology and deviant behavior associated with schizophrenia may be beyond the scope of social skills training to remediate. These include unusual, bizarre, and symptomatic behaviors that frighten others, or, at best, force others into defensive and avoidant stances. A number of studies have found that relapse and hospitalization were regularly preceded by increases in bizarre behavior, including incoherent speech, and aggression toward self or others (Miller, 1967; Passamanick, Scarpitti, & Dinitz, 1967). Ways to reduce the nuisance value of these bizarre, symptomatic behaviors need to be integrated with social skills training. Teaching the patient, for example, to talk to himself only in his own room may be an important first step in social skills acquisition. Paul and Lentz (1977) and Liberman, DeRisi,

King, Eckman, and Wood (1974) show clearly how a combination of symptom reduction and social rehabilitation can produce high yield in patient benefits and outcome.

MOTIVATIONAL DEFICITS

Many schizophrenics, in addition to suffering major interpersonal, instrumental role, and cognitive deficits, have a pervasive loss of affective expression and experience. Few reinforcers are available to strengthen their adaptive behavior. They describe being alienated from their feelings or feeling empty and devoid of emotions. "Anhedonia" is a term coined to describe the lack of pleasure in everyday life experienced by the schizophrenic. The emptiness of daily living is made worse by the schizophrenic's anxiety in the presence of others, with a consequent active avoidance of social relationships. Thus, the most important reinforcer for most of us—social relationships—is painful and aversive for most schizophrenics.

Just as the schizophrenic's thought processes are often jumbled, fragmented, and unconnected to reality, so is their quality and flow of emotions disrupted from real-life events. This apparent disruption of connectedness of affect to external reality produces, externally to the observation of others, inappropriate affect. In response to inner stimuli the schizophrenic may laugh and smile, cry, or show signs of fright and fear. Emptiness and a lack of feelings also are part of the schizophrenic experience, even more exasperating and exhausting than sadness and depression. The inward experience of emptiness parallels the outward signs of flatness and dullness of emotions. With a lack of connection of pleasure and emotional responsiveness to instrumental and interpersonal activities, the schizophrenic loses interest in the external world, has no motivation to pursue goal-oriented activities, and becomes lethargic, apathetic, and withdrawn.

The loss of affective responsiveness places a heavy burden on the family and professional help-givers who find their entreaties and encouragement to engage in daily life rebuffed or ignored. Active efforts to pull the withdrawn schizophrenic into social and recreational activities frequently has the effect of making worse the positive symptoms of the illness—delusions, hallucinations, incoherence (Wing, 1975). The effect of the social withdrawal, emotional dullness, and resistance to interpersonal involvement leads to a vicious cycle of greater and greater social isolation and increased negative symptoms of schizophrenia (apathy, slovenliness, and withdrawal). A corollary for the mental health profession is active avoidance by most therapists working with schizophrenic patients. The schizophrenic is usually relegated to brief, cursory visits, separated by long intervals, punctuated by prescriptions for neuroleptic medication—a treatment approach that is euphemistically termed "intermittent supportive therapy." Schizophrenics generally do not find social contact reinforcing and interactions with them are not usually rewarding for therapists.

Not only are positive reinforcers lacking in the lives of most schizophrenics, but they also are troubled by aversive stimuli. Instead of experiencing social relationships as rewarding, schizophrenics may attempt to escape or avoid relationships that are viewed by them as stressful and noxious. While no one enjoys criticism, schizophrenics may respond to censure in a magnified way, reflected in the massive disruptions of their task performance and flight from the situation. On the other hand, social censure can also facilitate a schizophrenic's performance if it is given immediately contingent upon incorrect responses; for example, criticizing a schizophrenic for slow responses to a reaction-time task will lead to more rapid responses (Garmezy, 1966).

Attempts to restore emotional reactivity to a schizophrenic requires Herculean efforts. Behavior therapists have used reinforcer sampling with only limited success (Paul & Lentz, 1977). Psychoanalysts such as Elvin Semrad have tried to help schizophrenics integrate their affects by taking a tour of the body—asking a patient, organ by organ, what, where, when, with whom, and how much bodily feeling was experienced. This was aimed at using awareness of bodily feelings as an aid in learning to acknowledge, recognize, and bear uncomfortable, but human, feelings (Adler, 1979).

IMPLICATIONS FOR CLINICAL INTERVENTION AND
SOCIAL SKILLS TRAINING

It is understandable why clinicians, subject to feelings of frustration, rejection, disappointment, and—if empathic—even emptiness, are reluctant to work therapeutically with schizophrenics on a regular basis over the long haul. But if the fear of relationships and flight from social reinforcers is a major feature of schizophrenia, then a tolerant, nonde-

manding, and long-term, reliable, and trusting relationship with a therapist who can demonstrate human feelings is just what is needed for
schizophrenics. One can sense the absurd inadequacy of providing social
skills training to schizophrenics for 8–12 weeks and then, with a pat on
the back, sending them off into the real world, where they are likely to
be victimized, ignored, and excluded.

Too much of behavior therapy and social skills training with schizophrenics is carried out in formats and durations for the convenience and
satisfaction of the clinicians, rather than for the needs of the patients.
Offering brief courses of social skills training enables therapists to rush
their results into print and presentations, garnering professional reinforcers along the way. Short-term therapy and training, often with
little or no follow-up, are also convenient for the needs of graduate
students who wish to obtain their doctorates in timely fashion and thus
dash off their dissertation research on schizophrenia and quickly move
to another part of the country, at the expense of schizophrenics' real
needs.

While we do not have data on the optimal duration of psychosocial
therapy for schizophrenics, on the basis of the long-term or intermittent
nature of the disorder one would assume that treatment needs to fit the
timetable of the patients' dysfunctions. Carefully implemented and
evaluated behavior therapy carried out with chronically and severely
impaired schizophrenics at the Camarillo/UCLA Clinical Research Unit
(Liberman, Wallace, Teigen, & Davis, 1974) and at the Adolf Meyer
Mental Health Center (Paul & Lentz, 1977) suggests that 6 months
minimum and perhaps as long as 2 to 4 years of treatment are necessary
to bring about clinically significant and durable outcomes.

It may be useful for behavior therapists to borrow some of the
perspective, commitment, and methods for building alliances from
psychoanalysts, if they wish to overcome the resistance of schizophrenic
patients to enter into social skills training and to remain with the
training long enough to reestablish relationships and emotional reactivity. Semrad, a warm, empathic analyst who trained generations of
psychiatrists to work with schizophrenics, attempted to establish safe,
trusting interpersonal environments that allowed the schizophrenic
patient sufficient comfort, sustenance, and gratification to make change
possible. He felt that the therapist's

> empathic understanding and grasp of the patient's distrust, vulnerabilities,
> pain, disorganization, and other needs and fears, helps create the necessary
> therapeutic setting. The awareness that the schizophrenic has an exquisite
> tendency to fragment and retreat to more primitive defenses and style of

> relating provides the therapist with the empathic framework in which he
> can decide how support, silence, activity, clarification, [and intervention] is
> appropriate and necessary from moment to moment and session to session.
> (Adler, 1979, pp. 132–133)

This long-term, tolerant commitment to working with the schizophrenic—termed the "holding environment" by another analyst, Winnicott (1965)—is similar to maintaining a shaping attitude, starting with
where the patient is at, and reinforcing small steps toward social re-
integration. This obviously is not a treatment suited to the hurried
needs of graduate students, psychiatric residents, or researchers whose
own contingencies of reinforcement compete with an immersion in a
time-consuming and emotionally exhausting program of social rehabilitation. However, one does not have to employ a nondirective, interpre-
tative stance for effectively building a therapeutic relationship with a
schizophrenic. By becoming a transparent, live person to the patient,
and accompanying the patient on forays into the real world (such as
bars, recreational events, and family settings), the therapist or trainer
can both construct an effective relationship and teach the patient useful
skills for community life. We have spent many evenings drinking beer
and eating pizza with schizophrenics while they were participating in
social skills training. This spontaneous, person-to-person, round-the-
clock relationship-building is also a feature of the PACT project (Stein
& Test, 1978) and the Mainstreaming Project (Mendel, Houle, & Osman,
1980).

In the Mainstreaming Project, which can serve as a model for *in vivo*
social skills training,

> severely impaired schizophrenics are placed in their own apartment in the
> community, surrounded by a matrix of ordinary people without mental
> illness and a normalizing environment. Special support is provided to each
> schizophrenic by a team of 3 individuals (usually graduate students in voca-
> tional rehabilitation and occupational therapy) who each spent up to 4 hours
> a day with the patient shopping, cooking, housekeeping, exercising, looking
> for a job, going to work, riding the bus, taking a driver's test, going to the
> doctor, and visiting with family. The patients are encouraged to meet and
> spend their time with nonpatients. They learn to cope with crises of
> loneliness, failure, disability, fear and impulse control in a normal setting
> and are given role modeling by their team members. (Mendel *et al.*, 1980,
> pp. 3–4)

As Brown suggests in Chapter 3 in this volume, it is time for us to leave
our hospital- and clinic-based social skills training studios, pack our

portable video equipment, and move into the real world for *in vivo* training of social and community life skills.

While taking a Semradian emotional tour of the body would not be against our cherished behavioral principles (and, in fact, would be consonant with a multimodal behavioral approach), we can teach emotionally expressive skills in ways more conventional and familiar to behavior therapists. For example, Brown and his colleagues at the UCLA/Sepulveda VA Medical Center in Los Angeles stimulate the experiencing of affects through homework assignments (see Chapter 3, this volume). Patients in their Life Skills Training Program are asked to write paragraphs about sadness- and anger-provoking events in which emotions were not fully experienced or expressed. Emotional retraining proceeds through several steps, and angry feelings usually preceding the experience of sadness. First, patients describe their feelings in writing, then in verbal expression, and then with nonverbal expressions added.

While schizophrenics are characterized by a constriction in their range and potency of reinforcers, they can be motivated to participate in social skills training by the creative use of positive and negative reinforcers. Money—a widely accepted, highly normative, generalized reinforcer—has been found to effectively reinforce schizophrenic patients' performance in role playing and in carrying out interpersonal assignments (Doty, 1975; Wallace, Chapter 2, this volume). Schizophrenic patients in the Camarillo/UCLA social skills training project received $2.00 for participating in each day's 5 hours of training and evaluation activities. Together with a heavy emphasis on establishing and maintaining close and collaborative therapeutic relationships, the financial reward helped to limit dropouts to only two out of a voluntary cohort of 30.

Another unusual source of motivation for use in social skills training comes from the experimental literature on social censure, cited above. While criticism and negative feedback tend to be viewed as harmful by behavior therapists, studies conducted on laboratory tasks suggest that, when clearly linked to incorrect response, critical feedback helps schizophrenics improve their performance. Two recent studies have demonstrated that exposure to a censured model resulted in positive behavioral changes in the social skills of chronic schizophrenics (Denicola, 1979). For censure to be beneficial, it must be presented contingent upon inappropriate behavior. It is likely that pairing praise for appropriate behavior with censure for inappropriate behavior will improve outcomes with schizophrenic patients. Important considerations are the quality of the relationship between the patient and the therapist who is giving criticism, the amount of psychopathology experienced by the patient, and the accurate perceiving and processing of the critical feedback (e.g., the patient will not benefit if he or she interprets the criticism in a delusional fashion). A series of controlled, single-case clinical experiments with schizophrenic patients indicates that various punishment methods were effective in improving social interaction and rational conversation when positive reinforcers had failed (Davis, Wallace, Liberman, & Finch, 1976; Fichter, Wallace, Liberman, & Davis, 1976; Liberman, Wallace, Teigen, & Davis, 1974; Patterson & Teigen, 1973). These data should be helpful to social skills trainers as they attempt to mold more effective intervention packages (Alevizos, Malloy, & Proctor, 1974).

COGNITIVE DEFICITS

The most intensively studied psychological aspects of schizophrenia have been cognitive and attentional deficits. These processes are often presumed to be fundamental or basic mediators of schizophrenic symptomatology and indicative of underlying neuropsychological vulnerabilities in persons predisposed to schizophrenia. In this section we will use the term "cognitive" broadly to refer to "all processes by which sensory input is transformed, reduced, elaborated, stored, recovered, and used" (Neisser, 1967, p. 4). This includes processes of sensation, perception, attention, memory, thinking, and related verbal and motor responses.

Clinical observations of schizophrenic patients have traditionally included mention of attentional disturbances. Both Kraepelin and Bleuler noted problems with attention as frequent accompaniments of the psychotic symptomatology. For example, Bleuler (1911/1950) observed:

> On the one hand it is evident that the uninterested or autistically encapsulated patients pay very little attention to the outer world. On the other hand, however, it is remarkable how many of the events which the patients seem to ignore are registered nevertheless. The selectivity which normal attention ordinarily exercises among the sensory impressions can be reduced to zero so that almost everything is recorded that reaches the senses. Thus, the facilitating as well as the inhibiting properties of attention are equally disturbed. (p. 68)

Subjective reports by schizophrenic patients during their actively psychotic periods highlight the problems experienced with selective attention. They seem overwhelmed by a flood of sensory input that they cannot control:

"I can't concentrate. It's diversion of attention that troubles me. . . . The sounds are coming through to me but I feel my mind cannot cope with everything. It's difficult to concentrate on any one sound. It's like trying to do two or three different things at one time."

"When I move quickly it's a strain on me. Things go too quick for my mind. They get blurred and it's like being blind. It's as if you were seeing a picture one moment and another picture the next."

"Things are coming in too fast. I lose my grip on it and get lost. I am attending to everything at once and as a result I do not really attend to anything."

"I'm a good listener but often I'm not really taking it in. I nod my head and smile but it's just a lot of jumbled up words to me."

"When people are talking I just get scraps of it. If it is just one person who is speaking that's not so bad but if the others join in then I can't pick it up at all. I just can't get in time with the conversation. It makes me feel open as if things are closing in on me and I have lost control." (McGhie & Chapman, 1961, p. 104)

These subjective accounts were quoted because they graphically illustrate the cognitive problems experienced by schizophrenics through an interpersonal context. They also represent a useful starting point for investigators seeking to conduct research on the phenomenon, namely, the gathering of data from the patients themselves on a phenomenological level (Freedman & Chapman, 1974). During the past 40 years, research in laboratory settings has quantified and categorized cognitive deficits experienced by schizophrenics through the use of a variety of performance tests. From this body of research emerges the possibility that the thought disorder characteristic of many schizophrenics is associated with fundamental attentional dysfunctions that may contribute to and underlie the disruption of rational, ordered thought and language (Maher, 1972; Rochester, 1978; Venables, 1978).

MEASUREMENT OF COGNITIVE DYSFUNCTION

A wide variety of performance tasks have been used to measure deficits in attention and information processing among schizophrenic patients. Among the most popular and productive performance tasks have been (1) simple reaction time after varying preparatory intervals, (2) vigilance, (3) competing information tasks, (4) span of apprehension, and (5)

short-term memory tasks. Some of the major attentional and information-processing deficits that have been reported among schizophrenic
patients relative to normal subjects are

1. Deficiencies in sustaining focused attention (Orzack &
Kornetsky, 1966; Shakow, 1963; Wohlberg & Kornetsky, 1973;
Zahn, Shakow, & Rosenthal, 1961)
2. Distractibility (McGhie, Chapman, & Lawson, 1965; Oltmanns, 1978; Oltmanns & Neale, 1975)
3. Slowness in initial processing of information in sensory
memory (Davidson & Neale, 1974; Neale, 1971; Saccuzzo, Hirt, &
Spencer, 1974)
4. Impaired detection of relevant stimuli imbedded in irrelevant noise (Rappaport, Hopkins, & Hall, 1972; Stilson & Kopell,
1964; Stilson, Kopell, Vandenberg, & Downs, 1966)
5. Inefficient active organization of information in short-term
memory (Koh, 1978; Traupman, 1975)

Experimental psychopathologists have proposed a range of possible
mechanisms to account for these and other deficits in schizophrenic
information processing. Drawing on Broadbent's (1958) early model of
normal functioning, some theorists have emphasized a deficiency of a
central filter mechanism early in the information-processing chain that
would normally screen out irrelevant stimuli and thoughts (McGhie,
1969; Payne, 1966; Venables, 1964, 1978). Others have posited that the
later response selection and organization phases are particularly deficient (Broen, 1968; Broen & Storms, 1967). Another prominent early
model emphasized slowness in the central processing of relevant information (Yates, 1966a, 1966b). These early explanatory models were
influential and suggestive of strategies for future investigations (Chapman & Chapman, 1973; Neale & Oltmanns, 1980; Nuechterlein, 1977a,
1977b). One recent methodological trend in this area that may yield
better isolation of the nature of schizophrenic deficits is the increased
use of techniques borrowed from information-processing studies of
normal populations (Neale & Oltmanns, 1980; Spring, Nuechterlein,
Sugarman, & Matthysse, 1977). At the same time, another promising
sign is greater recognition of special measurement problems that may
exist in applications of experimental psychology methods to the study of
cognitive differences between groups (Blaney, 1978; Chapman & Chapman, 1973, 1978).

While the stage or level of information processing at which schizophrenics have particular difficulty remains unclear, one common endpoint of many of the individual deficits would appear to be a state of

information overload (Hemsley, 1977). Deficient speed of processing from sensory storage, impaired separation of relevant and irrelevant information, and inefficient short-term memory organizational strategies might all result in a sensation of being overwhelmed by the information processing demands of everyday life.

RELATIONSHIPS BETWEEN COGNITIVE DEFICITS AND SYMPTOMATOLOGY

Viewing information overload as an endpoint of one or more specific processing deficits, Hemsley (1977) has suggested that some clinical phenomena in schizophrenics may represent attempts of the patient to cope with this state. This distinction between primary information-processing deficits and secondary symptomatic phenomena is, of course, reminiscent of Bleuler's separation of fundamental symptoms and accessory symptoms (Bleuler, 1911/1950). In this case, a state of information overload is substituted for Bleuler's postulation that a weakening of associative threads constitutes the fundamental cognitive deficit in schizophrenia. However, in this schema, adaptations to information overload characteristic of normal individuals are used to shed light on connections to clinical symptoms. Thus, the undifferentiated responding and delusion formation characteristic of schizophrenic patients is viewed as an exaggeration of the normal tendency to adopt a simplified information categorizing system under overload conditions. Similarly, incoherence and inappropriateness of speech might represent an extreme form of the intrusion of associated verbal responses occurring in normals who are overburdened by a high information presentation rate.

These connections between attempts to cope with a state of information overload and specific schizophrenic symptomatology remain plausible but speculative at this point due to the lack of a means of predicting and confirming which of the possible adaptations to this state will occur in individual schizophrenic patients. Presumably the severity of the underlying cognitive deficit and resultant level of overload may influence the type of adaptations attempted, but specific supportive data are lacking.

A connection between general level of cognitive performance deficit and global severity of schizophrenic symptomatology, however, has been demonstrated in some studies of antipsychotic medication. Several information-processing measures, including simple reaction time, a span of apprehension procedure, and a continuous performance test (Orzack, Kornetsky, & Freeman, 1967; Spohn, Lacoursiere, Thompson, & Coyne, 1977), have been found to be related to cross-sectional differences in symptomatic severity and to improvements in symptomatology with medication. Such relationships are consistent with the possibility that schizophrenic symptoms are mediated through disturbances in basic information-processing deficits.

Unfortunately, despite the advantages of longitudinal designs for clarifying relationships between basic information-processing deficits and the formation of schizophrenic symptoms, virtually all studies of adult schizophrenic cognitive deficits have involved cross-sectional comparisons. Increasing emphasis on the fluctuating symptomatic course characteristic of most schizophrenics has led to a conceptual distinction between cognitive deficits that are (1) *vulnerability-linked*, as evidenced by being present during both active symptomatic and remitted periods, and (2) those that are *symptom-linked*, as indicated by appearance or substantial exacerbation just prior to or during symptomatic periods (Cromwell & Spaulding, 1978; Zubin & Spring, 1977). Longitudinal comparisons of the cognitive functioning and the symptomatic status of schizophrenic and normal subjects at multiple points in time could directly examine whether various attentional and information-processing deficits are strongly linked to symptomatic status or are relatively stable, underlying characteristics of persons who have experienced a schizophrenic episode.

A conceptual bridge between these traitlike vulnerability indicators and the increasingly accepted diathesis–stress model of schizophrenia can also be suggested. If persistent attentional and information-processing dysfunctions in persons who have had a schizophrenic episode are found to be similar to deficits recently discovered among children at risk for schizophrenia (Asarnow, Steffy, MacCrimmon, & Cleghorn, 1978; Erlenmeyer-Kimling & Cornblatt, 1978; Marcus, 1972; Nuechterlein, 1980; Oltmanns, Weintraub, Stone, & Neale, 1978) and other first-degree relatives of schizophrenics (DeAmicis & Cromwell, 1979; Holzman, Proctor, Levy, Yasillo, Meltzer, & Hurt, 1974; Wood & Cook, 1979), the possibility that such deficits may be indicators of aspects of a diathesis to schizophrenia (or more generally to psychosis) would be supported. Thus, vulnerability-linked indicators of cognitive dysfunction would be potential indices of the susceptibility or diathesis for schizophrenia, while symptom-linked indicators would be implicated in symptom formation or caused by symptom exacerbation.

Currently, as a component of a longitudinal, prospective, follow-through study of carefully diagnosed schizophrenics at the Camarillo/ UCLA Clinical Research Center, Nuechterlein is gathering data on attentional and information-processing functioning using an adapted continuous performance test, span-of-apprehension task, and smooth-pursuit eye movements procedure. We expect this research to shed more light on the ability of these performance tests to discriminate vulnerability-linked from symptom-linked indicators of cognitive deficit.

COGNITIVE FUNCTIONING AND SOCIAL STIMULATION

Although the need to clarify the relationships between specific aspects of information processing and fluctuations in various schizophrenic clinical symptoms is clear, the global concept of information overload as an endpoint of specific information-processing deficits gives rise to a heuristically useful model of schizophrenic symptomatic relapse. Drawing on research at the Institute of Psychiatry in London (Brown & Birley, 1968; Brown et al., 1972; Vaughn & Leff, 1976; Wing & Brown, 1970), British investigators have postulated two complementary processes linking social stimulation and schizophrenic symptomatology (Hirsch, 1976; Leff, 1976; Wing, 1978). On the one hand, schizophrenics living in understimulating environments, such as large custodial institutions, are prone to develop negative symptoms such as apathy, social withdrawal, inactivity, and loss of self-care skills. These negative symptoms, or deficits in adaptive behavior, have been termed the "social breakdown" or "clinical poverty" syndrome. On the other hand, over-stimulating environments, such as highly critical or emotionally overinvolved relatives and suddenly introduced, total-push intensive treatment programs, may produce florid psychotic relapses. This dilemma of too little or too much social stimulation has been aptly described by Hirsch (1976): "The primary handicap of schizophrenics can be seen as an extraordinary vulnerability, like walking a tightrope, with the dangers of an understimulating social environment leading to the negative symptoms of social withdrawal and inactivity on the one side, and the dangers of overstimulation leading to florid symptoms and relapse on the other" (p. 461).

Conditions of overstimulation may operate by triggering or exacerbating a state of nervous system activity in vulnerable individuals that increases the danger of symptomatic relapse. For example, schizophrenic patients living with relatives high on EE tested within their homes showed higher levels of spontaneous fluctuations in the skin conductance response when their key relative entered the room than did patients with low-EE relatives (Tarrier, Vaughn, Lader, & Leff, 1979). Further investigations need to address the time course of such changes and the nature of any other psychophysiological systems that are also affected.

High levels of social stimulation could similarly lead to information overload in remitted schizophrenics who suffer from residual cognitive and attentional dysfunctions. Sensory flooding or information overload could, then, produce the physiological activity and neurochemical events that trigger symptomatic exacerbation in remitted patients with an underlying schizophrenic diathesis. Noxious social stimulation might interact with other processes to influence the type and severity of induced psychopathology as well. As a speculative example, moderately high levels of social stimulation might contribute to sufficient cognitive disorganization to result in delusion formation, while extremely high levels might lead to more complete disorganization and incoherence of thought and speech. Social withdrawal may be an escape adaptation by schizophrenics faced with the hyperarousal and information overload inherent in certain social situations. As Wing (1975) has noted of schizophrenics, "If he can't withdraw, if he is forced to interact by a socially intrusive environment, he is bound to show his abnormality in the form of delusions, speech disorder, or odd behavior" (p. 265).

Additional studies of the cognitive and psychophysiological mediators of the relationship between excessive social stimulation and symptomatic relapse are clearly needed. Earlier formulations (Garmezy, 1966) focusing on schizophrenic performance under laboratory conditions of social censure appear relevant, although not conceptualized in terms of relapse implications. Future studies should include an emphasis on reactions to relatives rated high on EE and real life event changes. Furthermore, cognitive and attentional assessment should control for psychometric artifacts that have clouded the interpretation of many early laboratory studies of social stimuli and schizophrenic cognition (Chapman & Chapman, 1973).

IMPLICATIONS FOR CLINICAL INTERVENTION AND SOCIAL SKILLS TRAINING

If schizophrenic patients do indeed experience the cognitive dysfunctions described above, then much of the work to date in social skills training—

emphasizing verbal and nonverbal *responding* to social challenges—may bypass the more critical psychological processes that are closely linked with attention, perception, and information processing. Focusing only on the topographical features of social skills—eye contact, gestures, voice volume, requesting the other to change, refusing an unreasonable demand—may lead to limited generalization partially because the cognitive processes that facilitate many different types of socially skilled behaviors in many different situations are not targeted for intervention. Thus, it may be more important to target the sensory input, selective focusing, and cognitive-processing precursors to verbal and nonverbal output. Similarly, since short-term memory seems to be structurally intact but mnemonic strategies inefficiently used in schizophrenia (Koh, 1978), teaching structured mnemonic techniques and supplying extra environmental triggers for recall might be useful.

Some of the relevant cognitive precursors of social skills have been identified by clinicians (Spivack, Platt, & Shure, 1976; Trower, Bryant, & Argyle, 1978; Wallace et al., 1980). They include problem recognition, problem definition, accurate perception of the relevant characteristics of the interpersonal situation, knowledge of social mores, information-processing capability, identifying short- and long-term goals, generating response alternatives, weighing the pros and cons of alternatives, evaluating and predicting potential consequences, choosing a reasonable alternative, and implementing an alternative and evaluating its effectiveness in achieving one's goals.

The social skills training program for schizophrenics developed by Wallace and his colleagues at the Camarillo/UCLA Clinical Research Center (see Wallace, Chapter 2, this volume) represents an important point of departure for clinicians who wish to incorporate cognitive problem-solving strategies in their social skills training. Wallace and his colleagues (Wallace et al., 1980) theorized that a socially skilled response is the end result of a chain of behaviors that begins with accurate reception of relevant interpersonal stimuli; moves to flexible processing of these stimuli to generate and evaluate possible response options from which a reasonable one is chosen; and ends with appropriate sending of the chosen alternative.

These workers have created an integrated assessment and training package, based on role playing of approximately 200 different interpersonal scenes in areas of hospital, community, friendship, and family relations. After each situation is role-played, the patient is asked a series of questions designed to assess his receiving and processing skills.

Errors or deficiencies in these cognitive skills call into action training techniques that are evaluated during the role play and, as in most conventional types of social skills training, are then remediated through instructions, modeling, prompts, coaching, and positive feedback.

Meichenbaum and his colleagues have described similar training paradigms, but for children with academic and behavioral problems. They have carried out think-aloud training designed to teach performance-related skills that have been identified through task analysis of the children's situations and goals. Among the skills taught through modeling, prompting, and feedback are

> (a) problem identification or self-interrogation skills ("What is it I have to do?"); (b) focusing attention and response guidance, which is usually the answer to self-inquiry ("Now, carefully stop and repeat the instructions"); (c) self-reinforcement involving standard-setting and self-evaluation ("Good, I'm doing fine"); and (d) coping skills and error-correcting options ("That's okay. . . . Even if I make an error I can go slowly"). Such cognitive training is conducted across tasks, settings, and people in order to ensure that children do not develop task-specific response sets, but, instead, develop generalized stratagems. (Meichenbaum & Asarnow, 1979, pp. 15–16)

While the preliminary results of the Camarillo/UCLA social skills training program, reported in Chapter 2 by Wallace, are promising, most of the empirical and clinical work applying cognitive strategies with deviant adult and child populations has yielded meager generalized outcomes (Denicola, 1979; Ledwidge, 1978; Meichenbaum & Asarnow, 1979). Self-instructional and self-evaluative training with schizophrenics has been disappointing. Most clinicians have reported that patients appear bored, fail to attend to or get involved with the training procedures, and do not reliably carry out assignments to practice the self-control skills outside of the training sessions. To improve the results of cognitive training, investigators teaching problem-solving strategies to retarded clients have recommended alterations in the training procedures, including (1) greater duration of training; (2) rationales for the purpose and usefulness of cognitive strategies; (3) fading of prompts and modeling from the trainer; (4) increased demand for and monitoring of mental involvement in the tasks; and (5) training across settings, problems, and persons. Since some of these recommendations have been incorporated into the Camarillo/UCLA social skills training program, the full report of the results and follow-up data from this program will serve as a further test of the utility of teaching cognitive and problem-solving skills to schizophrenics.

There are suggestions from the experimental psychopathology literature that additional tactics might be helpful in improving the learning of social skills by schizophrenics. These are outlined in Table 1-3 and include such procedures as use of brief, clearly focused sets of tasks; prominent posting of graphics that prompt patients to follow training procedures; repeated practice and overlearning; examining levels of autonomic responsiveness and potential for information overload through psychophysiological and cognitive tests; and allowing patients to temporarily escape or take time out from training when it becomes overstimulating. It would also be desirable for social skills trainers to recognize the diversity in the cognitive and attentional deficits and problems that schizophrenics demonstrate, since most studies indicate that only a subgroup of schizophrenics shows any given deficit. This recognition of diversity will require a more personalized system of training that takes into account each individual's cognitive deficits, assets, and needs.

TRAINING COGNITIVE SKILLS UNDERLYING SCHIZOPHRENIC VULNERABILITY

One final clinical implication that can be drawn from the experimental work done on cognitive processes in schizophrenia is perhaps a bit futuristic and speculative—the development of training methods for

TABLE 1-3. Some Cognitive Deficits Experienced by Schizophrenics and Suggestions for Remediating Them during Social Skills Training

Schizophrenic cognitive deficits	Training procedures for remediation of deficits
Showing associative intrusions in speech. (This may be explained by their failure to self-edit their tentative responses to words. It may be that schizophrenics have difficulty ignoring or dismissing inappropriate response options that occur to them, even though they may recognize that they are inappropriate. Thus, the schizophrenic cognitively perseverates or fixates on the same inappropriate response option until it is actually emitted.)	Employ mild censure contingent on inappropriate responding as well as praise for appropriate responding. Adapt thought stopping or some other intrusive stimulus that can break the schizophrenic's perseverating on inappropriate response options. Monitor thought processes by frequent questions, probes, and by having the schizophrenic think aloud.

TABLE 1-3. (*Continued*)

Schizophrenic cognitive deficits	Training procedures for remediation of deficits
Having difficulty sustaining focused attention over time.	Keep training tasks and steps brief and focused. Use frequent prompts to regain attentional focus.
Being more susceptible to irrelevant cues, being more susceptible to misinterpreting cues, and being more easily distractible.	Keep training setting uncluttered and devoid of distracting stimuli (sound attenuation).
	Post graphic charts for clear and simple visual cueing of cognitive strategies (e.g., post a list of response alternatives to social situations).
	Post a chart that has social skills training procedure and goals in view while, at the same time, the schizophrenic is hearing the same instructions by ear.
Having cognitive deficits that are made worse by requiring speeded responses to presentations of stimulus material.	Proceed slowly through the steps of clearly structured training procedures.
Overloading information may occur more readily when tasks are complex.	Conduct task analysis and break down tasks into similar substeps. Reduce novelty by many repetitions before moving to new material or scenes.
Tending to be influenced by stimuli in the environment that are most immediate.	Avoid preceding interferences with learning
	Give immediate feedback contingent upon performance in training. After overlearning has occurred, gradually introduce delays into feedback and then fade to self-evaluation and feedback.
Possibly developing exacerbation of psychotic symptoms if overstimulated by environment.	Pace training individually, keeping performance demands low and performance-contingent feedback positive.
	Examine level of autonomic responsiveness through psychophysiological recording and potential for information overload by information-processing tests (e.g., span-of-apprehension test).
	Monitor psychopathology by repeated administration of mental status exams and feedback results for clinical decisions on medication dose and pace of exposure to training.
	Allow schizophrenics to escape or take a time out from training when necessary.

improving basic psychological processes, such as sustained attention and selective attention, that may mediate some symptomatology and possibly may be linked to the underlying diathesis or vulnerability of individuals to schizophrenic disorder. The work by Nuechterlein, Asarnow, Erlenmeyer-Kimling, Holzman, and others, cited previously, suggests that certain attentional processes may be deficient in some first-degree relatives of schizophrenics and in remitted schizophrenics. If ongoing research confirms this suspected phenomenon and clarifies its role in the onset of schizophrenia, then clinicians could conceivably mount training efforts with individuals at risk for schizophrenia, aimed at strengthening these basic psychological and neurophysiological processes through behavioral interventions—monitoring, modeling, prompting, practice, contingent feedback. The analogy to biofeedback is possibly apt. This would certainly be an exciting development, for it would provide clinicians an unparalleled opportunity to engage in a truly preventive psychiatry.

THE OVERSTIMULATION HYPOTHESIS AND TREATMENT INTENSITY

As described by Wing, Brown, and their colleagues at the Institute of Psychiatry in London, schizophrenics who are exposed to overstimulating environments are presumably liable for exacerbation of their symptoms or relapse. This hypothesis is based upon data from studies on institutional and family factors bearing on the psychopathology of schizophrenics. Of concern is whether or not social skills training—especially in the intensive form with one or more training sessions per day—is overstimulating and likely to cause symptomatic flare-ups in vulnerable schizophrenics.

Since 1972, we have amassed clinical experience with over 100 schizophrenic patients who have participated in fairly intensive social skills training. We have had a few cases where symptoms flared up; this was usually at the very start of training with a patient who had previously spent a long period in an unstimulating and nondemanding environment. Perhaps upward of 10 patients out of 100 have initially balked at participating in the training. Our strategy has been to ease them into it and not force them to proceed until a solid working alliance has been forged. Fewer than five patients have had to drop out of the training or have absolutely refused to participate, even after a gradual induction and relationship building. On rare occasions, patients have experienced anxiety or depression, necessitating a brief period of "time out" from the training—usually 1 to 2 days. However, much more common than symptomatic exacerbation has been boredom and impatience with the structure and repetition of the training procedures.

Rather than overstimulation and symptom exacerbation, our cumulative experience has been that social skills training has been associated with reduction in psychopathology in over 90% of our patients. This is documented in the research reported by Wallace in Chapter 2, this volume. In addition to regular reductions in psychopathology as measured by the Present State Examination, the Brief Psychiatric Rating Scale, the Psychiatric Assessment Scale, and Global Impairment Ratings, we have found significant improvements in Minnesota Multiphasic Personality Inventory (MMPI) profiles (lowering from deviant to normal range on the Sc scale), and in the Whitaker Index of Schizophrenic Thinking (Liberman *et al.*, 1980).

How are we to explain this seemingly paradoxical finding that intensive social skills training does not produce exacerbation of schizophrenic symptoms? We think the explanation lies in the nature of the training; namely, that social skills training is not overstimulating, as it is practiced by well-trained and clinically sensitive behavior therapists. The goals of training are broken down into small steps so the performance demand at any one time is small and manageable. The training format is predictable, repetitive, and explained in advance. There is no effort—as in psychodrama—to emotionally arouse the patient since catharsis and abreaction are unimportant in the training process. The structure and clarity of the training process cuts down on the overall information processing difficulty level. Finally, as the patient participates in the training process, he or she is suffused with large doses of positive feedback, backed up by a warm and reliable therapeutic relationship. Despite this clinical experience that vindicates social skills training from the overstimulation caveat, it might be informative to monitor the autonomic responsivity levels and attentional functioning of patients undergoing this type of therapy by repeating electrodermal response and information-processing measures during the course of training.

AVOIDANCE AND ESCAPE AS GOALS OF
SOCIAL SKILLS TRAINING

Imbued with idealistic and optimistic zeal, behavior therapists have tended to target goals for schizophrenics that are aimed at equipping the patient to actively change his or her social environment. Thus, social skills training curricula for schizophrenics include goals such as initiating and maintaining conversations; overcoming obstacles to obtaining appointments with care-givers; getting satisfaction in consumer–marketplace interactions; expressing positive feelings to peers and family; and using eye contact, hand gestures, leaning forward, and good tone of voice to express feelings. Since these interpersonal goals are taught in a clear, step-by-step, structured manner with loads of positive feedback, there is little hazard of untoward overstimulation, arousal, information overload and symptomatic exacerbation during the training period. However, once the patient has left the protective security by clinically sensitive trainers and the psychiatric setting, employing a coping strategy of actively approaching others in the "big bad world" may lead to frustration, disappointment, anxiety, arousal, information overload, and symptomatic exacerbation. In most community aftercare programs, trained personnel are not available on the spot to guide the ex-patient's social interactions; they are only available to pick up the pieces once relapse has occurred.

Therefore, it behooves us to consider an additional coping strategy, one that promotes avoidance and escape decisions and responses for our

TABLE 1-4. Response Alternatives Used in the Social Skills Training Program

Compromising
Terminating rudely[a]
Terminating politely[a]
Ignoring criticism[a]
Getting angry
Repeating your request
Asking for assistance
Highlighting the importance of your need
Complying with the other's request
Refusing to comply with the other's request
Explaining your position
Asking for more information
Coming back later[a]
Acknowledging the other's position and . . . (use one of the above)

Note. After role-playing a scene, the patient is asked to choose one of these alternatives and then to evaluate its appropriateness for achieving short- and long-term goals. (Alternatives developed by C. J. Wallace and colleagues at the Camarillo/UCLA Clinical Research Center.)

[a]Indicate coping responses that involve avoiding or withdrawing from a stressful social situation.

schizophrenic patients. When we have identified certain characteristics and persistant stressors for a schizophrenic individual, it becomes possible to incorporate those situations into a training method that encourages the patient to identify the stressor (e.g., critical comments by key relatives), to determine how continued engagement with the stressful situation might endanger short- and long-term goals, to consider leaving the situation as a reasonable response option, and to practice this exit option through role playing. In Table 1-4 is shown the list of response alternatives used in the Camarillo/UCLA social skills training program. Perusal of the 14 generic alternatives indicates that four portray responses that might be considered escape from the situation. This is a step toward helping our patients learn how to back away gracefully from social situations and challenges that they may find stressful and overstimulating. In our normal, everyday commerce with friends, loved ones, coworkers, and passersby, we often modulate the stressfulness of our own interpersonal encounters by avoiding or escaping from them. Similarly, teaching our schizophrenic patients how to terminate or ignore potentially stressful situations may be in the service of normalizing their lives.

SUMMARY

Because social skills training with schizophrenics has failed to produce generalizable and durable results, there is a need for retooling the training methods. Helpful guidelines for making social skills training more effective with schizophrenics come from the literature on experimental psychopathology. A number of areas of research inquiry have yielded data that can be adapted and fit into social skills training—family factors, social and community stressors, psychopathology, motivational deficits, and cognitive deficits.

With the advent of a sensitive and reliable family interview, attitudes and emotions expressed by key relatives about a schizophrenic family member can now be used to determine a target group of schizophrenics who can be considered vulnerable for relapse. Patients coming from families who are rated high on criticism and overinvolvement are four times more likely to relapse than those who live with families who are not excessively critical or overinvolved. Data have also accumulated suggesting that communication deviance in parents predicts the onset of schizophrenialike symptoms in vulnerable offspring. Clinicians can no longer afford to ignore the family and its social processes in therapy efforts with schizophrenics. Methods, aimed at improving dysfunctional family interactions, are being tested for family therapy that train patients and relatives alike in mental health principles, communication skills, and problem solving.

Social and community stressors—termed "life events"—have been tentatively implicated in the relapse of chronic schizophrenics. These life events are more likely to occur during periods of economic downturn. The modest correlations obtained by researchers between the occurrence of stressors and the onset of illness suggest that recent life events alone are not sufficient to precipitate symptomatic flare-ups. The impact of life stressors is influenced by the individual's perception and cognitive processing of them, the person's coping skills and previous patterns of defense and sick role, and the person's social networks. Social skills trainers need to examine more closely the crucial events in the community that are related to relapse and breakdowns in social functioning. By developing a criterion-referenced approach to social skill assessment, a personalized system of training can be tailored to the specific deficits of each patient, which may be more effective in promoting generalization and durability of outcomes.

For too long, clinicians in the United States have avoided the important task of reliable and specific diagnosis in selecting patients for research projects. This diagnostic lucunae need not continue now that technology exists for making accurate diagnoses of schizophrenia. Greater attention paid to psychiatric assessment reveals the variation in the course of schizophrenia and the need to tailor treatment programs to the specific needs of a patient at a given point in the course of the illness. The timing of social skills training, preferably during periods of relative remission, becomes an important issue. Whether or not schizophrenics can benefit from social skills training while still experiencing psychotic symptoms may not be as relevant a query as how much benefit such patients can be expected to show. While brief regimens of social skills training are appealing and convenient for impatient, publication-hungry researchers, they will not suffice for making significant impacts on patients. The next decade of experience with social skills training with severely impaired patient populations will see much longer durations of training.

Motivational deficits have been noted in schizophrenics for as long as the disorder has been recognized and sorely challenge the fortitude of clinicians who attempt to engage this type of patient in any therapeutic modality. Even within the group of patients who are characterized as schizophrenic, there is great diversity in their responsiveness to tangible rewards and social reinforcers. This diversity and relative refractoriness to most incentives should instigate clinicians to go beyond offering different strokes for different folks to include measures for establishing social reinforcers, for using social censure contingent upon inappropriate behavior, for integrating normal role models into treatment, and for doling out money as a more potent reinforcer.

In schizophrenic disorders, there appears to be a dysfunction in one or more of the psychological processes that are subsumed under the term "cognition". As task demands increase—particularly in their complexity and speed requirements—the deficits in cognitive processes often increase. The efficient, synchronous meshing of sensory storage, recoding, selective attention, short-term memory organization, rehearsal, and response output is apparently impaired in most schizophrenics. Social skills trainers have only begun to identify cognitive processes as relevant for clinical intervention with schizophrenics. Work will proceed to develop methods for helping the schizophrenic to better regulate and integrate his perceptual, conceptual, and response processes.

To summarize some of the concepts that we have discussed, Figure 1-3 presents a heuristic schema depicting the possible interrelationships among environmental, cognitive, psychophysiological, and behavioral variables in the course of schizophrenic disorders. Realizing that any working model of such a complex interactive system will greatly oversimplify the natural situation, we present this diagram only as a heuristic guide to relationships that deserve systematic investigation.

The components of this diagram fall into four major categories: (1) external environment, (2) intrapersonal vulnerability characteristics, (3) intermediate states, and (4) outcome behaviors. The hypothesized noxious input from the social environment is represented by the concepts of stressors and life events, which are hypothesized to interact with preexisting characteristics of the vulnerable individual. Two broad classes of such intrapersonal vulnerability characteristics are included here, information-processing dysfunctions and physiological hyperreactivity. Of course, future research may specify more fully the nature of the personal characteristics linked to vulnerability to schizophrenia, but these two general areas seem to hold some promise at this time.

Noxious social stressors impinging on vulnerable individuals with information-processing deficits or physiological hyperreactivity would be expected to lead to transient, intermediate states of sensory or

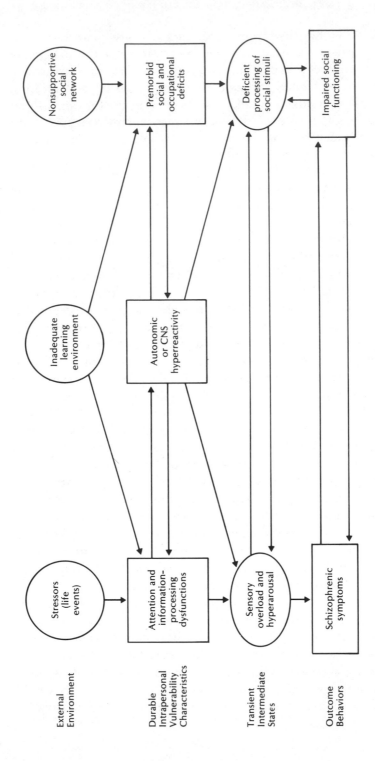

FIGURE 1-3. A hypothetical model of how environmental variables (round labels) may interact with durable, traitlike cognitive and psycho-physiological variables (square labels) to produce transient, statelike processes (oval labels), which, finally, lead to impairments in functioning and schizophrenia symptoms (rectangular labels). Course and outcome of schizophrenia, viewed from multiple social, occupational, and symptomatic dimensions, will thus vary greatly from individual to individual.

information overload and hyperarousal. Variations in the duration, quality, and strength of stressors and in the severity and type of vulnerability characteristics may influence the development of these intermediate states. Social learning opportunities and supportive social networks in the environment as well as social skills may cushion the full impact of social stressors on the vulnerable individual or enable the individual to better cope and resolve problems. Thus the vulnerable individual is not passively affected by social stressors and life events, but rather is able to actively utilize favorable environmental conditions and acquired social skills to modulate or eliminate stress. Presumably, active problem-solving efforts exert their effects by either aborting the development of or rapidly reversing sensory overload and physiological hyperarousal.

If information overload and hyperaroused physiological states do endure past some critical time period, they may contribute to the return of schizophrenic symptomatology. Likewise, such hyperarousal and overload states may lead to deficient processing of interpersonal stimuli and thus to impaired social and occupational functioning. The extent of impairment in the social and occupational realms also appears to be a function of premorbid learning environments and instrumental and social skill levels. Social and occupational outcomes are not necessarily correlated with symptomatic outcomes, since they are influenced by distinct preconditions.

Treatment of schizophrenic disorders could potentially be focused on any of the links and levels in these processes since the model describes interactions and mutual influence at each level. Thus, while past social skills training efforts have concentrated on altering behaviors at the outcome level, future strategies may more profitably be aimed at hypothesized precursors of these final outcomes.

ACKNOWLEDGMENTS

The preparation of this chapter was supported in part by NIMH Research Grant MH 30911, which funds the Mental Health Clinical Research Center for the Study of Schizophrenia. Robert Paul Liberman, principal investigator of the MHCRC, is responsible for the overall preparation of this chapter. Keith H. Nuechterlein is the primary contributor to the section on cognitive deficits. Charles J. Wallace is the developer of the cognitive problem-solving and information-processing model of social skills training used at the MHCRC. Liberman, Nuechterlein, Wallace, and Michael Dawson are responsible for the hypothetical model of schizophrenia illustrated in Figure 1-3. The authors appreciate the encouragement and support provided by Clinton Rust and Samuel Rapport, Executive Director and Medical Director, respectively, of Camarillo State Hospital.

REFERENCES

Adler, G. The psychotherapy of schizophrenia: Semrad's contributions to current psycho-analytic concepts. *Schizophrenia Bulletin, 1979, 5,* 130–134.

Alevizos, P. N., Malloy, T. E., & Proctor, S. Feedback variables in strategy acquisition: Some implications for behavior therapy. *Behavior Therapy, 1974, 5,* 514–522.

Asarnow, R. F., Steffy, R. A., MacCrimmon, F. J., & Cleghorn, J. M. An attentional assessment of foster children at risk for schizophrenia. In L. C. Wynne, R. L. Cromwell, & S. Matthysse (Eds.), *The nature of schizophrenia: New approaches to research and treatment.* New York: Wiley, 1978.

Birley, J. L. T., & Brown, G. W. Crisis and life changes preceding the onset or relapse of acute schizophrenia. *British Journal of Psychiatry, 1970, 116,* 327–333.

Blaney, P. H. Schizophrenic thought disorder: Why the lack of answers? In S. Schwartz (Ed.), *Language and cognition in schizophrenia.* Hillsdale, N.J.: Erlbaum, 1978.

Bleuler, E. *Dementia praecox or the group of schizophrenias* (J. Zinkin, trans.). New York: International Universities Press, 1950. (Originally published, 1911.)

Brenner, M. *Mental illness and the economy.* Cambridge, Mass.: Harvard University Press, 1973.

Broadbent, D. E. *Perception and communication.* London: Pergamon Press, 1958.

Broen, W. E. *Schizophrenia: Research and theory.* New York: Academic Press, 1968.

Broen, W. E., & Storms, L. H. A theory of response interference in schizophrenia. In B. A. Maher (Ed.), *Progress in experimental personality research* (Vol. 4). New York: Academic Press, 1967.

Brown, G. W., & Birley, J. L. T. Crisis and life changes and the onset of schizophrenia. *Journal of Health and Social Behavior, 1968, 9,* 203–214.

Brown, G. W., Birley, J. L. T., & Wing, J. K. Influence of family life on the course of schizophrenic disorders: A replication. *British Journal of Psychiatry, 1972, 121,* 241–258.

Brown, G. W., Bone, M., Dalison, B., & Wing, J. K. *Schizophrenia and social care.* London: Oxford University Press, 1966.

Chapman, L. J., & Chapman, J. P. *Disordered thought in schizophrenia.* New York: Appleton-Century-Crofts, 1973.

Chapman, L. J., & Chapman, J. P. The measurement of differential deficit. *Journal of Psychiatric Research, 1978, 14,* 303–311.

Chodoff, P., & Carpenter, W. T. Psychogenic theories of schizophrenia. In G. Usdin (Ed.), *Schizophrenia: Biological and psychological perspectives.* New York: Brunner/Mazel, 1975.

Cromwell, R. L., & Spaulding, W. How schizophrenics handle information. In W. E. Fann, I. Karacan, A. D. Pokorny, & R. L. Williams (Eds.), *Phenomenology and treatment of schizophrenia.* New York: Spectrum, 1978.

Davidson, G. S., & Neale, J. M. The effects of signal-noise similarity on visual information processing of schizophrenics. *Journal of Abnormal Psychology, 1974, 83,* 683–686.

Davis, J. R., Wallace, C. J., Liberman, R. P., & Finch, B. E. The use of brief isolation (time-out) to suppress delusional and hallucinatory speech. *Journal of Behavior Therapy and Experimental Psychiatry, 1976, 7,* 269–276.

DeAmicis, L., & Cromwell, R. L. Reaction time crossover in process schizophrenic patients, their relatives, and control subjects. *Journal of Nervous and Mental Disease, 1979, 167,* 593–600.

Denicola, J. *Cognitive behavioral and social skills training with schizophrenic inpatients.* Paper presented to the 25th annual meeting of the Southeastern Psychological Association, Atlanta, March 1979.

Doane, J. A., West, K. L., Goldstein, M. J., Rodnick, E. H., & Jones, J. E. Parental communication deviance and affective style as predictors of subsequent schizophrenia spectrum disorders in vulnerable adolescents. *Archives of General Psychiatry,* in press, 1981.

Doty, D. W. Role-playing and incentives in the modification of the social interaction of chronic psychiatric patients. *Journal of Consulting and Clinical Psychology*, 1975, *43*, 676–682.

Erlenmeyer-Kimling, L., & Cornblatt, B. Attentional measures in a study of children at high-risk for schizophrenia. In L. C. Wynne, R. L. Cromwell, & S. Matthysse (Eds.), *The nature of schizophrenia: New approaches to research and treatment.* New York: Wiley, 1978.

Falloon, I. R. H., Lindley, P., McDonald, R., & Marks, I. M. Social skills training of outpatient groups: A controlled study of rehearsal and homework. *British Journal of Psychiatry*, 1977, *131*, 599–609.

Fichter, M., Wallace, C. J., Liberman, R. P., & Davis, J. R. Improving social interaction in a chronic psychotic using "nagging" (discriminated avoidance): Experimental analysis and generalization. *Journal of Applied Behavior Analysis*, 1976, *9*, 377–386.

Freedman, B. J., & Chapman, L. J. Early subjective experience in schizophrenic episodes. *Journal of Abnormal Psychology*, 1974, *30*, 333–340.

Garmezy, N. The prediction of performance in schizophrenia. In P. Hoch & J. Zubin (Eds.), *Psychopathology of schizophrenia.* New York: Grune & Stratton, 1966.

Goldsmith, J. G., & McFall, R. M. Development and evaluation of an interpersonal skill-training program for psychiatric inpatients. *Journal of Consulting and Clinical Psychology*, 1975, *84*, 51–58.

Goldstein, A. A. *Structured learning therapy.* New York: Academic Press, 1973.

Goldstein, M. J., Rodnick, E. H., Jones, J. E., McPherson, S. R., & West, K. L. Familial precursors of schizophrenia spectrum disorders. In L. C. Wynne (Ed.), *The nature of schizophrenia.* New York: Wiley, 1978.

Hemsley, D. R. What have cognitive deficits to do with schizophrenic symptoms? *British Journal of Psychiatry*, 1977, *130*, 167–173.

Hersen, M., & Bellack, A. S. Social skills training for chronic psychiatric patients: Rationale, research findings, and future directions. *Comprehensive Psychiatry*, 1976, *17*, 559–580.

Hirsch, S. R. Interacting social and biological factors determining prognosis in the rehabilitation and management of persons with schizophrenia. In R. Cancro (Ed.), *Annual review of the schizophrenic syndrome* (Vol. 4). New York: Brunner/Mazel, 1976.

Hirsch, S. R., Gaind, R., Rohde, P. D., Stevens, B. C., & Wing, J. K. Double blind clinical trial of phenothiazines as a maintenance treatment for schizophrenia. *British Medical Journal*, 1973, *1*, 118–127.

Hogarty, G. E., Goldberg, S. C., & Schooler, N. R. Drugs and sociotherapy in the aftercare of schizophrenic patients: Two-year relapse rates. *Archives of General Psychiatry*, 1974, *31*, 603–608.

Holzman, P. S., Proctor, L. R., Levy, D. L., Yasillo, N. J., Meltzer, H. Y., & Hurt, S. W. Eye-tracking dysfunctions in schizophrenic patients and their relatives. *Archives of General Psychiatry*, 1974, *31*, 143–151.

Kayton, L., Beck, J., & Koh, S. D. Postpsychotic state convalescent environment and therapeutic relationship in schizophrenic outcome. *American Journal of Psychiatry*, 1976, *133*, 1269–1274.

Koh, S. D. Remembering of verbal materials by schizophrenic young adults. In S. Schwartz (Ed.), *Language and cognition in schizophrenia.* Hillsdale, N.J.: Erlbaum, 1978.

Ledwidge, B. Cognitive behavior modification: A step in the wrong direction? *Psychology Bulletin*, 1978, *25*, 217–224.

Leff, J. P. Schizophrenia and sensitivity to the family environment. *Schizophrenia Bulletin*, 1976, *2*, 566–574.

Leff, J. P., & Wing, J. K. Trial of maintenance therapy in schizophrenia. *British Medical Journal*, 1971, *3*, 599–604.

Liberman, R. P., & Davis, J. Drugs and behavior analysis. In M. Hersen, R. Eisler, & P. M. Miller (Eds.), *Progress in behavior modification.* New York: Academic Press, 1975.

Liberman, R. P., DeRisi, W. J., King, L., Eckman, T., & Wood, D. Behavioral measurement in a community mental health center. In P. Davidson, F. Clark, & L. Hamerlynck (Eds.), *Evaluating behavioral programs in community, residential, and educational settings.* Champaign, Il.: Research Press, 1974.

Liberman, R. P., King, L. W., DeRisi, W. J., & McCann, M. *Personal effectiveness: Guiding people to assert themselves and improve their social skills.* Champaign, Il.: Research Press, 1975.

Liberman, R. P., Lillie, F., Falloon, I. R. H., Hutchinson, W., & Harpin, R. E. *Social skills training with relapsing schizophrenics.* Unpublished manuscript, 1980.

Liberman, R. P., Wallace, C. J., Teigen, J., & Davis, J. R. Interventions with psychotic behaviors. In K. S. Calhoun, H. E. Adams, & E. M. Mitchell (Eds.), *Innovative treatment methods in psychopathology,* New York: Wiley, 1974.

Luria, R., & Meltzer, H. Y. *Standard Psychiatric History Schedule.* Chicago: Illinois State Psychiatric Institute/University of Chicago Clinical Research Center, 1977.

Maher, B. A. The language of schizophrenia: A review and reinterpretation. *Brisith Journal of Psychiatry,* 1972, *120,* 3–17.

Marcus, L. M. *Studies of attention in children vulnerable to psychopathology.* Unpublished doctoral dissertation, University of Minnesota, Minneapolis, 1972.

Marder, S. R., VanKammen, D. P., Docherty, J. P., Rayner, J., & Bunney, W. E. Predicting drug-free improvement in schizophrenic psychosis. *Archives of General Psychiatry,* 1979, *36,* 1080–1085.

McGhie, A. *Pathology of attention.* Middlesex, England: Penguin Books, 1969.

McGhie, A., & Chapman, J. S. Disorders of attention and perception in early schizophrenia. *British Journal of Medical Psychology,* 1961, *34,* 103–116.

McGhie, A., Chapman, J., & Lawson, J. S. The effect of distraction of schizophrenic performance: 2. Psychomotor ability. *British Journal of Psychiatry,* 1965, *111,* 391–398.

Meichenbaum, D., & Asarnow, J. R. Cognitive-behavior modification and metacognitive development: Implications for the classroom. In P. Kendall & S. Hollon (Eds.), *Cognitive-behavioral intervention: Theory, research, and prodecures.* New York: Academic Press, 1979.

Mendel, W. M. *Supportive care: Theory and technique.* Los Angeles: Mara Books, 1975.

Mendel, W. M. Personal communication, 1979.

Mendel, W., Houle, J., & Osman, S. *Mainstreaming: An approach to the treatment of chronically and severely mentally ill patients in the community.* Unpublished manuscript, 1980.

Miller, D. Retrospective analysis of post-hospital mental patients' worlds. *Journal of Health and Social Behavior,* 1967, *8,* 136–140.

Neale, J. M. Perceptual span in schizophrenia. *Journal of Abnormal Psychology,* 1971, *77,* 196–204.

Neale, J. M., & Oltmanns, T. F. *Schizophrenia.* New York: Wiley, 1980.

Neisser, U. *Cognitive psychology.* New York: Appleton-Century-Crofts, 1967.

Nuechterlein, K. H. Reaction time and attention in schizophrenia: A critical evaluation of the data and theories. *Schizophrenia Bulletin,* 1977, *3,* 373–428. (a)

Nuechterlein, K. H. Refocusing on attentional dysfunctions in schizophrenia. *Schizophrenia Bulletin,* 1977, *3,* 457–469. (b)

Nuechterlein, K. H. Sustained attention among children vulnerable to adult schizophrenia and among hyperactive children. In N. F. Watt, L. C. Wynne, E. J. Anthony, L. Erlenmeyer-Kimling, & J. E. Rolf (Eds.), *Children at risk for schizophrenia: A longitudinal perspective.* 1980.

Oltmanns, T. F. Selective attention in schizophrenic and manic psychoses: The effect of distraction on information processing. *Journal of Abnormal Psychology,* 1978, *87,* 212–225.

Oltmanns, T. F., & Neale, J. M. Schizophrenic performance when distractors are present: Attentional deficit or differential task difficulty? *Journal of Abnormal Psychology,* 1975, *84,* 205–209.

Oltmanns, T. F., Weintraub, S., Stone, A. A., & Neale, J. M. Cognitive slippage in children vulnerable to schizophrenia. *Journal of Abnormal Child Psychology*, 1978, *6*, 237–245.

Orzack, M. H., & Kornetsky, C. Attention dysfunction in chronic schizophrenia. *Archives of General Psychiatry*, 1966, *14*, 323–326.

Orzack, M. H., Kornetsky, C., & Freeman, H. The effects of daily administration of carphenazine on attention in the schizophrenic patient. *Psychopharmacologia*, 1967, *11*, 31–38.

Passamanick, B., Scarpitti, F. R., & Dinitz, S. *Schizophrenia in the community*. New York: Appleton-Century-Crofts, 1967.

Patterson, R. L., & Teigen, J. R. Conditioning and post-hospital generalization of non-delusional responses in a chronic psychotic patient. *Journal of Applied Behavior Analysis*, 1973, *6*, 65–70.

Paul, G. L., & Lentz, R. *Psychosocial treatment of the chronic mental patient*. Cambridge, Mass.: Harvard University Press, 1977.

Paul, G. L., Tobias, L. L., & Holly, B. L. Maintenance psychotropic drugs in the presence of active treatment programs. *Archives of General Psychiatry*, 1972, *27*, 106–115.

Payne, R. W. The measurement and significance of overinclusive thinking and retardation in schizophrenic patients. In P. H. Hoch & J. Zubin (Eds.), *Psychopathology of schizophrenia*. New York: Grune & Stratton, 1966.

Rappaport, M., Hopkins, H. K., & Hall, K. Auditory signal detection in paranoid and nonparanoid schizophrenics. *Archives of General Psychiatry*, 1972, *27*, 747–752.

Rochester, S. R. Are language disorders in acute schizophrenia actually information processing problems? *Journal of Psychiatric Research*, 1978, *14*, 275–283.

Saccuzzo, D. P., Hirt, M., & Spencer, T. J. Backward masking as a measure of attention in schizophrenia. *Journal of Abnormal Psychology*, 1974, *83*, 512–522.

Shakow, D. Psychological deficit in schizophrenia. *Behavioral Science*, 1963, *8*, 275–305.

Spivack, G., Platt, J. J., & Shure, M. B. *The problem-solving approach to adjustment*. San Francisco: Jossey-Bass, 1976.

Spohn, H. E., Lacoursiere, R. B., Thompson, K., & Coyne, L. Phenothiazine effects on psychological and psychophysiological dsyfunction in chronic schizophrenics. *Archives of General Psychiatry*, 1977, *34*, 633–644.

Spring, B., Nuechterlein, K. H., Sugarman, J., & Matthysse, S. The "new look" in studies of schizophrenic attention and information processing. *Schizophrenia Bulletin*, 1977, *3*, 470–482.

Stein, L. I., & Test, M. A. *Alternatives to mental hospital treatment*. New York: Plenum Press, 1978.

Stilson, D. W., & Kopell, B. S. Visual recognition in the presence of noise by psychiatric patients. *Journal of Nervous and Mental Disease*, 1964, *139*, 209–221.

Stilson, D. W., Kopell, B. S., Vandenbergh, R., & Downs, M. P. Perceptual recognition in the presence of noise by psychiatric patients. *Journal of Nervous and Mental Disease*, 1966, *142*, 235–247.

Tarrier, N., Vaughn, C. E., Lader, M. H., & Leff, J. P. Bodily reactions to people and events in schizophrenics. *Archives of General Psychiatry*, 1979, *36*, 311–315.

Tolsdorf, C. C. Social networks, support, and coping. *Family Process*, 1976, *15*, 407–418.

Traupman, K. L. Effects of categorization and imagery on recognition and recall by process and reactive schizophrenics. *Journal of Abnormal Psychology*, 1975, *84*, 307–314.

Trower, P., Bryant, B., & Argyle, M. *Social skills and mental health*. Pittsburgh: University of Pittsburgh Press, 1978.

Vaughn, C. E., & Leff, J. P. The influence of family and social factors on the course of psychiatric illness. *British Journal of Psychiatry*, 1976, *129*, 125–137.

Venables, P. H. Input dysfunction in schizophrenia. In B. A. Maher (Ed.), *Progress in experimental personality research* (Vol. 1). New York: Academic Press, 1964.

Venables, P. H. Cognitive disorder. In J. K. Wing (Ed.), *Schizophrenia: Towards a new synthesis*. London: Academic Press, 1978.

Wallace, C. J. *Social skills training for relapsing schizophrenics.* NIMH Research Grant No. MN30911, 1977–1979.

Wallace, C. J., Nelson, C., Liberman, R. P., Lukoff, D., & Aitchison, R. A. Review and critique of social skills training with schizophrenics. *Schizophrenia Bulletin,* 1980, *6,* 42–64.

Wing, J. K. Impairments in schizophrenia: A rational basis for social treatment. In R. D. Wirto, G. Winokur, & M. Roff (Eds.), *Life history research in psychopathology.* Minneapolis: University of Minnesota Press, 1975.

Wing, J. K. Clinical concepts of schizophrenia. In J. K. Wing (Ed.), *Schizophrenia: Towards a new synthesis.* London: Academic Press, 1978.

Wing, J. K., & Brown, G. W. *Institutionalization and schizophrenia: A comparative study of three mental hospitals 1960–1968.* Cambridge, England: Cambridge University Press, 1970.

Wing, J. K., Cooper, J. E., & Sartorius, N. *The measurement and classification of psychiatric symptoms.* London: Cambridge University Press, 1974.

Winnicott, D. W. *The maturational processes and the facilitating environment.* New York: International Universities Press, 1965.

Wohlberg, G. W., & Kornetsky, C. Sustained attention in remitted schizophrenics. *Archives of General Psychiatry,* 1973, *28,* 533–537.

Wood, R. L., & Cook, M. Attentional deficit in the siblings of schizophrenics. *Psychological Medicine,* 1979, *9,* 465–467.

Yates, A. J. Data processing levels and thought disorder in schizophrenia. *Australian Journal of Psychology,* 1966, *18,* 103–112. (a)

Yates, A. J. Psychological deficit. In P. R. Farnsworth (Ed.), *Annual review of psychology.* Palo Alto, Calif.: Annual Reviews, 1966. (b)

Zahn, T. P., Shakow, D., & Rosenthal, D. Reaction time in schizophrenic and normal subjects as a function of preparatory and intertrial intervals. *Journal of Nervous and Mental Disease,* 1961, *133,* 283–287.

Zubin, J., & Spring, B. Vulnerability—a new view of schizophrenia. *Journal of Abnormal Psychology,* 1977, *86,* 103–126.

Zubin, J., Sutton, S., Salzinger, K., Salzinger, S., Burdock, E. I., & Peretz, D. A biometric approach to prognosis in schizophrenia. In P. Hoch & J. Zubin (Eds.), *Comparative epidemiology of the mental disorders.* New York: Grune & Stratton, 1961.

2

THE SOCIAL SKILLS TRAINING PROJECT OF THE MENTAL HEALTH CLINICAL RESEARCH CENTER FOR THE STUDY OF SCHIZOPHRENIA

CHARLES J. WALLACE

The purpose of this chapter is to describe the results of a project conducted at the Mental Health Clinical Research Center (MHCRC) for the Study of Schizophrenia comparing an intensive regimen of social skills training for chronic, recidivist schizophrenics with an equally intensive control therapy. Consistent with the focus of the MHCRC on the problems of relapse and rehospitalization of chronic schizophrenics, the design and implementation of the project were guided by three considerations. First, social skills training was to be expanded from its usual focus on behaviors such as eye contact and voice volume to a focus on problem-solving skills. The untested assumption was that an increase in problem-solving skills would be more relevant to forestalling relapse and/or rehospitalization than an increase only in such discrete, narrowly defined behavior as eye contact. Second, the effects of the training were to be evaluated for a follow-up period that was long enough to determine the impact of training on rates of relapse and rehospitalization. Third, patients were to be selected for participation who were clearly diagnosed as schizophrenic and who were at risk for relapse.

Charles J. Wallace. Mental Health Clinical Research Center for the Study of Schizophrenia, Rehabilitation Research and Training Center for Mental Illness, Brentwood Veterans Administration Medical Center–UCLA Department of Psychiatry–Camarillo State Hospital, Camarillo, California.

OVERVIEW

The design of the project was a comparison of the effects of 9 weeks of intensive inpatient social skills training with a similarly intensive 9 inpatient weeks of a control therapy designed on a basis of a holistic health rationale. Twenty-eight male caucasian patients participated in the project, 14 in the social skills treatment (SST) and 14 in the holistic health treatment (HHT). All patients lived on the same hospital unit for the 9 weeks of their treatment. They were admitted to the unit in cohorts of six with three assigned at random to each of the two treatments. All patients had been diagnosed as schizophrenic on the basis of the relatively stringent criteria of the Present State Examination (PSE). All patients had been hospitalized at least once previously, and all but four patients (two in SST and two in HHT) had been living with relatives who had been high in expressed emotion (EE).

The two treatments were conducted for 5 days a week from 2 to 6 hours daily. SST consisted of

1. daily 2-hour morning sessions designed to increase problem-solving skills
2. thrice-weekly afternoon sessions designed to generalize training to new persons and places
3. twice-weekly afternoon trips to the surrounding community to provide an opportunity to complete homework assignments
4. twice-weekly evening sessions designed to increase problem-solving skills in noninterpersonal areas
5. weekly meetings of patients and their families designed to increase family communication skills

HHT consisted of

1. daily 2-hour morning sessions of a standardized routine of yoga, jogging, and meditation
2. thrice-weekly afternoon sessions designed to develop positive expectations about recovery and provide a rationale that schizophrenia is a response to stress and can be controlled by identifying and reducing stressors
3. twice-weekly afternoon trips to the surrounding community
4. twice-weekly evening sessions designed to increase self-esteem and provide a rationale for considering schizophrenia as a growth experience
5. weekly family therapy sessions

Except for the family therapy, all therapists rotated between SST and HHT on a daily basis.

After the 9 weeks of inpatient treatment, all patients were discharged to appropriate aftercare facilities. They were provided active aftercare treatment that began with five contacts per week and eventually declined to two per month with termination 2 years after discharge.

The effects of the treatments were evaluated with a variety of dependent measures. These included self-report and interview-based measures of psychopathology, self-report and role-played measures of social skills, and paper-and-pencil and role-played measures of problem-solving skills. All dependent variables were administered pre-, post-, and 9 months after treatment. Additionally, the interview-based measures of psychopathology were administered biweekly during the inpatient phase and, along with several self-report measures, at 1, 3, 6, 12, 18, and 24 months posttreatment.

SUBJECTS AND SETTING

The process of selecting patients for participation in the project began with a regular review by project personnel of the lists of caucasian male admissions to two local neuropsychiatric facilities. A prospective participant was contacted if he had been diagnosed schizophrenic at admission, had been living with a first-degree relative for at least 1 of the previous 3 months, had no evidence of alcohol or drug abuse, had no history of serious assault, had no continuous and severe psychotic symptoms for 1 year or longer, had not been hospitalized more than 1 year consecutively of the past 5 years, and had no evidence of organic brain syndrome. The purpose of the project was explained, and, if the patient was agreeable, the PSE was administered. The PSE is a highly structured mental status examination that requires fulfilling several stringent criteria before assigning a diagnosis of schizophrenia. The criteria are similar to the National Research Diagnostic Criteria and to the criteria of current symptomatology required by DSM-III for a diagnosis of schizophrenia. The interviewer not only had extensive training and experience in administering the PSE, but his accuracy in scoring the interview was continually assessed.

If the prospective patient was diagnosed schizophrenic on the basis of the PSE, relatives with whom the patient had been living just prior to admission were contacted and, if they were agreeable, the Camberwell Family Interview was administered. The Camberwell Family Interview has been used in a series of studies conducted in England during the past

20 years to determine the relationship between family members' EE and the probability of relapse and/or rehospitalization. The results from the studies have consistently indicated that returning after hospitalization to an environment that is high in EE significantly increases the probability that the patient will relapse in 9 months, relapse being defined as an increase of symptomatology as measured by the PSE.

Each first-degree relative was interviewed separately; his or her EE was rated on the basis of the number of hostile comments made about the patient, the tone of voice used in describing the patient, and the degree of overinvolvement with the patient's day-to-day activities. If one or both of the first-degree relatives were determined to be high in EE, the patient and the relatives were asked to join the project, with the specific date of entrance to be set when five patients who fulfilled the same criteria had also been selected. Patients were to be admitted to the project in cohorts of six with three assigned at random to each of the treatments. However, it was not always possible to locate within a reasonable period of time six patients who fulfilled all of the admission criteria. Hence, for several patients, the criterion of a high EE rating was ignored. Additionally, two patients from the first cohort (one in HHT and one in SST) withdrew from the project before completion of the inpatient phase. Thus, the final complement of participants consisted of 28 patients (14 assigned at random to SST and 14 to HHT) divided into five cohorts with six in all but the first cohort. All patients fulfilled the criteria for entrance into the project except that four patients (two in SST and two in HHT) were not living with first-degree relatives who were high in EE (one was low in EE and three were not living with any family members).

All patients lived on the Clinical Research Unit at the Camarillo–NPI Research Program (Camarillo State Hospital) during the 9 weeks of inpatient treatment. The unit has been described in detail in other publications (Liberman, Wallace, Teigen, & Davis, 1974). However, to briefly review, the unit is a 12-bed inpatient facility that provides intensive treatment for a variety of behavior disorders. The unit is relatively "richly" staffed (a 14-member nursing staff plus a full-time psychiatrist, psychologist, social worker, and research associate), and patients are treated with a combination of standardized and individualized behavioral programs. Standardized programs include a comprehensive, three-tier token economy designed to maintain and enhance daily living skills plus various programs designed to decrease assault and property destruction, increase grooming skills, and increase appropriate eating skills. All 28 patients were treated only with the standardized programs, and they moved up and down the tiers of the token economy as their performance and the contingencies dictated.

SOCIAL SKILLS TRAINING

The daily schedule for each of the 9 weeks of SST is presented in Figure 2-1. The objective of the procedures was to teach patients problem-solving skills. Problem-solving skills were defined in terms of a model of socially skilled behavior (Figure 2-2) that was developed from the available research literature (D'Zurilla & Goldfried, 1971; Spivack, Platt, & Shure, 1976). A socially skilled response to a problem situation was

FIGURE 2-1. Weekly schedule for all patients in SST and HHT procedures.

Time		Monday	Tuesday	Wednesday	Thursday	Friday
6:45–9:30	MORNING	up; groom; breakfast				→
9:30–11:30		therapy —				→
11:30–12:30	AFTERNOON	lunch; credit system task				→
12:30–2:00		therapy —			→	interviews with psychiatrist
2:00–5:00		trip to town for generalization	grounds privileges	trip to town for generalization	grounds privileges	grounds privileges
5:00–7:00	EVENING	dinner; credit system task				→
7:00–9:00		✕	training sessions	family therapy	training sessions	✕

presumed to be the outcome of a process that began with accurate receiving of the parameters of the situation, moved to flexible processing of the information to generate and evaluate possible responses, and ended with effective sending of the chosen response. "Accurate receiving" was defined as correct recognition of the interpersonal partner's status, emotions, and messages. "Flexible processing" was defined as generating possible responses and evaluating each one's consequences in terms of the impact on the partner's emotions and behaviors. "Effective sending" was defined in terms of behaviors such as appropriate eye contact, voice volume, latency of response, posture, and gestures.

Problem situations were differentiated into instrumental versus friendship/dating situations. "Instrumental" situations were defined as those in which the interpersonal interaction was necessary to achieve a noninterpersonal goal, such as having a check mailed or renting an apartment. "Friendship/dating" situations were defined as those in which the goal was maintenance or enhancement of the interpersonal interaction. Receiving, processing, and sending skills were defined for each type of situation as indicated in Tables 2-1 to 2-6.

MORNING SESSIONS

All three patients per cohort who were assigned to SST participated with two therapists as a group. Approximately the first 4½ weeks of the sessions were devoted to training skills in instrumental situations; the last 4½ weeks were devoted to friendship/dating situations.

The basic format of the sessions dealing with instrumental situations is presented in Figure 2-3. Six scenes were scheduled to be role-played and recorded each day. The scenes were grouped into those that portrayed situations dealing with peers and staff in the hospital (40 scenes); those that portrayed situations dealing with various community agents such as physicians, social workers, shopkeepers, and apartment

FIGURE 2-2. Model of socially skilled behavior.

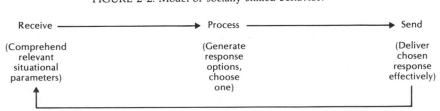

TABLE 2-1. Receiving Skills for Instrumental Situations

1. Identify the interpersonal partner's status
2. Identify the interpersonal partner's emotion
3. Comprehend the message
4. Identify the long-term goal
5. Identify the short-term goal

TABLE 2-2. Processing Skills for Instrumental Situations

1. Generate response options
2. Predict impact of each option on the interpersonal partner's emotions
3. Predict impact of each option on the interpersonal partner's behaviors
4. Predict impact of each option on achievement of short-term goal
5. Predict impact of each option on achievement of long-term goal
6. Select best option

TABLE 2-3. Sending Skills for Instrumental Situations

1. Eye contact
2. Voice
   a. Volume
   b. Fluency
3. Latency
4. Posture
5. Hand gestures
6. Facial expression

TABLE 2-4. Receiving Skills for Friendship/Dating Situations

1. Identify the interpersonal partner's status
2. Identify the interpersonal partner's emotion
3. Identify the main topic
4. Identify other possible topics

TABLE 2-5. Processing Skills for Friendship/Dating Situations

1. Identify short-term goal
2. Identify long-term goal
3. Determine if continue conversation or terminate
4. Determine if time to relinquish or resume leadership of conversation
5. Identify appropriate level of self-disclosure

TABLE 2-6. Sending Skills for Friendship/Dating Situations

1. Eye contact
2. Voice
   a. Volume
   b. Fluency
3. Latency
4. Posture
5. Hand gestures
6. Facial expression
7. Nonverbal active listening skills
8. Verbal active listening skills
9. Open- and closed-ended questions

owners (48 scenes); and those that dealt with family difficulties (51 scenes). The first two groups of scenes, which were the same for all cohorts, had been selected on the basis of a quasi-systematic study whose results suggested that the scenes were potentially important for adjustment to the hospital and the community. The family scenes were different, of course, for each patient, and were constructed on the basis of information provided by the family members during the Camberwell Family Interview and by the patient.

The introduction and setting of each scene plus instructions to the confederate were typed on a data sheet, as exemplified by Figure 2-4. The introduction and setting included a brief description of the context of the scene, the person with whom the role player was to be interacting, and the short- and long-term goals to be achieved. One of the three patients was selected to be the role player and one of the therapists was selected to be the confederate. One of the remaining two patients was designated "other 1" with the last patient designated "other 2." The role play began with the therapist reading the setting and starting the video-recorder. Depending upon the instructions to the confederate, the interaction could stop after the patient's response or could continue for several exchanges.

Receiving Questions (Instrumental Situations)

Once the scene had ended, the video-recorder was stopped and the patients were asked six questions, designed to assess their accurate receiving of the situational parameters. The questions in their order of administration were

1. Who spoke to [role player]? ("other 1")
2. What did [confederate] say? (role player)

3. What was [confederate] feeling? ("other 2"; pleasant, pre-occupied, angry)

4. What was the short-term goal? ("other 2")

5. What was the long-term goal? (role player)

6. Did [role player] get his long- and short-term goals? ("other 2")

As exemplified by Figure 2-4, a short notation of each question plus the correct answers were written on the data sheet. The therapist compared

FIGURE 2-3. Format of morning sessions for instrumental situations.

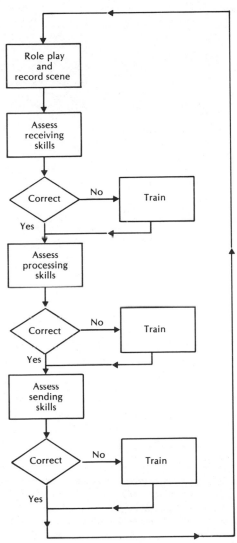

Now that you have found an apartment to rent it is necessary to get yourself settled in your new place. In this next situation, your overall or long-term goal is to arrange for the gas, electric, and telephone hookups. Your immediate or short-term goal is to borrow your neighbor's phone so that you can call the utility companies. You have just rented a new apartment and need to call the phone company to have a phone put in, the gas company to turn your gas on, and the electric company to turn on the electricity. You decide to ask your neighbor if you can borrow their phone for these three quick calls. You go next door, knock on their door and say, "Hello, my name is _____. I just moved in the apartment next door and I was wondering if I could use your phone for just a moment to call the utility company." Neighbor says, "Bug-off, man." (He is angry.)

Date: _____ RP: _____ O^1: _____ O^2: _____

Question	Patient		Answer	Trials
1. Who	O^1	Neighbor		
2. Say	RP	Bug-off		
3. Feeling	O^2	Angry		
4. STG	O^1	Use phone		
5. LTG	RP	Get utilities hooked up		
6. Get	O^2	N/A		
7. Name	O^1	GA-O _____ Action only _____ Can't _____ MA-O 4 Label only _____		
8. Feel	O^2	Angry		
9. Do	O^1	Still won't let you use phone		
10. Get STG	O^2	No		
11. Get LTG	O^1	Not here		
12. Use why	O^2	No Don't get STG or LTG yet		
13. Do	RP	Replay video GA-RP SA-RP Alt ____ ____ ____ ____ ____ SA-RP 1-P Trials ____ ____ ____ ____ ____ Okay, good-bye		
14. Get STG	RP		Answer	Trials
15. Get LTG	RP		No	
16. Good/why	RP		Not yet	
			Yes; at least you're out of unpleasant situation.	
17. MA-RP	RP	Performed as GA-RP Suggest ____ Model ____ Coach ____		
18. Best alt	RP	GA-RP ____ GA-O ____ MA-O ____ SA-RP ____		

19. Sending
   replay
   (best alt)
	RP	Sending skill ____ Model ____ Coach ____		

FIGURE 2-4. Example of data sheet used in training instrumental social skills. Abbreviations: RP, patient chosen as role player; O^1, patient chosen as "other 1"; O^2, patient chosen as "other 2"; STG, short-term goal; LTG, long-term goal; alt, alternative; MA-O, the number of the alternative that must be role-played and then processed by the patient chosen as O^1;

each patient's answers with the correct ones; if an answer was incorrect, the relevant portion of the setting was reread, and the patient was asked the question again. If the patient's answer was still incorrect, the correct answer was provided and the patient was prompted to repeat it in response to the question. Mistakes were recorded on the data sheet.

Processing Questions (Instrumental Situations)

After completion of the six receiving questions, the focus of the session was changed to assessing and training processing skills. The first processing question was directed to the patient designated as "other 1" and was designed to assess the skills of generating alternate responses. The question was, "Name one thing [role player] could have done when [confederate] said _____." The patient was expected to respond by selecting one of 13 alternate responses listed in Table 2-7 that were written on a large poster taped to a wall in the training room. (Prior to the session, the patients had received 3 days of training in recognizing and generating each of the 13 alternatives as well as the three emotions.) If the patient responded with a description of an activity (e.g., "yell at the other

TABLE 2-7. Alternate Responses Used with Instrumental Situations

Number	Response
1.	Compromise
2.	Terminate rudely
3.	Terminate politely
4.	Highlight the importance of your request
5.	Get angry
6.	Repeat your request
7.	Ask for assistance
8.	Comply with other's request
9.	Refuse to comply with other's request
10.	Explain your position
11.	Ask for more information
12.	Come back later (ask for an appointment)
13.	Acknowledge the other's position and . . . (use one of the above)

MA-RP, the number of the alternative that must be role-played and then processed by the patient chosen as RP; GA-O, the number of the alternative that was spontaneously generated by the patient chosen as O[1]; GA-RP, the number of the alternative that was spontaneously generated by the patient chosen as RP; SA-RP, the number of the alternative that could be suggested by the therapist to RP in the event that the spontaneously generated alternative (GA-RP) was ineffective.

person"), he or she was asked to role-play the action with the confederate and was then asked to supply the appropriate label (e.g., get angry). If an incorrect label was provided, the patient was asked to reconsider the 13 alternatives and attempt to answer correctly. If the answer was still incorrect, the therapist modeled the behavior that matched the incorrect label and then supplied the correct label, which the patient was asked to repeat. If, on the other hand, the patient responded with a label (e.g., get angry), he or she was asked to role-play with the confederate the behavior that would match the label. If the role-played behavior did not match the label, the patient was asked to reconsider the label and then try to answer the question again. If the answer was still incorrect, the therapist provided the label for the behavior that was actually role-played, modeled the behavior that correctly matched the label originally generated by the patient, and then asked the patient to role-play the modeled behavior.

In order to keep the training as consistent as possible from cohort to cohort, each scene was constructed with an alternate response that was to be used in the next part of the assessing and training of processing skills. For example, the number 4 (in Figure 2-4) indicated to the therapist that the alternate response to be considered was "highlighting the importance of the request." This alternative, which was selected for many scenes as an ineffective albeit commonly used response, was introduced to the "other 1" patient by saying, "I'd like you to consider _____ [alternative]. Would you please role-play _____ [alternative]?" If the role-played behavior did not match the suggested alternative, the therapist modeled the correct behavior and asked the patient to role-play again.

Once the alternative had been correctly role-played, the "other 1" and "other 2" patients were asked questions designed to assess their ability to generate and evaluate the consequences of the just considered and role-played alternative. The questions in their order of administration were

> 1. If you were to _____ [alternative], what would the other person feel? ("other 2")
> 2. If you were to _____ [alternative], what would the other person do? ("other 1")
> 3. Would you get your short-term goal? ("other 2")
> 4. Would you get your long-term goal? ("other 1")

As with the receiving questions, the correct answers were written on the data sheet. The therapist compared the answers with the correct ones; if an answer was incorrect, the correct consequence was modeled by the confederate and the patient was asked to identify the consequence. If the patient's answer was still incorrect, the correct answer was provided and the patient was prompted to repeat it in response to the question. Mistakes were recorded on the data sheet.

Once the four questions had been answered, the focus of the session shifted to the role player whose skills were assessed in processing the alternative that had actually been used during the initial, tape-recorded role play. The videotape was rewound and the patients viewed the original role play. The role player was then asked the following questions:

1. What do you do?
2. Did you get your short-term goal?
3. Did you get your long-term goal?

If the role player mislabeled the alternative that had been used, he was asked to reconsider the label and try to answer the question again. If the answer was still incorrect, the correct label was provided and the patient was prompted to repeat it in response to the question. If the answer to either of the questions concerned with the attainment of the goal was incorrect, the tape was replayed, the relevant section highlighted, and the question was repeated. If the answer was still incorrect, the correct answer was provided and the patient was prompted to repeat it in response to the question.

If the role player had used an inadequate alternative (i.e., one that failed to achieve either the long- or short-term goal), the therapist asked him to role-play another alternative that was listed on the data sheet and had been selected as being the most effective for that situation. The scene was again role-played and videotaped, and the role player was again asked the three questions listed above.

Sending Questions (Instrumental Situations)

Once an effective alternative had been role-played, the focus of the session shifted to assessing and training sending skills. The videotape of the effective alternative was replayed, and the role player was asked to evaluate eye contact, voice volume, fluency, latency, posture, and hand gestures. If, in the therapist's judgment, one of the behaviors was inadequate, the role player was instructed to replay the effective alternative and attempt to improve the deficient sending skill. If the behavior was still not improved, the therapist modeled the adequate sending skills and asked the role player to try again. If the behavior was still inadequate, the scene was replayed again with the therapist directly coaching the role player.

Once the deficient sending skill was adequately performed, the session moved on to the next scene. Since there were six scenes per session, each of the three patients was designated as the role player, "other 1," and "other 2" for two scenes. Because the sessions were fairly lengthy, coffee breaks were provided after each set of two scenes.

Module One (Friendship/Dating Situations)

After the 4½ weeks of training in instrumental situations, the focus of the sessions shifted to training problem-solving skills in friendship/ dating situations. The first 3 days of training were designed to teach patients to recognize and generate three additional emotions (bored, sad, uncomfortable), four nonverbal active listening skills (e.g., head nods, leaning forward), and three levels of self-disclosure (high, medium, and low).

The training was divided into five modules designed so that the skills taught in new modules were added to the ones taught in previous modules. The training format was similar to that used with the instrumental situations. The introduction and setting for each scene were typed on a data sheet, one of the two therapists was designated as the confederate, and the patients were designated as role player, "other 1," and "other 2." Each scene was videotaped, and patients were asked questions at the end of the role play as it was being played back. Data sheets were used to structure the therapists' activities and to record the mistakes made by the patients in answering the various questions. Figure 2-5 presents a data sheet used with the last module that includes all of the questions addressed to the patients.

The first module was designed to teach patients to recognize possible topics and to use them in initiating conversations. Nine scenes were used to practice the skills; they were the same for all but the first cohort (the first cohort was used to "pilot" the training for the friendship/dating situations and the procedures were different in several respects from those used with the other cohorts). Each scene was introduced by the therapist and role-played for one or two exchanges. At the conclusion of the role play, the "other 1" and "other 2" patients were asked five questions in the following order:

You're standing in a long checkout line at a supermarket and decide to start a conversation with the man standing behind you. (Confederate: begin pleasant, then, get uncomfortable; wandering eye contact, fidgety body movements. All these scenes are to last 60–75 meters.)

Date: _____ RP: _____ O^1: _____ O^2: _____

Patient	Question	Answer	Trials
O^1	1. Who		
O^2	2. Main topic		
O^1	3. Feeling		
O^2	4. Short-term goal		
O^1	5. Long-term goal		

Stop video after RP's first statement and ask:

RP	6. What topic area did role player choose?	
O^1	7. Can you think of another topic area? How might you use that topic area as an opening line? (Have patient stand and demonstrate in role-play situation.)	
RP	8. Did you use an open-ended question? (If no, ask #9.)	
O^2	9. Can you think of an open-ended question that could have been used? (Have patient stand and role-play use of question.)	

Instruct other to say "stop" after each question that is asked by the role player. Ask if it was open- or closed-ended. If the patient neglects to stop you after a question, mark a "1" under incorrect, replay last 4–5 meters of the tape and point out when the question occurred.

		Correct	Incorrect
O^1	10. Role player asked a question?		
	Open or closed?		

Stop video every 10–15 meters and ask the following:

		Correct	Incorrect
RP	11. What level of self-disclosure should you be at?		
O^1	12. Did role player want to continue or terminate?		
	What cues told you this? (Ask only occasionally.)		
O^2	13. Did confederate want to continue or terminate?		
	What cues told you this? (Ask only occasionally.)		
RP	14. Is one person doing most of the talking or is it 50–50?		
O^1	15. Is it time to change the topic?		
O^2	What are some possible topic areas to change to?		

After each change in topic on tape, stop and ask:

		Correct	Incorrect
O^1	16. Has role player changed the topic?		
O^2	What topic did he or she change to?		

Stop tape any time to reinforce active listening skills, gestures, good open-ended questions, and appropriate laughter.
(O should play the confederate whenever feasible.)

FIGURE 2-5. Example of data sheet used in training friendship social skills.

1. Who spoke to [role player]? ("other 1")
2. What was the main topic? ("other 2")
3. What was [confederate] feeling? ("other 1")
4. What was the short-term goal? ("other 2")
5. What was the long-term goal? ("other 1")

Incorrect answers resulted in the therapist rereading the relevant portion of the setting and repeating the question. If the patient's answer was still incorrect, the correct answer was provided, and the patient was prompted to repeat it in response to the question.

The videotape was then replayed and stopped after the role player's first response. The role player was asked, "What topic area did you choose?" If the answer was incorrect, the tape was replayed and the question was repeated. If the answer was still incorrect, the correct answer was provided and the patient was prompted to repeat it in response to the question.

The "other 1" patient was then asked, "Can you think of another topic area?" He was also asked to role-play the use of the topic area to initiate a conversation. If the patient could not think of or identify a correct topic area, the introduction and setting were reread and he was instructed to reconsider the specific elements of the situation as possible topic areas. If the answer was still incorrect, the correct answer was provided and the patient was prompted to repeat it in response to the question. If the role play was incorrect, instruction was given in the correct use of the topic area and a request was made to role-play again. If the response was still incorrect, modeling and coaching were used to obtain the correct role play.

The focus of the remainder of the replay of the videotape was on the sending skills of the role player. Deficient sending skills resulted in a sequential application of instructions, modeling, and coaching as necessary to achieve the performance of an appropriate sending skill.

Module Two (Friendship/Dating Situations)

The second module was designed to add the use of open- and closed-ended questions to the skills taught in the previous module. Three scenes were used; the format of role playing and questioning was the same as in the previous module except that the role player and the "other 2" patient were each asked one additional question. The role player was asked, "Did you use an open-ended question?" If the answer was incorrect, the definitions of open- and closed-ended questions were reviewed and the question was repeated. If the answer was still incorrect, the correct answer was provided and the patient was prompted to repeat it in response to the question. If the response during the initial role play was a closed-ended question, the "other 2" patient was asked, "Can you think of an open-ended question that could have been used?" The patient was also asked to role-play the answer. If the role-played answer was incorrect, the definitions of the two types of questions were reviewed and the patient was asked to role-play again. If the answer was still incorrect, the therapist used either modeling or coaching or both as necessary to achieve the correct response during another role play.

Module Three (Friendship/Dating Situations)

The third module was designed to add to the skills taught in the previous modules the use of verbal active listening skills plus the recognition of the interpersonal partner's level of self-disclosure and comfort/discomfort. Nine scenes were used with a changed format that expanded the role play from a few exchanges to 3 to 4 minutes of conversation. The same questions were asked at the end of the role play as were asked in the previous modules. In addition, the "other 1" patient was asked to closely attend to the playback of the scene and indicate with the word "stop" whenever the role player had asked a question. After the "other 1" patient had so indicated, he was asked if the role-played question had been open- or closed-ended. If the "other 1" patient did not recognize the question as an open- or closed-ended one, the definitions were reviewed and the question repeated. If the answer was still incorrect, the correct answer was provided and the patient was prompted to repeat it in response to the question. A tally was kept on the data sheet of the number of times the "other 1" patient correctly recognized that the role player had asked a question and correctly identified its type.

Also during the playback, the tape was stopped approximately every 10 to 15 meters and each of the patients was asked another question. The role player was asked, "At what level of self-disclosure should you be?" To provide a rationale to answer this question, the patients had been told that their self-disclosure should be at approximately the same level as that of their interpersonal partner. Thus, the answer to this question required that the role player recognize the level of the partner's self-disclosure. If the role player's answer was incorrect, the definitions of the levels of self-disclosure were reviewed, the tape replayed, and the questions repeated. If the answer was still incorrect, the correct answer was provided and the patient was prompted to repeat it in response to the question.

The "other 1" patient was asked, "Did [role player] want to continue or terminate?" To provide a rationale to answer this question, the patient had been told that little eye contact, little speech in response to questions, and/or fidgeting and shifting of body position away from the interpersonal partner all indicated possible discomfort that might be lessened by a change in topic or termination of the conversation. Thus, the answer to the question required that the "other 1" patient recognize nonverbal cues of discomfort. If the answer was incorrect, the indications of discomfort were reviewed, the tape replayed, and the question repeated. If the answer was still incorrect, the patient was provided with the answer and prompted to repeat it in response to the question.

The "other 2" patient was asked, "Did [confederate] want to continue or terminate?" Incorrect answers were corrected as indicated for the similar question asked of the "other 1" patient.

Module Four (Friendship/Dating Situations)

The fourth module was designed to add the skills of taking turns as the leader of the conversation to the skills taught in the previous modules. Eight scenes were used; the format of role playing and questioning was the same as in previous modules except that the duration of the conversations were increased and an additional question was asked of the role player when the tape was stopped at approximately every 10 to 15 meters. The question was "Is one person doing most of the talking or is it 50–50?" If the role player's answer was incorrect the tape was replayed and the question repeated. If the answer was still incorrect, the correct answer was provided and he was prompted to repeat it in response to the question.

Module Five (Friendship/Dating Situations)

The fifth module was designed to add the skills of changing topics and terminating conversations to the skills taught in the previous modules. Thirty scenes were used; the format of the questioning and role playing was the same as that used in previous modules except an additional question was asked of both the "other 1" and "other 2" patients when the tape was stopped at approximately 10 to 15 meters. The "other 1" patient was asked, "Is it time to change the topic?" To provide a rationale to answer this question, the patients were told at the beginning of the module that the interpersonal partner's emotion was a cue to continue with or change topics. Specifically, the partner's discomfort or boredom was a signal to change topics, sadness was a signal to proceed with caution, and anger or continued boredom after a change in topics was a signal to terminate. If the "other 1" patient's answer was incorrect, the relationship between the parnter's emotion and continuing or terminating was restated and the question repeated. If the answer was still incorrect, the correct answer was provided and the patient was prompted to repeat it in response to the question.

In addition to stopping the tape every 10 to 15 meters, the tape was stopped by the therapist whenever the role player changed topics. The "other 1" patient was asked, "Has [role player] changed the topic?" If the answer was incorrect, the tape was replayed and the question repeated. If the answer was still incorrect, the patient was provided with the correct answer and prompted to repeat it in response to the question. The "other 2" patient was asked, "What topic did [role player] change to?" An incorrect answer was corrected using the routine previously described.

AFTERNOON SESSIONS

The thrice-weekly afternoon sessions were designed to generalize the skills learned in the morning session to new places and interpersonal partners. Sessions were conducted on the Clinical Research Unit with the three patients and the two morning therapists as a group. For the instrumental situations, three scenes were selected from the six that had been role-played in the morning, one per patient as role player. Each scene was role-played in three variations. First, the scene was enacted in the same manner as in the morning session. After the enactment, the two non-role-playing patients were asked

1. Who spoke to [role player]?
2. What did [confederate] say?
3. What was the short-term goal?
4. What was the long-term goal?
5. Did [role player] get his short- and long-term goal?

An incorrect answer resulted in the therapist's providing the correct answer and prompting the patient to repeat it in response to the question. An inadequate role play was corrected by the therapist's using instructions, modeling, or coaching as necessary to prompt an adequate performance.

Second, the same sceme was role-played with a new interpersonal partner (generally a member of the unit's nursing staff) who responded in the same manner as the original confederate. The same questions were asked of the two non-role-playing patients.

Third, the same scene was role-played with the new interpersonal partner responding in a spontaneously different manner than that of the first two role plays. The same questions were asked after the role play.

For the friendship/dating modules, the same routine was followed except that the question about what the partner said was changed to "What was the main topic?" The duration of the role play was also longer, and fewer than three scenes might be used since there might not have been three scenes role-played during the morning session.

AFTERCARE SESSIONS

The three patients again participated as a group in the Wednesday afternoon sessions that were designed to help them consider solutions to the problems that they were likely to face when they were discharged from the project. The format was a group of discussion of topics that was organized as shown in Table 2-8. The discussion was guided by questions appropriate to each topic that were designed to stimulate patients' identification of possible problems and solutions.

TABLE 2-8. Topics of Aftercare Sessions for SST Group

Week	Topic
1.	Introduction to Aftercare Program
2.	Income
3.	Living arrangement
4.	Use of time
5.	Vocational training and education
6.	Employment
7.	Psychiatric treatment
8.	Signs of impending crisis
9.	Individual planning, arrangements, and visits to aftercare facilities

HOMEWORK ASSIGNMENTS

The patients were requested to select and complete homework assignments designed to prompt them to use the skills developed in the morning and afternoon sessions with new interpersonal partners and in new places and situations. Thirty-six assignments were developed: nine with in-hospital partners (e.g., after receiving a cup of black coffee, ask the nurse to put in sugar), nine with community agents (e.g., request change for a $5 bill at a drug store without buying an item), nine with family members (e.g., at a family therapy session, discuss your weekend schedule with your parents), and nine appropriate to the friendship/dating modules (e.g., approach a staff member with special interests and ask an open-ended question and expand the topic by asking at least two other open-ended questions). At the end of each Monday and Thursday afternoon session, patients in cohorts three, four, and five were prompted to select two assignments (the procedures were "piloted" by cohorts one and two and were different in several respects from those used with the later cohorts). On Mondays, patients were asked to select one each from the community and in-hospital assignments; on Tuesday, one each from the friendship/dating and in-hospital assignments; on Wednesdays, one each from the family and community assignments; and on Thursdays, one each from the friendship/dating and family assignments. The chosen assignments were noted on data sheets and were reviewed with patients at the beginning of the following day's morning session. No contingencies other than praise were arranged for completion of the assignments. The opportunity to complete the community assignments was given on Monday and Wednesday afternoon. All of the patients not restricted to the unit were driven to the surrounding community, dropped off at a common point, and asked to rendezvous 1 hour later for coffee in a local restaurant.

TUESDAY EVENING SESSIONS

The Tuesday evening sessions were designed to provide information about solutions to noninterpersonal, community-survival problems. The format, which was the same for all cohorts, was a group discussion of 10 topics organized as shown in Table 2-9. Additionally, there were tasks for each topic area that were to be completed during the session. For example, for the topic of transportation, the patients used a local map

TABLE 2-9. Topics of Tuesday Evening Sessions for SST Group

Week	Topic
1.	Recreational planning; good grooming
2.	Food preparation
3.	Locating and moving into an apartment
4.	Job interviews
5.	Transportation
6.	Maintenance of clothing
7.	Medical services
8.	Money management
9.	Checking and savings accounts

and bus schedule to plan their transportation for their destinations, and they completed a worksheet on appropriate methods of transportation for different situations.

THURSDAY EVENING SESSIONS

The Thursday evening sessions were designed to assist patients to cope with anger and anxiety. The format, which was the same for all cohorts, was a group discussion of the topics listed in Table 2-10. Additionally, there was either role plays or tasks for each topic that were to be completed during the sessions. For example, for the anger- and stress-control rehearsal, each patient selected a situation that was stressful or anger-provoking and then role-played the situation with the therapist.

TABLE 2-10. Topics of Thursday Evening Sessions for SST Group

Week	Topic
1.	Generate rights of children, criminals, and themselves
2.	Passive, assertive, aggressive behavior
3.	Self-talk and emotions
4.	Anger and stress control: Family scenes I
5.	Anger and stress control: Family scenes II
6.	Anger and stress control: Nonfamily scenes
7.	Long-term goal planning I
8.	Long-term goal planning II
9.	Review

The role play was videotaped and the patient practiced out loud, while watching the videotaped self-statements designed to control the anger. The patient then practiced the statements covertly while the tape was replayed. Finally, the situation was again role-played with the patient practicing the self-statements while experiencing the provocation directly.

FAMILY THERAPY SESSIONS

The patients and their relatives met weekly in a multiple family group. The first two sessions were spent on discussions of schizophrenia, its causes, course, and treatment. Information was translated to a lay person's level of understanding, with schizophrenia presented as a series of severe problems in working, self-care, thinking, and feeling. The remaining seven sessions were designed to improve family communication skills. For the first half of each session, families listened to didactic discussions and watched demonstrations. For the second half, each family role-played the skills, which consisted of expressing positive and negative feelings and feedback, making positive requests, using active listening skills, and coping with symptoms.

HOLISTIC HEALTH TRAINING

The daily schedule of sessions was the same as that for the SST group. The procedures were based upon the rationale, presented to the patients in great detail, that schizophrenia was a response to stress. Relapse could be forestalled or even prevented by increasing one's physical capacity to deal with stress and by using one of several stress-reduction techniques.

MORNING SESSIONS

All three cohorts who were assigned to HHT participated with two therapists as a group. The session consisted of 30 minutes of yoga, 1.8 miles of walking and jogging, and 20 minutes of meditation. The yoga routine was audiotaped so that it could be used by all therapists. Patients were initially coached in the proper execution of the postures and were prompted to follow the routine as necessary.

The 1.8-mile jogging and walking route wound around the hospital grounds. At first, patients traversed the route at a brisk walk; however, as their endurance increased, short stretches of slow jogging were added. If it was raining or if the patients chose to do so, the jogging/walking was dropped for 2 of the 5 days in favor of aerobic exercise in the hospital gymnasium.

Patients were trained to meditate beginning with 5 days of listening to meditation music with eyes closed for 20 minutes. The intent was to acclimate the patients to lying quietly with eyes closed. The following 5 days introduced patients to chanting by having them repeat out loud, in unison, "om shanti" for 5 minutes. Each patient was also asked to select his own mantra for private chanting. Subsequent sessions consisted of 5 minutes of chanting their personal mantras.

TUESDAY AND THURSDAY AFTERNOON SESSIONS

The sessions were designed to assist patients in developing stress-control techniques. The sessions were conducted on the unit with the three patients and the two morning therapists as a group. The format was a structured group discussion of 16 topics organized as shown in Table 2-11.

Each session began with a 15-minute to 20-minute audiotape that provided the information about the day's topic. Handouts designed to complement the material were distributed and were to be read while listening to the tape. At the end of the tape, the therapists conducted a structured group discussion following a discussion guide. A six-item, multiple-choice quiz provided a check on the comprehension of the material. If any answer was incorrect, the relevant material was reread. The session ended with an art therapy assignment based on that day's topic—for example, "draw an environment containing many of your relapse stressors," or "draw the feeling of relaxation you get while meditating."

MONDAY AFTERNOON SESSIONS

The sessions were designed to develop positive beliefs and expectations about successful recovery. The format of the session was the same as

TABLE 2-11. Topics of Tuesday and Thursday Afternoon Sessions for HHT Group

Week	Topic
1.	Define holistic health
1.	Stress and ulcers
2.	Recognize stress
2.	Define causes of stress
3.	Meditation training
3.	Managing stressors: Universal stressors
4.	Managing stressors: Your relapse stressors
4.	Aerobic exercise
5.	Stress filter: Meditation
5.	Stress filter: Medication
6.	Stress filter: Nutrition I
6.	Stress filter: Nutrition II
7.	Developing constructive coping responses I
7.	Developing constructive coping responses II
8.	Developing constructive coping responses III
8.	Aftercare life-style and goals I
9.	Aftercare life-style and goals II
9.	Review

that of the Tuesday and Thursday sessions and covered the topics shown in Table 2-12.

AFTERCARE SESSIONS

The three patients again participated as a group in the Wednesday aftercare sessions. The same topics were followed in the same order as with the SST group. The sessions, however, were not focused on identifying and solving possible problems.

TRIPS TO THE SURROUNDING COMMUNITY

There were no homework assignments for the HHT group; however, they accompanied the SST patients on the trips to the surrounding community.

TABLE 2-12. Topics of Monday Afternoon Sessions for HHT Group

Week	Topic
1.	Introduction to HHT program
2.	Split-brain theory
3.	Symptoms and Split-brain I
4.	Symptoms and Split-brain II
5.	Positive beliefs about living with your own schizophrenia
6.	Positive life goals I
7.	Positive life goals II
8.	Staying well in the community
9.	Fears about readjustment

TUESDAY EVENING SESSIONS

The Tuesday evening sessions were designed to develop the rationale that schizophrenia can be considered as an experience that can contribute to personal growth. The format was a group discussion of nine topics organized as shown in Table 2-13.

THURSDAY EVENING SESSIONS

The Thursday evening sessions were designed to increase the patient's self-esteem. The format was a group discussion of nine topics organized as indicated in Table 2-14.

TABLE 2-13. Topics of Tuesday Evening Sessions for HHT Group

Week	Topic
1.	Schizophrenia as a growth experience
2.	A close look at your schizophrenic experience
3.	Schizophrenia and social change: Handsome Lake
4.	Schizophrenia and personal change
5.	Schizophrenia and healing: The shaman
6.	Schizophrenia and religion: Mysticism
7.	Schizophrenia and art: Perceptual alteration
8.	Schizophrenia and art: Artists with visions
9.	A closer look at your schizophrenic experience

TABLE 2-14. Topics of Thursday Evening Sessions for HHT Group

Week	Topic
1.	Importance of self-esteem
2.	Nature walk
3.	Coat of arms
4.	"Who am I" collage
5.	Magic circle
6.	Commercial for myself
7.	Magic circle
8.	Self-esteem tree
9.	Maintaining self-esteem in the community

FAMILY THERAPY SESSIONS

The patients and their families met weekly in a multiple family group. The sessions were conducted by an experienced, psychodynamically oriented psychiatrist who provided encouragement to the families to confront conflicts, discuss them, ventilate feelings, make future plans, and gain insight into their relationships. No attempt was made to limit the scope or format of the sessions.

MEDICATION

The type and amount of medication was individually prescribed for each patient based on each one's history of the effects of previous medication and on the results of the biweekly administrations of the Psychiatric Assessment Scale (PAS) and Brief Psychiatric Rating Scale (BPRS) (see following). Additionally, all but the last cohorts of patients participated in an experiment designed to replicate a previous finding (Van Putten & May, 1978) that a patient's subjective reaction to medication can predict later clinical improvement as measured by rating scales completed by psychiatrists, nurses, and significant others. In the week just after the administration of the pretreatment measures, all medication was discontinued on Tuesday and test doses of chlorpromazine were given on Friday and Saturday. At specified times after administration of the medication, structured interviews were conducted to determine the patient's subjective reactions to the medication. The previous medication was reinstated on Sunday and treatment began on Monday.

AFTERCARE

After the inpatient phase, all patients were discharged to appropriate aftercare facilities and were placed in the care of the appropriate community agency. All placements were coordinated by the MHCRC social worker, who also provided active aftercare services designed to assist patients and their relatives to obtain maximum services from the various community agencies. The frequency of contact by the MHCRC social worker began at five contacts per week for the first 2 weeks, declined to two per week by the 8th week after discharge, and faded to two per month by the 9th month, with termination of services 24 months after discharge. All questions and/or contacts initiated by either a patient or a relative were logged and answered. All requests for assistance were answered if the MHCRC social worker considered it appropriate to do so in view of the patient's and family's relationships with various community agencies.

THERAPISTS

All therapists rotated between the two therapies on a daily basis, with the same therapists conducting both morning and afternoon sessions. The patients were always transported into the surrounding community by the same two therapists, and all Tuesday and Thursday evening sessions were conducted by two therapists (one conducted the SST session on Tuesday and the other conducted the HHT session; they reversed their assignments for the Thursday session). The SST family therapy was conducted by three therapists who conducted no other sessions with the patients; the HHT family session was conducted by another set of three therapists who also conducted no other sessions with the patients. Thus, except for the family therapy, each therapist's time was equally divided between the SST and HHT groups.

DEPENDENT MEASURES

The dependent measures and their frequencies of administration were as shown in Table 2-15.

The confederate test of social skills was the same as that used by Goldsmith and McFall (1975). Each patient conversed with same- and

TABLE 2-15. Dependent Measures

Measure	Frequency	Rater
Brief Psychiatric Rating Scale (BPRS)	Biweekly and every follow-up	Psychiatrist
Psychiatric Assessment Scale (PAS)	Biweekly and every follow-up	Psychiatrist
Clinical Global Impressions (CGI)	Biweekly and every follow-up	Psychiatrist
Nurses' Observation Scale for Inpatient Evaluation (NOSIE-30)	Weekly as inpatient	Nursing staff
Nurses' Global Impressions (NGI)	Weekly as inpatient	Nursing staff
Interpersonal cognitive problem-solving skills (MEPS, Options, Consequences)	Pre- and post- and 9-month follow-up	Staff
Rathus Assertiveness Schedule	Pre- and post- and 9-month follow-up	Patient
Social Anxiety and Distress Scale (SAD)	Pre- and post- and 9-month follow-up	Patient
Fear of Negative Evaluation Scale (FNE)	Pre- and post- and 9-month follow-up	Patient
Minnesota Multiphasic Personality Inventory (MMPI-168)	Pre- and post- and every follow-up	Patient
Symptom Check List 90 (SCL-90)	Pre- and post- and every follow-up	Patient
Confederate test of social skills	Pre- and post- and 9-month follow-up	Staff and patient
Role-play test of social competence	Pre- and post- and 9-month follow-up	Staff
Shipley–Hartford IQ Test	Pre- and post- and 9-month follow-up	Patient
Tennessee Self-Concept Test	Pre- and post- and 9-month follow-up	Patient
In-therapy process assessments	Daily as inpatient	Staff
Katz Social Adjustment Scale (KAS)	Pre- and 9-month follow-up	Patient and family
Present State Examination (PSE)	Pre- and post- and 9-month follow-up	Psychiatrist
Aftercare information	Biweekly after discharge	Staff

Note. Follow-ups were scheduled at 1, 3, 6, 9, 12, 18, and 24 months posttherapy.

opposite-sex partners separately for 5 minutes each. The patient was given four tasks to perform during the conversation (e.g., ask the confederate to join you socially for a cup of coffee) and was confronted with four demands made by the partner (e.g., forget the patient's name). At the end of the conversation, the patient rated his own discomfort and skills on a 9-point scale; the confederate also rated the patient's discomfort and skill and completed the Impact Message Inventory. Each conversation was videotaped.

The role-play test of social skills used four instrumental scenes, two of which had been used in the training and two of which had not. The test format was much the same as the training format. The introduction and setting were read for each scene, and the role play continued for only one exchange between confederate and patient. The patient was then asked the six receiving and five processing questions, with no feedback given about the correctness of the answers. The role play and answers were videotaped.

The aftercare information was collected every 2 weeks by the MHCRC social worker during one of the regularly scheduled contacts with each patient. A standardized interview was developed with questions designed to elicit information about any changes since the last biweekly interview in the adequacy of self-care skills; the number of days of working, training, or schooling; the number of contacts with health care providers other than the MHCRC; the number of contacts with family members; the type and dosage of medication or illicit street drugs; the quality of life style; and the quality and quantity of stressful life events.

RESULTS

As of this writing, follow-up information is still being collected on all cohorts. The role-play and confederate tests of social skills, the tests of interpersonal cognitive problem-solving skills (MEPS, Options, Consequences), the Rathus, the SAD, and the FNE have yet to be scored. However, the PAS, BPRS, MMPI-168, SCL-90, CGI, NGI, and NOSIE-30 have all been scored, and analyzed with a one-way analysis of covariance for the posttest differences among the treatments and cohorts, with the pretest scores as the covariance. The results of these preliminary analyses indicate that there were no significant differences among the five cohorts or between the two treatment groups on the adjusted post-, unadjusted post-, or premeasures. However, there was a decline on all measures of psychopathology appropriate to schizophrenic patients (e.g., the PAS, MMPI Sc scale, BPRS items 4, 8, 15) that was equal for all five cohorts and for both groups. In other words, both groups and all cohorts were equal in symptomatology at the start of training and received equal benefit from their inpatient stay.

As of this writing, three patients from the SST group and nine from the HHT group have relapsed, relapse defined as a substantial increase in scores on the PAS. Two patients in each of the treatment groups were discharged with persisting symptoms of such intensity that they could not later relapse. Thus, the results indicate that significantly ($\chi^2 = 6.0$, $df = 1$, $p < .02$) fewer patients in the SST group (25%, 3/12) have relapsed or been rehospitalized than in the HHT group (75%, 9/12). Unfortunately, these rates are somewhat difficult to interpret at this stage of the analyses. The data have not been analyzed to determine if the SST group actually increased in social skills compared to the HHT group. Additionally, differences in the aftercare placements and treatment given to the two groups plus differences in compliance with the medication regimes prescribed at discharge have not been analyzed. Without these analyses, the differences could be attributed to several variables.

DISCUSSION

The project was specifically designed to incorporate several differences between it and the past studies of the effects of social skills training with chronic schizophrenics. First, all participants were diagnosed as schizophrenic using a set of relatively stringent criteria with the diagnostic information elicited and scored in a reliable manner. Although this may limit the generalizability of the results, it is arguably better than applying the techniques to a group of patients whose varying diagnoses may interact with the treatment to produce a positive outcome for one type of diagnosis and a negative outcome for another. The fact that diagnosis and its possible interaction with treatment has so often been ignored may help to explain some of the contradictory findings of past studies.

Second, all participants were at risk for relapse, based on their past histories of hospitalization and, except for four patients, on their families' high levels of EE. Although this too limits the generalizability of the results, at least the population to whom the results do apply will be relatively well defined.

Third, the training regimen was relatively extensive and intensive. In view of the MHCRC's focus on relapse and rehospitalization, a decision was made to design the training so that it might have a maximum impact on these problems. The training was viewed as a package of techniques organized to teach problem-solving skills. If the package was proven to be effective, further research could be conducted to identify the effective elements.

Fourth, the follow-up period was relatively long, with frequent and comprehensive measurement. The goal was to clearly describe the outcome of the training monitored over a period of time that was sufficient to allow relapse or rehospitalization to occur. Past research had indicated that 48% of chronic schizophrenics relapse within 1 year after discharge and 80% within 2 years, even if patients continue their medication. Additionally, to provide a meaningful clinical outcome for all participants, a relatively active aftercare program was implemented. The program also provided the services necessary to keep patients in contact with the project so that they could be followed after discharge.

Fifth, the training techniques were specified as thoroughly as possible. The goal was to standardize the procedures so that all cohorts could be treated in the same manner and therapists could rotate between the two treatments, thus removing the potentially confounding variable of differences among therapists. The standardization also reduced both the amount of therapist training and the variance among therapists in the application of the treatment.

Sixth, the focus of the social skills training was deliberately shifted from changing behaviors such as eye contact to improving problem-solving skills. The results of studies that have investigated the relationships between social and environmental variables and relapse seemed to indicate that a broader range of behaviors (e.g., instrumental role performance) was correlated with outcome. Thus, the training was expanded to encompass these variables. However, the relationship between the outcome of schizophrenia and social competence is relatively untested. In the past, the relationship has been based upon retrospective studies of various diagnostic categories and heterosocial competence during adolescence. The inference that adolescent heterosocial competence is related to trainable social or problem-solving skills (be it eye contact or generating response options) is unwarranted; to infer that such skills are related to outcome is equally unwarranted. For example, if social or problem-solving skills are disrupted by an exacerbation of symptoms, which also leads to rehospitalization, then the best therapeutic strategy might be to treat the symptoms. If a disruption of skills precedes an exacerbation of symptoms, then the best strategy might be to improve the skills. On the other hand, there may be no relationship between these skills and outcome, with the level of skill associated only with a long-term outcome, such as quality of life, that is unrelated to relapse or rehospitalization. What is needed is prospective longitudinal data about the relationships between social or problem-solving skills and outcome, the latter defined in several ways. These data are scheduled to be collected as part of a new project of the MHCRC, and may shed light on the relevance of these training techniques to improving outcome in schizophrenia.

ACKNOWLEDGMENTS

The author would like to thank the many people who have contributed to this project. Connie Nelson, Chris Ferris, Portia Loughman, and Dave Lukoff were therapists for both treatments. Connie also designed the friendship/dating modules; Chris designed the homework assignment procedures; Portia coordinated all aspects of data collection; and Dave designed the holistic health treatment. Sandy Rappe designed and implemented all aftercare procedures for both treatment groups. Mike Marshall prescribed medication and conducted family therapy sessions. Bob Aitchison, Bob Liberman, and Ian Falloon designed and conducted the family therapy sessions for the social skills group. Bob Liberman recruited subjects, prescribed medication, and generally rode herd on the project in his role as principal investigator of the MHCRC.

This work was supported in part by Grant No. MH30911 from the National Institute of Mental Health.

REFERENCES

D'Zurilla, T. J., & Goldfried, M. R. Problem solving and behavior modification. *Journal of Abnormal Psychology*, 1971, *78*, 107–126.

Goldsmith, J. R., & McFall, R. M. Development and evaluation of an interpersonal skills training program for psychiatric inpatients. *Journal of Abnormal Psychology*, 1975, *84*, 51–58.

Liberman, R. P., Wallace, C. J., Teigen, J., & Davis, J. Interventions with psychotic behaviors. In K. S. Calhoun, H. E. Adams, & K. M. Mitchell (Eds.), *Innovative treatment methods in psychopathology*. New York: Wiley, 1974.

Spivack, G., Platt, J. J., & Shure, M. B. *The problem solving approach to adjustment*. San Francisco: Jossey-Bass, 1976.

Van Putten, T., & May, P. R. A. Subjective response as a predictor of outcome in pharmacotherapy: The consumer has a point. *Archives of General Psychiatry*, 1978, *35*, 477–480.

3

MAINTENANCE AND GENERALIZATION ISSUES IN SKILLS TRAINING WITH CHRONIC SCHIZOPHRENICS

MURRAY BROWN

Despite the advent of long-acting neuroleptics, chronic schizophrenic patients fail to stay out of the hospital or to function adequately in the community. Antipsychotic medications have not stopped the "revolving-door" pattern of discharge and readmission to psychiatric facilities. Relapse and rehospitalization rates indicate that 30% to 40% of schizophrenic patients discharged to the community are readmitted within the first year, rising to 50% to 60% within 2 years (Mosher 1971; Talbott, 1974). This has been paralleled by a 30% rise in the annual rate of readmission of schizophrenic persons to state or county hospitals in recent years (Goldberg, Schooler, Hogarty, & Ropes, 1977).

Traditionally, the chronic patient is discharged from the hospital with little or no effort made to provide either continuity of care or assistance in the process of learning to function in the community. The development of community mental health centers, once thought to impact upon the revolving-door syndrome, has not provided a solution. One recent study of all consecutive admissions of schizophrenics to a typical community mental health center found that 45% were readmitted within 6 months of discharge (Evans, Goldstein, & Rodnick, 1973). After a 3- to 5-year follow-up, only 25% to 35% of patients have not required readmission (Kohen & Paul, 1976). Although drug treatment ameliorates acute symptomatology and is often necessary for maintaining remission of disabling schizophrenic symptoms, it alone cannot

Murray Brown. Mental Health and Behavioral Sciences Education, Sepulveda Veterans Administration Medical Center, Sepulveda, California, and Department of Psychiatry, UCLA School of Medicine, Los Angeles, California.

combat the patterns of recidivism and sustained chronicity. In addition, side effects of neuroleptics, especially akinesia, akathisia, and the extra-pyramidal syndrome, contribute to patients' noncompliance with their medications regime (Van Putten, 1974). Even among those who take their medications reliably, 48% relapse within 2 years (Hogarty, Gold-berg, & Schooler, 1974). Thus neuroleptics neither prevent relapse nor maintain patients' adaptation to community-living situations. Drugs do not teach daily living and coping skills necessary for survival and main-tenance in the community. As most schizophrenic patients need to learn or relearn these skills, greater emphasis must be placed on the develop-ment and implementation of psychosocial interventions for the chronic schizophrenic patient.

Within the past 10 to 15 years two therapies have been developed that increase the performance of instrumental role behaviors and inter-personal skills. As Strauss and Carpenter (1974) have indicated, pre-morbid levels of these behaviors and skills are important predictors of competence in subsequent social adjustment, clinical outcome, and quality of interpersonal life for the schizophrenic patient. One therapy, the token economy, has been used primarily with inpatients and its effectiveness in increasing instrumental role behaviors has been well documented (Hersen & Bellack, 1976a; Kazdin, 1977; Paul & Lentz, 1977).

The second therapy, alternately known as "personal effectiveness training," "structural learning therapy," and "social skills training," was also developed from a behavioral perspective and uses techniques such as shaping, positive reinforcement, modeling, behavioral rehearsal, feedback, and prompting. This treatment approach has been used with both inpatients and outpatients to increase a broad spectrum of behav-iors labeled "social skills." The effectiveness of social skills training with a schizophrenic population has been demonstrated and evaluated in a number of studies recently reviewed by Wallace, Nelson, Liberman, Richison, Lukoff, Elder, and Ferris (1980).

Though preparation for community living through social skills training is an accepted and validated treatment strategy for chronic schziophrenic patients, maintenance of patients in adaptive community living is accomplished via an organized chronic care delivery system. It is evident that chronic patients have a number of special and unique problems, such as high vulnerability to stress, difficulty coping with demands of everyday living, extreme dependency needs, and difficulty securing an adequate income (Committee on Psychiatry and the Community, 1978). A comprehensive treatment and rehabilitation program needs to be community-based and structured to provide continuity of care and optimal adaptation to community living. There must be a continuum of services with easy access and reentry balancing an active outreach with the encouragement of independence. Specific recommendations from a conference sponsored by the Group for the Advancement of Psychiatry (Committee on Psychiatry and the Community, 1978) include a 24-hour crisis stabilization facility, active outreach, functional (*in vivo*) evaluation, training in the skills of everyday living, a variety of special living arrangements, prevocational evaluation and clinical work adjustment programs (sheltered workshops), socialization networks, functional maintenance programs, and an assortment of indirect services such as *in vivo* community consultation–education, and interagency collaboration and referral. Without such treatment and rehabilitation programs, community living may be as institutionalizing as the worst state hospital.

This chapter will review the pilot program of life and social skills training begun at Sepulveda Veterans Administration (VA) Medical Center. The program is developing inpatient and community-based procedures for training chronic schizophrenic patients in social skills, competency-based community living skills, and symptom management. The program objective is to increase community tenure and quality of life experience through a combination of detailed practical training procedures in a variety of community settings. Specific program content, training approaches, outcome, and community follow-up will be reviewed in the context of maintenance and generalization of clinical gains.

BACKGROUND: COMMUNITY-BASED TREATMENT

In order to examine existing programs designed to improve community living of chronic schizophrenics, evaluation criteria must differentiate satisfactory and unsatisfactory function and performance in the community. Paul and Lentz (1977) have suggested broad functional criteria "to bring patients to documented performance levels of resocialization and instrumental roles needed to care for themselves and freely interact with available local communities, and to reduce bizarre motoric and cognitive behaviors to the level required for community tolerance and safe interaction" (p. 5). Rehospitalization as a criterion for relapse is not consistently reliable as police/emergency units, community mental health agencies, board-and-care operators, families, and patients have different expectations of and criteria for rehospitalization. Many patients, though not hospitalized, continue to live at levels of marginal social and instrumental role function. Measures to evaluate symptom level and psychosocial adjustment must also be considered in outcome assessment of community programs for chronic patients.

A variety of residential treatment programs have been developed for patients living in the community (Mosher & Menn, 1978; Polak, 1978). These programs demonstrated effective alternatives to hospitalization but revealed that treatment differences between experimental and comparison patients in hospitalization rates and psychosocial functioning disappeared during follow-up intervals ranging from 6 to 24 months.

However, patients can be kept out of the hospital and psychiatric symptomatology can be reduced while they remain in contact with a community treatment program. Recent studies involving intensive psychosocial training and support show that improvement in the social and community living skills of chronic patients can be obtained for the duration of their treatment involvement (Fairweather, Sanders, Maynard, & Aessler, 1969; Lamb & Goertzel, 1972).

Some of the successful preliminary attempts at environmental engineering have been reviewed by Greenblatt and Budson (1976). The community programs they reviewed included the Ft. Logan Mental Health Center in Denver, Colorado, the Program for Assertive Community Training (PACT) in Madison, Wisconsin, the Southern Arizona Mental Health Center, Berkeley House in Boston, and Soteria in San Francisco. These programs range from family and home care to halfway houses. In general patients appear to make gains in socialization, ability to work and function satisfactorily, and not become burdens to their families. The authors conclude that about 80% of those patients discharged from halfway house programs make the transition to community life successfully and have lower rehospitalization rates than might be expected.

In a very promising study, Test and Stein (1978) demonstrated modest increases in the social skills of chronic psychiatric patients and at the same time reduced recidivism rates below those of hospitalized and alternative community controls. Unselected groups of patients seeking hospital admission were randomly assigned to the community treatment program or to a hospital treatment condition. The community treatment consisted of patients living independently (e.g., rooms or apartments) in the community and receiving intensive help and guidance in socializing, community living, and employment by an interdisciplinary, professional mental health staff. Of importance for generalization of learning, all coping skills were taught *in vivo* (e.g., shopping skills were taught in a supermarket). Furthermore, the staff was highly mobile and assertive, with virtual 24-hour availability to the patient and to the community to provide support during times of crisis, and keep the patient in treatment.

The results of this intensive approach revealed that during the course of the 14-month treatment, patients involved in the community program showed significantly less unemployment, higher competitive income, more independent living, and better social relationships than hospital-treated controls. Significant differences were found regarding rehospitalization rates, as experimentals were rarely hospitalized while the controls experienced a 46% rate of rehospitalization. Stein and Test (1978) conclude from their experience with PACT that when community programming is inadequate, the hospital is forced into serving as the primary locus of treatment for the patient rather than being utilized for the more appropriate specialized role it is capable of performing. Unlike other studies utilizing high expectancy treatments, the experimental patients involved in the Stein and Test study were significantly less symptomatic and spent significantly fewer days in the hospital than controls. Thus, it appears that intensive community-based programs that focus specifically on the teaching of community living skills do not have to result in increased hospitalizations as long as assertive crisis intervention and supportive procedures are provided to both the community and patients on a 24-hour basis. It should be noted, however, that as in other programs, Test and Stein (1978) have reported that differences in results in favor of the community treatment group disappeared by the end of a 14-month posttreatment follow-up period. During the follow-up period patients were linked to existing social and mental health agencies that were expected to take responsibility for the patients' continuing care. The gains in social skills displayed by patients in community treatment, although significantly better than those displayed by controls, were at best modest. Community-based programs can offer promise to the chronic schizophrenic patient. However, durability of patients' gains requires a lifelong linkage with an active chronic care delivery system.

LIFE SKILLS PROGRAM

The Life Skills Training Program at the VA Medical Center (VAMC), Sepulveda, is the result of years of clinical experience in attempting to remotivate patients to live outside the hospital. The majority of the psychiatric patients cycle through the hospital, the community, and back to the hospital repeatedly. This occurs with a very large proportion of the VAMC, Sepulveda, patients, as suggested by the findings of Rose, Hawkins, and Apodaca (1977). They found that 79% of the applicants for psychiatric inpatient status were revolving-door patients. Of these patients, 80% had been discharged within the past year, 50% within the preceding 5 months and 32% within the last month. Approximately 70% of all admissions to the psychiatric service at VAMC, Sepulveda, are diagnosed as having schizophrenia—a population with the greatest potential for benefiting from a life skills program. As shown in a study by Gross (1975) with the veterans at the Los Angeles Outpatient Clinic, the needs of both Vietnam-era and older veterans can be classified as life skills problems: earning a living, paying the bills, getting along with others, and using leisure time well. The problems surveyed fell into the same prioritization for both Vietnam and the older veterans: (1) mood, (2) health, (3) activities, (4) money, (5) work/training, and (6) interpersonal problems—all related to self-maintenance.

Health Care for American Veterans (1977) recommended that the VA take the lead in creating programs for long-term care and alternatives to institutionalization. The life skills program was developed as such an alternative within the VA system.

In conjunction with occupational therapists and rehabilitation counselors, conceptual designs and practical components of this program were refined over a 4-year period. A research design was constructed to test the feasibility of implementing a life skills program within the VA and to test the immediate impact of such training on schizophrenic patients. This has involved the development of an original assessment instrument—the Life Skills Inventory (LSI), standardization of the program content, and running several pilot groups to refine the process of the training and the LSI.

The inpatient training takes place in an occupational therapy suite with two large conference rooms, two offices, and a fully equipped kitchen, pantry, and dining room. There are five psychiatric wards, each with a census of approximately 30 beds. Patients are referred to the program from the wards but sleep and participate in their respective ward's activities when not in the life skills program. In order to be accepted into the program patients had to meet established research criteria for the diagnosis of chronic schizophrenia (*Diagnostic and Statistical Manual of Mental Disorders*, 3rd ed., 1980; Feighner, Robins, Guze, Woodruff, Winokur, & Muñoz, 1972). These diagnostic criteria are

1. A chronic illness with at least 6 months of continuous symptoms prior to the screening evaluation without return to the premorbid level of psychosocial adjustment

2. Absence of a period of depressive or manic symptoms sufficient to qualify for affective disorder or probable affective disorder

3. At least three of the following manifestations:

a. Absence of alcoholism or drug abuse within one year of onset of psychosis

b. Onset of illness prior to age 40

c. Active phase of illness with significant impairment in self-care, social adjustment, or work history

d. Family history of schizophrenia

4. Characteristic schizophrenic symptoms, at least one of the following:

a. Thought insertion

b. Thought broadcasting

c. Thought withdrawal

d. Delusion of being controlled

e. Other bizarre delusions

f. Delusions accompanied by hallucinations

g. Auditory hallucinations with a commentary or narrative style

h. Incoherence, derailment, poverty of speech, or marked illogicalness

5. Residual symptoms, at least two of the following:

a. Social isolation or withdrawal

b. Marked impairment in role function (i.e., work, school)

c. Eccentric, odd, or peculiar behaviors

d. Impairment in personal hygiene and grooming

e. Blunted, flat, or inappropriate affect

f. Speech that is tangential, depressive, vague, overelaborate, or circumstantial

g. Unusual perceptual experiences (e.g., recurrent illusions)

h. Bizarre ideation or magical thinking (i.e., telepathy, ideas of reference, clairvoyance)

The major questions to be addressed in this research study revolve around the issue of skill maintenance and generalization.

• Can chronic patients learn life skills and retain them up to one year?

• Do life skills graduates have fewer and/or shorter rehospitalizations than other chronic schizophrenic patients?

• Do life skills graduates have more hope for the future, better clinical status, and higher levels of functioning than a control group of chronic schizophrenic patients?

The materials for the program consist of guide books describing the content and application of the teaching model, informational handouts, worksheets, and pamphlets for the patients to keep in a binder. The training manual for each module sets forth the procedures and content of each session for the week, relates the content to the coaching–modeling–rehearsing–feedback theoretical model (Goldsmith & McFall, 1975) and includes suggestions for daily homework assignments. Once the patient is in the community and needs to review something (e.g., tenant rights, how to read a bank statement, or a recipe that serves six cheaply), the binder serves as a reference book.

The program runs 7 weeks, with a different content module each week. Patients meet 5 days a week, 4 hours per day (9:00–11:00 A.M. and 1:00–3:00 P.M.) excepting federal holidays. The content of each module was developed by a staff person with expertise and experience in a given topic area, such as nutrition or finances.

Personnel for the pilot program consists of three full-time clinical and research staff persons. Occupational therapists donate their time, periodically suspending their other responsibilities and programs in order to lead a given module. Volunteer service funds were made available for purchasing utensils for the occupational therapy life skills kitchen and the staff donated money for group meals in the community and snacks during the program. There are 10 regular consultants who participate in the program, providing art or movement therapy, dietetics, vocational counseling, and social work services. Community consultants who participate in the program without reimbursement include the Employment Development Department and Security Pacific Bank personnel.

Interpersonal Skills was chosen as the first module because of its manifest relevance to all other modules. Unless a person can approach another for a basic request, or use a telephone in a relatively assertive manner, he is unlikely to survive in the community. The functional use of the content of the other seven modules depends to a large extent on some mastery of the first interpersonal week.

The interpersonal skills model allows any life skills content area or individual needs to be the subject of the role-playing/training situation.

Therefore, if a patient has just had an unresolved encounter with another person, this interaction is dealt with immediately in the personal effectiveness (PE) (Liberman, King, DeRisi, & McCann, 1975) format. At the beginning of each session, therapists clearly delineate the behaviors they expect to elicit and socially reward in the course of that particular session. If there is a homework assignment, the session begins with the homework review. Praise is given to the patients for just the effort of attempting the homework. A typical assignment in the first week might be to have a 3-minute conversation with a stranger in the hospital canteen.

This discussion of small gains and their reward in and out of the role-playing situation is crucial for this therapy. Throughout contact with the patients the coach solicits appropriate positive feedback from patients and other coaches. Aside from the theoretical and empirical evidence to support this positive approach it seems apparent that this behavioral style is essential to raising the battered, low self-esteem and low levels of motivation characteristic of chronic psychiatric patients. After the homework review a role-playing scene is immediately constructed either as a result of difficulty with homework, from prepared content (as prescribed in the module content guide) or from some unanticipated situational demand.

The motivational characteristic of schizophrenia makes it essential that nonapathy is rewarded and the PE structure does that. Immediate role playing helps to "energize" the patient. Over time, it is hoped, the patients feel an effort is worth making and are conscious of this in a self-esteem boosting manner. Every effort is made to practice realistic content in the role-playing scenes. Wherever possible people whom the patients would actually have difficulty dealing with appropriately in real life are incorporated into the role-play scenes.

The content of the interpersonal skills module also attends to the individual (topographical) deficits of each subject. That is, one patient may have very poor eye contact or another talk too softly to be heard. Each is praised by the therapists and the other patients whenever improvement is shown. The patient's performance of these skills and others (assertiveness, making a request, starting a social conversation) is never said to be "poor"; rather, they are told a skill "needs work" to improve.

The second week, *Nutrition and Meal Planning I,* is more readily described according to the behavioral rehearsal model. The skills of cooking are more concrete performances than verbal interpersonal performances and thus better suited to the behavioral rehearsal model.

Briefly, the behavior rehearsal model, as described by McFall and Lillesand (1971) consists of four stages: coaching the patient on the session subject, modeling the subject, allowing the patient to rehearse the subject, and then giving feedback as the patient demonstrates what he has learned. These four stages structure the teaching methods for each module. The organization and content of each module are structured around behavioral objectives for each session.

In order for the patients to participate fully in rehearsing all aspects of meal preparation, a field trip to a supermarket gives the therapist the opportunity to model appropriate shopping techniques and allows patients opportunities to rehearse them *in vivo*. The kitchen is used to prepare and serve meals, and practice cleaning up. Eating a meal patients have prepared themselves is a form of positive reinforcement for them. It may also serve as an enticement for staying in the program.

The *Nutrition II* module (week 5) expands upon the material covered in the first nutrition module, such as planning a week's meals and changing recipe quantities. It also presents housekeeping skills, including changing bed linen, using the laundromat, and cleaning the bathroom and kitchen. This week culminates in cooking a three-course meal. The week emphasizes easily prepared meals designed to be suitable for the possibly sparse living conditions these socially and economically deprived patients will likely encounter.

The four remaining modules are described briefly below. Each also presents appropriate audiovisual aids, leaflets and worksheets for the patient's notebook, and one field trip. The field trip is an important element of each module as it helps the patient to generalize the new behaviors outside the hospital setting.

The *Health and Hygiene* module (week 3) focuses on self-care, attire, self-medication, how to seek information about health problems, and the importance of keeping medical appointments, taking medication, and dental care. Patients also view a sex educational movie and discuss sexual hygiene and problems. Patients who are on major tranquilizers learn what these medications do and that they are taking major tranquilizers because they have had a major mental illness. Side effects are also discussed and reviewed. Usually the chief of psychopharmacology participates in this week's module. During this week therapists intermittently prompt patients to repeat the name and dose of the medication they are taking and to understand the reasons for their medication ("It helps to make me think clearly"; "Alters me so I'm not so up and down in mood"; "This drug stops me feeling so bad").

The *Managing Money* module (week 4) includes basic arithmetic necessary for making change and budgeting monthly expenses and income. It covers how to estimate weekly and monthly expenses such as rent, food, recreation, and transportation, how to avoid debts, and how to budget for making payments on time. A field trip to a bank is scheduled. The patients list their own resources and budget realistic expenditures for the future. Different board and care prices, travel expenses, ways of saving money, and consumer awareness issues are discussed. In this module as in other modules, cartoons and comic characters, easily remembered acronyms, and other attention and memory aids are used.

The *Prevocational* module materials include worksheets, interest and job preference checklists, job application forms, and two excellent pamphlets from the Employment Development Department related to getting a job. The major problem with the content is that the patients who are ready to return to some type of employment are given all the attention, time, and assistance. Those who are not or may never be ready for even sheltered workshop employment are left out. That is, there is no flexibility regarding the levels of patients' skills and their needs in the area.

The content of this week begins with assessing one's interests and skills, gathering information, rehearsing telephone calls to potential employers, filling out job applications and role-playing job interviews. Homework assignments include filling out applications and bringing information relevant to getting a job. The structured format fits well with the interpersonal and role-playing aspects of the module.

The *Community Resources and Social Networks* (week 7) module utilizes the newspaper section listing community activities, entertainment and recreation, Lazarus's circle of acquaintances and friends, and a consumerism pamphlet published by the Department of Motor Vehicles. The week begins with defining a fulfilling social network, where to meet people, a review of conversation skills, and practices dealing with the opposite sex or critical parents when home on the weekends. The group makes a box lunch and takes the bus to a satellite VA community center and to a library. Afterward they evaluate the positive things done on the field trip. On another day, the group goes somewhere else, such as a museum of their choice. Homework is assigned daily on finding some activity to attend in the community. Anxiety situations are dealt with as they arise, as there is a lot of predischarge and separation anxiety during the last week of the program. The patients also rehearse problem solving in terms of deciding how to use leisure time, who to see socially, budgeting for recreation (e.g., movies), and dealing with the frustration of being given the runaround when attempting to get information from others.

HALFWAY HOUSE COMPONENT

Part of the success of the life skills pilot program may be reflected in the reaction of the ward treatment staff. Prior to the program, patients were to be discharged directly to whatever community placements were available. Afterward staff members were concerned that the life skills training participants be discharged to appropriate community placements where they could practice and maintain their newly acquired or reinforced life skills. The program experience had not only raised the patients' expectations but the staff's expectations as well. This resulted in an expansion of the program to include a halfway house as a component of the life skills program. The goal of this component is to further develop and generalize competence in daily living skills. A maximum of four residents live in the house for a contractual 2-month stay. Potential participants are screened by an interdisciplinary team and must meet the following criteria:

1. Be capable of and interested in moving to independent community life
2. Be male and age 20 to 50
3. Have no substance abuse problems
4. Be capable of or on self-medication
5. Be employable, employed, attending school, or in another occupational activity (e.g., sheltered workshop)

Each resident participates with the staff in setting his own goals and in program planning and evaluation. The level of the program is geared to the initial level of competence and needs of each resident. Using an individualized training framework, the program attempts to provide for the unique needs of patients. Repeated practice and positive reinforcement are central to building the problem-solving skills necessary for community living.

The halfway house gives the residents a transitional group-living experience wherein they can further improve their skills, begin to generalize them to nonward situations, rebuild a supportive social network in the community, and reduce their stigmatization and isolation from other citizens. They are responsible for their own housekeeping, meal planning, shopping, recreation, and possibly finding work or returning to school.

The program is supervised by two part-time mental health associates who maintain a weekly 5-day activity schedule 8:00 A.M. to 6:00 P.M. Monday through Friday. They are on call at all other times and maintain telephone contact twice a day on the weekends. Since the house is located on the peripheral grounds of the hospital, the psychiatric officer of the day is available for any emergencies. Structured training sessions and *in vivo* teaching methods that improve spontaneous interactions in the natural environment promote generalization of skills. As the residents learn to employ independent living skills, supervision and teaching interactions are gradually faded and reduced in structure so that natural aspects of community living maintain normalization of behavior.

Of the 34 life skills program graduates, 10 have been placed in the halfway house. After their time in the house, two returned to their families, one was placed in a cooperative house, one is living in an apartment, and two have not been discharged. Four are currently living in the house.

During the halfway house placement patients begin to make contact with groups in the community that are not part of the hospital service network, such as potential employers, special interest agencies, recreational and educational resources, and church groups. The focus on social networks may also include brief family therapy interventions and reducing the social stigma of patients through educating significant others in the community.

DATA ANALYSIS

Over the past 4 years, seven pilot groups have gone through the training. There have been 34 graduates, 13 dropouts, and one suicide. Those graduates who have been rehospitalized since discharge from the program usually look better clinically than on their prior admissions and have shorter lengths of stay.

There were no control groups run during the pilot-phase years.

The patients we have been working with met DSM-III (1980) and Feighner *et al.* (1972) criteria for chronic schizophrenia and have an average chronicity of 5 years. It has been a major research flaw in schizophrenia studies that the criteria for acceptance of patients diagnosed as schizophrenic were unreliable and variable. With the World Health Organization diagnostic studies (Liberman, Wallace, Vaughn, & Snyder, 1979) there is now some acceptable degree of reliability for a schizophrenia diagnosis as such. In addition, the Present State Examination became part of the diagnostic evaluation in 1980. We can, therefore, safely say that if our life skills approach helps this relatively tightly defined group of psychotic patients, then life skills may be worth considering for the majority of chronic schizophrenic patients. Aside from the criteria for schizophrenia the team had no clear clinical criteria to specify who amongst the patients would be more likely to succeed with a life skills approach. The literature suggests that social and familial factors predict relapse in schizophrenia far better than strictly psychiatric clinical criteria. At the moment there are no clear behavioral criteria to identify those most likely to benefit from a life skills program. Hopefully, these social and familial factors that have been found to predict relapse can be related to behavioral/skills factors in the future.

To date, the program has had a 29% dropout rate. Due to the paucity of follow-up data and the changes in the test battery over the seven pilot runs, only score means and ranges are presented.

The LSI is a combined cognitive and behavioral-item instrument. It reflects the content of the modules and the cognitive and behavioral skills the patients are expected to learn. By late 1978, the LSI and the modules had become fairly set and no significant changes have been made. The LSI consists of 29 multiple-choice and fill-in written questions and 12 behavioral tests ranging from separating fixed and variable expenses to cooking noodles and boiling an egg. The items and possible total score have been revised over time but it has not been validated via administration to control and nonschizophrenic groups. Validity and interrater reliability tests are presently being constructed and will be implemented in the near future. Given these caveats, the percentage scores are given in Table 3-1.

Two depression scales are included in the test battery. The Hamilton Rating Scale for Depression (HRSD) (Hamilton, 1967) is a brief interview rated by the clinician. All ratings were done by the author (a potential bias that is now corrected by a blind rater). A score of less than 10 reflects normal to mild depression, and over 40, extreme depressive symptomatology. The second scale is the Zung Self-Rating Depression Scale (SDS) (Zung, 1965). A score of 50 and below reflects normal

TABLE 3-1. Life Skills Inventory, Life and Social Skills Training Program Mean Performance Scores

Administration	n	Percentage correct mean	Range
pre-	34	65	30–87%
post-	33	77.5	38–94%
3rd month	3	56	48–66%
6th to 7th month	6	84.8	63–99%

conditions, 50 to 60 reflects mild to marked depression, 60 to 70, moderate to severe status. The lack of change from pre- to posttest may be due to the time lag in self-perceived change. The statistical data for both of these scales are shown in Table 3-2.

The Social Anxiety Questionnaire (SAQ) is a brief self-rating of anxiety-provoking situations. The mean score for schizophrenics is 42 (Falloon, Lindley, McDonald, & Marks, 1977). See Table 3-3.

In light of the importance of mood, vigor, and hope for the future as indicators of improvements in chronic schizophrenic patients, several changes were made in the test battery. Two scales were added after the first two pilot groups were run. One scale was developed at VAMC, Sepulveda, the Future Outlook Inventory (Gunn & Pearman, 1970). The general outlook factor is given in standardized percentile scores. The other addition is the Profile of Mood States (POMS) developed by McNair, Lorr, and Droppleman (1971); results of both tests are shown in Table 3-4.

The lack of follow-up data is due to the lack of adequate personnel

TABLE 3-2. Hamilton Rating Scale for Depression (HRSD) and Zung Self-Rating Depression Scale (SDS), Life and Social Skills Training Program Mean Performance Scores

Test	Administration	n	Mean	Range
HRSD	pre-	24	34.6	2–62
	post-	29	16	2–62
	3rd month	3	39.3	24–52
	6th to 7th month	6	26	12–36
Zung SDS	pre-	31	57	34–75
	post-	27	57	29–74
	3rd month	3	50.3	44–59
	6th to 7th month	5	43.8	26–69
	12th month	5	53.8	28–64

TABLE 3-3. Social Anxiety Questionnaire, Life and Social Skills Training Program Mean Performance Scores

Administration	n	Mean	Range
pre-	30	44.6	3–81
post-	35	37	7–72
3rd month	3	53	45–63
6th month	5	32.6	7–60
12th month	5	38.2	3–60

to implement the evaluation component of the program. It cannot be stressed enough that the limited number of cases and poor follow-up data obviates the possibility of making a statistically meaningful statement about the LSI's validity or reliability or of the effect of life skills training on subject groups. However, the existing data do suggest the LSI is already fairly reliable, has internal consistency, content and face validity, and perhaps criterion validity. A VA merit review grant funded for 2 years will provide a mechanism to do more thorough follow-up of life skills graduates and yield longitudinal data.

In review, the data reflect the type of patient generally accepted into the program, especially the type that self-selects to complete a 7-week program. This profile indicates these patients are somewhat anxious, slightly to moderately depressed, and already have a fairly good array of instrumental skills upon entry. This is suggested by the follow-up scores, which are seen to be higher than posttest results. It appears skills were muted or masked during the inpatient stay and reappeared after patients became well enough to be placed in the community (whether or not they used their skills—i.e., were placed in board-and-care homes). However, patients do demonstrate improvement in their clinical status during the program (within the 7 weeks) and appear to maintain these gains up to a year past discharge.

Because of limited resources, the patients were not as fully assessed as they would be for individual behavioral therapy, with a full analysis of their deficits and assets related to a detailed life history. However, the first week of therapy (which was concerned with teaching interpersonal content) revealed the behaviors and attitudes of the patients that needed to be emphasized in the following weeks of therapy. It is also important to acknowledge that a behavioral rehearsal approach

TABLE 3-4. Future Outlook Inventory (FOI) and Profile of Mood States (POMS), Life and Social Skills Training Program Mean Performance Scores

Test	Administration	n	Mean[a]	Range[b]
FOI	pre-	21	56.3	10–95
	post-	21	64.8	10–100
	7th month	1	60	
	12th month	5	55	5–90
POMS				
Tension	pre-	24	48.8	30–62
	post-	17	42.4	30–55
	7th month	1	42	—
	10th to 12th month	5	39	34–48
Depression	pre-	24	50.5	32–74
	post-	17	46.7	34–69
	7th month	1	56	—
	10th to 12th month	5	42.6	36–52
Anger	pre-	24	51.2	37–69
	post-	17	47.2	37–68
	7th month	1	37	—
	10th to 12th month	5	48	37–62
Vigor	pre-	24	47.4	33–72
	post-	17	48.1	39–62
	7th month	1	45	—
	10th to 12 month	5	52.4	39–66
Fatigue	pre-	24	53.2	35–74
	post-	17	49.2	34–68
	7th month	1	55	—
	10th to 12th month	5	44.4	37–55
Confusion	pre-	24	50.4	33–67
	post-	17	47.3	33–64
	7th month	1	51	—
	10th to 12th month	5	42.2	35–52

[a]Means for Future Outlook Inventory given as percentiles; means for Profile of Mood States given as mean T scores for each factor over time.
[b]Range for Future Outlook Inventory given as percentiles.

would not suffice without individual clinical matters being incorporated into the group. This has been supported by experience so far. Individual attention is needed to deal with the problems of each patient from day to day, to keep him functioning and motivated to attend the life skills training—quite aside from teaching him new skills or resurrecting disused skills he may have possessed. It seems there is no possibility of patients such as these being taught in a classroom situation by a teacher unfamiliar with the unpredictable manifestations of psychosis. This may seem obvious, but given the optimistic flavor of some of the behavioral literature, it bears reiterating.

FOLLOW-UP

Some clinical follow-up data have been accumulated through correspondence and telephone contacts with all but two of the discharged subjects. During October and November 1979, data were collected by contacting the patient or his parents. Information was requested regarding six areas: living arrangements, employment, socialization, medical status, feeling about life skills program (i.e., consumer satisfaction), and general mental status. The following percentages lump together patients who left the hospital in 1977 with those who were discharged or placed in the halfway house, February 1980. That is, patients from the earlier groups had more time to regress, be rehospitalized, or to succeed than those more recently discharged.

As for living arrangements, 19% live with their parents and another 19% live in board-and-care facilities. In apartments, cooperative housing, or hotels—that is, independent living—there are 30% of all life skills graduates. Six percent (6%) have unknown arrangements. Thirteen percent (13%) are presently living in the halfway house (and have been for 2 months) and 13% are awaiting discharge.

Employment or other occupational activities break into two major trends: either the patient has enough disability money on which to live without working or he has to earn a living. Thus, 69% are not engaged in work or work-related activities. Of those working, 9% are employed in regular jobs, 3% do volunteer work, and 6% are enrolled in college. The status of 13% is unknown.

Socialization falls into four broad, almost intuitive, categories. Rather than list the activities, the group or individual nature of the activity suggest the category. Generally, those living with parents can be considered to have significant others. Because friends may or may not be involved enough to qualify as significant others without evidence to that effect they are counted as friends only. Fifteen percent (15%) have significant others, 31% have friends or acquaintances, and 22% have no friends or group activities. Unknown social situations constitute 37%.

Medical–psychiatric status relates primarily to compliance with medication. These are all self-report data, and the desirable answer is self-evident. So given this caveat, 63% are complying and taking their medication and 9% are not complying. Another 18% are unknown.

More data need to be collected on the quality, location, and length of stay for every rehospitalization since discharge from life skills. From first-hand knowledge and follow-up interviews, the following estimates may be made: 37% have been hospitalized at least once; 28% have never been rehospitalized (probably because of the high stability of board-and-care placements), 26% have not been discharged or are living in a halfway house, and the status of 16% is unknown. At this time the data have not been analyzed for length of community tenure.

DISCUSSION

There are many studies in the literature that support the premise that intensive social skills training can lead to chronic schizophrenic patients acquiring a level of social skill competence that enables them to remain in the community with lower relapse rates. Individual differences exist among different programs, each emphasizing a more selective focus on either topographical features, token economy, communication skills, level of emotional expression of family members, structural remotivation groups, daily living skills, attention-focusing techniques or *in vivo* training centers. All support the need for psychosocial rehabilitation of chronic patients whose primary needs seem to center around adjustment or readjustment to the demands of community living. Though preparation for community living is a general treatment strategy, community caretakers and institutions oftentimes paradoxically promote a custodial, dependent patient model of care. Some patients, while chronically disabled, are only partially disabled and with support can increase functioning socially, at work or school, in the family, or in a social network. Quality of life experience should be a criterion of successful rehabilitation just as much as lower rehabilitation rates. Maintenance and generalization strategies should be designed to promote growth and sustain functioning to the maximum degree possible for each individual. Schizophrenic patients, especially those of low socioeconomic status, often have never learned adequate life skills and social repertoires. Thus the need for such training exceeds both the articulated demand and the present extent to which it is provided. As Paul (1969) noted, for these patients to stay in the community, rehabilitation, must focus upon resocialization, including the development of *self-maintenance*, interpersonal interaction, and communication skills. "Self-maintenance" refers to those skills of daily living that require more than the ability to be assertive or hold a conversation—skills such as grooming, self-medication, and meal preparation. Yet the majority of research on social skills for schizophrenics is strictly limited to the interpersonal, assertive, social skills.

In their excellent review of the literature, Hersen and Bellack (1976a) point out that "there appears to be little effort toward directly teaching patients new skills . . . [and] the tacit assumption that the patient has the social response in his repertoire" (p. 560). Behavioral approaches have been mainly token economy programs, with little lasting effect. In summarizing single-case and group-comparison clinical studies of (assertive) social skills training Hersen and Bellack (1976a) state that when training "approximates (via behavioral rehearsal) real life situations there is greater likelihood that in-hospital changes will transfer to the patient's natural environment following discharge" (p. 571). One of the more comprehensive and widely quoted reviews of psychosocial treatment approaches to schizophrenia suggested that therapy should be in a structured setting with clear goal setting and emphasize small incremental improvements in the patient's clinical conditions (May & Tuma, 1976). Yet the targets of training are consistently interpersonal, assertive, and communication skills (Bellack, Hersen, & Turner, 1976; Hersen & Bellack, 1976b; Hersen, Eisler, Miller, Johnson, & Pinkston, 1973; Hersen, Turner, Edelstein, & Pinkston, 1975). Interpersonal, assertive, and communication skills are certainly important and represent a common deficit in schizophrenic patients. The three major social skills training programs, structured learning therapy (Goldstein, Martens, Hubben, Van Belle, Schaaf, Wiersima, & Goldhart, 1973), personal effectiveness training (Liberman et al., 1975), and interpersonal skill training as developed by Goldsmith and McFall (1975), all utilize the same basic components. These are (1) coaching or instruction, (2) modeling, (3) rehearsal or practice, and (4) feedback or reinforcement.

Unfortunately, factors other than the techniques or content of a skills training program may influence the patient's prognosis. Vaillant (1978) found nonschizoid premorbid adjustments a major prognostic factor differentiating 51 remitting schizophrenics from 128 unimproved patients over a 10-year follow-up interval. Falloon et al. (1977) found differential outcomes for patients in a skills therapy program. The schizophrenic patients improved slightly after treatment but lost all improvement at follow-up. Falloon concluded that behavioral discussion groups are effective and are enhanced by modeling and rehearsal, although the problem of generalizing change to *in vivo* situation remains.

Liberman *et al.* (1979), in research utilizing the Camberwell Family Interview, found that the best single predictor of symptom relapse in the 9 months after hospital discharge was the level of emotion expressed by a relative toward the patient at the time of the patient's hospitalization. Specifically, critical comments and emotional overinvolvement have been the best predictors of relapse. Unmarried males living with parents who are high on the expressed emotion scales constitute the highest vulnerability target group. They can be helped by reducing the amount of face-to-face contact with such parents after discharge and the parents can be trained to become less critical and less emotionally involved.

Compliance with medication regimens is an important factor in skills maintenance and generalization as well as in predicting relapse. In fact, such compliance is a skill that bears practice and requires such maintenance. In the Sepulveda program, as patients in the life skills program begin to improve clinically and to raise their expectations of themselves, they attempt to have medication reduced or stopped and express a desire not to take medication after discharge. This material is addressed in the health module primarily. However, after leaving the hospital setting there is little reinforcement given for staying on their drug treatment regimen. There is often little reinforcement for their improved interpersonal daily living skills upon return to an impoverished psychosocial environment as well.

Not only may terminating one's medication negatively affect social competence, but lack of opportunity and positive reinforcement for practicing social competence may result in self-termination of medication. This situation has been studied from the perspective of predicting hospitalization. Serban, Gidynski, and Melnick (1975) found antisocial behavior separated high from low socially competent subjects and that interpersonal relationships played a minimal role in predicting readmission of chronic patients since their life-style tends to be devoid of significant interpersonal contact. Predictions of rehospitalization of chronic schizophrenic patients appear to be related to antisocial behavior and poor relations with sexual partners and neighbors, as opposed to social performance (employment, occupation, marital status). Serban suggests existing community programs are of little value for the chronic patient marginally adapted to the community between hospitalizations. He suggests that readmissions could be reduced if the specific needs of each patient were met by more active aftercare programs.

The maintenance of gains made in social skills must be paralleled by skill generalization to situations and people outside the hospital. That is, if gains are to be maintained, then the patient must have the chance to use those skills and be reinforced positively for doing so. The reverse is also true. Patients must generalize their skills to the outside world if they are to maintain the skill improvement made in the hospital. In order to provide the optimal opportunity for such generalization and maintenance of skills, community living arrangements must be designed so as to support positive attitudes toward active rehabilitation.

GENERALIZATION OF SKILLS IN THE COMMUNITY

An important consideration in evaluating the effectiveness of any type of therapy is whether or not the improvements achieved extend to other situations, for long durations, and to behaviors not specifically treated. The term "generalization" describes the extension or transfer of improvement beyond the immediacy of treatment. Generalization is a term derived from learning theory and used by behavior therapists to evaluate the spread and durability of treatment effects. There are three major parameters of generalization. "Stimulus generalization" refers to behavioral gains that transfer to different situations or settings. "Response generalization" refers to the spread of treatment effects to behaviors that were not originally targeted as foci for intervention. The third parameter is the durability of behavior change over time.

Generalization should not be assumed to be an automatic by-product of treatment. Rather, ways to facilitate generalization should be incorporated into treatment and then the extent of generalization assessed. Treatments that effect change in limited situations or for short periods of time may be of little usefulness to therapists pursuing the goal of reintegrating a patient into his family, job, and community. Similarly, treatments that affect only those behaviors directly treated are less beneficial than treatments that promote a spreading of therapeutic responses. Although the generalization issue is relevant to the evaluation of therapy for all patients, it is most critical in working with chronically impaired psychotics. Problems with generalization in psychotic patients have been well documented by clinicians and researchers alike (Kazdin & Bootzin, 1972; Liberman, Wallace, Teigen, & Davis, 1974; Paul, 1969; Wallace, 1976).

A behavioral approach to community rehabilitation of schizophrenics is described by Lehrer and Lanoil (1977). It emphasizes provisions for the smooth transition of patients from institutional to community life with sufficient incentive to maintain involvement. They described a setting called "The Club," which concentrates on natural or intrinsic reinforcers. Program components include a prevocational day program, the work-for-pay program, and special recreation. Programs are designed to avoid any opportunities for failure and there are no time limitations on program participation. Particular attention has been devoted to motivating patients to come to the club and to engage in prevocational activities. They use such natural consequences as attention, approval, recognition, and status as forms of reinforcement, in contrast to the more commonly used token economy.

Lehrer and Lanoil's work (1977) demonstrated the increasing sophistication of community psychiatric rehabilitation. Fountain House also demonstrates the shifting priorities of community programs, as it moves from a social-meeting plan to a systematic program of work-readiness and vocational training (Beard, Malamud, & Rossman, 1978). Other community programs on a similar format, like Mainstreaming (Mendel, Houle, & Osman, 1980), have developed increasingly specific behavioral goals for patients in a variety of areas. These more specific behavioral goals require training sites and training managers or technicians who know how to use both natural sources of reinforcement and specific, stepped training techniques to achieve behavioral changes for their clients. New strategies are being employed that aim at strengthening the linkage of hospital treatment to aftercare services.

Since the social environment of chronically disabled schizophrenics living in the community has been shown to affect relapse rates, it should be the focus for interventions aimed at fostering generalization (Liberman, DeRisi, King, Eckman, & Wood, 1974). Behavior therapy approaches, with their emphasis on consistent uses of reinforcement contingencies and ongoing monitoring of behavior, offer workable models for the maintenance and rehabilitation of the chronic mental patient in the community. Generalization of treatment effects in chronic psychotics can be promoted by the following operations:

1. Select as target behaviors in the treatment setting those that will continue to be reinforced in the natural milieu. These functional

behaviors will be strengthened even after treatment has ended.

2. Pair praise, acknowledgment, approval, and other social reinforcers with tangible reinforcers, such as tokens and other rewards. In this manner, naturally occurring social reinforcers will maintain behavioral gains after discharge.

3. Gradually fade out the tangible reinforcers, eventually relying solely on the more naturally occurring social reinforcers.

4. Simulate the natural environment with its stimulus characteristics in the treatment milieu, and reinforce adaptive behavior under these simulated conditions. Examples of simulating the real world in the hospital are having facilities for patients to cook their own meals, perform meaningful work, wash their own clothes, and use the telephones and public transportation.

5. Gradually draw in the natural environment; for instance, schedule increasing amounts of time in the community for patients as they approach discharge.

6. Train relatives and caretakers to carry out the reinforcement program begun in the hospital. This brings elements of the treatment situation into the aftercare milieu. Family therapy and education of community agents are opportunities for emphasizing and strengthening skills of every day living.

7. Teach patients to provide self-reinforcement for their own behavioral goals. Strategies of self-control can foster durability of improvement as well as helping to prevent new problems, stresses, and difficulties from mounting to the point of requiring professional intervention.

8. Use intermittent and delayed schedules of reinforcement as the treatment proceeds. These schedules build in a certain amount of uncertainty in the patient's expectations of positive feedback, thereby freeing the patient from over dependence on therapists and increasing the durability of improvement.

9. Use overtraining in strengthening the adaptive behaviors that are the goals of treatment. Overlearning occurs through large numbers of treatment sessions. Reinforcement for redundant practice well beyond the point of acquisition of new behaviors protects against relapse. This is particularly important in patients who start with minimal social skills or who have been behaviorally impoverished through long years of residence in institutions.

10. Involve the patient in setting the goals of treatment and in choosing from among alternative treatment methods. This helps to shift the perceived locus of control from external to internal, and makes

more likely that the patient will attribute clinical progress to his or her own efforts.

The behavioral problems of chronic psychotics are lifelong, with the vicissitudes determined by ecological, economic, biological, and therapeutic factors. We can blame the long-term, clinical failures of some of our patients on aftercare environments that prompt and reinforce maladaptive behavior, or on our insufficient and poorly planned efforts to anticipate and program for generalization. We have well-documented, successful models for generalization; however, we must begin applying them in customary clinical practice and delivery of mental health services. This will require sophistication in community organization and in the development of mechanisms for interagency communication and coordination. Behavioral and community approaches deemphasize the fixed entities view of disordered behavior and leave open the possibility that many adverse end states can be averted by effective community treatment, support, and acceptance.

REFERENCES

Beard, J. H., Malamud, T. J., & Rossman, E. Psychiatric rehabilitation and long-term rehospitalization rates: The findings of two research studies. *Schizophrenia Bulletin*, 1978, 4 (4), 622–635.

Bellack, A. S., Hersen, M., & Turner, S. M. Generalization effects of social skills training with chronic schizophrenics: An experimental analysis. *Behaviour Research and Therapy*, 1976, 14, 391–398.

Committee on Psychiatry and the Community. *The chronic mental patient in the community.* New York: Group for the Advancement of Psychiatry, Vol. 10, publication no. 102, 1978.

Diagnostic and statistical manual of mental disorders (3rd ed.) (DSM-III). Washington, D.C.: American Psychiatric Association, 1980.

Evans, J. R., Goldstein, M. J., & Rodnick, E. H. Premorbid adjustment, paranoid status, and patterns of response to phenothiazine in acute schizophrenia. *Schizophrenia Bulletin*, 1973, 3, 24–37.

Fairweather, G. W., Sanders, D. H., Maynard, H., & Aessler, D. L. *Community life for the mentally ill: An alternative to community care.* New York: Aldine, 1969.

Falloon, I., Lindley, P., McDonald, R., & Marks, I. M. Social skills training of outpatient groups: A controlled study of rehearsal and homework. *British Journal of Psychiatry*, 1977, 131, 599–609.

Feighner, J. P., Robins, E., Guze, S. B., Woodruff, R. A., Winokur, G., & Muñoz, R. Diagnostic criteria for use in psychiatric research *Archives of General Psychiatry*, 1972, 26, 57–63.

Goldberg, S. C., Schooler, N. R., Hogarty, E. E., & Ropes, M. Prediction of relapse in schizoprehnic outpatients treated by drug and sociotherapy. *Archives of General Psychiatry,* 1977, *34,* 171–184.

Goldsmith, J. B., & McFall, R. M. Development and evaluation of an interpersonal skills-training program for psychiatric inpatients. *Journal of Abnormal Psychology,* 1975, *84,* 51–58.

Goldstein, A. P., Martens, J., Hubben, J., Van Belle, H. A., Schaaf, W., Wiersima, H., & Goldhart, A. The use of modeling to increase independent behavior. *Behaviour Research and Therapy,* 1973, *11,* 31–43.

Greenblatt, M., & Budson, R. A symposium, follow-up studies of community care. *American Journal of Psychiatry,* 1976, *133* (8), 916–921.

Gross, C. *Characteristics and problems of a veteran outpatient population.* Los Angeles: Veteran Need Identification Project, Los Angeles Outpatient Clinic, 1975.

Gunn, R., & Pearman, H. E. An analysis of the future outlook of hospitalized psychiatric patients. *Journal of Clinical Psychology,* 1970, *26* (1), 99–103.

Hamilton, M. Development of a rating scale for primary depressive illness. *British Journal of Social and Clinical Psychology,* 1967, *6,* 278–296.

Health care for American veterans. Washington, D.C.: National Research Council, 1977.

Hersen, M., & Bellack, A. S. Social skills training for chronic psychiatric patients: Rationale, research findings, and future directions. *Comprehensive Psychiatry,* 1976, *17,* 559–580. (a)

Hersen, M., & Bellack, A. S. A multiple baseline analysis of social skills training in chronic schizophrenics. *Journal of Applied Behavior Analysis,* 1976, *9,* 239–245. (b)

Hersen, M., Eisler, R. M., Miller, P., Johnson, M., & Pinkston, S. Effects of practice, instructions, and modeling on components of assertive behavior. *Behaviour Research and Therapy,* 1973, *11,* 447–451.

Hersen, M., Turner, S. M., Edelstein, B. A., & Pinkston, S. G. Effect of phenothiazine and social skills training in chronic schizophrenics. *Journal of Clinical Psychology,* 1975, *31,* 588–594.

Hogarty, G. E., Goldberg, S. C., & Schooler, N. R. Drug and sociotherapy in the aftercare of schizophrenic patients: II. Two-year relapse rates. *Archives of General Psychiatry,* 1974, *31,* 603–608.

Kazdin, A. E. *The token economy: A review and evaluation.* New York: Plenum, 1977.

Kazdin, A. E., & Bootzin, R. R. The token economy: An evaluation review. *Journal of Applied Behavior Analysis,* 1972, *5,* 1–30.

Kohen, W., & Paul, G. L. Current trends and recommended changes in extended-care placement of mental patients: The Illinois system as a case in point. *Schizophrenia Bulletin,* 1976, *2,* 575–594.

Lamb, H. R., & Goertzel, V. High expectations of long-term ex-state hospital patients. *American Journal of Psychiatry,* 1972, *129,* 471.

Lehrer, P., & Lanoil, J. Natural reinforcement in a psychiatric rehabilitation program. *Schizophrenia Bulletin,* 1977, *3,* 297–303.

Liberman, R. P., DeRisi, W., King, L., Eckman, T., & Wood, D. Behavioral measurement in a community mental health center. In P. Davidson, F. Clark, & L. Hamerlynck (Eds.), *Evaluating behavioral programs in community, residential and educational settings.* Champaign, Ill.: Research Press, 1974.

Liberman, R. P., King, L. W., DeRisi, W., & McCann, M. *Personal effectiveness: Guiding people to assert their feelings and improve their social skills.* Champaign, Ill.: Research Press, 1975.

Liberman, R. P., Wallace, C., Teigen, J., & Davis, J. Behavioral interventions with psychotics. In K. S. Kalhoun, H. E. Adams, & E. M. Mitchell (Eds.), *Innovative treatment methods in psychopathology.* New York: Wiley, 1974.

Liberman, R. P., Wallace, C. J., Vaughn, C. E., & Snyder, K. L. *Social and family factors in the course of schizophrenia: Towards an interpersonal problem-solving therapy for schizophrenics and their families.* Paper presented at the Conference on Psychotherapy of Schizophrenics: Current Status and New Directions, Yale University School of Medicine, New Haven, Conn., April 9, 1979.

May, P. R. A., & Tuma, A. H. A follow-up study of the results of treatment of schizophrenia. In R. L. Spitzer & D. R. Klein (Eds.), *Evaluation of psychological therapies.* Baltimore: Johns Hopkins Press, 1976.

McFall, R., & Lillesand, D. Behavioral rehearsal with modeling coaching in assertion training. *Journal of Abnormal Psychology,* 1971, 77, (3), 313–323.

McNair, D., Lorr, M., & Droppleman, L. *EITS manual for the profile of mood states.* San Diego: Educational & Industrial Testing Service, 1971.

Mendel, W., Houle, J., & Osman, S. Mainstreaming: An approach to the treatment of chronically and severely mentally ill patients in the community. *Hillside Journal of Clinical Psychiatry,* 1980, 2(1), 95–178.

Mosher, L. R. Madness in the community. *Attitude,* 1971, 1, 2–21.

Mosher, L. R., & Menn, A. Z. Lower barriers in the community: The Soteria model. In L. I. Stein & M. A. Test (Eds.), *Alternatives to mental hospital treatment.* New York: Plenum, 1978.

Paul, G. L. Chronic mental patient: Current status—future directions. *Psychology Bulletin,* 1969, 71, 81–94.

Paul, G. L., & Lentz, R. J. *Psychosocial treatment of chronic mental patients: Milieu vs. social-learning programs.* Cambridge, Mass.: Harvard University Press, 1977.

Polak, P. R. A comprehensive system of alternatives to psychiatric hospitalization. In L. I. Stein & M. A. Test (Eds.), *Alternatives to mental hospital treatment.* New York: Plenum, 1978.

Rose, S., Hawkins, J., & Apodaca, L. The decision to admit: Criteria for admission and readmission at a VA hospital. *Archives of General Psychiatry,* 1977, 34, 418–421.

Serban, G., Gidynski, C., & Melnick, E. Social performance and readmission in acute and chronic schizophrenics: Comparison of two approaches. *Behavioral Neuropsychiatry,* 1975, 7, 6–12.

Stein, L. I., & Test, M. D. (Eds.). *Alternatives to mental hospital treatment.* New York: Plenum, 1978.

Strauss, J. S., & Carpenter, W. T. The prediction of outcome in schizophrenia: II. Relationships between predictor and outcome variables. *Archives of General Psychiatry,* 1974, 31, 37–42.

Talbott, J. A. Stop the revolving door: A study of recidivism to a state hospital. *Psychiatric Quarterly,* 1974, 48, 159–167.

Test, M. A., & Stein, L. I. Training in community living: Research design and results. In L. I. Stein & M. A. Test (Eds.), *Alternatives to mental hospital treatment.* New York: Plenum, 1978.

Vaillant, G. E. A 10-year follow-up of remitting schizophrenics. *Schizophrenia Bulletin,* 1978, 4, 78–85.

Van Putten, T. Why do schizophrenic patients refuse to take their drugs? *Archives of General Psychiatry,* 1974, 31, 67–72.

Wallace, C. J. Assessment of psychotic behavior. In M. Hersen & A. Bellack (Eds.), *Behavioral assessment: A practical handbook.* Oxford: Pergamon, 1976.

Wallace, C. J., Nelson, C., Liberman, R. P., Richison, R., Lukoff, D., Elder, J., & Ferris, C. A review and critique of social skills training with schizophrenic patients. *Schizophrenia Bulletin,* 1980, 6, 42–64.

Zung, W. A self-rating depression scale. *Archives of General Psychiatry,* 1965, 12, 63–70.

4

BEHAVIORAL FAMILY THERAPY FOR SCHIZOPHRENIA

IAN R. H. FALLOON
JEFFREY L. BOYD
CHRISTINE W. MCGILL

INTRODUCTION

FAMILY COMMUNICATION AND SCHIZOPHRENIA

Disturbed family relationships have long been associated with families of schizophrenic patients. Harry Stack Sullivan (1927) first suggested links between schizophrenic symptoms and family interaction. He proposed a possible etiological link between a disturbed family environment during childhood and the subsequent onset of schizophrenia in adult life. This hypothesis heralded a large volume of subsequent research that sought to pinpoint the specific family behavior that spawns the schizophrenic breakdown of one family member. The enormous complexity of this mission has not daunted researchers, who have painstakingly stuck to the task of unraveling the process of family interaction. Despite their valiant efforts, only limited conclusions concerning the nature of etiological factors in schizophrenia can be drawn from the data. Very little of this wealth of information about families with a schizophrenic member has been translated into clinical intervention and even less into demonstrably effective treatment methods. A brief review of some of these studies may be relevant to the development of an effective family therapy program for schizophrenic patients.

Ian R. H. Falloon, Jeffrey L. Boyd, and Christine W. McGill. Department of Psychiatry and the Behavioral Sciences, University of Southern California School of Medicine, Los Angeles, California.

Fromm-Reichmann (1948) coined the phrase "schizophrenogenic mother," hereby directing attention toward the maternal role in schizophrenia. Earlier, Kasanin, Knight, and Sage (1934) found evidence of maternal overprotection or rejection in 27 of 45 (60%) schizophrenics. He also noted that the schizophrenics tended to have been sickly children and that the overprotective response might well have been a response to biological vulnerability. Subsequent studies have supported the view that mothers of schizophrenics tend to be more overprotective than mothers of other mentally ill persons (Alanen, 1958; Gerard & Siegel, 1950; Lidz, Fleck, & Cornelison, 1965; Lu, 1961; Reichard & Tillman, 1950; Tietze, 1949). Not only are mothers overprotective, but it has been suggested that they dominate decision making within the family and act in an intrusive way with their schizophrenic offspring (Kohn & Clausen, 1956; Laing & Esterson, 1964). Lidz, Cornelison, Fleck, and Terry (1957) described a similar pattern of dominant mothers with complementary weak, passive fathers and termed it "marital skew." However, this "abnormal" pattern of parental decision making represents a normal state of affairs in lower socioeconomic families and has not been substantiated as a pattern specific to schizophrenic families in later research (Kohn & Clausen, 1956).

Another pattern of family interaction described by Lidz and his colleagues has been found more consistently in parents of schizophrenics. He uses the term "marital schism" to describe discordant, distrustful marital relationships where the parents are so involved in their own needs and conflicts that they tend to ignore the needs of other family members and may scapegoat or impose unrealistic expectations on schizophrenic members. Once again, this pattern of interaction has not appeared limited to schizophrenic families (Waring & Ricks, 1965). Bowen's description of "emotional divorce," where both parents appear remote, cold, and lacking in mutual understanding, may be a more accurate stereotype of marriages where offspring suffer from schizophrenia (Bowen, Dysinger, & Basamania, 1959; Waring & Ricks, 1965). In one form or another, marital discord has been consistently found in families with schizophrenic members, in both descriptive (Bowen et al., 1959; Fleck, Lidz, & Cornelison, 1963; Laing & Esterson, 1964; Lidz & Lidz, 1949; Tietze, 1949) and empirical studies (Alanen, 1958, 1966; Cheek, 1965; Ferreira & Winter, 1965; Gerard & Siegel, 1950; McGhie, 1961).

The mediating links between parental discord and psychiatric disturbance in children have not been clearly demonstrated. Some studies have indicated that parents' behavior is more negative in the presence of schizophrenic offspring than with nonschizophrenic siblings (Mishler & Waxler, 1968; Sharan, 1966). These findings illustrate the difficulty of establishing causality in interactional research. Many family therapists have abandoned the unidirectional view of causality and have instead conceptualized the family in terms of systems theory (von Bertalanffy, 1968). The family is viewed as a social system of interlocking parts. Disturbance of any component of the system will lead to disturbance in all other parts and necessitate an adaptation process to regain the steady state. The family systems approach gives rise to several concepts relevant to family treatment. Jackson (1959) used the concept of homeostasis to explain why family relationships with severely distorted interaction patterns may, nonetheless, achieve some stability. Behavior therapists have used the concept of reciprocity in contingencies of reinforcing and aversive exchanges between marital couples (Liberman, 1970; Stuart, 1969).

Wynne (Wynne, Ryckoff, Day, & Hirsch, 1958) has outlined a phenomenon he calls "pseudomutuality," where the family of a schizophrenic maintains a closed interactive system in which all needs must appear to be met and where independent goals, open disagreement, and contacts with the extrafamilial social network are discouraged. The lack of contact with the social network, even at times of stress, that is frequently found in families of schizophrenics offers some validation for this concept (Tolsdorf, 1976).

Bowen (1966) has graphically described the blurring of the individuals' boundaries within an undifferentiated ego mass that occurs in families of schizophrenics where considerable difficulties are encountered by the individual who is attempting to develop as a self-sufficient person. Although providing a very interesting model, no empirical studies have been conducted to support the systems theory approach to family interaction.

The second major area of research into the family interaction of families with a schizophrenic member has involved detailed observation of communication skills. These studies derived from the work of the anthropologist Gregory Bateson, who described an incongruity of verbal and nonverbal communication leading to a confusion of informative and affective messages (Bateson, Jackson, Haley, & Weakland, 1956). While, once again, these defects are probably not specific to schizophrenia (Sluzki & Vernon, 1971), a lack of effective interpersonal communication skill must compound the difficulty families encounter when interacting with a schizophrenic member. In order to sustain adequate interpersonal communication, accurate perception and processing of relevant social and environmental clues is required (Falloon, 1978). Disorders of attention as well as a variety of cognitive deficits that mediate against accurate interpersonal perception have been reported in schizophrenic patients (Buss & Lang, 1965) and their parents as well (McConaghy, 1959). Singer and Wynne (1966a) noted a variety of verbal communication defects in the parents of schizophrenics that were less frequent in parents of normal or neurotic offspring. These included disruptions, vagueness, irrelevant remarks, lack of closure, and other speech abnormalities that suggested underlying attentional and cognitive defects. This work was partially replicated by Hirsch and Leff (1975), who attributed the differences between the groups to greater verbosity among parents of schizophrenics. However, verbal excess may itself indicate a lack of clarity in communication (Woodward & Goldstein, 1977). Thus, it could be hypothesized that the parents of schizophrenics have an underlying cognitive deficit that leads to communication difficulties, to marital and family discord, and may be inherited to a more severe degree in the schizophrenic offspring. The difficulties in communication between parents and their schizophrenic offspring are significantly greater than with nonschizophrenic offspring (Mishler & Waxler, 1968). Parents speak in a more pedantic way to the schizophrenic child, suggesting that they may be trying to assist him or her to understand them.

The third series of family interaction studies has examined the problem-solving behavior of schizophrenics and their families. These studies have suggested reduced efficiency in problem solving compared to families with normal offspring (Ferreira & Winter, 1965; Haley, 1968; Lerner, 1965, 1967; Reiss, 1967, 1968, 1969). However, differences have not been specific to families of schizophrenics but have been evident in families with other disturbed offspring as well. It seems probable that the communication and cognitive difficulties noted in these families mediate against clarity of problem definition, listing potential solutions, weighing the consequences, choosing the best alternative, and planning the appropriate responses.

In summary, there appears no clear evidence for a specific pattern of family interaction associated with the development or etiology of schizophrenia. But the evidence available from interaction research suggests that in families containing a schizophrenic member, particularly where the identified patient has poor prognostic features, certain family factors are probably more frequent. These include

1. Discord between parents
2. Overprotective, intrusive mothers
3. Deficiencies in parents' communication skills
4. Poor problem-solving abilities

The implications of this research for family intervention strategies suggest methods that enhance agreement between parents, improve family communication skills (in particular, the appropriate expression of positive and negative feelings), increase the social distance between schizophrenic and overinvolved family members, and teach problem-solving strategies.

THE FAMILY MILIEU

All these studies have tended to examine family interaction, with the aim of eventually unraveling schizophrenic family communication and, thereby, curing the disorder. However, after considerable optimism with the advent of effective medication and enlightened social policy, the pendulum is swinging back to a view that, in many cases, schizophrenia is a chronic disorder, with handicaps that may be minimized only through long-term social support and low-dosage medication (Gunderson, 1978; Stein, 1978; Wing, 1977). The crucial issues are how to provide optimal community support and how to derive maximum benefits from long-term neuroleptic medication while avoiding the harmful effects. The role of family support has been investigated extensively by Brown and coworkers at the Institute of Psychiatry in London. A study of patients discharged from long-term institutional care revealed a greater relapse rate in those who returned to live with parents and spouses than those who lived with less emotionally involved relatives or in residential care facilities (Brown, Carstairs, & Topping, 1958; Brown, Monck, Carstairs, & Wing, 1962). Two subsequent studies conducted a decade apart helped specify the qualities in the family atmosphere that appeared to determine the outcome. Families where the emotions ran high and family members expressed high levels of criticism and hostility or markedly overinvolved, intrusive attitudes were clearly associated with a high rate of relapse. Those families where members expressed more tolerant attitudes, with warmth and realistic concern, tended to provide a supportive milieu for the patient and, consequently, fewer relapses were reported. These studies employed an interview with each family member as the source of data and assumed that the attitudes expressed toward the patient reflected family interaction patterns, at least at times of stress (Brown, Birley, & Wing, 1972; Vaughn & Leff, 1976a). Combining data from these two studies, it was noted that the impact of a highly emotional relative could be substantially reduced where the social distance between patient and relative could be increased to the point where less than 35 hours per week were spent together in the same room. An equally powerful protector was adequate antipsychotic drug therapy. The combination of these two factors, social distance plus drug therapy, appeared capable of reducing relapse rates during a 9-month postdischarge period from a striking 92% to about 15%. This was similar to the rate of relapse found in the low-"expressed-emotion" (EE) homes, where drug therapy appeared to be of little additional value in preventing relapses (Vaughn & Leff, 1976a).

COMMUNITY MANAGEMENT OF SCHIZOPHRENIA: INDIVIDUAL VERSUS FAMILY-ORIENTED APPROACH

This suggests several potentially therapeutic strategies. The most parsimonious would be the provision of adequate continuation medication through methods that may enhance compliance (i.e., minimally effective dosage to reduce unpleasant side effects, rapid follow-up of missed appointments, home visits where necessary, the use of long-acting intramuscular preparations for persistent noncompliance, and education of the patient about the nature and rationale for his treatment). This can be combined with vocational counseling to enable the patient or emotionally expressive (high-EE) family members to find work-related activities outside the home and thereby reduce the time spent in face-to-face contact. The provision of day care, activity centers, and residential care facilities may likewise enable separation from family influences. Supportive care, as described by Mendel (1975), constitutes a model of aftercare for the schizophrenic that combines these strategies with supportive psychotherapy to assist the patient with his here-and-now problems of living. He emphasizes the importance of continuity of care and long-term support. These concepts have received substantial empirical support. Hogarty and his colleagues (Hogarty, Goldberg, Schooler, & Ulrich, 1974a, 1974b) reported a successful interaction between drugs and intensive social casework that became apparent only after 18 months of treatment. Stein and Test (1978) achieved excellent results while actively providing support for schizophrenics in the community environment, but noted a considerable reduction in benefits after their extensive help was phased out. Several other innovative programs that have provided extrafamilial supportive living arrangements have shown considerable promise (Fairweather, Sanders, Maynard, & Cressler, 1969; Mosher, Menn, & Matthews, 1975; Polak, Deever, & Kirkby, 1977; Sanders, Smith, & Weinman, 1967). The value of continued medication in preventing relapse has been clearly established in several double-blind follow-up trials (Englehardt & Freedman, 1970; Falloon, Watt, & Shepherd, 1978a; Hirsch, Gaind, Rohde, Stevens, & Wing, 1973; Leff & Wing, 1971). There is less evidence for the benefits of supportive psychotherapy continued after discharge from hospital, although in a well-controlled study, psychotherapy for schizophrenic patients during their hospital stay did not measurably alter their postdischarge course, in contrast to the substantial ability of phenothiazines and electroconvulsive therapy to reduce rehospitalization (May, 1968; May, Tuma, & Dixon, 1976; May, Tuma, Yale, Potepan, & Dixon, 1976). However, in community-based therapy, visits to the psychiatrist to obtain medication are always accompanied by supportive psychotherapy of some kind. It is clearly impossible to succeed in providing continued medication compliance without developing a therapeutic alliance with the patient.

At this point, the long-term community management of schizophrenics is at a relatively early stage of development. Several major concerns exist. First, treatment may need to be lifelong in many cases (Mendel, 1976). Secondly, irreversible side effects, such as tardive dyskinesia, appear more frequently when antipsychotic medication is continued for several years (Simpson, 1977). Reduction in the amount of medication ingested may lessen the severity of extrapyramidal adverse effects. However, the plasma levels of antipsychotic drugs are poorly correlated to ingested dosage (Cooper, Simpson, & Lee, 1976). In fact, high plasma levels may be associated with aggressive behavior, and improvement may result from a lowering of the dosage to achieve levels of less than 300 ng/ml (Curry, Marshall, Davis, & Janowsky, 1970). Another feature observed in isolated cases is rapid metabolism of ingested medication through enzyme induction that results in nondetectable plasma levels and negligible clinical effects (Cooper *et al.*, 1976). Thus, although drug therapy is highly effective in most patients, there remain many unanswered questions of considerable clinical significance.

Thirdly, the provision of adequate vocational rehabilitation is often limited by the patient's learning ability and motivation, as well as by community resources and the economic climate—for example, unemployment levels, funding of sheltered employment programs (Lamb, 1979). Residential care is seldom ideal and, while there is often greater tolerance of aberrant behavior within the residence, the community is generally less tolerant, and the lack of adequate personalized support often leads to a reduction in social functioning (Lamb & Goertzel, 1977). Finally, despite apparently ideal community care conditions, compliance with all aspects of the program is difficult to sustain over long periods, so that the people who require maximal support ultimately receive very little.

A family-oriented program, on the other hand, offers an approach that may avoid many of the difficulties encountered in patient-oriented programs. A stable reduction in family emotional tension might be expected to lead to a stable reduction in psychopathology and relapse rate, a reduced need for continuation medication, and less pressure for the provision of vocational and residential facilities. This formulation assumes that (1) family therapy can reduce EE to low levels, and (2) that the EE factors are themselves directly associated with psychopathology. A pilot study of a highly specific family therapy approach that reduced the EE levels in two out of three families (Falloon, Liberman, Lillie, & Vaughn, 1981) supports the feasibility of this approach. However, in addition, the patients received considerable extrafamilial training in social and interpersonal skills, and it was not possible to isolate improvement in the patient from changes in the attitudes of the family. Vaughn and Leff (1976b) point out that the most frequent hostile criticisms parents made about the patients concerned lifelong traits, including poor social skills and lack of expression of feelings—not current symptom-related behavior.

PSYCHOSOCIAL STRESS, COPING, AND RELAPSE

A series of studies, examining the impact of life events on the course of schizophrenic illness, indicates that the risk of relapse is significantly increased during the 3 weeks following a stressful life change (Brown &

Birley, 1968). Once again, adequate antipsychotic medication offers some protection against this stress, but it is not in itself sufficient (Leff, Hirsch, Gaind, Rohde, & Stevens, 1973).

To date, no study has examined extra- and intrafamilial stress factors concurrently. Zubin and Spring (1977) have outlined a theory of vulnerability to explain the interaction between stress and psychopathology. Ongoing family stress and superimposed life events may summate until they exceed a threshold above which a relapse of florid symptoms may be inevitable. Very high levels of day-to-day family stress may exceed the threshold without the added impact of life events, while low family stress may require the presence of a major stressful life event to exceed the threshold and trigger a relapse. Leff and Vaughn (1980) found surprisingly few life events associated with relapse in high-EE families, whereas low-EE patients did not relapse, despite experiencing many life events. Efforts to enhance the ability to cope with life crises have not yet been evaluated. Studies of the coping mechanisms of schizophrenics have highlighted their ineffective problem-solving skills as well as lack of assistance from the family until after relapse has occurred (Tolsdorf, 1976). This suggests that another useful family intervention may involve teaching effective strategies for coping with intermittent major stressful events to both the patient and his family network. In addition, patients and their families could be taught to improve their recognition of the signs of excessive stress and imminent relapse so that they can intervene appropriately to reduce stress and prevent a full-blown relapse.

PREPARING FAMILIES FOR COMMUNITY CARE

Most schizophrenic patients and their families are ill prepared for the primary care task that community-oriented psychiatry has placed upon them (Lamb, Hoffman, Hoffman, & Oliphant, 1976). The burden on families has been shown to be considerable (Grad & Sainsbury, 1968). This burden may be eased where antipsychotic medication is provided in adequate dosage (Stevens, 1973) and where specific community support is provided for the care of patients in the community (Stein & Test, 1978). Apart from the general inadequacy of support services, patients and families have extremely limited knowledge of their illness, and it is apparent that many difficulties in community management programs are associated with insufficient understanding of the nature of the disorder and the rationale for treatment (Creer & Wing, 1974; Soskis, 1978). In order to further harness the caring support of the family network, basic education about schizophrenia may be an important first step. Such education has been considered highly beneficial by patients and their families in our pilot studies. In addition to educating the nuclear family about schizophrenia, it may be helpful to promote a similar understanding among the wider social network of extended family and friends.

This review of the family factors related to the course of schizophrenia suggests that an effective family intervention should

1. Educate the family and social network about the nature and management of schizophrenia, so that family members can more readily provide a caring, supportive milieu and encourage treatment compliance, based on a clear understanding of the basic principles of primary care for schizophrenia
2. Teach more effective nonverbal and verbal communication (in particular, the appropriate expression of dissatisfaction and concern), in order to reduce hostile criticism and overinvolvement
3. Teach more effective problem-solving skills, so that family members can learn to identify and cope with stressful life events, as well as reduce the level of family tension

EVALUATION OF FAMILY THERAPY OUTCOME WITH SCHIZOPHRENICS

The paucity of adequately controlled outcome studies of family therapy is in striking contrast to the plethora of studies of treatment process. Extensive reviews by several authors (DeWitt, 1978; Massie & Beels, 1972; Wells & Dezen, 1978; Wells, Dilkes, & Trivelli, 1972) have described only two adequately designed studies that have compared family therapy with schizophrenic patients with adequately controlled alternative treatment modalities. Neither dealt exclusively with a schizophrenic population. Two recent studies not included in these reviews involve family therapy in broadly defined populations of schizophrenics.

Langsley and his colleagues at the University of Colorado Medical Center treated 150 randomly selected cases of acute psychiatric illness with crisis-oriented family therapy that aimed to avoid hospital admission. A matched control group of 150 similar cases where the identified patient had been admitted to hospital for conventional treatment was selected. The family intervention employed directive and supportive strategies to guide the family through the crisis and to help the patient return to his or her previous level of social functioning. The families were taught effective methods of coping with the present situation without scapegoating or extruding the patient from the family group. The average duration of treatment was 3 weeks, consisting of about five office visits, a home visit, and 24-hour telephone contact. Treatment began at the moment of referral to hospital. Drugs were used for symptom relief of any family member. The family was informed of the short-term nature of the crisis treatment. When long-term therapy was indicated, referrals were made to other services. It is not clear how the family crisis unit and other community agencies collaborated in the follow-up care, although it appeared that the family crisis unit continued to assist whenever a crisis occurred throughout the 2-year follow-up period.

An 18-month follow-up of 80% of the original sample indicated that not only could hospitalization be avoided on a short-term basis, but that in many cases, hospitalization could be reduced over a much longer period (Langsley, Machotka, & Flomenhaft, 1971). In an earlier report, it is suggested that the family approach may greatly reduce the costs associated with hospital care, although no detailed cost-effectiveness study was reported (Langsley, Pittman, Machotka, & Flomenhaft, 1968). The measures of social adjustment showed no advantage for the family therapy group, although a measure of clinical status suggested that family-treated patients had less symptomatic impairment at follow-up. However, no detailed information on drug therapy is provided, and it is not clear how this may have contributed to the differential clinical outcome.

Although no diagnostic breakdown is given for the main study, a subgroup of 25 families of schizophrenic patients who had participated in the family treatment was compared with an unmatched group of 25 schizophrenics who received the control treatment. A rating of life events and coping indicated that the schizophrenic families who received family therapy had experienced fewer crises and managed to cope with them better than the controls (Langsley, Pittman, & Swank, 1969).

The main study, while generally supportive of the family therapy approach, is limited in the specific conclusions that can be drawn with regard to the treatment of schizophrenia. As Wells and Dezen (1978) have noted, the independent variable, family therapy, is confounded with the dependent variable, hospital admission. With the designs employed, it is not possible to conclude whether the more favorable results of family therapy are the result of merely avoiding hospitalization— which may have been achieved by several other methods (e.g., individual crisis intervention, day hospital care)—or were specific to the family orientation.

In a similarly flawed study of community-based family therapy as an alternative to hospitalization, Rittenhouse (1970) employed family interventions designed to improve family communication skills with subjects who were considered in need of hospitalization. Seventy-two (72) subjects were randomly assigned to either family therapy or hospital milieu and were followed up at 3, 6, and 12 months. Again, the family approach showed a reduced readmission rate but no differences on social adjustment and clinical ratings were found between the two approaches. The outcome of schizophrenics in this sample was not specified.

These two studies enable us to conclude that family interventions are an effective alternative to hospitalization for patients with a wide variety of psychiatric disturbances. This may be viewed as merely shifting the primary care role from the nursing professionals at the hospital to the family care givers at home. The support provided to the family is praiseworthy and may be seen as a major step in developing viable community care, but there is no clear indication that such short-term therapy has any lasting impact on the course of schizophrenic illness through preventing further relapses, or that changes in family communication patterns are produced that may benefit other family members.

The reluctance of family therapists to examine diagnostic variables probably derives from the systems concept of the sick family, in which the designated patient is considered the carrier of family pathology. Although family therapists have sought to abandon the use of patient-oriented diagnoses, they have been slow to develop alternative family-oriented classifications (Reiss, Costell, Jones, & Berkman, 1980). Diagnosis as a means of precise classification of individual schizophrenic patients has suffered from a somewhat similar lack of generalizability. In a recently concluded study of family therapy by Goldstein, Rodnick, Evans, May, and Steinberg (1978), schizophrenic patients were selected on the basis of the New Haven Schizophrenic Index. This index gives a broad definition of schizophrenia. Almost half the patients classified as schizophrenic using this scheme would not be so classified using a more conservative method, such as the Present State Examination/CATEGO method (Wing, Cooper, & Sartorius, 1974), or the flexible system for diagnosis developed by the Washington, D.C., group in the International Pilot Study of Schizophrenia (Carpenter, Strauss, & Bartko, 1973; Strauss & Gift, 1977). Symptoms such as confusion, depersonalization, visual hallucinations, and paranoid ideation (not delusional) are given the same weighting as auditory hallucinations, delusions, and thought disorder. Clearly, reliable diagnosis is essential to all psychiatric research.

Goldstein's study (Goldstein *et al.*, 1978), despite this crucial limitation, is well designed. Ninety-six (96) schizophrenic patients, the majority suffering their first hospital admission, were followed up for 6 months after being treated with family therapy, or standard aftercare, combined with either high-dosage fluphenazine enanthate or low-dosage fluphenazine enanthate. The family therapy consisted of six sessions and was conducted during the first 6 weeks after discharge from the hospital. The therapists were provided with clear-cut objectives that included (1) getting both the patient and family to accept the fact that the patient had suffered a psychotic illness; (2) identifying precipitating life stresses at the time of onset of the psychosis; (3) getting the family to consider similar stressful events that might occur in the future; and (4) teaching the family ways to minimize or avoid these potential stresses. No attempt was made to alter the structure of family relationships or to directly improve family communication. The drug therapy was parenteral, thereby controlling for ingestion compliance factors. The high dosage was 25 mg every 2 weeks, and the low dosage 6.25 mg over the same interval.

The results were evaluated in terms of prevention of rehospitalization and ratings of psychopathology using the Brief Psychiatric Rating Scale (Overall & Gorham, 1962) at the end of treatment (i.e., 6 weeks) and at 6 months after discharge from hospital. At 6 weeks, the results tended to favor patients who received family therapy, while at 6 months the main effect was for the high-dosage medication. Forty-eight percent of low-dose-plus-no-family-therapy patients relapsed, while not one high-dose-plus-family-therapy patient had relapsed at 6 months ($p <$ .01). The remaining two groups who received either high-dose medication (17%) or family therapy alone (22%) showed similar partial protection from relapse.

The analysis of symptom ratings was less clear and showed no differences between the treatment groups on measures of florid schizophrenic symptoms (conceptual disorganization, unusual thought content, hallucinations). However, measures of associated symptoms, such as social withdrawal and anxiety–depression, suggested a detrimental effect that could be attributed to the high-dose medication. These unwanted effects of long-acting parenteral medication have been reported by other investigators (deAlarcon & Carney, 1969; Andrews, 1973;

Falloon, Watt, & Shepherd, 1978a, 1978b). Unfortunately, the lack of a measure of social functioning precluded assessing the severity of the residual functional impairment associated with the medication in this study. The authors concluded that such symptomatology is a small price to pay for avoiding hospitalization; however, social withdrawal and negative affect may, in many cases, be as undesirable as rehospitalization. It is interesting to note that at the completion of family therapy, social withdrawal was reduced in the high-dosage group, suggesting that continued therapy may have countered the negative effects of medication. The merits of long-acting phenothiazines have recently been questioned (Falloon *et al.*, 1978b), and it is probable that oral preparations are more effective adjuncts to psychosocial therapy.

A further analysis along the poor-versus-good premorbid adjustment variable in the Goldstein *et al.* (1978) study suggested that males in the good premorbid group obtained excellent results irrespective of treatment, while poor premorbid men benefited most from the combination of family and adequate drug therapy. The validity of the premorbid distinction as a predictive variable for women did not hold up in this study.

It may be concluded that this study suggests a beneficial interaction between family therapy and drug therapy. However, it is hardly surprising that a 6-week course of family therapy proved to be less significant a factor at 6 months than drug therapy continued over the entire period. It is more remarkable that so few sessions of crisis-oriented family therapy should have produced a favorable trend still evident over 4 months later. The impact of a longer period of family therapy that also attempts to induce durable changes in family interaction patterns remains an exciting prospect. A further question raised by this study is whether a lower dosage of medication might prove effective when combined with family therapy of longer duration. However, it would seem advisable to start with a standard dose and then gradually reduce it while monitoring the clinical state. Serial plasma levels of orally administered antipsychotic drugs that would help in the titration of optimal dose levels may soon be readily available (Cooper *et al.*, 1976). Oral medication is more readily titrated and is probably associated with less severe side effects. In addition, its noninvasive mode of administration makes it more acceptable to patients.

Gould and Glick (1977) have reported the outcome of another study of brief family therapy (four sessions) on hospitalized schizophrenics. Two family therapy conditions were compared with two

groups who did not receive family therapy. Assignment was not randomized, but the groups were reasonably well matched on sociodemo-
graphic characteristics. The authors concluded that the presence of
family members during inpatient treatment was associated with better
posthospital adjustment and that the brief family therapy did not show
any additional benefits. The family therapy was conducted by trainees
under the supervision of an experienced family therapist and focused
mainly on discharge planning issues. In addition to the family sessions,
patients all received phenothiazine medication, individual psychotherapy
one to three times a week, two sessions of group therapy per week, a
role play group, a treatment planning group, a discharge planning
group, and a variety of occupational therapy groups. It is not surprising
that the effects of the family therapy intervention could not be partialed
out from this rich therapeutic program. But despite the gross methodological inadequacies, this study does suggest the value of family concern
and support for schizophrenic patients returning to the community.

To date, the published studies of family therapy have tended to
focus predominantly on crisis intervention issues related mainly to
admission and discharge from hospital. Despite extremely short-term
family intervention, extremely promising results have been achieved. It
is not clear whether changes in family interaction and communication
patterns have occurred with this short-term family therapy to account
for the lasting benefits that have been reported. The need for a well-
controlled study of family therapy of longer duration that, in addition to
dealing with life crises issues, also addresses communication disturbances within the family system, is clearly the next step in this research
endeavor.

BEHAVIORAL FAMILY THERAPY: A PILOT STUDY

In a pilot study conducted at the Bethlem Royal and Maudsley Hospitals
in London, Ian Falloon, in collaboration with Robert Liberman, devised a
family therapy method that took as its theoretical basis the family EE
findings of the Medical Research Council Social Psychiatry Unit (Falloon
et al., 1981). The principal goal of this method was to reduce the levels of
EE in key relatives. Strategies were directed at changing patterns of
negative criticism and hostility toward the patient and reducing overdependent bonding between relatives and patients. This family therapy
formed an integral part of a larger intervention approach that sought to

increase social distance through teaching independent living skills during a 10-week inpatient social skills training program (Liberman, Lillie, Falloon, Vaughn, Harpin, Leff, Hutchinson, Ryan, & Stoute, 1978). All patients were maintained on antipsychotic medication.

Three male schizophrenic patients (diagnosed using the Present State Examination) with poor premorbid adjustment and histories of frequent schizophrenic relapses were chosen for this pilot study. Each patient had been living with a parent who was high on EE prior to his admission. All three families consisted of a single-parent household, although in one case, the parent lived with a stable partner. Twenty sessions, each of 2 hours' duration, were held on a twice-weekly schedule while the patients were in hospital, followed by five sessions at weekly intervals after their discharge. Family therapy was conducted in a multi-family group. The impact of family therapy was evaluated using a single-case multiple-baseline method. During the first 10 sessions, an educational approach was employed that focused on providing clear information about the nature of the schizophrenic illness and the rationale for combined biological and psychosocial therapies. Patients and families were invited to share their experiences of schizophrenia and to clarify their concerns and misunderstandings. The importance of regular medication in preventing relapse was emphasized, together with psychosocial methods to reduce and cope with environmental stresses that may precipitate relapse. Families were told that although there was no evidence that they had caused their son's illness, they nevertheless may contribute to an improved outcome by providing a supportive milieu.

Following the educational sessions, the families were instructed in more effective communication and problem-solving skills. These skills included attending to and expressing positive feelings to one another, and expressing dissatisfaction with specific behavior in a constructive manner. Specific conflict situations also were identified for each family that involved issues such as coping with symptomatic behavior, getting the patient to help with chores, sharing recreational interests, living independently, and reducing unrealistic expectations. New skills were taught using a behavioral social-learning format of repeated role rehearsal of a specific interpersonal situation, with demonstration of alternative strategies by therapists and other family members, feedback, coaching, and social reinforcement. Following practice in the therapy session, families practiced the new strategies after the sessions or on home visits at weekends.

The effectiveness of these methods was evaluated in terms of the frequency that new behavior generalized outside the sessions. In all three families, a substantial increase in specific positive family interactions was noted after the baseline period. A Camberwell Family Interview carried out 6 weeks after the last family session revealed a reduction in EE from high to low levels in two of the three families, with reports of substantial changes in family interaction.

The conclusions that could be drawn from this pilot study were limited by the concurrent, intensive, patient-oriented social skills training. But, the findings suggest that significant changes in interactive patterns that have been clearly linked to poor prognosis can be accomplished through a method that directly addresses the communication deficits of the families. The effects of this therapy were undoubtedly diluted by having the patient and family separated (except for weekend visits) during the greater part of the treatment program, so that opportunities to practice alternative communication skills in the intact family were greatly reduced. However, these preliminary results, together with those of the recent study by Goldstein et al. (1978), suggest that family therapy may be one of the most promising psychosocial intervention strategies in the community treatment of schizophrenia. It was hypothesized that appropriate interventions in selected families may prevent the establishment of a chronic, relapsing course in family members suffering from schizophrenia. Since 1977, development of behavioral family methods at the University of Southern California and the University of California, Los Angeles, Mental Health Clinical Research Center for the Study of Schizophrenia have continued. The family interventions have been refined and a carefully controlled outcome study has been launched with support from the National Institute of Mental Health. The remainder of this chapter will describe the family therapy interventions and the research in progress.

THE FAMILY THERAPY PROGRAM

The goal of the family therapy program is to provide comprehensive, long-term community care for persons suffering from schizophrenia by utilizing natural support systems. To this end, the major interventions involve increasing the social and interpersonal competence of both the patient and the family members with whom he or she lives. It is hypothesized that schizophrenia is a stress-related biological illness that can be effectively treated by combining drug therapy with psychosocial interventions. Thus, family interventions address the difficulties of long-term drug therapy as well as teaching coping mechanisms that are effective at reducing environmental stress. Two major sources of stress are specifically addressed: (1) disturbed family relationships, and (2) life events. Families who have severe deficits in their ability to cope with these stressors are selected for the program and, after detailed behavioral analysis of their assets and deficits, begin an intervention program of 2 years duration. The specific interventions include (1) education about schizophrenia, (2) carefully monitored neuroleptic medication, (3) communication training, (4) problem solving, and (5) crisis intervention.

TREATMENT SETTING

The family sessions are conducted in the home. Although home visiting is costly, there are many advantages to this approach. First, generalization of behavior from one setting to another is a problem that is seldom addressed adequately by clinic-based community treatment programs. The problem is compounded in the treatment of schizophrenia by evidence of low levels of transfer of learned skills across settings with this population (Liberman, McCann, & Wallace, 1976). *In vivo* family sessions not only enhance generalization in the natural environment, but also take advantage of the family unit as a powerful agent for effecting social learning and reinforcement.

Secondly, failed appointments, which frequently frustrate therapists and reduce the effective delivery of therapeutic interventions, are minimized. Poor compliance with clinic-based therapy programs has been a major problem in the community care of schizophrenics that has not been effectively resolved.

Thirdly, in the home setting the therapist is able to gain a substantial knowledge of family behavior patterns and idiosyncratic aspects of the family's daily life that may not be demonstrable in the clinic. Family systems theorists have placed much emphasis on the generality of family communication, which has tended to obscure the fact that each individual's responses are situation-specific. Home visits often clarify family stresses that have confounded other therapists. Frequently therapists have been surprised how well certain patients function in the home environment, while showing minimal levels of competence in the clinic. On the other hand, unremitting family stress is often readily explained by atrocious living conditions.

A further advantage of *in vivo* family therapy is the ability to involve family members, friends, and neighbors, who would be unlikely to attend clinic sessions. The broader impact of therapy on the social network provides greater opportunities for creating community support systems outside the family. This is of particular importance in the single-parent family.

TREATMENT SCHEDULE

Patients are recruited for the family therapy program following acute hospitalization and/or exacerbation of florid schizophrenia symptomatology. They are stabilized on medication and receive weekly individual supportive care sessions at the clinic for approximately 1 month. During this time data is collected from both the index patient and other family members. Each family member is interviewed with the semistructured Camberwell Family Interview (Vaughn & Leff, 1976b). Information on family members' coping mechanisms at times of crisis enables the interviewer to classify families into high or low EE categories. Those families in the high-EE group enter the family intervention program after further assessment of family communication, problem solving skills, psychopathology, and social function.

The treatment schedule extends over a 2-year period. During the first 3 months, 1-hour sessions are held weekly; from 3 to 6 months sessions taper to biweekly; from 6 to 9 months sessions diminish to every 3rd week. The rationale for this approach is related to data on risk of relapse, which indicate that patients are most vulnerable to symptomatic exacerbations in the 3 months following an acute episode, and although they remain at risk throughout the subsequent 2-year period, few relapses occur after 9 months postdischarge. Patients who have not relapsed within 9 months postdischarge are relatively unlikely to relapse in the following 15 months.

After 9 months of active treatment, therapists continue to reduce their intensive support as the family gains competence and a monthly maintenance schedule is implemented to the 2-year mark, with crisis intervention available whenever necessary. Care is comprehensive and any further need for hospitalization or emergency care is provided by the program. The monthly sessions may include multifamily group sessions at the clinic, with families encouraged to meet together more often in their homes. The goal is to construct a community-based social network and support group in a population that suffers from social isolation of significant proportions.

FAMILY EDUCATION SESSIONS

The first two sessions of the family program are educational in nature and attempt to provide the family and index patient with information on the nature, course, and treatment of schizophrenia. A didactic format is utilized, with visual aids and handouts. The family is asked to share their perceptions and experiences and the index patient is encouraged to discuss his or her individual symptomatology and interpersonal difficulties in a supportive atmosphere.

"Schizophrenia" is defined as a major mental illness with biological and psychosocial components that cause problems of daily functioning in many of the following areas: (1) personal care, (2) interpersonal relationships, (3) work/study, (4) social and leisure activities, (5) decision making. Target symptoms, such as hallucinations, delusions, and thought disorders are reviewed by the therapists in the context of reviewing major diagnostic categories. Surprisingly, this is more often than not the first time such information has been imparted directly to the family or index patient and it is a powerful tool in correcting family misunderstanding about mental illness. This lack of understanding frequently underlies much of the criticism and overinvolvement shown toward the index patient.

Theoretical material related to the etiology and treatment of schizophrenia is tailored to the family's level of comprehension. For example, some families may request a critique of the literature on dopamine pathways, while others are satisfied with the knowledge that disordered brain chemistry alters the patient's ability to process thoughts properly. Current research studies are reviewed as well as media trends. Families frequently ask about highly publicized new treatments, such as megavitamin therapy and dialysis treatment. The absence of a body of empirical data on these modes of treatment is noted and it is reiterated that while there is no known cure for schizophrenia at present, highly effective treatment to prevent subsequent relapse and deterioration is currently available.

The genetic literature suggesting a biological transmission of inherent schizophrenic factors is reviewed, particularly the twin studies. Although risk of schizophrenia increases 10-fold in first-degree relatives, procreation is not discouraged. With the precise mechanism of genetic transfer still unknown, families are advised that probability exists of increased genetic vulnerability. Genetic theory, coupled with multiple environmental factors, is posited as an explanation of the etiological determinants of schizophrenia. Families are reassured that there is little evidence of implicating child-rearing practices in causing the illness. However, since stress has been identified as influential on the course of schizophrenia, the importance of family support in minimizing both intrafamilial and external stressors is emphasized.

Family members are encouraged to ventilate feelings of frustration, anger, or guilt about schizophrenia or its management, with the therapists adopting an emphatic, supportive position. Patients and their families are urged to adopt realistic yet hopeful expectations for the future. Family goal adjustment is often essential in reducing criticism and hostility leveled at the patient for his or her lack of attainment of parental expectations. Return of premorbid levels of function and drug or therapy "cure" are two notions that are discouraged as unrealistic short-term goals. The family is seen as the cornerstone of supportive care and stress-reduction management as well as the base of planning for long-term rehabilitation goals. Thus, the rationale for family therapy is that integration of the biopsychosocial models occurs optimally in the family system.

The second family education session addresses the importance of neuroleptic medication in the treatment of schizophrenia. The rationale for the use of optimal low-dose maintenance medication is presented in terms of the need for modification of the combined effects of stress and biochemistry. Families are given a brief overview of all drugs commonly prescribed for psychiatric disorders. The different types of major tranquilizers are outlined, along with a description of symptoms most likely to respond to them. Statistics showing a 70% risk of relapse without medication as opposed to a 30% risk with medication indicate the benefits of medication in preventing return of florid symptomatology.

With medication compliance a major problem in the schizophrenic population and with individual differences in drug absorption a further complicating issue, monthly blood plasma levels are drawn to monitor drug efficacy. Side effects of drug therapy are enumerated as well as methods of minimizing them. The possibility of irreversible unwanted effects, such as tardive dyskinesia, is described as a potential risk of long-term pharmacotherapy.

Families are advised not to tamper with the medication schedule without discussing changes with the prescribing physician. The potential dangers of street drugs such as amphetamines, LSD, and PCP on the course of schizophrenia are detailed. A neutral position is maintained on the use of alcohol and marijuana in moderation, while warnings are issued to the schizophrenic patient of possible synergistic effects with neuroleptics.

Families are given written handouts outlining all material covered in the educational sessions. They are encouraged to ask questions and discuss any recent media coverage specific to schizophrenia. After completion of the educational sessions, families are asked to fill out a questionnaire to indicate their fund of knowledge. The increase in family awareness is usually accompanied by improved attitudes expressed about the patient. Patients are sometimes disturbed when initially told of their diagnosis, but subsequently accept this information and begin to adopt the role of an assertive, informed consumer. Although no more than two sessions are devoted in their entirety to this process, periodic review and further education continue throughout the treatment program.

COMMUNICATION TRAINING

On completion of the two family-education sessions, the next 12 *in vivo* sessions are geared to the need for improvement in family patterns of communication. Specific training strategies are employed to shape effective expression of positive and negative feelings, reflective listening, making requests, and reciprocity of conversation. This is tailored to the families' unique communication deficits as evinced in pretreatment interactional assessment. Week-to-week problems are pinpointed during a brief (10–15 minute) individual session with the index patient while the cotherapist meets with the rest of the family. The remainder of the session is spent with the entire family.

The following important elements of communication are addressed: (1) nonverbal behavior such as voice tone and volume, body language and eye contact, and facial expression; (2) verbal content, its appropriateness, clarity, and specificity; (3) expression of "I" statements of feelings; (4) reciprocity of conversation, including empathic listening, timing of response, and transitional statements. Generalized expression of positive or negative affect is discouraged in favor of praise or criticism for specific behavior. The importance of the immediacy of reinforcement is stressed.

One of the most powerful interventions is the repeated rehearsal of difficult family situations. Improved communication is shaped in rehearsal through the use of instruction, modeling, coaching, social reinforcement, and performance feedback. Family tension is diffused or slowed down by this process. Role reversal is another strategy sometimes used, wherein one family member assumes the role of another. Role play of extrafamilial situations is likewise of great value in preparing family members for anticipated stressors. Family members are trained to set up their own role rehearsal, to model and provide feedback and coaching.

Families are encouraged to practice newly learned communication techniques between sessions. Homework assignments are given, which include rehearsal of specific skills on a daily basis. Reports of these efforts are kept on family worksheets, which are reviewed at the beginning of each session. Individual journals are kept as further evidence of generalization. Family members are prompted to show retention of skills and therapists look for spontaneous performance of new communication skills during the sessions.

The therapist maintains a role as a teacher, modeling appropriate communication skills, offering much support and reassurance in a noncritical nonjudgmental manner. Although it is sometimes extremely difficult to find behavior to reinforce, every effort is made to focus on that which can be positively reinforced, while prompting alternative expression at the same time.

THE PROBLEM-SOLVING MODEL

When families show some mastery of basic communication skills, the problem-solving model is introduced as an effort at stress reduction at family crisis points. Problem solving is used to modify both familial tension as well as extrafamilial stressors. Family members are taught to (1) come to an agreement on the specific definition of the problem;

(2) generate at least five possible solutions or alternatives to the problem without judging their relative merits; (3) evaluate the positive and negative aspects of each alternative; (4) agree upon the best solution or combination of solutions; (5) plan and carry out the agreed-upon solution; (6) review and praise efforts at implementing the solution.

Families are encouraged to further structure their brainstorming efforts by writing down all suggestions. This maximizes group participation and focuses attention on the task. The therapist initially provides much active guidance, which is gradually withdrawn as the family masters the technique. The problem-solving method seeks to diffuse the burden of coping with a problem to all members of the family system and to draw on the strengths and resources of the family. Homework assignments are assigned with the goal that eventually the family will utilize the problem-solving model at the time of major life events, as well as in planning strategies for dealing with individual and family goals.

ADDITIONAL BEHAVIORAL STRATEGIES

Few families have an adequate repertoire of coping skills for dealing with the behavioral disturbances often associated with schizophrenia. Such specific problems as medication compliance, reduction of side effects, dealing with persistent delusions or hallucinations, or when to seek professional intervention are commonly raised by families. Behavioral management strategies that are taught to families include (1) contingency contracting; (2) token economy reinforcement schedules; (3) shaping; (4) time-out; (5) limit setting; (6) identification of warning signals of impending relapse.

DESIGN OF CONTROLLED STUDY

In order to assess the effectiveness of the family therapy program, a controlled-outcome study was designed. It was not feasible to compare the program with a no-treatment control. The most appropriate comparison was thought to be a therapy program that provided similar intensive support, with optimal medication and crisis intervention. In addition, it was considered important that the control program approximate the community care provided for persons suffering from schizophrenia by agencies of the highest quality. Ideally the control therapy would have excluded family participation. However, exclusion of family contact and support would not have been compatible with excellent community management. For these reasons the control therapy that we developed was based on individual supportive psychotherapy with family contact and support when necessary.

The design of this study is depicted in Figure 4-1 and calls for the random assignment of 40 index patients and their families to one of two treatment conditions: family therapy (20 cases) or supportive psychotherapy (20 cases). In either event, treatment consists of an initial

FIGURE 4-1. Summary of design.

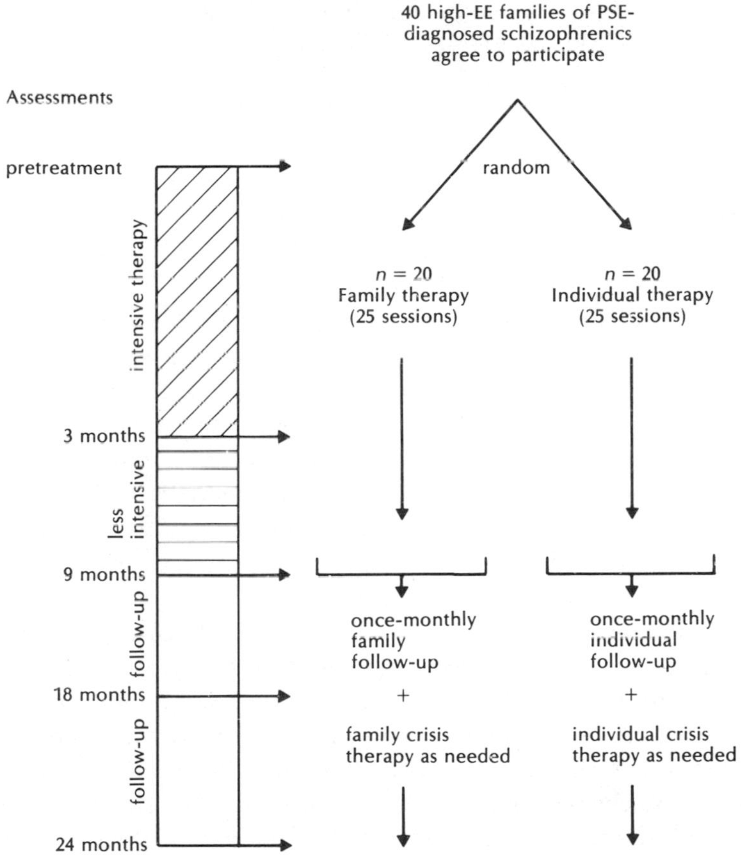

intensive phase of weekly therapy sessions, tapering gradually to a less intensive phase of monthly follow-up visits after 9 months. A total of 40 sessions are provided over a 2-year period. Therapists are available for additional crisis intervention sessions at all times throughout the study. If patients require hospital care, therapists continue to treat them in an inpatient unit and therapy sessions continue after discharge.

An extensive battery of dependent measures is administered to each index patient and his or her parent(s) before treatment and at the end of months 3, 9, 18, and 24, to independently assess communication deviance and affective communication style, level of EE, family problem-solving skills, family burden, psychopathology, and social adjustment. In addition, psychopathology is rated by the therapist at each session and family ratings of tension in the home and family problems are obtained. Ongoing data are also being gathered regarding significant life events and coping efforts by family members via biweekly, semistructured interviews over the telephone.

PATIENT SELECTION

All patients entered into the study have been diagnosed as schizophrenic using the Present State Examination (PSE) and CATEGO classification system (Wing, *et al.*, 1974).

This is a conservative instrument for diagnosing schizophrenia, reflecting the European phenomenological approach and similar to the DSM-III classification of schizophrenia. Most of our index patients have scored positively on the PSE's "nuclear syndrome," indicating the presence of one or more of the following symptoms: thought insertion, thought broadcasting, thought withdrawal, auditory hallucinations in the third person, delusions of control, delusions of alien penetration, and primary delusions. Patients suffering their first episode of schizophrenia are included as well as more chronic cases.

In addition to having a positive diagnosis of schizophrenia, index patients must be 18 to 45 years old and live with or be in daily contact with one or both parents. Prior to beginning the study proper, all parents and key relatives living at home are administered the abbreviated version of the Camberwell Family Interview (Vaughn & Leff, 1976b) by a trained interviewer. At least one person must be demonstrate a high level of EE. Finally, English must be the language spoken at home.

TREATMENT CONDITIONS

Regardless of the treatment condition, certain aspects of treatment are the same for all index patients. Specifically, a vigorous attempt has been made to maintain all patients on an adequate dosage of neuroleptic medication. Due to its relative lack of severe side effects and the availability of a practical laboratory procedure for assaying blood levels, chlorpromazine has been used most frequently. In cases where poor compliance has persisted despite persuasive efforts, the intramuscular long-acting phenothiazine, fluphenazine decanoate, has been employed. Tablet forms of high-potency neuroleptics, such as fluphenazine and haloperidol, have been used on rare occasions when sedation or other side effects necessitated discontinuing the chlorpromazine.

Pharmacologic aspects of treatment are managed by a psychiatrist, who is blind to treatment conditions, through monthly patient visits to the clinic. These visits are for medication purposes only, and the psychiatrist does not intervene in other aspects of treatment. At these times the patients are rated for psychopathology, using the Brief Psychiatric Rating Scale (BPRS), and "target symptoms" (two or three specifically chosen schizophrenic symptoms that a given patient displays when relapsed). Ratings of common side effects and a neurological assessment for signs of extrapyramidal effects and dyskinesias are conducted. Blood samples are drawn by a registered nurse for purposes of assaying blood levels of medication.

Another aspect of treatment available to all index patients is rehabilitation counseling. All patients are encouraged to meet with an experienced rehabilitation counselor for four 1-hour sessions at some time during the first 9 months of treatment to discuss vocational or educational plans, leisure-time activities, sheltered workshops, specific problems such as how to fill out a job application, or obtain appropriate Social Security benefits.

Patients assigned to the family therapy condition receive family sessions in their homes. Patients receiving supportive psychotherapy are seen in the clinic. Treatment is aimed at providing support for the patient in coping with problems of daily living and maximizing his or her level of functioning. Interventions aimed at exploring psychodynamic developmental processes are minimized. Assistance is provided in obtaining financial support, developing a social network, and coping with symptoms. Family problems may be addressed in the individual sessions, and family members are interviewed individually when they attend the clinic with the index patient. Discussions are usually brief and consist of giving and seeking information on the patient's condition, and providing direct advice on management problems. At no time are family members and index patient seen conjointly, and although support and reassurance are given, specific communication and problem-solving training is avoided.

The components of the two treatment conditions are summarized in Table 4-1.

THERAPISTS

The three authors are the primary therapists for all study patients. To control for therapist variables such as professional training, skill, and experience, a balanced design has been employed, with each therapist treating an equal number of family and individual cases. Each of the authors is an experienced psychotherapist with at least 5 years of experience working with chronically ill psychiatric patients and their families. In addition to the primary therapist, the family therapy sessions are sometimes conducted with a cotherapist, usually a trainee (psychiatric resident, clinical psychology intern, psychiatric nurse, etc.). The primary therapists consult extensively among themselves on virtually a daily basis to discuss case management issues and specific therapeutic techniques. Role playing is employed in a weekly seminar to teach trainees specific behavioral techniques, as well as to generate ideas on how to deal with special problems as they arise in therapy sessions.

MAJOR ASSESSMENT PROCEDURES

The most important outcome data concern the relative effectiveness of family versus individual therapy in forestalling or preventing schizophrenic relapse. Here the crucial problem is how to define relapse. The usual definition, psychiatric rehospitalization, is inadequate since rehospitalization frequently occurs for reasons not specifically related to schizophrenia (e.g., acting-out behavior, suicidal ideation, loss of family support, etc.). Conversely, it is not uncommon for a full-blown relapse into florid schizophrenic symptomatology to be treated on an outpatient

TABLE 4-1. Components of Family versus Individual Therapy

Therapeutic ingredients	Family	Individual
Neuroleptic medication	+++	+++
Individual supportive psychotherapy	+	+++
Crisis intervention	++	++
Rehabilitation counseling	++	++
Family contact/sessions at home	+++	±
Family education	+++	±
Family communication and problem solving	+++	±

Note. +++ denotes major intervention; ++, moderate invervention; +, minor intervention; ±, employed when necessary only.

basis. For these reasons, we define "relapse" in a clinical manner: specifically, a return to florid symptomatology in a previously symptom-free patient, or a marked exacerbation of existing schizophrenic symptoms. Toward this end, target symptoms are defined for each patient based on their symptom picture at full relapse. These symptoms are carefully chosen to be specifically schizophrenic (e.g., delusions of control, thought broadcasting, auditory hallucinations). Target symptoms such as depression, agitation, or social withdrawal are avoided because they could occur in nonschizophrenic conditions as well. Target symptoms are rated on a 7-point scale by a psychiatrist blind to treatment conditions. When the target symptoms are present in severity comparable to previous relapses, a new relapse is considered to have occurred.

In addition to assessing relapses, various other outcome measures are being collected. Social adjustment of index patients, as well as key relatives living at home, is assessed at baseline (pretreatment) and at the end of months 3, 9, 18, and 24, using the Social Adjustment Scale, Self-Report Form developed by Weissman, Paykel, and Seigel (1972). At these times a 64-item Hopkins Symptom Checklist (Lipman, Covi, Rickels, Uhlenhuth, & Lazar, 1968) is completed by each family member, providing a measure of family distress as manifested by symptoms such as depression, anxiety, somatization, and so forth. In addition to these self-report instruments, two behavioral assessment procedures are conducted at baseline and at the end of the 3rd month of treatment, in order to assess if changes in family communication and problem solving have taken place. The first of these is the Consensus Rorschach, where family members are scored for communication deviance using Singer and Wynne's (1966b) method. The second is the Family Confrontation Test (Goldstein, Judd, Rodnick, Alkire, & Gould, 1968). In this procedure families are asked to discuss a current family problem (elicited beforehand) for 10 minutes and to try to arrive at a solution. A verbatim transcript is later rated for problem-solving skills and emotional communication. The latter rating is essentially an interpersonal analogue of the expressed emotion concept. The Camberwell Family Interview EE scales were not designed as measures of change and have not been employed as outcome variables in this study.

Various data are also being collected on an ongoing basis, in an attempt to investigate some of the factors that may be causally related to relapse. The relationship between significant life events and symptomatic exacerbations is being investigated via biweekly telephone interviews. Using a semistructured approach, stressful events and major life changes are elicited, as well as family members' cognitive and behavioral responses to them. The data obtained in this way can be combined with the relapse data and serial BPRS ratings to elucidate the role psychosocial stressors and coping styles play in schizophrenic relapse. Monthly determinations of medication blood levels can also be analyzed to examine the part that neuroleptics play in preventing relapse and/or reducing the impact of stressful life events.

PRELIMINARY FINDINGS

At the time this chapter was written 27 index patients had begun the study. Of these, 10 receiving family therapy and 10 receiving individual therapy had completed the 3-month intensive phase of treatment (and some considerably more). Although it would be inappropriate to perform statistical analyses on so few patients, some of the early findings can be summarized here in a nonstatistical manner.

The 10 patients receiving family therapy have been in treatment an average of 8 months and, at this point, none have relapsed. The 10 patients in individual therapy have averaged 9 months in treatment and of them seven have relapsed, with one having relapsed twice. Although the sample size is small, these findings are encouraging with respect to the efficacy of behavioral family therapy.

The observations of the therapists have been supported by preliminary behavioral test findings that suggest that emotional communication and problem-solving skills of the families receiving *in vivo* therapy have improved after 3 months, while the control families show no positive changes.

The social adjustment data show a similar but less striking pattern. Nine of the 10 patients receiving family therapy showed improvement at the 3-month point on a global measure of social adjustment derived from the self-report Social Adjustment Scale. Six of 10 patients receiving individual therapy showed improvement at that point.

Minimal differences were found on the global index of symptomatology derived from the Hopkins Symptom Checklist. Seven of the 10 family patients showed improvement after 3 months, compared to 5 of the 10 individual patients.

Although no quantitative analysis has been performed with the life events data, our clinical observation is that there seems to be a definite relationship between stressful life events and exacerbations of schizophrenic symptomatology. Typically, we have noted a 2- to 3-week delay after a life event before symptoms return or worsen. This pattern seems to be more definite for the patients receiving family therapy. Our hypothesis at this point is that the family therapy serves to reduce the level of tension in the home, as well as the level of EE, thereby reducing the contribution to exacerbations that these important family factors normally make. Thus, for these families significant life events would play a larger role. For patients receiving individual therapy these pernicious family factors continue to contribute to exacerbations and relapses even in the absence of a significant life event.

CONCLUSIONS

An extensive review of the community management of schizophrenia revealed that although etiological variables are not clearly understood, there is adequate empirical data to support the view that the social competence of family members with whom a person suffering from schizophrenia is living is a significant prognostic factor. In particular, defects in emotional expression and problem-solving skills appeared to be associated with a poor prognosis and a high risk of relapse. Furthermore, it was considered that a lack of information about the nature and treatment of schizophrenia contributed to this deficiency.

A family-oriented treatment approach has been developed over the past 5 years, which was thought to be particularly efficacious with families where there is a high level of EE and an inadequate reserve of coping mechanisms to deal with the behavioral management of a chronic illness. Two methods based on social learning theory have been employed: (1) communication training, and (2) structured problem solving. These techniques, coupled with continued family education about schizophrenia, carefully monitored neuroleptic medication, and effective crisis intervention form the basis of the family therapy program. The goal is to maintain persons suffering from schizophrenia at their highest level of social function while reducing stress and preventing further relapse. One of the salient features of the program is that family sessions are conducted *in vivo*.

The preliminary findings of a controlled outcome study that compares the *in vivo* family approach with an individual approach conducted in the clinic are presented. These suggest that there may be specific benefits associated with the family therapy. Behavioral observations indicate that measurable changes in family communication and problem solving are achieved by the 3rd month of treatment in the majority of families. However, it should be stressed that the data presented represent progress after a mere one-eighth of the treatment duration, and although promising, must be viewed with great caution.

REFERENCES

Alanen, Y. O. The mothers of schizophrenic patients. *Acta Psychiatrica Scandinavica*, 1958, *33*, Suppl. 124, 1-361.

Alanen, Y. O. The family in the pathogenesis of schizophrenic and neurotic disorders. *Acta Psychiatrica Scandinavica*, 1966, *42*, Suppl. 189.

Alarcon, R. de, & Carney, M. W. P. Severe depressive mood changes following slow-release intramuscular fluphenazine injection. *British Medical Journal*, 1969, *3*, 564-567.

Andrews, W. N. Long-acting tranquilizers and the amotivational syndrome in the treatment of schizophrenia. In M. H. King (Ed.), *Community management of the schizophrenic in chemical remission*. Amsterdam: Exerpta Medica, 1973.

Bateson, G., Jackson, D. D., Haley, J., & Weakland, J. H. Toward a theory of schizophrenia. *Behavioral Science*, 1956, *1*, 251-264.

Bertalanffy, L. von *General systems theory*. New York: Braziller, 1968.

Bowen, M. A family concept of schizophrenia. In D. Jackson (Ed.), *The etiology of schizophrenia*. New York: Basic Books, 1966.

Bowen, M., Dysinger, R. H., & Başamania, B. The role of the father in families with a schizophrenic patient. *American Journal of Psychiatry*, 1959, *115*, 1017-1020.

Brown, G. W., & Birley, J. L. T. Crises and life changes and the onset of schizophrenia. *Journal of Health and Social Behavior*, 1968, *9*, 203-214.

Brown, G. W., Birley, J. L. T., & Wing, J. K. Influence of family life on the course of schizophrenic disorders: A replication. *British Journal of Psychiatry*, 1972, *121*, 241-258.

Brown, G. W., Carstairs, G. M., & Topping, G. G. The post-hospital adjustment of chronic mental patients. *Lancet*, 1958, *2*, 685-689.

Brown, G. W., Monck, E. M., Carstairs, G. M., & Wing, J. K. Influence of family life on the course of schizophrenic illness. *British Journal of Preventive Social Medicine*, 1962, *16*, 55–68.

Buss, A., & Lang, P. Psychological deficit in schizophrenia: I. Affect, reinforcement, and concept attainment. *Journal of Abnormal Psychology*, 1965, *70*, 2–24.

Carpenter, W. T., Strauss, J. S., & Bartko, J. J. Flexible system of diagnosis of schizophrenia: Report from the WHO international pilot study of schizophrenia. *Science*, 1973, *182*, 1275–1278.

Cheek, F. E. The father of the schizophrenic. *Archives of General Psychiatry*, 1965, *13*, 336–345.

Cooper, T. B., Simpson, G. M., & Lee, J. H. Thymoleptic and neuroleptic drug plasma levels in psychiatry: Current status. *International review of neurobiology* (Vol. 19). New York: Academic Press, 1976.

Creer, C., & Wing, J. K. *Schizophrenia at home*. Surrey: National Schizophrenia Fellowship, 1974.

Curry, S. H., Marshall, J. H. L., Davis, J. S., & Janowsky, D. J. Chlorpromazine plasma levels and effects. *Archives of General Psychiatry*, 1970, *22*, 289–296.

DeWitt, K. N. The effectiveness of family therapy. *Archives of General Psychiatry*, 1978, *35*, 549–561.

Engelhardt, D. M., & Freedman, N. Maintenance drug therapy: The schizophrenic patient in the community. In A. Kiev (Ed.), *Social psychiatry*. London: Routledge & Kegan Paul, 1970.

Fairweather, G. W., Sanders, D. H., Maynard, H., & Cressler, D. L. *Community life for the mentally ill: An alternative to institutional care*. New York: Aldine, 1969.

Falloon, I. R. H. Social skills training for community living. *Psychiatric Clinics of North America*, 1978, *1*, 291–305.

Falloon, I. R. H., Liberman, R. P., Lillie, F. J., & Vaughn, C. Family therapy with relapsing schizophrenics and their families: A pilot study. *Family Process*, 1981.

Falloon, I. R. H., Watt, D. C., & Shepherd, M. A comparative controlled trial of pimozide and fluphenazine decanoate in the continuation therapy of schizophrenia. *Psychological Medicine*, 1978, *8*, 59–70.(a)

Falloon, I. R. H., Watt, D. C., & Shepherd, M. The social outcome of patients in a trial of long-term continuation therapy in schizophrenia: Pimozide vs. fluphenazine. *Psychological Medicine*, 1978, *8*, 265–274.(b)

Ferriera, A. J., & Winter, W. D. Family interaction and decision making. *Archives of General Psychiatry*, 1965, *13*, 214–223.

Fleck, S., Lidz, T., & Cornelison, A. Comparison of parent–child relationships of male and female schizophrenic patients. *Archives of General Psychiatry*, 1963, *8*, 1–7.

Fromm-Reichman, F. Notes on the development of treatment of schizophrenics by psychoanalytic psychotherapy. *Psychiatry*, 1948, *11*, 263–273.

Gerard, D. L., & Siegel, J. The family background of schizophrenia. *Psychiatric Quarterly*, 1950, *24*, 47–73.

Goldstein, M. J., Judd, L. L., Rodnick, E. H., Alkire, A. A., & Gould, E. A method for studying social influence and coping patterns within families of disturbed adolescents. *Journal of Nervous and Mental Disease*, 1968, *147*, 233–251.

Goldstein, M. J., Rodnick, E. H., Evans, J. R., May, P. R. A., & Steinberg, M. Drug and family therapy in the aftercare treatment of acute schizophrenia. *Archives of General Psychiatry*, 1978, *35*, 1169–1177.

Gould, E., & Glick, I. D. The effects of family presence and brief family intervention on global outcome for hospitalized schizophrenic patients. *Family Process*, 1977, *4*, 503–510.

Grad, J., & Sainsbury, P. The effects that patients have on their families in a community care and a control psychiatric service: A two-year follow-up. *British Journal of Psychiatry*, 1968, *114*, 265–278.

Gunderson, J. E. *In favor of psychosocial treatment of schizophrenia*. Paper presented at the annual meeting of the American Psychiatric Association, Atlanta, May 1978.

Haley, J. Testing parental instructions to schizophrenics and normal children: A pilot study. *Journal of Abnormal Psychology*, 1968, *73*, 559–565.

Hirsch, S. R., Gaind, R., Rohde, P. D., Stevens, B., & Wing, J. K. Outpatient maintenance of chronic schizophrenic patients with long-acting fluphenazine double-blind placebo trial. *British Medical Journal*, 1973, *1*, 633–637.

Hirsch, S. R., & Leff, J. P. *Abnormalities in the parents of schizophrenics*. London: Oxford University Press, 1975.

Hogarty, G. E., Goldberg, S. C., Schooler, N. R., & Ulrich, R. F. The collaborative study group: Drug and sociotherapy in the aftercare of schizophrenic patients: II. Two-year relapse rates. *Archives of General Psychiatry*, 1974, *31*, 603–608.(a)

Hogarty, G. E., Goldberg, S. C., Schooler, N. R., & Ulrich, R. F. Drug and sociotherapy in the aftercare of schizophrenic patients: III. Adjustment of non-relapsed patients. *Archives of General Psychiatry*, 1974, *31*, 609–618.(b)

Jackson, D. D. Family interaction, family homeostasis and some implications for conjoint family psychotherapy. In J. Masserman (Ed.), *Individual and family dynamics*. New York: Grune & Stratton, 1959.

Kasanin, J., Knight, E., & Sage, P. The parent–child relationship in schizophrenia. *Journal of Nervous and Mental Disease*, 1934, *79*, 249–263.

Kohn, M., & Clausen, J. A. Parental authority behavior and schizophrenia. *American Journal of Orthopsychiatry*, 1956, *26*, 297–313.

Laing, R. D., & Esterson, A. *Sanity, madness and the family*. London: Tavistock, 1964.

Lamb, H. R. The new asylums in the community. *Archives of General Psychiatry*, 1979, *36*, 129–134.

Lamb, H. R., & Goertzel, V. The long-term patient in the era of community treatment. *Archives of General Psychiatry*, 1977, *34*, 679–682.

Lamb, H. R., Hoffman, F., Hoffman, A., & Oliphant, E. No place for schizophrenics: The unwelcome consumer speaks out. *Psychiatric Annals*, 1976, *6*, 688–692.

Langsley, D., Machotka, P., & Flomenhaft, K. Avoiding mental hospital admission: A follow-up study. *American Journal of Psychiatry*, 1971, *127*, 1391–1394.

Langsley, D. G., Pittman, F. S., Machotka, P., & Flomenhaft, K. Family crisis therapy: Results and implications. *Family Process*, 1968, *7*, 145–158.

Langsley, D. G., Pittman, F. S., & Swank, G. E. Family crises in schizophrenics and other mental patients. *Journal of Nervous and Mental Disease*, 1969, *149*, 270–276.

Leff, J. P., Hirsch, S. R., Gaind, R., Rohde, P. D., & Stevens, B. C. Life events and maintenance therapy in schizophrenic relapse. *British Journal of Psychiatry*, 1973, *123*, 659–660.

Leff, J. P., & Vaughn, C. The interaction of life events and relatives' expressed emotions in schizophrenia and depressive neurosis. *British Journal of Psychiatry*, 1980, *136*, 146–153.

Leff, J. P., & Wing, J. K. Trial of maintenance therapy in schizophrenia. *British Medical Journal*, 1971, *3*, 599–604.

Lerner, P. M. Resolution of intrafamilial role conflict in families of schizophrenic patients: I. Thought disturbance. *Journal of Nervous and Mental Disease*, 1965, *141*, 342–351.

Lerner, P. M. Resolution of intrafamilial role conflict in families of schizophrenic patients: II. Social maturity. *Journal of Nervous and Mental Disease*, 1967, *145*, 336–341.

Liberman, R. P. Behavioral approaches to family and couple therapy. *American Journal of Orthopsychiatry*, 1970, *40*, 106–118.

Liberman, R. P., McCann, M. J., & Wallace, C. J. Generalization of behavior therapy with psychotics. *British Journal of Psychiatry*, 1976, *129*, 490–496.

Liberman, R. P., Lillie, F., Falloon, I. R. H., Vaughn, C. E., Harpin, R. E., Leff, J., Hutchinson, W., Ryan, P., & Stoute, M. *Social skills training for schizophrenic patients and their families.* Unpublished manuscript, 1978. (Available from Clinical Research Center, Box A, Camarillo, Calif.)

Lidz, T., Cornelison, A. R., Fleck, S., & Terry, D. The intrafamilial environment of schizophrenic patients: II. Marital schism and marital skew. *American Journal of Psychiatry,* 1957, *114,* 241-248.

Lidz, T., Fleck, S., & Cornelison, A. *Schizophrenia and the family.* New York: International Universities Press, 1965.

Lidz, R. W., & Lidz, T. The family environment of schizophrenic patients. *American Journal of Psychiatry,* 1949, *106,* 332-345.

Lipman, R. S., Covi, L., Rickels, K., Uhlenhuth, E. H., & Lazar, R. Selected measures of change in outpatient drug evaluation. In D. H. Efron (Ed.), *Psychopharmacology: A review of progress, 1957-1967* (U.S. Public Health Service Publication No. 1836). Washington, D.C.: U.S. Government Printing Office, 1968.

Lu, Y. C. Mother-child role relations in schizophrenia. *Psychiatry,* 1961, *24,* 133-142.

Massie, H. N., & Beels, C. C. The outcome of family treatment of schizophrenia. *Schizophrenia Bulletin,* 1972, *6,* 24-36.

May, P. R. A. *Treatment of schizophrenia.* New York: Science House, 1968.

May, P. R. A., Tuma, A. H., & Dixon, W. J. Schizophrenia: A follow-up study of results of treatment: I. Design and other problems. *Archives of General Psychiatry,* 1976, *33,* 474-478.

May, P. R. A., Tuma, A. H., Yale, C., Potepan, P., & Dixon, W. J. Schizophrenia: A follow-up study of results of treatment of schizophrenia: II. Hospital stay over two to five years. *Archives of General Psychiatry,* 1976, *33,* 481-486.

McConaghy, N. The use of an object-sorting test in elucidating the hereditary factor in schizophrenia. *Journal of Neurology, Neurosurgery and Psychiatry,* 1959, *22,* 243-246.

McGhie, A. A comparative study of the mother-child relationship in schizophrenia. *British Journal of Medical Psychology,* 1961, *34,* 195-208.

Mendel, W. *Supportive care: Theory and technique.* Los Angeles: Mira Books, 1975.

Mendel, W. *Schizophrenia: The experience and its treatment.* San Francisco: Jossey-Bass, 1976.

Mishler, E. G., & Waxler, N. E. *Interaction in families.* New York: Wiley, 1968.

Mosher, L. R., Menn, H., & Matthews, S. Soteria: Evaluation of a home-based treatment for schizophrenia. *American Journal of Orthopsychiatry,* 1975, *45,* 455-469.

Overall, J. E., & Gorham, D. R. The Brief Psychiatric Rating Scale. *Psychological Reports,* 1962, *10,* 799-812.

Polak, P. R., Deever, S., & Kirkby, M. W. On treating the insane in sane places. *Journal of Community Psychology,* 1977, *5,* 380-387.

Reichard, S., & Tillman, C. Patterns of parent-child relationships in schizophrenia. *Psychiatry,* 1950, *13,* 247-257.

Reiss, D. Individual thinking and family interaction: II. A study of pattern and recognition and hypotheses testing in families of normals, character disordered and schizophrenics. *Journal of Psychiatric Research,* 1967, *5,* 193-211.

Reiss, D. Individual thinking and family interaction: III. An experimental study of categorization performance in families of normals, character disordered and schizophrenics. *Journal of Nervous and Mental Disease,* 1968, *146,* 384-403.

Reiss, D. Individual thinking and family interaction: IV. A study of information exchange in families of normals, character disordered and schizophrenics. *Journal of Nervous and Mental Disease,* 1969, *149,* 473-490.

Reiss, D., Costell, R., Jones, C., & Berkman, H. The family meets the hospital: A laboratory forecast of the encounter. *Archives of General Psychiatry,* 1980, *37,* 141-154.

Rittenhouse, J. Endurance of effect: Family unit treatment compared to identified patient treatment. *Proceedings of the 78th annual convention of APA,* 1970, 535-536.

Sanders, R., Smith, R. S., & Weinman, B. S. *Chronic psychosis and recovery*. San Francisco: Jossey-Bass, 1967.

Sharan, S. N. Family interaction with schizophrenics and their siblings. *Journal of Abnormal Psychology*, 1966, *71*, 345–353.

Simpson, G. M. Neurotoxicity of major tranquilizers. In L. Raizin, H. Shiraki, & N. Greerie (Eds.), *Neurotoxicity*. New York: Raven Press, 1977.

Singer, M. T., & Wynne, L. C. Communication styles in parents of normals, neurotics, and schizophrenics. *Psychiatric Research Reports*, 1966, *20*, 25–38.(a)

Singer, M. T., & Wynne, L. C. Principles for scoring communication defects and deviances in parents of schizophrenics: Rorschach and TAT scoring manuals. *Psychiatry*, 1966, *29*, 260–288.(b)

Sluzki, C. E., & Vernon, P. E. The double bind as a universal pathogenic situation. *Family Process*, 1971, *10*, 397–410.

Soskis, D. A. Schizophrenic and medical inpatients as informed drug consumers. *Archives of General Psychiatry*, 1978, *35*, 645–647.

Stein, L. I. *Cessation of a treatment program for schizophrenia*. Paper presented at the annual meeting of the American Psychiatric Association, Atlanta, 1978.

Stein, L. I., & Test, M. A. (Eds.). *Alternatives to mental hospital treatment*. New York: Plenum, 1978.

Stevens, B. C. Role of fluphenazine decanoate in lessening the burden of chronic schizophrenics on the community. *Psychological Medicine*, 1973, *3*, 141–158.

Strauss, J. S., & Gift, T. E. Choosing an approach for diagnosing schizophrenia. *Archives of General Psychiatry*, 1977, *34*, 1248–1253.

Stuart, R. B. Operant–interpersonal treatment for marital discord. *Journal of Consulting and Clinical Psychology*, 1969, *33*, 675.

Sullivan, H. S. The onset of schizophrenia. *American Journal of Psychiatry*, 1927, *7*, 105–134.

Tietze, T. A study of mothers of schizophrenic patients. *Psychiatry*, 1949, *12*, 55–65.

Tolsdorf, C. C. Social networks, support, and coping: An exploratory study. *Family Process*, 1976, *15*, 407–418.

Vaughn, C. E., & Leff, J. P. The influence of family and social factors on the course of psychiatric illness: A comparison of schizophrenic and depressed neurotic patients. *British Journal of Psychiatry*, 1976, *129*, 125–137.(a)

Vaughn, C. E., & Leff, J. P. The measurement of expressed emotion in the families of psychiatric patients. *British Journal of Social and Clinical Psychology*, 1976, *15*, 157–165.(b)

Waring, M., & Ricks, D. Family patterns of children who became adult schizophrenics. *Journal of Nervous and Mental Disease*, 1965, *140*, 351–364.

Weissman, M. M., Paykel, E. S., & Siegel, R. *Social adjustment scale: Rationale, reliability, validity and scoring*. Unpublished manuscript, 1972.

Wells, R. A., & Dezen, A. E. The results of family therapy, revisited: The nonbehavioral methods. *Family Process*, 1978, *17*, 151–186.

Wells, R. A., Dilkes, T. C., & Trivelli, N. The results of family therapy: A critical review of the literature. *Family Process*, 1972, *7*, 189–207.

Wing, J. K. *The management of schizophrenia in the community*. Lecture to American College of Psychiatrists, Atlanta, February 1977.

Wing, J. K., Cooper, J. E., & Sartorius, N. *The measurement and classification of psychiatric symptoms*. London: Cambridge University Press, 1974.

Woodward, J. A., & Goldstein, M. J. Communication deviance in the families of schizophrenics: A comment on the misuse of analysis of covariance. *Science*, 1977, *197*, 1096–1097.

Wynne, L. C., Ryckoff, I., Day, J., & Hirsch, D. Pseudo-mutuality in the family relations of schizophrenics. *Psychiatry*, 1958, *21*, 205–220.

Zubin, J., & Spring, B. Vulnerability: A new view of schizophrenia. *Journal of Abnormal Psychology*, 1977, *86*, 103–126.

II

SOCIAL SKILLS TRAINING WITH OTHER POPULATIONS

The five chapters comprising this part are all concerned with social skills training on select populations. In general, the procedures utilized are similar to the procedures described in the first section of this book, although the training is usually much shorter in duration and less intense. While the training procedures are often quite similar across populations, the content of the training differs, depending upon the particular deficits exhibited by the various populations.

Chapter 5, by Hersen, Bellack, and Himmelhoch, begins with their review of behavioral theories concerning the etiology of and maintaining factors in depression and a selective review of behavioral approaches to the treatment of depression. The authors then go on to describe their treatment program for unipolar depressed women. Treatment is individually based and consists of 12 weekly sessions of 60 minutes' duration. These 12 sessions are followed by six to eight booster sessions distributed over a 6-month period. Because the treatment is individually based, more flexibility and individualized tailoring is found in this program than was found in the programs described in the previous section. The authors describe their program as consisting of four separate components: (1) skills training, (2) social perception training, (3) practice, and (4) self-evaluation and self-reinforcement. The skills training component consists of a series of procedures (e.g., modeling) that are similar to those already described in the previous part. Although the authors label the practice component as a separate component, this component resembles closely the practice procedures generally regarded as part of social skills training by other authors. "Social perception" is defined as (1) knowledge about the meaning of various response cues and familiarity with social mores, (2) attention to the relevant aspects of interactions, including the context and interpersonal response cues proved by the partner, (3) information-processing capabilities, and (4) the ability to accurately predict interpersonal consequences. Social perception training generally consists of information giving and role playing. This social perception training component resembles the receiving and processing components in Wallace's tripartite model of social skills. The fourth component of Hersen, Bellack, and Himmelhoch's program involves self-evaluation and self-reinforcement. Subjects are trained to evaluate their responses more objectively and to use self-reinforcement in order to maintain their responding. Data of a preliminary nature indicate that this social skills training leads not only to improved interpersonal functioning and mood, but to the reduction of vegetative symptomology usually associated with unipolar nonpsychotic depression.

The social skills training program described in Chapter 6 was developed at the Behavior Training Clinic at the Providence Veterans Administration Medical Center. It is a group-based treatment utilizing two cotherapists. It includes many of the response acquisition procedures (such as modeling, role rehearsal, etc.) that are characteristic of most social skills training programs. Treatment is based upon a 10-lesson manual that provides the content of the treatment. The number and length of treatment sessions has varied because, as the authors note, the practical considerations involved in doing clinical research sometimes require such flexibility in the delivery of services. That is, a social skills training program with inpatients might be delivered on a daily basis over a brief period of time because the average length of time before discharge on such a unit dictates a brief time frame, while a program involving outpatients may meet less frequently over an extended period of time because of the patients' employment schedule. The social skills training program developed at the Behavior Training Clinic has been evaluated in a number of studies. In general, the results from these studies indicate that the program leads to significantly more improvement in social competency (as measured by self-report and laboratory-based observations) than a medication maintenance and supportive therapy regimen, a bibliotherapy program, a sensitivity group program, and a specific cognitive intervention labeled "covert reinforcement." There is also evidence that these gains in social competency are maintained over a considerable period of time and some suggestive evidence is presented that would indicate that there is some generalization to the natural environment. One problem associated with the studies emanating from the Behavior Training Clinic is that they have employed heterogeneous groups of patients as subjects. Consequently, it is impossible to ascertain the effectiveness of this program with certain subtypes of patients. Another problem with these studies is that most of the evidence for the utility of the Behavior Training Clinic program is based on laboratory assessment protocols and consequently the long-term clinical impact of this program is still unclear. The authors, however, do report some correspondence between the laboratory-based assessment measures and measures derived in more naturalistic settings.

Jacobson begins Chapter 7 with a review of the literature on communication skills and marital satisfaction. He concludes his review with the statement that the literature does not shed much light on the relative importance of communication versus other dimensions of marital behavior in light of their contribution to marital satisfaction but points out that the literature does clearly show that communication skills are related to marital satisfaction. Jacobson next outlines intervention strategies and training procedures used to teach communication skills. The training procedures include the familiar strategies of instruction, modeling, feedback, and homework. However, much to his credit, Jacobson provides useful clinical advice and hints on how to implement these strategies with married couples. He divides the content of behavioral communication training programs into soft and hard skills. "Soft" skills promote closeness and intimacy, whereas "hard" skills are task-oriented, problem-solving skills that are used to resolve conflicts, negotiate behavior change, and alter status quo. Jacobson describes the teaching of various soft skills such as listening skills, validation, feeling talk, negative feeling expression, and positive feeling expression, and provides examples of how each skill may be used.

The hard skills, or problem-solving skills, are next reviewed. Jacobson stresses problem solving as a special form of communication and discusses various techniques that can be used to handle a couple's resistance to problem solving. He emphasizes the distinction between the problem definition phase and the problem solution phase and the importance of not muddling these in treating distressed couples. He next provides guidelines and procedures for both defining problems and arriving at solutions. Finally, Jacobson briefly reviews the research on the effectiveness of behavioral communication training.

The fact that many individuals would consider the title "Self-Monitoring and Reactivity for Individuals with Brown Hair" unusual, but find nothing unusual in the title "Assertion Training for Women," MacDonald finds disturbing in Chapter 8. What MacDonald finds disturbing is the assumption that membership in a certain demographic category somehow qualifies one as an appropriate candidate for a particular therapeutic intervention. In a thorough review of the literature, MacDonald examines the validity of the assumption that there are differences between the actual assertion levels of men and women. She comes to the conclusion that the behavioral data suggest that there are no differences between the level of assertion of men and women when sex is treated as individual difference variable. She further concludes that there are probably sex differences in the antecedents and consequences of assertion when sex is treated as a stimulus variable. That is, MacDonald feels that the data suggest that women are confronted at least more frequently, and perhaps more fundamentally, with rights infringements situations than are men, and that when women defend their rights at a level equivalent to a level exhibited by men, their behavior is more likely to be either disregarded or negatively sanctioned. The implication that MacDonald draws from her review is that it is inappropriate to view assertion training for women as a correct strategy to alleviate women's oppression. She states that the oppression of women is not due to a lack of assertive skills, but is rather an institutional problem. MacDonald further states that if treatment strategies are to be more effective they should be directed toward environmental antecedent and consequent events.

Although MacDonald's conclusions are specific to assertion training for women, they have direct implications for the whole field of social skills training. That is, it is important for social skills trainers and researchers to carefully examine the assumption that their particular subject population lacks adequate social skills. Furthermore, there is a need to obtain empirical justification that the skills that are being taught in their social skills training programs will be reinforced by the community.

French and Tyne begin Chapter 9, "The Identification and Treatment of Children with Peer-Relationship Difficulties," by noting that the interest in changing children's level of social competency is spurred on by the findings that a child's status within the peer group appears to be predictive of later psychological adjustment. French and Tyne differentiate three types of out-group or at-risk children: isolated, neglected, and rejected. They contend that the differentiation of these various types of out-group children is dependent upon the identification procedures employed. They urge investigators to employ multiple identification strategies, including teachers' judgments, observational ratings, peer nominations (both positive and negative), and peer ratings. In their review of intervention programs, the authors remark that the content of the social skills treatment programs in this area also rests mainly on the clinical intuition of the investigators rather than on any empirical data. French and Tyne are also concerned about the fact that there is very little data with respect to the relative efficacy of various training procedures and possible interactions with different treatment content. They note that though some programs appear to teach skills using an inductive process, while other programs appear to be more deductive in their approach, no well-controlled studies have been conducted to test the relative efficacy of such approaches. The authors also review the treatment-outcome studies conducted in each of the three areas of out-group children. They conclude that there appears to be more success in treating isolated children than neglected or rejected children. This may be due to the fact that there is greater pathology in neglected and rejected children than in isolated children. In fact, parenthetically, no good data exist indicating that social isolation is an interpersonal problem of any significance. In addition, in treating isolated children one is only concerned about the behavior of the isolate, while with neglected and rejected children one must change the targeted child's behavior such that other children's perceptions of that child will be modified.

Although each of the chapters in this part deals with different targeted populations one is struck by the similarity of the problems in each area. Several of these problems will be addressed in the next part of this book: (1) how to determine the content of a social skills training program (i.e., the skills to be taught); (2) the identification and assessment of the target population; and (3) measuring the clinical significance of a therapeutic intervention.

5

SKILLS TRAINING
WITH UNIPOLAR DEPRESSED WOMEN

MICHEL HERSEN
ALAN S. BELLACK
JONATHAN M. HIMMELHOCH

THEORETICAL ISSUES IN DEPRESSION

In a recent review of the literature, Kovacs (1979) has argued that "the behavior and cognitive therapies are the most exciting recent treatment modalities in the area of depressive disorders, which, for over a decade, has relied primarily on pharmacological interventions" (p. 496). Almost all of the behavioral approaches to depression have been an elaboration of the single theme: loss of positive reinforcement. However, Wolpe (1979) ties in such loss in neurotic depression with conditioned anxiety response habits. It was Ferster's (1965) functional analysis of depression, described in his seminal article, "Classification of Behavioral Pathology," which generated a surge of interest in the behavioral analysis of depressive states. Ferster was most impressed by the reduced adaptive behavioral repertoire of the depressed person, and viewed such an individual's behaviors as being on an extinction schedule. Adaptive behaviors were no longer positively reinforced, and consequently their rate of occurrence progressively declined. Ferster outlined three possible situations that lead to a reduction in positive reinforcement: (1) when reinforcement is contingent on a large amount of behavior; (2) when many behaviors function as preaversive stimuli (i.e., where

Michel Hersen. Western Psychiatric Institute and Clinic, University of Pittsburgh School of Medicine, Pittsburgh, Pennsylvania.

Alan S. Bellack. Clinical Psychology Center, University of Pittsburgh, Pittsburgh, Pennsylvania.

Jonathan M. Himmelhoch. Western Psychiatric Institute and Clinic, University of Pittsburgh School of Medicine, Pittsburgh, Pennsylvania.

they have been consistently and contingently related to an aversive state such as anxiety, leading to a decreased frequency in their occurrence); and (3) when there is a sudden shift in reinforcement contingencies (such as when an adolescent moves from the protection of his home and peer group into the adult world).

Costello (1972) has challenged Ferster's hypothesis with the obverse suggestion that depression is caused by a general loss of reinforcer effectiveness. In Costello's view the depressive's reduced behavioral repertoire is not contingent on loss of positive reinforcement, but is caused by the biochemical or neurologic changes that rob each and every reinforcer of their effectiveness, disrupting the entire chain of behaviors leading up to reinforcement. Costello's hypothesis must be carefully considered because it suggests that no psychotherapy, whatever its theoretical grounding, can begin to work unless reinforcer effectiveness returns (i.e., unless the biochemical or neurologic substrate of depression has been at least partly altered). Klerman, DiMascio, Weissman, Prusoff, and Paykel's (1974) data strongly support this theoretical position, which prima facie begs for investigation of combined pharmacologic–behavioral approaches to depression (cf. Weissman, 1979).

Nevertheless, Ferster's work remains key, no matter whether the approaches borne by his hypothesis are used in the presence or in the absence of effective antidepressant medications. His work has already served as an impetus to many clinical reports of successful behavioral treatments of depression (e.g., Burgess, 1969; Hersen, Eisler, Alford, & Agras, 1973). However, there still are relatively few empirical data to support these anecdotal successes.

In considering the etiology of depression (i.e., so-called neurotic or reactive depression), Wolpe (1979) categories his cases into four types. The first category is depressed as "a consequence of severe and prolonged anxiety that is directly conditioned." The second category is depressed as "a consequence of anxiety based on erroneous, self-devaluative conditions." The third category develops depression "in the context of anxiety-based inability to control interpersonal situations." The fourth category is said to become depressed "in the context of excessively prolonged and severe responses to bereavement." Treatment for each of the categories described is somewhat different. For the third category, treatment recommended by Wolpe is assertive training, or what now is referred to as social skills training.

LEWINSOHN'S WORK

While Lewinsohn (1975) follows Ferster's central formulation concerning the relationship between a reduced behavioral repertoire in depression and loss of positive reinforcement, he adds an important refinement. In his eyes, it is not the total amount of positive reinforcement that is critical in depression, but the amount of response-contingent positive reinforcement. In other words, large amounts of positive reinforcement may be available to the depressed individual, but if such reinforcement is not response-contingent, the individual may still remain depressed, because noncontingent reinforcement does not contribute to maintaining a behavioral repertoire (cf. Liberman & Raskin, 1971).

Lewinsohn's group was the first to study the relationship of response-contingent reinforcement to depression (Libet & Lewinsohn, 1973) in their investigation of the relationship between pleasant activities and mood (Lewinsohn & Graf, 1973; Lewinsohn & Libet, 1972). In Lewinsohn's view, engaging in pleasant activities represents one example of response-contingent reinforcement. In one study, his group found a significant correlation between pleasant activities and mood in a college student population. Moreover, correlations between pleasant activity and mood were not significantly different from depressed, nondepressed psychotic patients, or normal controls. In another study, Lewinsohn and Libet (1972) recruited a more heterogeneous population from the community at large, and replicated their earlier findings. The consistent finding of a significant relationship between mood and number of pleasant activities in widely varying populations not only supported Lewinsohn's position, but generally supports the behavioral view of depression (cf. Lewinsohn & Amenson, 1978). Lewinsohn (1975) specifically concluded from these investigations that the depressed individual's social environment reinforces his or her depressed behavior through expressions of sympathy and concern that inadvertently results in its maintenance. After a while, social support is negatively reinforced by the depressed individual's behavior, which then leads to desertion of the depressed subject by other persons in the social environment. Hostility, one of the central etiologic themes of the psychoanalytic theory of depression, is seen as elicited by the low rate of response-contingent positive reinforcement. The resulting social isolation further reduces positive reinforcement, and the depressed individual is then catapulted into an extinction schedule, and into a full-fledged depressive episode.

But Lewinsohn (1975) then goes considerably beyond the central idea of response-contingent reinforcement in developing his theoretical position. He is one of the few behavioral theorists who attempts to deal directly with the symptoms of dysphoria, guilt, and helplessness, so characteristic of full-blown depressive episodes. While he conceptualizes such behavior as unconditioned responses to a reduced or low rate of positive reinforcement, he also uses the two-factor theory of emotions in his explanation. Physiological states such as dysphoria, fatigue, and so forth, are cognitively interpreted in depressed terms variously as feeling inadequate, evil, unlikable, or guilty.

Finally, Lewinsohn posits another major and entirely original factor in the etiology of depression. He suggests that the depressed individual's instrumental behavioral repertoire and his or her social skills are deficient. The concept of social skill is then tied in with that of response-contingent reinforcement. Social skill is "the complex ability both to emit behaviors which are positively and negatively reinforced and not to emit behaviors which are punished or extinguished by others" (Libet & Lewinsohn, 1973). Because social skill is defined in terms of its consequences, the basic unit includes the behavior of the subject and the responses of significant others to that behavior.

The above theoretical notions suggest that depressed individuals will emit fewer behaviors, elicit more behaviors from others than they emit, interact with fewer individuals, emit fewer positive reactions to others' behavior, and have longer action latencies than nondepressed individuals. Each prediction is predicated on the assumption that depressed individuals have become socially unskilled and, therefore, are no longer able to elicit positive reinforcement from others. Libet and Lewinsohn (1973) have tested these predictions by comparing depressed and nondepressed college students, and have found that depressed individuals do indeed evidence a lower activity level, a narrower interpersonal range, a lower rate of emitted positive reactions, and a longer action latency than control subjects. They also discovered that depressed people are more sensitive to aversive interpersonal stimulation, and have especially long action latencies following a negative social interaction. Moreover, when participating in groups, depressed individuals tend to emit fewer actions following, the group's most aversive, undepressed member's interaction.

Lewinsohn and Shaffer (1971) also investigated social skill deficiencies in the depressed individual's natural environments (i.e., their homes). In this circumstance the depressed person was seen to have little ability to elicit positive reinforcement from other family members.

Most recently, Sanchez and Lewinsohn (1980) have provided additional empirical support for Lewinsohn's theoretical position. That is, a correlation of −.50 was found between assertiveness and depression in 12 depressed outpatients over a 12-week period. Thus, on days when assertive behavior was displayed, depression was less intense. Moreover, in a separate analysis, it was found "that rate of emitted assertive behavior may indeed be better able to predict subsequent level of depression than level of depression can predict subsequent rate of emitted assertive behavior." This suggests "that therapeutic interventions that increase levels of emitted assertive behavior may prove useful in the treatment of depression" (p. 120).

TREATMENT TECHNIQUES

Lewinsohn's (1975) treatment package involves a 3-month time-limited contract, beginning with an assessment period that includes determination of a traditional diagnosis, evaluation of the severity of depression and suicide potential, functional analysis of depressed and other important behaviors, and formulation of treatment goals.

The functional analysis is aimed at identifying those behaviors that create problems because of excessively high or excessively low frequency, and at identifying those aspects of the environment that maintain depressive behaviors. Home visitors are often part of this assessment. Social skill problems can be assessed in a group therapy setting. Interpersonal behavior patterns are recorded during each session. Success or failure of each subject's attempts to change behavior are monitored and fed back to the group.

Lewinsohn's two basic therapeutic goals are to increase pleasant activities and to improve social skills. In the first case, he applies the Premack Principle, which states that a high-frequency behavior can be used to increase the rate of a low-frequency behavior. This can be done by making sure the high-frequency behavior immediately follows the occurrence of a desired low-frequency behavior, thus serving as a positive reinforcer. In a typical example, a patient is expected to carry out homework goals in a graduated fashion prior to the succeeding treatment session. If the goals have been accomplished, the therapist will listen to depressive talk. If not, the therapist will end the session after 10 to 15 minutes.

To improve social skills, the second major goal, the therapist identifies social behaviors that reduce positive reinforcement and promote depression and then provides the patient feedback about these patterns.

Lewinsohn's twofold treatment approach, focusing on both pleasant activities and social skills, represents a step forward in relating treatment to theory and empirical data. However, the sophistication of his therapeutic interventions does not match the sophistication of his assessment measures. The development of more specific therapeutic techniques for increasing social skills of depressed patients is clearly needed.

McLean, Ogston, and Grauer (1973) have recently attempted to deal with this shortcoming in a controlled study using Lewinsohn-derived treatment approaches. Twenty depressed patients were divided into two groups. The experimental group was taught social learning principles, stressing positive communication with spouses in addition to implementation of behavioral contracts. The controls received medication, group psychotherapy, and/or individual psychotherapy. Social learning principles were taught directly using homework assignments geared toward promoting generalization. Spouses were included in the treatment so the patient could receive and give feedback on the effects of their reciprocal interactions. Pre- and postmeasurements revealed the experimental group to be less depressed and, on the basis of blindly rated audio recordings of behavior in their homes, to have significantly reduced their negative responses. The control group was somewhat more depressed at the end of treatment and did not change its style of interpersonal interaction. The authors suggest that an important part of treatment involved the patients' realizations that symptoms varied according to their social effectiveness, and that they could improve their social skill and control their depression.

In a more comprehensive study, McLean and Hakstian (1979) evaluated the effects of 10 weeks of psychotherapy, behavior therapy, drug therapy, and relaxation therapy for 178 moderately depressed clients. Drug therapy consisted of amitriptyline graduated to a fixed dose of 150 mg/day. Behavior therapy, as in McLean's earlier study, consisted of a social skills approach. The results of this study favored behavior therapy on nine of 10 measures at the conclusion of 10 weeks of treatment.

However, such superiority was greatly diminished at the 3-month follow-up.

Although McLean's studies answer some of the methodological problems in Lewinsohn's approach to the depressive syndromes, many problems still remain, which have weakened the fiber not only of his approach, but of all of the behavioral approaches. Behavioral researchers frequently have used subjects in their studies who may not have been clinically depressed according to usual criteria. For example, Lewinsohn's own subjects were either college students or individuals from the community solicited through advertisements (MacPhillamy & Lewinsohn, 1974). The relationship of data collected from college students and volunteer subjects to that collected from psychiatric patients is unknown. A second problem still concerns the need for more controlled experimentation with long-term follow-up and maintenance treatment. Anecdotal reports may produce testable hypotheses, but these hypotheses must be tested on a clinically depressed population.

Nevertheless, the techniques of social skill training offer a precision and replicability that could go a long way in solving those methodological problems that have been the bugaboo of recent ambitious studies attempting to determine the role of psychotherapy in the treatment of neurotic depression.

SOCIAL SKILLS TRAINING

It is presently possible to adopt social skill interventions sophisticated enough to test Lewinsohn's twofold hypothesis on a psychiatric population of subjects with clinically significant depression. This could be accomplished by combining techniques developed in other treatment situations with those more rudimentary techniques developed by Lewinsohn. This combination of techniques has recently become known as social skills training.

Social skills training is based on the notion that a depressed patient (1) once possessed the requisite responses in his or her repertoire but lost them as a function of anxiety, (2) never had the requisite responses in his or her repertoire in the first place, or (3) lost the responses during the course of a psychiatric illness and/or lengthy institutionalization (see Hersen & Bellack, 1976). Therefore, irrespective of the origin of social skill deficits, a reeducation period is needed for the patient. A number of component techniques are used during the course of skills training, including instructions, feedback, social reinforcement, modeling, coaching, behavior rehearsal, and graded homework assignments (see Hersen, Eisler, Miller, Johnson, & Pinkston, 1973). These techniques have been shown to be effective in modifying unassertive behavior in psychiatric patients in both analogue and clinical research studies (Hersen & Bellack, 1978). This approach requires a careful behavioral analysis of deficits. Actual training involves considerable practice in the consultation room in the form of role playing. Frequently the therapist models the appropriate responses, followed by additional patient practice. Social reinforcement is provided by the therapist for improved responses to a variety of interpersonal situations. The therapist then encourages the patient to practice his or her newly developed repertoire in a natural environment. Homework assignments are graded in a way that the patient is likely to receive reinforcement (i.e., from the natural environment) for his or her efforts. The testing of these techniques to improve the social skills of depressives on antidepressant medications seems to be strongly suggested by the results of Weissman and Klerman's combined psychopharmacology–psychotherapy investigations.

Liberman and Davis (1975) have argued:

> A collaboration between researchers in behavior analysis and clinical psychopharmacology also promises to lead to a more reliable, valid and comprehensive classification of behavior disorders based upon differential response to environmental and chemical interventions. The identification of various subgroups within the large, clinical populations referred to as schizophrenic, hyperkinetic, and depressed would promote behavioral-biological research and contribute to the state of the art when we will be closer to predicting what treatment in which setting is most effective for a specific individual. (pp. 326–327)

Finally, Lewinsohn (1975) himself points out the need for controlled research where pharmacological and behavioral therapies of depressives not only could be compared to each other, but where their additive effects could be evaluated as well. Such combined approaches are beginning to be used in a number of psychiatric situations (e.g., see Liberman & Davis, 1975; Turner, Hersen, & Alford, 1974), but they probably hold their greatest promise in the treatment of the depressive syndrome.

In considering a comprehensive treatment, there are two core areas of maladaptation in the depressed patient. First, there is depressive symptomatology, usually neurovegetative, which when present destroys any possibility of successful learning. Second, there are cognitive, instrumental, and social skill deficits that form an omnipresent background against which depressive symptoms wax and wane. In the initial Klerman et al. (1974) investigation, in which the additive effects of psychotherapy and drugs were assessed, there were essentially no drug/psychotherapy interaction effects, supporting the idea that these two core areas operate somewhat independently from one another. Medication seemed to relieve symptoms and prevent relapse; psychotherapy seemed to slowly improve social adjustment (after 8 months). However, the investigators actually initiated psychotherapy some 2 months after a course of amitriptyline had already been administered. Moreover, psychotherapy was not precisely defined. And, even though social skills of patients improved, therapeutic intervention was not directly targeted for such change. By contrast, the social skills approach to be described is specifically directed toward improving social and interpersonal adjustment. A combination of pharmocologic and social skills intervention promises to be a treatment strategy likely to be effective in both of these core treatment areas. This hypothesis is bolstered by the recent findings of Weissman, Prusoff, DiMascio, Neu, Goklaney, and Klerman (1979) showing the benefits of combining interpersonal psychotherapy and amitriptyline in delaying possible return of depressive symptoms. However, it should be pointed out that in this investigation by Weissman and her colleagues, both amitriptyline and interpersonal psychotherapy were equally effective in the initial treatment of acutely depressed, nonpsychotic outpatients.

SOCIAL SKILLS TRAINING PROGRAM

TRAINING FOCUS

Social skills training is a structured learning therapy. It is designed to develop the specific skills necessary to perform effectively in interpersonal situations. By "perform effectively," we mean the maximization of positive reinforcement, while keeping social punishment at a minimum. This conception presumes that the individual may reap some negative consequences from others in the process of standing up for personal rights and maintaining a healthy adjustment. This sense of balance seems to be especially important for depressed patients, who often are either overly demanding of others or are overly submissive. The former style results in excessive social punishment. The latter seems to be an effort to avoid punishment at all costs, and results in a dearth of positive reinforcement.

Our social skills training program primarily deals with three types of social skills, each of which has special relevance for depressed women: positive assertion, negative assertion, and conversation skills. "Positive assertion" refers to the expression of positive feelings to others. There are four major subcategories of positive assertion: (1) giving compliments, (2) expressing affection, (3) offering approval and praise, and (4) making apologies. Depressed patients generally do not spontaneously make these important responses to others. They often have the requisite verbal content in their repertoires or can easily learn what to say. The major training tasks are (1) to stimulate the patient to make the responses at the appropriate times, and (2) to shape the appropriate paralinguistic components. Because of their dysphoric mood, these patients have great difficulty with voice intonation and inflection. Consequently, their responses generally lack a sense of warmth, enthusiasm, and the positive feeling tone necessary to make these responses effectively.

"Negative assertion" refers to the expression of displeasure and standing up for one's rights. Four categories of negative assertion are included in our training program: (1) refusing unreasonable requests, (2) requesting new behavior from others, (3) compromise and negotiation, and (4) expressing disapproval and annoyance. These responses seem to play a critical role in the dysphoric mood experienced by depressed patients (Sanchez & Lewinsohn, 1980). Considerable time in training is devoted to development of coordinated delivery of the verbal, paralinguistic, and nonverbal components of each category. Once again, paralinguistic features are especially difficult to train. However, the verbal content of these responses also presents problems. The stressful nature of negative assertion situations has a disruptive effect. It interferes with concentration and makes it difficult for the person to generate appropriate statements. Many depressed patients also are reluctant to make these responses, fearing a negative reaction from the interpersonal partner. Modification of these faulty cognitions is a central part of the training. The depressed person must be taught that the reactions will generally be less negative than expected and that they will be less painful than continued passivity and submission.

The third target area is conversational skill. This includes the ability to initiate, maintain, and gracefully end conversations. Depressed patients often have a restricted range of social interactions (Libet &

Lewinsohn, 1973). This training is designed to correct the difficulty and, as a result, increase the receipt of social reinforcement. An important aspect of this training is to teach the patient how to be more positively reinforcing to others. Patients are taught to use social reinforcement, agreement, and encouragement. They are also taught to inhibit "sick talk," and to avoid complaining and whining.

Social skills are situationally specific (Bellack & Hersen, 1978). Training the patient to be assertive or conversant in one situation will not necessarily generalize to other people or situations. Thus, we provide training on each target behavior in each of four social contexts: (1) with strangers, (2) with friends, (3) with family members (or in heterosocial interactions), and (4) at work or school. The four social contexts are appraised as to their significance for the patient. Generally, one or two present no problem or are of little significance. The remaining areas are treated in order of increasing significance. This arrangement is followed in order to develop basic skills and achieve some success before tackling the most difficult issues.

Next, an assessment is conducted to determine precisely who the person has difficulty with, in what particular types of interactions, and in which of the four social contexts. For example, a patient might be having difficulty initiating conversations with attractive males (i.e., potential dating partners), but not with unattractive males or with females. She might be unable to refuse unreasonable requests from her employer, but be able to resist such requests from her mother. Conversely, she may be unable to express positive feelings toward her mother. These specific deficits are ordered hierarchically, and trained in order of increasing difficulty as each social context is confronted.

COMPONENTS OF TRAINING

The training program consists of four separable components: (1) skills training, (2) social perception training, (3) practice, and (4) self-evaluation and self-reinforcement. Each is applied to each of the social contexts selected for treatment.

Skills Training

This component involves the set of procedures that has typically been called "social skills training" in the literature (cf. Bellack & Hersen, 1977, 1978, 1979). It is the basic strategy for training each of the specific response skills. The three other training components are designed to reinforce the preliminary changes produced by skills training, and ensure that the newly learned behaviors are used *in vivo* and maintained.

Before beginning skills training, it is necessary to conduct a careful assessment. As indicated above, it is necessary to determine the specific responses to target with which interpersonal partners in which social contexts. Some of these data can be gathered by careful interviewing. The patient is the best source of data about her own distress, and she can identify the situations which are most painful for her. She can also indicate sources of difficulty and the relevance of various issues. However, patients can only provide a biased and limited report. They often do not know how they come across to others, why they fail in social interactions, and precisely which response elements they perform poorly. Consequently, it is necessary to observe the patient in action. This is accomplished by having her role-play various interactions.

Our pretreatment assessment battery is presented in Table 5-1. It includes a 16-item role-play test, which covers each of the general target areas, each social context, and a variety of interpersonal partners (e.g., employers, parents). The therapist formulates preliminary hypotheses about what treatment should cover based on these role-play responses, various self-report data, and a psychiatric interview (the Hamilton Rating Scale). These hypotheses are refined in the first therapy session by a more focused interview. At this point, the therapist determines the specific contexts, responses, and interpersonal partners to target, and formulates a tentative hierarchy to guide the order of training. Finally, specific plans for skills training are developed by having the patient role-play with the therapist. This last step allows the

TABLE 5-1. Assessment Battery

Type	Description
Self-report	Beck Depression Inventory
	Lubin Depression Adjective Check List
	Hopkins Symptom Checklist
	Wolpe–Lazarus Assertiveness Scale
	Eysenck Personality Inventory
Observer ratings	Raskin Eligibility Depression Scale
	Hamilton Rating Scale for Depression
	Paykel *et al.* Assessment of Social Adjustment
Behavioral	16-Item Role-Play Test (extended interaction)
Significant other	Katz Adjustment Scale—Relative

therapist to determine the precise verbal, nonverbal, and paralinguistic elements that must be trained. Of course, assessment is a continuing process throughout the course of treatment. Frequent modifications are made in the plan as the therapist gathers more information, as the patient develops new skills, as problems and roadblocks crop up, and as the patient's life situation changes.

Training proper begins once the final assessment step is completed and the therapist identifies a precise starting point (e.g., a specific behavior in a specific context). The first step is to describe the target to the patient and provide a rationale for its use in the designated manner. The rationale is critical if the patient is to appreciate the importance of the behavior and work diligently. It should emphasize the social value of performing the response in the desired fashion. For example, "The next thing we need to work on is eye contact. It is important that you look straight at people when you tell them that you are displeased. If you do, they'll know you are serious and not to be taken lightly. If you don't, they'll think that you are unsure of yourself and can be bullied. OK? Do you understand why it is so important? Good." The therapist should be certain that the patient's assent is based on understanding and agreement, not lip service.

Once the patient agrees to the importance of the behavior, instructions are provided as to how the response should be performed. Instructions should be specific and succinct. For example, "I want you to look at my face for the entire time that you speak. You don't need to look directly at my eyes. Let your gaze shift slowly from my forehead, to my nose, to my mouth, and back to my forehead. But, keep looking at my face. OK? Good." Vague instructions, such as, "Look at me when you talk," will not produce the requisite response. Extended instructions with convoluted rationales and if–then clauses are confusing, and the patient will typically recall only a small portion. The therapist must be careful to avoid overcomplicating the task by attempting to give too much qualification or dealing with exceptions to the role. These special cases should be covered only after the basic skill is mastered. Whenever possible, instructions should specify what the patient should do, not what they should not do.

Social skills are much like motor skills (e.g., bicycle riding, swimming). They cannot be learned solely by didactic instruction. Proper performance must be observed and performed. The bulk of skills training is devoted to serial trials of observation and performance. Often, instructions will not be sufficient to convey how the response is to be performed. The therapist then models appropriate performance. The modeling display is presented in a role-play format. The therapist portrays the patient and the patient enacts the relevant interpersonal partner. Before role playing begins, the therapist should clearly specify the aspect of his or her response to which the patient should attend. If not, the patient is likely to attend to an irrelevant component. The interaction should be kept very brief. One or two sentences is ample. Longer interactions at this preliminary stage result in distraction and confusion. Simplicity is the guiding word whenever new behaviors are presented. After the modeling display, the therapist questions the patient to be sure she attended to the proper element and understands how it is to be performed. Repeated modeling displays are sometimes required.

The next step is the most important: role playing. Here, the patient attempts to perform the target response in a simulated interpersonal scenario. The parameters of the scenario are first carefully specified. For example, "I'll play your boss. It's about 4:30 P.M. and you're getting ready to leave. You have a date tonight and you're in a hurry. I'm going to ask you to stay late to get some work done and you're going to refuse." The therapist then reviews how the response is to be performed. "Remember, you indicate that you understand the problem and that you would like to help, but that you have a prior commitment and can't stay." This instruction should be relatively simple and cover only the immediate target. The patient can only be expected to master one response element at a time. The various response parameters must be taught sequentially. The therapist and patient then role-play the interaction. Initial trials should be kept brief, and the therapist should portray a cooperative partner. Resistance and complications can be added in subsequent trials.

Following the role play, the therapist provides feedback and positive reinforcement. The feedback should be specific and limited to the behavior under focus. Problems with other response components should be ignored. Moreover, feedback should be couched in positive terms. It should emphasize positive aspects of the response and how it could be improved. The patient and the response should never be criticized! Also, feedback should always contain some positive reinforcement. The therapist must point out some positive aspect of the response. Effort or improvement can be reinforced, even if the response is of poor quality. An appropriate feedback response is as follows: "That was a good try. I liked the way you looked at me when you spoke. You really looked as if you meant what you said. Let's try it again, and this time let's work some more on your volume. I'd like you to try and speak a little louder. It will make you even more convincing."

Repetition is a fundamental feature of skills training. No response is adequately mastered after a single trial. Even a successful role play must be repeated. We require our therapists to perform at least two to five repetitions of each scenario. Feedback and reinforcement follow each repetition. When difficulties are encountered, further instructions and modeling can also be provided. If the patient does not master the response after five trials, some modification in the procedure is required. In some cases, simpler versions of the response can be presented or the target can be broken down into elements. These procedures are especially useful in training verbal content. In teaching paralinguistic response features, it often is helpful to let the patient hear herself by listening to a tape recording of the previous role-play interaction. This type of feedback seems to be more informative than verbal descriptions of intonation or voice volume.

The therapist should recognize that some patients will never achieve mastery of certain responses. It is counteproductive to continue hammering away after a plateau is reached. The goal of training is the minimally acceptable response. This is the least that must be done to achieve a goal. Once this point is reached, the therapist should consider moving on to the next response. Continued attempts to push the patient beyond her ability will be highly punishing to the patient, as well as frustrating for the therapist. It is more likely to result in termination than in a breakthrough.

Social Perception Training

Current approaches to social skills assessment and training have placed almost exclusive emphasis on motoric response components. It generally has been presumed that the quality of interpersonal performance depends (almost) entirely on the response skills in the person's repertoire. However, this conception only accounts for part of the variance in social skills. While the individual cannot perform effectively without the requisite response capability, the mere presence of such skills in the repertoire does not insure effective performance. More specifically, the individual must know *when* and *where* to make various responses, as well as *how* to make them. This aspect of interpersonal skill has been referred to as social or interpersonal perception (Morrison & Bellack, 1978). It includes: (1) knowledge about the meaning of various response cues and familiarity with social mores; (2) attention to the relevant aspects of the interaction, including the context and the interpersonal response cues provided by the partner; (3) information-processing capability; and (4) the ability to accurately predict interpersonal consequences. (Bellack, 1979, p. 98)

Social perception training is a vital component of social skills training, although it is the least formalized component. It does not consist of specific strategies to be implemented in a prescribed fashion. Rather, there are a number of general strategies that are intermittently applied throughout training. The foremost and most consistently employed technique is information giving. The therapist is a teacher. He or she teaches the patient about social interactions: what to expect from others, what various responses mean, when responses can be made, and so forth. Every response skill that is trained is placed in the context of when, where, and why it should be made. This information is imparted while giving the rationale for responses, in the context of feedback, in general discussions about how the responses can be utilized, in giving homework assignments (see "Practice," below), and in reviewing reports of how homework was carried out. The patient is not simply given factual information, but is taught to attend to the social environment and the interpersonal partner.

A second vehicle for development of social perception skills is the therapist's role-play performance. As training progresses on individual skills, the therapist presents more difficult responses, such as resisting the patient's attempts to compromise. These variations give the patient practice in interpreting and responding to different social cues. The therapist specifically points out the cues that were varied and illustrates how they are discriminative for different counterresponses. During the later stages of training, the therapist can prompt the patient for the same type of analyses (e.g., "What would you do if I hesitated and gave a weak response to your question?"). A related strategy is for the therapist to model a range of responses around a common theme and have the patient provide an appropriate counter to each variation. For example, in the context of requesting a raise, the therapist could portray an employer who is ambivalent, hostile, understanding but not complying, too busy to discuss the issue, and so forth. Of course, the therapist would attempt to vary paralinguistic and nonverbal response elements as well as verbal content.

Practice

The gains made in sessions have a low probability of being maintained if they are not overlearned. There is ample evidence demonstrating that newly learned responses drop out under stress, replaced by well-established patterns (Bellack, 1980). Therefore, it is vital to insure extensive practice of new social skills. Repeated role-play trials in sessions serve this purpose. However, it is also critical for the patient to practice newly learned responses in the natural environment. *In vivo* practice facilitates generalization, as well as contributing to overlearning.

Beginning with the second session, the patient is given a homework assignment at the conclusion of every session. The assignment is based on the skills learned during that particular session. It is worked out jointly with the patient, to help insure compliance. There are several vital guidelines to be used in generating assignments. First, the instructions must be specific or the task will not be performed in the desired manner. "Try to meet some new people this week," is not adequate. An appropriate task is as follows, "The homework for this week is to start conversations with three different people at work who you know by sight, but have never met. The best place would be the employee cafeteria or the elevator. I want you to do at least one by Tuesday, and the second by Thursday. Remember, you can keep it brief. Smile and say something about the situation. OK? Any questions? Good luck."

Second, the patient must be able to perform the assignment adequately. Of course, she should have the opportunity to do it. It also should be geared to her skill level; she should already have achieved a degree of competence on the response. Homework is designed to overtrain, not provide basic instruction. Finally, the assignment should be in keeping with the patient's overall level of functioning and state of depression. Initial assignments should not demand substantial behavioral changes, even if the patient has learned the specific social skill responses needed.

The third guideline is that the homework assignment should lead to reinforcement. There should be a high probability that the patient will be successful. The therapist must consider the likelihood that the interpersonal partner will not respond favorably. This often is independent of the patient's skill level. For example, a long-standing pattern of maladaptive communication with a husband is not likely to be quickly changed. Such difficult problems must be reserved for later in the course of treatment, when the depression is somewhat abated, skills are more refined, and the patient is better able to accept only partial success.

One final note on homework needs to be articulated. The patient should monitor homework performance and keep a diary or record form. The previous assignment is briefly discussed at the beginning of each therapy session. The patient should be heartily reinforced for effort. Reports of noncompliance are followed by a reminder of the importance of completing assignments and a quick shift to the current training focus. The patient should not be scolded, preached at, or given support and sympathy for failure to comply.

Self-Evaluation and Self-Reinforcement

Depressed individuals have been shown to make inappropriately negative evaluations of their behavior (Rehm, 1977). Therefore, patients are liable to perceive their efforts as inadequate. They may also fail to perceive environmental reinforcement of their homework performance, and view partial success as failure. Either occurrence could mitigate the effects of treatment. To prevent this, subjects are trained to evaluate their responses more objectively and to use self-reinforcement (cf. Bellack, 1976; Bellack, Glanz, & Simon, 1976; Fuchs & Rehm, 1977). Beginning with the second content area hierarchy, patients are requested to evaluate each of their role-played responses and assign a letter grade to the response (i.e., A, B, C, D, F). Grades of A or B are followed by the emission of a positive self-statement such as, "I did that pretty well. I'm really learning."

Initially, patients tend to grade themselves quite negatively. The therapist corrects any inappropriately low evaluations by providing more appropriate and objective criteria. For example, "I think that was a strong B. We were focusing only on verbal content that time, and you made a clear statement of your feelings." The therapist also prompts for and models appropriate positive self-statements. Patients are instructed to perform similar self-evaluative and self-reinforcing operations for homework responses. Specific criteria are supplied when the assignment is given (e.g., "Give yourself an A if you state your preference and have a firm tone of voice, a B if your tone is only moderately firm. Don't worry about his response when you grade yourself. Just focus on how you presented yourself.").

STRUCTURE OF TRAINING

Our training program is divided into two parts: (1) primary treatment, and (2) maintenance. The primary phase consists of 12 weekly sessions of 60 minutes' duration. Training is conducted in the format of individual therapy. An overview of the session-by-session course of training is presented in Table 5-2. The first session is devoted to an introduction of the patient to treatment and preliminary assessment and treatment planning. It is important to provide the patient with a clear and cogent rationale for the treatment. Most patients expect therapy to entail open-ended discussion of their symptoms and some critical life issues. They generally must be persuaded of the logic of the social skills model as well as the structured aspect. This must be accomplished right at the beginning of treatment. It is difficult to establish or reinstate the structured approach if the patient is reinforced for self-exploration and bemoaning her fate.

Skills training begins in the second session. Each session begins with a review of homework, followed by two to five role plays of each of three different scenarios. The session concludes with a brief summary and a homework assignment. The schedule presented in Table 5-2 projects two sessions for each of the first two problem areas and three sessions each for the third and fourth areas. In practice, training generally covers only two or three areas. Moreover, there often is one area or issue (e.g., a particular work or marital problem) that requires as

TABLE 5-2. Session-by-Session Plan of Treatment

Session	Treatment
1	Overview and rationale
	Assessment
	Preliminary treatment planning
2, 3	Train on first problem area
4, 5	Train on second problem area
	Introduce social perception training
	Introduce self-evaluation and self-reinforcement
6, 7, 8	Train on third problem area
9, 10, 11	Train on fourth problem area
12	Summarize accomplishments
	Plan for future problems
13–18	Problem solve and review

much as half of all training sessions. Training in social perception skills and self-evaluation and self-reinforcement begin at about session 4, although this is somewhat flexible. The final session must contain a summary of accomplishments and plans for dealing with probable problems in the future. New responses should not be introduced in this session unless they are likely to be mastered without further training. Plans should also be made for the maintenance phase of treatment.

Twelve weeks is a relatively brief period of time in which to produce durable changes. Aside from the comparatively small amount of therapist–patient contact in this period, the patient does not have an opportunity to try out new skills in the face of a diversity of real-life problems. Consequently, we administer six to eight booster sessions over the following 6 months. These sessions follow a p.r.n. schedule, averaging about one per month. The first few often are scheduled at shorter intervals than those at the end of this period. New material is not presented in these sessions. Rather, they focus on review and problem solving. The patient is given further role-play practice on difficult issues, and established skills are translated to newly developed problems. The goal is to reestablish skills that have begun to fade and to help the patient in her own efforts to use her skills to handle new problems.

INTERPERSONAL STYLE

Before concluding the description of our training program, a word is required about the interpersonal style or tone of the therapy. While the procedure is highly structured, it does not follow a lockstep sequence. It is presented in a conversational manner, and involves considerable discussion between therapist and patient. However, discussion is focused on the training tasks except when there is a crisis situation. The therapist never lets the protocol interfere with the dictates of good clinical judgment. In a similar vein, the atmosphere is definitely not cold or harsh. The therapist must be warm, empathic, and express high personal regard for the patient. He or she actively and continuously works at maintaining a positive therapeutic atmosphere. The therapist is directive, but is not dictatorial. The patient is made to feel that the therapist understands her and is working toward alleviating her distress, even when the focus of the interaction shifts away from direct discussion of her most prominent concerns. Operationally, the therapist provides extensive positive reinforcement, secures patient input on the content of treatment, and expresses understanding of patient concerns. The therapist is not critical, does not ignore patient complaints, and does not impose values or force the patient into directions she does not wish to pursue.

PRELIMINARY DATA

Let us now present some preliminary results of our social skills approach developed for unipolar nonpsychotic depressed females. In pilot work we first conducted before receiving funding for our National Institute of Mental Health (NIMH) project, four such female patients were given social skills treatment (Wells, Hersen, Bellack, & Himmelhoch, 1979). Ages ranged between 19 and 45. Each of the patients received 12 weekly 1½-hour treatment sessions. Treatment administered was directed to improving assertiveness with regard to deficits in family interactions, work interactions, interactions with friends, and interactions with strangers. The treatment protocol was the same as that previously described for the initial treatment phase.

Results of this investigation appear in Table 5-3. Inspection of this table indicates both improvement in specific behavioral measures tapping social skills as well as marked improvement on self-report and psychiatric rating scales of depression. As argued by Wells et al. (1979),

These results indicate that social skills training holds promise as a treatment approach for depressed individuals. This type of approach would appear to be especially appropriate for unipolar (nonpsychotic) patients, whose premorbid personalities are frequently anxious, shy, and socially deficient. Teaching these individuals more effective social behavior should increase the amount of positive reinforcement they self-generate, resulting in decreases in acute depression and, possibly, a decreased probability of future depressive episodes. (p. 1332)

Let us now look at preliminary results of the social-skills-plus-placebo treatment from our NIMH project. Five unipolar (nonpsychotic) female depressives were administered social skills training and received placebos (Hersen, Bellack, & Himmelhoch, 1980). Ages ranged between 25 and 57. Skills training consisted of instructions, role playing, feedback, modeling, positive reinforcement, social perception instruction, correct self-evaluation, and homework assignments. All five patients received 12 1-hour sessions during initial treatment. Three also received

TABLE 5-3. Behavioral Measures, Self-Report Scales, and Psychiatric Rating Scales for Four Depressed Patients Receiving Social Skills Training

Measures[a]	Patient 1			Patient 2			Patient 3			Patient 4		
	Pre-	Mid-	Post-	Pre-	Mid-	Post-	Pre-	Mid-	Post-	Pre-	Mid-	Post-
Behavioral												
Overall assertiveness (5-point scale)	2.9	3.6	4.4	2.7	3.1	3.8	3.5	3.9	3.8	2.2	3.5	3.7
Eye contact[b]	.11	.64	.86	.16	.64	.72	.61	.99	.95	.32	.68	.89
Speech duration (in seconds)	.47	7.1	5.3	3.5	3.7	5.3	6.6	7.8	8.4	2.4	3.8	3
Response latency (in seconds)	2.4	1.2	.7	1.2	.7	.5	1.5	.9	.8	1.1	.6	.5
Intonation (5-point scale)	2.8	3.8	4.4	4.2	4.1	3.8	3.7	4.1	4.6	3.8	5	4.3
Self-report												
Wolpe–Lazarus (assertiveness)	18	23	25	6	19	16	15	17	18	14	21	25
Beck (depression)	15	4	11	25	22	16	20	17	15	21	8	0
Lubin (depression)	14	10	13	14	9	11	19	13	14	25	12	7
Psychiatric rating												
Hamilton (depression)	24	7	11	31	18	19	30	22	16	19	7	4

Note. From "Social Skills Training in Unipolar Nonpsychotic Depression" by K. C. Wells, M. Hersen, A. S. Bellack, and J. M. Himmelhoch, *American Journal of Psychiatry*, 1979, *136* (10), 1331–1332. Copyright 1979 by the American Psychiatric Association. Reprinted by permission.
[a] For overall assertiveness, eye contact, speech duration, intonation, and the Wolpe–Lazarus Assertiveness Scale, increasing scores indicate improvement. For response latency and the Beck, Lubin, and Hamilton depression scales, decreasing scores indicate improvement.
[b] Eye contact was measured in seconds for each role-playing situation and is expressed as the ratio of eye contact to speech duration.

maintenance treatment for 6 months (one session per month) following initial treatment. One patient was in maintenance treatment for 3 months (one session per month).

Results of treatment are presented in Table 5-4. This table shows that there were improvements seen in self-report, psychiatric rating scales, and behavioral measures of depression and assertiveness level. As noted by Hersen *et al.* (1980), social skills training led not only to improved interpersonal functioning and mood, but it significantly reduced vegetative symptomatology associated with unipolar nonpsychotic depression.

CONCLUSION

In the preceding pages we have presented the rationale for social skills training with depressed women, described our training program, and presented some preliminary data on its effectiveness. In concluding, we

TABLE 5-4. Self-Report Scales, Psychiatric Rating Scales, and Behavioral Measures for Five Depressed Patients Receiving Social Skills Training

Measures	Initial treatment			Maintenance treatment	
	Baseline	6 weeks	12 weeks	3 months	6 months
Patient 1					
BDI	18	15	5	2	3
DACL	69	73	71	78	78
WLAS	20	22	23	21	25
Hamilton	28	15	12	2	2
Raskin	10	8	5	3	3
OA (5-point scale)	p 3.25	p 3.63	p 3.75	p 3.88	p 4.38
	n 2.75	n 3.63	n 3.75	n 3.75	n 3.88
Patient 2					
BDI	19	0	2	1	0
DACL	67	78	82	80	78
WLAS	8	18	16	25	25
Hamilton	22	9	4	2	1
Raskin	6	4	3	1	3
OA (5-point scale)	p 3.38	p 3.38	p 3.25	p 3.38	p 3.38
	n 2.88	n 3.50	n 3.63	n 3.75	n 4.00

(Continued)

TABLE 5-4. (*Continued*)

Measures	Initial treatment			Maintenance treatment	
	Baseline	6 weeks	12 weeks	3 months	6 months
Patient 3					
BDI	20	1	8	9	11
DACL	50	89	84	60	71
WLAS	15	20	20	18	23
Hamilton	28	10	1	11	10
Raskin	6	5	3	5	4
OA (5-point	p 2.50	p 3.25	—	p 3.25	p 3.75
scale)	n 2.14	n 3.75	—	n 3.13	n 3.75
Patient 4					
BDI	10	9	0	1	—
DACL	80	89	89	88	—
WLAS	16	20	23	23	—
Hamilton	16	6	2	0	—
Raskin	5	3	3	3	—
OA (5-point	p 4.13	p 4.63	p 4.13	p 4.38	—
scale)	n 4.13	n 4.13	n 3.88	n 3.88	—
Patient 5					
BDI	36	21	7	—	—
DACL	58	71	84	—	—
WLAS	17	19	25	—	—
Hamilton	21	12	2	—	—
Raskin	6	4	4	—	—
OA (5-point	p 4.00	p 4.50	—	—	—
scale)	n 3.38	n 3.88	—	—	—

Note. Abbreviations: BDI, Beck Depression Inventory; DACL, Depression Adjective Check List; WLAS, Wolpe-Lazarus Assertiveness Scale; OA, overall assertiveness. For the BDI, Hamilton, and Raskin scales, decreasing scores indicate improvement. For the DACL, WLAS, and OA, increasing scores indicate improvement. The notation of "p" refers to scenes requiring positive assertion; "n" refers to scenes requiring negative assertion.

would like to underscore the tentative nature of our program. It has been developed on the basis of the existing literature, pilot efforts, and clinical intuition. Neither the entire package nor the specific elements have been empirically evaluated. The program is gradually evolving as a function of our clinical experience. We expect our current project to demonstrate the effectiveness of the overall package. Even if our optimism is justified, the reader should be careful not to reify each and every aspect of the package as currently specified. Conversely, any future tests of the program should be based on careful adherence to our blueprint. This is not to say that other versions of social skills training should not be developed. Rather, the literature can best progress if the precise nature of any treatment procedures are documented and evaluations of specific therapies are based on their protocols.

ACKNOWLEDGMENTS

Preparation of this chapter was facilitated by Grant No. MH 28279-01A1 from the National Institute of Mental Health.

REFERENCES

Bellack, A. S. A comparison of self-monitoring and self-reinforcement in weight reduction. *Behavior Therapy*, 1976, 7, 68–75.

Bellack, A. S. Behavioral assessment of social skills. In A. S. Bellack & M. Hersen (Eds.), *Research and practice in social skills training*. New York: Plenum Press, 1979.

Bellack, A. S. Anxiety and neurotic disorders. In A. E. Kazdin, A. S. Bellack, & M. Hersen (Eds.), *New perspectives in abnormal psychology*. New York: Oxford University Press, 1980.

Bellack, A. S., Glanz, L. M., & Simon, R. Self-reinforcement style and covert imagery in the treatment of obesity. *Journal of Consulting and Clinical Psychology*, 1976, 44, 490–491.

Bellack, A. S., & Hersen, M. *Behavior modification: An introductory textbook*. Baltimore: Williams & Wilkins, 1977.

Bellack, A. S., & Hersen, M. Chronic psychiatric patients: Social skills training. In M. Hersen & A. S. Bellack (Eds.), *Behavior therapy in the psychiatric setting*. Baltimore: Williams & Wilkins, 1978.

Bellack, A. S., & Hersen, M. (Eds.). *Research and practice in social skills training*. New York: Plenum Press, 1979.

Burgess, E. P. The modification of depressive behaviors. In R. D. Rubin & C. M. Franks (Eds.), *Advances in behavior therapy*. New York: Academic Press, 1969.

Costello, C. G. Depression: Loss of reinforcers or loss of reinforcer effectiveness? *Behavior Therapy*, 1972, 3, 240–247.

Ferster, C. B. Classification of behavioral pathology. In L. Krasner & L. P. Ullmann (Eds.), *Research in behavior modification*. New York: Holt, Rinehart & Winston, 1965.

Fuchs, C. Z., & Rehm, L. P. A self-control behavior therapy program for depression. *Journal of Consulting and Clinical Psychology*, 1977, 45, 206–215.

Hersen, M., & Bellack, A. S. Social skills training for chronic psychiatric patients: Rationale, research findings, and future directions. *Comprehensive Psychiatry*, 1976, 17, 559–580.

Hersen, M., & Bellack, A. S. (Eds.). *Behavior therapy in the psychiatric setting*. Baltimore: Williams & Wilkins, 1978.

Hersen, M., Bellack, A. S., & Himmelhoch, J. M. *Treatment for unipolar depression with social skills training*. Unpublished manuscript, 1980.

Hersen, M., Eisler, R. M., Alford, G. S., & Agras, W. S. Effects of token economy on neurotic depression: An experimental analysis. *Behavior Therapy*, 1973, 4, 392–397.

Hersen, M., Eisler, R. M., Miller, P. M., Johnson, M. B., & Pinkston, S. G. Effects of practice, instructions, and modeling on components of assertive behavior. *Behaviour Research and Therapy*, 1973, *11*, 443–451.

Klerman, G. L., DiMascio, A., Weissman, M., Prusoff, B., & Paykel, E. S. Treatment of depression by drugs and psychotherapy. *American Journal of Psychiatry*, 1974, *131*, 186–191.

Kovacs, M. Treating depressive disorders: The efficacy of behavior and cognitive therapies. *Behavior Modification*, 1979, *3*, 496–517.

Lewinsohn, P. M. The behavioral study and treatment of depression. In M. Hersen, R. M. Eisler, & P. M. Miller (Eds.), *Progress in behavior modification* (Vol. 1). New York: Academic Press, 1975.

Lewinsohn, P. M., & Amenson, C. S. Some relations between pleasant and unpleasant mood-related events and depression. *Journal of Abnormal Psychology*, 1978, *87*, 644–654.

Lewinsohn, P. M., & Graf, M. Pleasant activities and depression. *Journal of Consulting and Clinical Psychology*, 1973, *41*, 261–268.

Lewinsohn, P. M., & Libet, J. Pleasant events, activity schedules, and depression. *Journal of Abnormal Psychology*, 1972, *79*, 291–295.

Lewinsohn, P. M., & Shaffer, M. Use of home observations as an integral part of the treatment of depression: Preliminary report and case studies. *Journal of Consulting and Clinical Psychology*, 1971, *37*, 87–94.

Liberman, R. P., & Davis, J. Drugs and behavior analysis. In M. Hersen, R. M. Eisler, & P. M. Miller (Eds.), *Progress in behavior modification* (Vol. 1). New York: Academic Press, 1975.

Liberman, R. P., & Raskin, D. E. Depression: A behavioral formulation. *Archives of General Psychiatry*, 1971, *24*, 514–523.

Libet, J., & Lewinsohn, P. M. Concept of social skill with special reference to the behavior of depressed persons. *Journal of Consulting and Clinical Psychology*, 1973, *40*, 304–312.

MacPhillamy, D. J., & Lewinsohn, P. M. Depression as a function of levels of desired and obtained pleasure. *Journal of Abnormal Psychology*, 1974, *83*, 651–657.

McLean, P. D., & Hakstian, A. R. Clinical depression: Comparative efficacy of outpatient treatments. *Journal of Consulting and Clinical Psychology*, 1979, *47*, 818–836.

McLean, P. D., Ogston, K., & Grauer, L. A behavioral approach to the treatment of depression. *Journal of Behavior Therapy and Experimental Psychiatry*, 1973, *4*, 323–330.

Morrison, R. L., & Bellack, A. S. *The role of social perception in social skill*. Unpublished manuscript, University of Pittsburgh, 1978.

Rehm, L. P. A self-control model of depression. *Behavior Therapy*, 1977, *8*, 787–804.

Sanchez, V., & Lewinsohn, P. M. Assertive behavior and depression. *Journal of Consulting and Clinical Psychology*, 1980, *48*, 119–120.

Turner, S. M., Hersen, M., & Alford, H. Effects of massed practice and meprobamate on spasmodic torticollis: An experimental analysis. *Behaviour Research and Therapy*, 1974, *12*, 259–260.

Weissman, M. M. The psychological treatment of depression: Evidence for the efficacy of psychotherapy alone, in comparison with, and in combination with pharmacotherapy. *Archives of General Psychiatry*, 1979, *36*, 1261–1269.

Weissman, M. M., Prusoff, B. A., DiMascio, A., Neu, C., Goklaney, M., & Klerman, G. L. The efficacy of drugs and psychotherapy in the treatment of acute depressive episodes. *Amerian Journal of Psychiatry*, 1979, *136*, 555–558.

Wells, K. C., Hersen, M., Bellack, A. S., & Himmelhoch, J. M. Social skills training in unipolar nonpsychotic depression. *American Journal of Psychiatry*, 1979, *136*, 1331–1332.

Wolpe, J. The experimental model and treatment of neurotic depression. *Behaviour Research and Therapy*, 1979, *17*, 555–565.

6

SOCIAL SKILLS TRAINING FOR PSYCHIATRIC PATIENTS: TREATMENT AND OUTCOME

PETER M. MONTI
DONALD P. CORRIVEAU
JAMES P. CURRAN

The purpose of this chapter is twofold. Our initial purpose is to provide, in sufficient detail, a description of our own social skills treatment program. We will describe the specific skills and components (e.g., starting conversations, giving criticism, refusing unreasonable requests, etc.) that comprise our training manual as well as several response acquisition training procedures used in our social skills program. While a complete how-to manual is beyond the scope of this chapter, we hope to share with the reader our experience in developing a systematic social skills program, including procedural nuances and clinical issues that typically arise in the course of such a program. The second purpose of this chapter is to describe the results of our own outcome research evaluating the efficacy of social skills training with psychiatric populations.

THE SOCIAL SKILLS TREATMENT PROGRAM

BASIC STRUCTURE

Our social skills training package is a semistructured program designed specifically for use in a group format. The program for our social skills groups is geared to a social skills training manual consisting of a series

Peter M. Monti, Donald P. Corriveau, and James P. Curran. Veterans Administration Medical Center/Brown University Medical School, Providence, Rhode Island.

of 10 lessons or chapters. After a particular lesson or chapter is presented in the group context, each patient is given a copy of that chapter to read and to keep for future reference. Each respective chapter represents a general category or type of social skill.

Since the initial development of our social skills training program 5 years ago, we have experimented with various schedules for our group format. While a daily schedule of group meetings appeared ideal for our inpatient and day hospital populations, few outpatients were interested in such an intensive approach. This problem was easily solved by incorporating two independent group schedules. Our social skills groups designed primarily for outpatients are scheduled over the course of 10 consecutive weeks, with a single 1½-hour session per week. Social skills groups designed for inpatients and day hospital patients are typically scheduled for a total of 20 sessions, approximately 1 hour each in duration, over the course of 4 weeks. These groups are scheduled Monday through Friday and are offered on a monthly basis. By scheduling our inpatient groups on such a regular basis, we have found an increased referral rate from our inpatient unit staff.

Our social skills training groups are always led by two cotherapists, one male and one female, who alternate two specific responsibilities. On any specific session, one therapist is primarily responsible for presenting the information contained in the chapter for that day. The other therapist, in addition to being a backup as a role model or role-play partner, is mainly responsible for processing group dynamics. After a debriefing session, which follows every group meeting, both therapists take an active role in communicating clinically important information to other hospital treatment personnel (e.g., nurses, psychiatrists, social workers, etc.). Entries describing the material covered during any particular session as well as any observations by the therapists regarding skills deficits or acquisitions are entered in the patients' charts. Additionally, we have placed on the inpatient ward a journal in which our therapists describe clinically important material that may be relevant to the inpatient staff. We find this active communication between our therapists and our inpatient staff particularly helpful in facilitating their cooperation. As we shall describe in a later section, members of our inpatient and day hospital staff are requested to take an active role in several aspects of our social skills training program. Although the training groups are time-limited, our therapists are available for follow-up work with these patients as well as for individualized behavioral programs.

Since our social skills training program was designed primarily as a support service, potential candidates for our social skills groups are typically referred by mental health workers from our outpatient, day hospital, or inpatient units. Potential candidates are then given a standard interview (the Initial Screening Interview, a copy of which is obtainable from Donald P. Corriveau) by a member of our treatment staff. The interviewer is typically one of the cotherapists who will be leading the group. The major purpose of this interview is to assess and record particular interpersonal deficits of each patient. Care is given to obtaining important baseline information regarding situational factors that may govern these deficits. A second purpose of the interview is simply to judge whether a particular patient appears appropriate for a social skills group. Following this interview, patients are scheduled for an extensive behavioral assessment (see Chapter 11 for a description of our assessment protocol).

Since the relative success of the entire group experience rests heavily upon the success of the first group session, we will present an in-depth analysis of what typically occurs in our initial session. After introducing themselves to the group members, therapists begin by delineating the major goals and objectives of the social skills program. Essentially, they describe that the major objective in social skills training is to increase group members' abilities and competency in dealing with a variety of interpersonal situations and/or to decrease any anxiety or discomfort that they may be experiencing in interpersonal situations. To set the mood or atmosphere of the group experience as well as to counter any stereotypic bias or expectation of what may be encountered in group therapy, patients are assured that the group's orientation will be very practical, here and now, low-pressured, and probably even enjoyable. Patients are told that they will be able to set their own pace and level of involvement and that they will not be coerced into discussing or revealing any subject matter that they are not willing to provide. Through the use of several examples, therapists discuss how every patient will inevitably find some element within the program to be particularly helpful. They note, for example, how some individuals might be well versed in starting conversations but these same individuals experience difficulty in providing criticism to others. Therapists also state that they will attempt to tailor the learning experiences of the group to best match the specific needs of individual group members. The patients, in turn, are encouraged to present their own problematic interpersonal situations in order to make the group experience as relevant as possible. Therapists also discuss how the social skills training program will, it is hoped, contain new strategies and methods of dealing with difficult interpersonal situations. Most importantly, therapists emphasize that the goal of the program is not to instruct patients how to behave but rather to increase the patients' own options and opportunities so that they themselves will make their own decisions. Therapists also describe how social skills, like other motor skills, such as riding a bicycle or playing tennis, must be learned and acquired through practice, not by simply reading or listening.

Although therapeutic salesmanship is clearly important in establishing group morale, therapists should not describe social skills training as a panacea for all psychological problems. While social skills training may provide a general benefit in helping patients with many aspects of their own lives, it is clearly not a cure-all prescription. Patients are forewarned that the skills acquired through our training program will not assure success in every interpersonal situation. To place the value of skills training in perspective, the patients are told that in general the acquisition of social skills will help to increase the possibility of success in obtaining one's goals. Although the potential benefits and limitations of social skills training as discussed above can be easily presented in a few minutes, these important messages are repeated frequently throughout the entire treatment program.

The next activity in the first session of our training program is a group-building exercise. Although the establishment of rapport is an important element in any form of group therapy, this process is especially germane in a social skills training group where patients are either socially inadequate or are reportedly uncomfortable or anxious in social situations. Although there are several good group-building exercises available for group therapy leaders, we invariably present the following exercise. Therapists instruct patients to group themselves into pairs, sequentially assign either the letter A or B to each patient, and give the following directions: "For the next 5 minutes, I would like each person designated A to talk and get to know person B. Try to find something interesting about this person." After this 5-minute exercise, each person designated A is requested to report his or her findings to the group. During this reporting process, therapists provide contingent praise to each narration, complimenting in particular those patients who report interesting and unique features about their partner. Next, roles are reversed and the exercise is repeated. Although this exercise is admittedly a simple one, it is very nonthreatening and serves several important purposes. Patients appear more comfortable following this exercise and therapists have a unique opportunity to begin establishing baseline data for each of their patients with respect to skills deficits. In this exercise, therapists also develop a reliance on group exercises per se and introduce patients to the topic of starting conversations, the first chapter of the social skills manual.

The final exercise scheduled for the first session of our group is a role play performed by both cotherapists. Patients are introduced to the role play by the group leader as follows:

> Imagine that [name of cotherapist] and myself are very close friends. Although I really like this individual, he [or she] has a very bad habit of borrowing my car without ever offering to pay or reimburse me for the gasoline. In fact, he [or she] has occasionally returned my car with the gas indicator registering empty. Imagine now that he [or she] is returning the keys to my car after having borrowed it again. Remember that my goal in this situation is to request that he [or she] no longer borrow my car without helping defray the cost of the gasoline used. He [or she] says to me, "Here are the keys to your car."

During this role play, the group leader purposefully portrays a very passive individual who is apparently too anxious to make the appropriate request. The group leader then turns to the group members and asks whether or not the goal of this situation was met. After a short discussion highlighting the inadequacies of the leader's behavior, the group leader says that he or she will try a new way of handling the situation. In the second role play, the group leader becomes very aggressive and both cotherapists portray a heated argument. At this point, the therapist turns to the group and again asks whether his or her goal was met. A dramatic enactment of an aggressive response will typically lead some group members to state that the group leader had not met his or her goal, while other patients maintain a different point of view, reflecting sentiments such as, "I wish that I had the guts to act like that!" At this point, the group leader would parenthetically conclude that in a way the goal was met of having the other person stop borrowing the car without returning the gasoline. By stressing the arguments invariably presented by several group members, however, the group leader would emphasize that a second, perhaps more important goal, that of maintaining an important friendship, was clearly compromised by such an aggressive response. After a short discussion of this issue, a third role play, enacting an appropriately constructive criticism, is used to illustrate a more skillful and assertive response to this problematic situation.

These successive role plays serve several important purposes. First, although we attempt to keep our terminology to a bare minimum, we find it particularly useful to provide descriptions and examples of passive, aggressive, and assertive styles of responding. Secondly, the role play demonstrates modeling. As described in the next section, modeling procedures generally serve to supply information and to specifically contrast skillful with nonskillful responses. Lastly and most importantly, these role plays also initiate a very important therapeutic process: that of learning to conceptualize goals. Many of our patients appear to have difficulty in identifying and delineating short- versus long-term consequences of a situation. Before providing further descriptions of our 10-chapter treatment program, let us first direct our attention to the major training procedures used throughout our social skills training program.

MAJOR TREATMENT PROCEDURES

Instruction

Skilled behavioral components are initially introduced by instructions in the form of general rules. Therapists describe general strategies for optimizing interpersonal effectiveness and systematically summarize the major components of these strategies. When discussing these rules, therapists employ various visual aids, including a blackboard and handouts. Most importantly, therapists provide a strong rationale for each of these rules, illustrating how they will likely lead to increased interpersonal effectiveness.

Modeling

As illustrated in our description of the first session, modeling is a procedure used to illustrate various ways of handling interpersonal situations. In particular, modeling serves to contrast the most likely consequences of inappropriate and appropriate responses to certain social situations. Throughout the course of our program, modeling procedures are initially employed when a new social skill is presented, usually at the introduction of each new chapter. Modeling procedures are also implemented on an impromptu basis whenever patients appear to have difficulty understanding the information presented and discussed in the group meetings. In addition to the modeling procedures conducted by the cotherapists, we also employ video systems, which are particularly well suited to the presentation of preprogrammed scenarios. Both live and video forms of modeling are effective in illustrating material, and if possible both procedures should be used. Alternating between live and video modeling will increase group members' interest and attention and is also helpful in familiarizing patients with the video equipment itself (especially when video feedback will be incorporated into the program).

Behavioral Rehearsal

While modeling procedures are used more frequently in the earlier sessions of the training program, therapists are trained to progressively increase their reliance on behavioral rehearsal, the most important training procedure found in our program. While modeling procedures serve to supply information, behavioral rehearsal appears to be the major vehicle through which new skills can be acquired. In essence, behavioral rehearsal offers patients a unique opportunity to practice new skills, to receive constructive criticisms in areas of potential improvement, and to receive social praise for using these skills. During the first few sessions of any group, behavioral rehearsals are typically done with the patient and one of the cotherapists. Before behavioral rehearsals are implemented, patients are requested to describe any problematic situation in which they have difficulty performing a particular skill. For those patients who cannot supply such situations spontaneously, hypothetical situations are provided. After a few sessions, patients seem to catch on to the purpose of this procedure and therapists can then encourage behavioral rehearsals between two patients.

Role Reversal

In presenting new skills to our patients, it is occasionally common to hear notes of pessimism such as, "That sounds nice but in my case it simply won't work! My wife would get very angry if I tried to be assertive with her." The therapists might ask to challenge this pessimism with a role-reversal procedure as follows: "Well, let's see. You play the part of your wife and I'll respond to you in an assertive fashion." While placing himself in the role of his wife, the patient might have difficulty in responding angrily to an assertive therapist. Role-reversal procedures appear to illustrate to patients the fact that skillful responses are typically not antagonistic. In general, role-reversal procedures help to increase patient expectations that socially skillful responses are more likely to lead to success.

Reinforcement and Shaping Procedures

Our experiences show clearly that our most effective therapists are those who effectively employ principles of operant conditioning in their group sessions. In particular, effective therapists are those who seem to rely heavily upon social reinforcement and shaping procedures. While we attempt to foster the use of praise as a reinforcer, therapists are also cautioned against indiscriminant and noncontingent use of this procedure. If therapists should provide praise unconditionally, patients are quick to perceive the insincerity of this feedback and praise would quickly lose any reinforcement value. Conversely, if therapists provide only critical feedback without any positive reinforcement, patients will soon find the group to be an aversive experience. Hence, our therapists are trained to find some element in patients' responses that are appropriate and skillful and to amply praise patients on these elements before mentioning potential areas of improvement. When therapists have difficulty in finding skillful elements of a patient's response, the patient should at least be commended for participating in the behavioral rehearsal. It should be noted that while some patients are reluctant to participate in the behavioral rehearsals, their behavior can usually be shaped with adequate social reinforcement.

Another important source of reinforcement can be found among the group members themselves. This valuable resource should be gradually developed and monitored consistently by the therapists; otherwise, unwarranted criticism from group members may severely dampen the participation of other patients. To effectively develop this powerful source of reinforcement, therapists should begin every discussion following a particular behavior rehearsal by initially asking whether other group members can find something skillful and appropriate in the particular patient's response. In order to develop this source of reinforcement early in the group program, therapists should initially solicit the opinions of complimentary patients and avoid requesting the opinions of patients who appear unduly critical. (Cynical behavior itself may be conceptualized as a social skill deficit that therapists might later focus on as a target variable for certain patients.)

As mentioned earlier, our most successful therapists are those who attend closely to the process of shaping desirable responses. A patient's initial response in a behavioral rehearsal often falls somewhere short of his or her potential for a maximally effective response. Therapists should not only shape successive approximations to obtainable target behaviors within each set of behavioral rehearsals, but they should also shape a gradual acquisition of social skills throughout the entire training program. This is not an easy responsibility. Some of the patients appear more skillful in the group setting than they appear in their own environment, while the opposite is sometimes true for other patients. Thus, in discussing obtainable goals with patients (especially when discussing *in vivo* exercises), therapists should consistently avail themselves of data from as many sources (patients' family, friends, and staff personnel) as possible.

Another important source of reinforcement intimately related to shaping processes should be noted. As a social skills training group develops and patients acquire new skills, performances of these new responses in front of other people appear to contain their own intrinsic rewards. Many patients report that they always knew what they wanted to do or say in certain situations but could never do so, mostly because they feared failure or other forms of personal discomfort. Other patients begin to realize that they have more skills than they once thought, and consequently, they become more eager to use and apply them. Similarly, when patients acquire new skills or strategies for handling potentially problematic social situations, they concurrently report a new sense of control over their environment. Obviously, success in dealing with one's environment has its own reinforcement value. If therapists can systematically shape these desirable behaviors, the acquisition of a repertoire of social skills produces intrinsic rewards, which often become multiplicative. To enhance the overall effectiveness of a social skills training program, therapists should attempt to insure a series of initial successes by discussing clearly obtainable goals with their patients. Following these early successes, therapists may then gradually shape a series of more difficult behavioral skills.

Feedback Procedures

Another training procedure that we include in our social skills program includes several feedback procedures. As with other motor skills, the acquisition of social skills is greatly accelerated by appropriate feedback.

While praise and shaping procedures are used to reinforce patients' attempts at skillful behavior, further improvement typically requires appropriate constructive criticism. Hence, feedback should accompany each behavioral rehearsal.

Although therapists must take the initial responsibility in providing constructive criticism to their patients, another useful source of feedback comes from other group members. This is a unique learning opportunity available only through the group experience. The utility of this source of feedback is maximized when attention is directed to role-play partners within each of the behavioral rehearsals. As patients engage in behavioral rehearsals with other patients, it is particularly effective to ask the role-play partner how he or she felt during a particular role play. As an example, consider a patient who is practicing to criticize his boss. During a series of behavioral rehearsals, the patient might try several different approaches and the role-play partner could be asked how he or she would react to each of the different responses.

Another valuable source of feedback can be obtained by the use of video recording equipment. Video recordings have the unique potential of providing immediate, descriptive, and objective feedback, and if necessary, can be repeated quite frequently. When a series of videotaped behavioral rehearsals show improvement from the patients' first attempt to the last attempt, the illustration of this accomplishment can be particularly reinforcing. Moreover, patients also find it rewarding to compare recent videotaped segments as they are recorded in latter sessions of the program with earlier behavioral rehearsals. Although there is some initial anxiety produced by the sight of video equipment in the group setting, patients soon appear to enjoy seeing themselves on the video monitor and their anxiety is short-lived. As discussed in an earlier section, the same video equipment may also be used to present modeling tapes. This dual purpose of employing video equipment deserves special consideration as a modern clinical tool. At the very least, the use of multiple modes of presentation (role plays by therapists, role plays by patients, videotaped models, and other audiovisual aids), will, as in many teaching situations, increase the attention span of its recipients.

Homework

While the therapeutic procedures discussed above all promote the acquisition of social skills, there is no guarantee that treatment gains will generalize outside the group setting. In our effort to increase both the durability and generalization of treatment effects, we have placed particular emphasis on homework assignments. The purpose of these assignments is to engage patients in practicing their social skills in real-life social situations. Assignments are programmed in every treatment chapter and are given to the patients at the end of each session. The first 15 to 20 minutes of each session is typically devoted to a discussion of the previous session's assignment. Every patient is requested to discuss his or her relative success and/or failure for each particular assignment. When patients report that a particular attempt appeared unsuccessful, suggestions for different strategies are discussed and new behavioral rehearsals are implemented to provide further practice.

As might be predicted, we typically encounter motivational problems on the part of some of our patients with their participation in doing homework assignments. For some of our reluctant patients, the notion of homework seems to remind them of schoolwork, which they may resent. In our experience, patients seem much less resistant to these assignments when we simply avoid the word "homework" and replace it with the word "exercise." For other patients, exercises represent a request for them to engage in behaviors (e.g., starting a conversation with a stranger) that they have been actively avoiding for years. Patients must be continually reminded that the acquisition of a social skill can be achieved only through active practice. As part of general shaping procedures, therapists should take an active part in planning these assignments with their individual patients.

In order to facilitate the availability of practice opportunities for our inpatients, therapists regularly maintain lines of communication with the clinical staff on our inpatient unit. Clinical staff are informed as to what material was presented on any particular day and are encouraged to assist patients in practicing these particular skills. Although homework assignments are not the easiest training procedure to implement in a social skills training program, their potential for addressing generalization of behavior change would appear to mandate their inclusion in any social skills program.

Adjunct Role Playing

Another procedure that we have incorporated to increase generalization of behavior change deserves some attention. While the majority of patients eventually become comfortable in practicing certain behaviors with both the therapists and other group members, their performance in other social settings, especially with novel people, remains a point of difficulty. As a case in point, one of our patients completed all of his homework assignments that were requested of him but would not practice any situations with anyone but his wife. In order to increase the breadth of this patient's social contacts, we incorporated into the group the assistance of other personnel, called "adjunct role players." We typically train several undergraduate psychology students to serve as role models and to attend certain group sessions with the express purpose of interacting with patients in certain behavioral rehearsals. If, for example, a particular patient has difficulty in a situation such as a job interview, we have several adjunct role players play the part of a potential employer.

While we have had consistently positive experiences with the addition of new faces within the group setting, we should caution against indiscriminant use of adjunct role players. As with other forms of psychotherapy, social skills training includes important therapeutic relationships between patients and therapists. Significant rapport must be established and maintained for patients to be able to discuss intimate interpersonal problems, which are often very sensitive in nature. Clearly, judicious implementation of an adjunct role-playing component must be timely and should never be overdone.

Other Training Procedures

At least on an operational level, the procedures described above represent a major portion of our social skills training program. An effective integration of these treatment components is central to a successful program. In addition to these treatment procedures there are several components that could fall under the rubric of nonspecific treatment variables. Although little research has specifically examined these so-called nonspecific treatment factors within a social skills training program (e.g., sex and age of therapists and patients, skill level of therapists), they may account for some of the treatment effectiveness. The amount of structure provided within each social skills program is also an important consideration. Social skills training procedures are very structured compared to other forms of group therapy. Yet, social skills therapists should be highly trained and experienced clinicians who are sufficiently flexible to adequately deal with all clinical issues that arise in the group. (We will discuss our own training procedures for social skills therapists in a later section of this chapter.) We also recommend that therapists themselves be socially skillful. Besides serving in several leadership capacities, therapists inevitably become important role models. It appears crucially important to provide role models who appear to possess sufficient skill in dealing effectively with their own problematic social situations.

Another therapeutic goal, which we have not yet specifically discussed but which is nonetheless formally integrated into our social skills training program, is what we refer to as the conceptualization of goal-directed behavior. A surprising number of our patients appear to have considerable difficulty in conceptualizing the distinction between short- and long-term consequences of their behavior. These individuals, who coincidentally often express a bifurcated view of their environment, are often fixed upon only the short-term consequences of their social interactions. For these individuals, specific exercises designed toward examining a situation and delineating both short- and long-term goals within these situations has important clinical utility. Procedures to promote the development of this cognitive skill were illustrated in our earlier presentation of what is typically done during the first session of any social skills training program. In addition to these procedures, we also include in our comprehensive treatment package a lesson that includes several elements found in contemporary cognitive-behavior therapy. These elements will be discussed in more detail in the following section, describing our treatment manual.

TREATMENT MANUAL

While a complete therapist's training manual is beyond the scope or intention of this chapter, this section will present and briefly discuss the major skills addressed in our treatment program. The 10 general skill categories included in our patient manual shoud be conceived as general content areas, each including several skill components. While the presentation of our treatment program may, at first glance, provide an illusion of a completely structured program, therapists nonetheless attempt to provide an individualized program tailored for each patient. In presenting these major content areas, we will discuss some of the more common difficulties that arise in our attempts to promote these skills.

Lesson 1: Starting Conversations

To introduce the topic of starting conversations, therapists begin by discussing the important role of this skill. Patients are reminded about the importance of communication in establishing both intimate and casual relationships as well as the role of communication in everyday life. This discussion typically provides therapists with baseline data with respect to patients' potential deficits in this area and patients quickly perceive the relevance of this skill. Following this discussion, therapists describe five general points that should be helpful in effectively starting conversations. First, therapists illustrate the importance of finding an appropriate time and place for beginning a conversation. Next, therapists discuss the appropriateness of various conversational topics. Interestingly, some patients invariably reveal the misconception that any conversation based upon small talk would probably be perceived as trite and meaningless. These patients are assured that many meaningful conversations can begin with small talk, if only to get things going.

The third general strategy for appropriate conversational skill focuses upon various amounts of self-disclosure. Patients are reminded that while appropriate levels of self-disclosure are important in establishing close friendships, too much self-disclosure may, at times, be inappropriate. The fourth point discussed in this session cautions patients against the use of close-ended statements. Group members are reminded of the value of relevant questions in maintaining an interesting conversation. Lastly, patients are instructed on appropriate ways of ending a conversation gracefully.

Although these general strategies appear to represent a good deal of information, the use of appropriate models (and if possible, the use of videotaped scenarios) can quickly highlight the major issues. Therapists are urged to incorporate behavioral rehearsal procedures in this session as soon as possible. Therapists may elect to be the role-play partner themselves or may assign this responsibility to other patients. Since these therapeutic procedures are rather new to most patients, mild apprehension is not uncommon. During the rehearsals, some patients may feel somewhat upset over prolonged silences by their partners. A natural reaction is that they are not doing a good job. In most cases, the duration of these silences is not atypical and video feedback is particularly useful in highlighting the actual appropriateness of their conversations. Another common reaction by some patients is that although they appear to be following the rules correctly, they still have difficulty maintaining a conversation. An analysis of these patients' conversations will typically show that they are either engaging in several close-ended statements or are posing questions in such a way as to yield simple yes or no answers. Again, the use of video feedback is particularly helpful in illustrating both the strengths and weaknesses of various conversational styles.

Lesson 2: Nonverbal Behavior

In this lesson patients are presented several examples of both appropriate and inappropriate elements of nonverbal behavior. For example, therapists illustrate appropriate posturing by initially modeling extreme rigidity as well as excessive fidgeting during the course of an interaction. Similarly, therapists illustrate appropriate eye contact by first showing complete lack of eye contact during a conversation as well as by illustrating excessive blinking and staring. Similar models employed to contrast appropriate and inappropriate elements are also applied to head nods, smiling, and gesturing.

Although the presentation of these skills appears rather straightforward and concise, an important purpose of this lesson is to provide patients with feedback with respect to their nonverbal cues. Some patients, for example, might generate cues that most individuals might perceive as abrasive without really being aware of this. Constructive criticism should prove particularly helpful for these patients.

Lesson 3: Giving and Receiving Compliments

The lesson on giving and receiving compliments begins by discussing the importance of compliments. Patients are reminded that most people enjoy receiving compliments; yet, people often seem to take significant others for granted and often fail to compliment them as often as they should. Patients are given a brief course on behavior modification by reminding them how they can maintain and increase desirable behaviors in others by simply praising them contingently. In describing general strategies patients are instructed to state their compliments in terms of their own feelings rather than in terms of absolute facts. Patients are also instructed to pick out something specific to include in the compliment. After these points are presented and discussed, patients then participate in behavioral rehearsals. Finally, patients are simply instructed to always accept a compliment given to them. Through examples, patients are shown how misguided modesty may often prove to be discomforting to the person providing the compliment.

Lesson 4: Negative Thoughts and Self-Statements

In several respects, this lesson stands apart from other lessons. First, the material was developed primarily from a cognitive-behavior therapy orientation and, as such, treatment sessions focus primarily upon cognitive processes. Less attention is directed toward actual behavior change. Secondly, therapeutic procedures such as behavioral rehearsal and modeling, used extensively throughout all other lessons, are not employed in sessions devoted to this material. The primary focus of this lesson is in demonstrating the influence of cognitive self-statements on behavior. In particular, the deleterious effects of negative self-statements in preventing skillful behavior is discussed. The essential purpose of this discussion is to allow patients to pinpoint when and where they actually engage in negative self-statements. We find this lesson to be the single most difficult lesson to present successfully. Not all patients readily grasp the significance of the vicious cycle between cognitions and behavior. Once patients are able to identify and articulate their negative self-statements, the responsibility of the therapists is then to introduce methods by which patients can either eliminate negative self-statements or at least attenuate their impact. Therapists often suggest that patients attempt to challenge these self-statements, which, more often than not, appear irrational to some degree.

Although behavioral rehearsals are not particularly adaptable to this lesson, therapists are urged to use many examples. Judging by our patients' response to this lesson, it is clear that attention to cognitive processes is particularly important. Therapists are trained to include therapeutic elements similar to Ellis's Rational–Emotive Therapy as well as Meichenbaum's Self-Instructional Training.

Lesson 5: Giving Criticism

In introducing this lesson, patients are reminded that while most people have a natural inclination to avoid hurting the feelings of others, it is often necessary to provide constructive criticism. While some people may try to avoid expressing criticism altogether, negative results, such as the accumulation of resentment, are likely to result. In further highlighting the importance of giving criticism, patients are reminded that other people may be irritating us possibly without them knowing it. If we do not provide criticism when it is called for, we may, as a consequence, be making it more difficult for the other person to change his or her behavior. As a central theme to this lesson, patients are also reminded that the goal of being assertive includes standing up for one's rights, but not at the expense of others. Patients are instructed that this lesson includes skills in giving and expressing constructive criticism to others without unduly hurting their feelings.

Either through modeling tapes or role plays, patients are presented with the following five suggestions for enhancing the effectiveness of a criticism:

1. State the criticism in terms of your own feelings, not in terms of absolute statements.
2. Try not to criticize the entire person, but rather try to direct your criticism at specific aspects of his or her behavior.
3. Try to request specific behavior change. If there is something specific that the other person could do to ameliorate the situation, try to request it specifically. Don't assume that he or she will know how to appease you.
4. Within the conversation, try to both start and finish on a positive note. In other words, try to diminish the overall negativeness of your conversation by sandwiching these statements with either compliments or some type of positive regard.
5. Don't let your tone of voice become angry. If your goal is actually to change his or her behavior, a heated argument will probably not result in obtaining your short- and long-term goals.

In this lesson, patients may be somewhat overwhelmed by the number of points presented. Given both the importance of providing criticism in everyday life, as well as the considerable range of appropriate responses to many situations, therapists should spend considerable time planning behavioral rehearsals for all patients. The effectiveness of this training procedure can also be greatly enhanced by the use of adjunct role players.

Lesson 6: Receiving Criticism

Perhaps because of the pervasiveness of critical statements in everyday life, most patients are eager to acquire new skills in handling criticism directed at them. Initial discussion of this lesson includes the distinction between what we call assertive criticism and manipulative criticism. Patients are instructed that manipulative or aggressive criticism appears to be directed at the person rather than at elements of his or her behavior. Aggressive criticism appears to be more a reflection of the other person's emotional state than an appropriate reaction to the recipient's behavior. In handling aggressive criticism, patients are initially instructed to never deny the criticism. Patients are reminded that argumentation will typically not lead to long-term goals. One specific strategy that is illustrated includes the technique of fogging; that is, finding some element in the criticism that can be agreed with and stating it even more directly. A second related strategy includes requesting that the other person specify, in concrete and behavioral terms, exactly what elements of behavior are unsatisfactory. Paradoxically, this appears to take away much of the negative impact of a potential argument.

Next, patients are shown a different strategy to deal with assertive criticism. First, they are instructed to behave as if the criticism is not something to get upset about. They are further instructed to sincerely question the other person in order to clarify the content and nature of the criticism. A final strategy applicable to either type of criticism is to have the patients propose a workable compromise, if one is available. Usually, this consists of proposing some type of behavioral change that might satisfy the criticism.

Lesson 7: Listening Skills and "Feeling Talk"

This lesson focuses on two separate skills. Listening skills include all the verbal and nonverbal cues that suggest that one is attentive to a conversant dialogue. Therapists typically model inappropriate listening skills by portraying a hypothetical conversation where one individual is continually looking at his watch, yawning quite frequently, and generally looking away from his partner. Most importantly, patients are told that good listeners have a knack of perceiving the feelings of others. Therapists might describe an example where a friend is describing the good time that he had at a recent wedding. While the person with only moderate listening skills might ask for details about the bride's dress, food, decor, and so forth, a truly good listener would ask how the person actually enjoyed himself.

As a general strategy for establishing good listening skills, therapists suggest the sharing of similar experiences or feelings with a conversational partner. Patients are especially cautioned about the importance of timing and several examples of appropriate and inappropriate timing are illustrated.

The second general social skill included in this lesson is "feeling talk." In essence, this discussion focuses upon appropriate self-disclosure. The material typically illustrates how a mutual exchange of important feelings and experiences is a major way in which people learn to trust each other and represents an important process by which friendships are established.

Lesson 8: Being Assertive in Business Situations

The major purpose of this lesson is to present a wide variety of situations that many people find potentially problematic. Although new skills are not introduced in this lesson, these sessions usually present a brief review of all prior skills presented in earlier lessons. One type of situation typically presented in these sessions involves interactions with salespersons. Therapists present assertive strategies to deal with common sales pressure as well as methods for returning defective or undesirable merchandise. Often, patients will also describe difficulties in employer–employee relationships. Therapists instruct patients to recall the points for appropriately receiving criticism, both assertive and manipulative, and rules for refusing unreasonable requests. Additionally, therapists describe important skills that may be used in the job interview. We find the use of adjunct role players as hypothetical interviewers particularly effective in allowing patients to practice describing their qualifications and interests for a hypothetical position.

Lesson 9: Close Relationships

Both lessons 9 and 10 are devoted to reviewing the major skills described above as well as to incorporating group members' real-life problematic situations. This lesson specifically focuses on difficulties that often arise in close relationships. Patients are reminded that frequent contact with a particular person will often increase the likelihood of having some elements of that person's behavior produce an irritating effect on us. Consequently, patients are warned about the danger of letting things build up. A common strategy designed to ameliorate this problem is simply to provide appropriate constructive criticism at an early point in this sequence. Invariably, patients comment on the difficulty of expressing negative criticism to an individual close to them for fear of hurting that person's feelings. Patients are reminded that if the behavior of that other person continued to be irritating, the long-term consequence to the relationship may be more damaging. Moreover, patients are reminded that although negative criticism may initially hurt the other individual, negative criticism should also be constructive and, in the long run, may benefit that individual. Patients are urged to provide real-life examples that might have occurred to them recently, and are then requested to use appropriate criticism during behavior rehearsals.

Lesson 10: Intimate Relationships

Discussion of material in this lesson is typically directed toward special problematic situations and difficulties encountered between couples or very close friends. Patients are reminded how people have a general tendency to take each other for granted. While the frequency of criticism may tend to increase over the course of the relationship, the frequency of positive statements or compliments often diminishes. Patients are instructed that if they themselves initiate more frequent compliments, a reciprocal effect will probably occur.

Therapists also discuss the importance of providing both positive as well as negative feedback in these intimate relationships. While patients are apt to point to the difficulty and potential discomfort that they might produce with their sexual partner, they are reminded of the potential long-term consequence of an improved sexual relationship.

While the material included in this chapter is clearly sensitive in nature, patients quickly perceive the importance of skillful behavior in nearly all aspects of their lives. As is true of any successful social skills training session, therapists should present themselves as resource people who wish to present various strategies for dealing with difficult situations.

THERAPIST TRAINING

Although our social skills training groups are quite structured, adequate therapist training—regardless of the amount of prior clinical experience of prospective therapists—is crucially important. In our program, we have been fortunate in obtaining the services of a variety of medical center staff (psychiatric nurses, social workers, psychiatric residents, and psychology interns) as social skill therapists. Our experience has shown the importance of instituting a vigorous training program as well as a consistent monitoring process. Training usually begins by having prospective therapists participate in a social skills training program headed by a therapist/trainer. Although the information provided in these mock sessions is greatly compacted, prospective therapists are encouraged to present real-life examples and to participate in behavior rehearsals. Prospective therapists are shown several preprogrammed videotapes illustrating several examples of modeling and behavioral rehearsal procedures. We also present a library of role plays that we have found useful in prior social skills training groups. While the specific intent of these training sessions is to present both the content as well as the therapeutic procedures found in our groups, prospective therapists also seem to benefit from having participated in this mock social skills training program. During these sessions, prospective therapists share major responsibility as a therapist. Our therapist-training staff relies heavily on behavioral rehearsal as a mechanism to insure appropriate therapist behavior in our program. Shaping and reinforcement procedures are often used to increase prospective therapists' reliance on the use of specific behavioral rehearsal and the avoidance of discursive discussions.

Regardless of prior clinical experience, we invariably require that all prospective skill therapists participate in an actual social skill group as an observer. Patients are not unduly uncomfortable with this procedure and quickly relate to the prospective therapist as a regular group member. Although the observer does not share other therapists' responsibilities, he or she participates in a debriefing process with the therapists following every session. When a prospective therapist appears ready to assume the responsibility of a cotherapist, this individual is paired with an experienced social skill therapist. While the apprentice therapist shares half of the responsibility of providing didactic information to the group, an experienced therapist proves to be an important backup.

As mentioned earlier, we are always concerned about the quality and consistency of our social skills program. Hence, we actively monitor the behavior of our therapists. This is mainly achieved by providing weekly therapists' meetings between all social skills therapists and senior people from our clinical staff. Senior staff, on an unannounced schedule, sit in on some of the social skills groups. Besides providing valuable data with respect to the performance of each of our therapists, the procedure allows a further check on the amount of consistency throughout our social skills program.

While we obviously place considerable emphasis on the importance of following a prescribed protocol in delivering social skills training, therapists are reminded that this form of training is, indeed, a form of psychotherapy. Within our own therapist-training procedures, we continually stress the importance of integrating potential benefits of social skills training with the patients' overall treatment program. To accomplish this goal, prospective therapists are trained to secure active lines of communication with all treatment staff. In other words, our social skills therapists are strongly encouraged to engage all treatment staff in the process of increasing our patients' social competence. The next section of this chapter will describe four studies in which we have systematically tested the effectiveness of our program.

TREATMENT-OUTCOME STUDIES

STUDY I

Our first treatment-outcome study was designed to test the effectiveness of our social skills training package and to compare its effectiveness to typical outpatient treatment at the Providence Veterans Administration (VA) Mental Hygiene Clinic. Since such treatment typically involves supportive psychotherapy and/or medication maintenance, the typical treatment comparison basically served as a nonspecific treatment control group.

The initial subject pool for this study consisted of approximately 1200 male psychiatric outpatients receiving treatment at the mental hygiene clinic. All patients proceeded through two screening processes prior to assignment into this study. The first screening process consisted of the identification of patients who were labeled as having social relationship problems according to our computerized information system (the MultiState Information System) (Laska, 1974). This system catalogues demographic and problem-oriented data that are collected on all mental hygiene clinic patients as they are interviewed for admission into the clinic. The second screening consisted of providing the therapists (psychiatrists and social workers) working in the mental hygiene clinic with lists of their patients who had been so identified by our information system and asking them to nominate those who might be suitable for our intensive social skills training program. The final sample included 80 patients. After giving their informed consent, patients were assessed and then randomly assigned to either a social skills training group or a typical mental hygiene clinic treatment group ($n = 40$ per group). Patients assigned to the control group were told that due to problems with the availability of therapists, they would have to wait several weeks before being assigned to a social skills training group. Patients assigned to the social skills training group began group treatment. At posttreatment all patients were readministered the assessment measures and control patients were offered group treatment. Thirteen patients in each group did not complete either the treatment or the assessment procedures. To determine whether the patients who completed treatment differed from those who were lost through attrition, *t*-tests were performed on pretreatment data. No significant differences were found. The final number for each group was 27. The groups were roughly equivalent in age (range 24–70 years, mean 47 years), education level (range 3–19 years, mean 11 years), and diagnostic category (16 psychotics, 38 neurotics).

Due to the availability of both therapists and patients, the study was run in six cohorts that were replications of each other. Each social skills group plus its respective control group constituted one cohort of the study. In each cohort, each of 14 patients was randomly assigned to either the social skills training group or the control group. Approximately four patients in each cohort were lost to attrition. Patients assigned to the social skills treatment group participated in 10 weekly sessions of 1½ hours. Social skills training was conducted in small groups of approximately five to seven patients led by male and female cotherapists who were either social workers, psychologists, or psychiatric nurses assigned to the clinic. Treatment sessions were based on our 10-chapter treatment manual and treatment was conducted as described in the previous section of this chapter. Different pairs of cotherapists conducted the treatment in the various cohorts of this study. The therapists were extensively trained in the principles and techniques of social skills training by the authors, who also provided close supervision of the therapists throughout treatment. Weekly supervision meetings were conducted with the therapists to discuss any special difficulties that they might have been having and to ensure that treatment was conducted as specified. Patients assigned to the control group continued to receive supportive psychotherapy and/or medication maintenance throughout the 10-week treatment period.

Assessment consisted of patients completing a revision of Richardson and Tasto's Social Anxiety Inventory (1976), relabeled the Social Reaction Inventory (SRI) by Curran, Corriveau, Monti, and Hagerman (1980), and each individually participating in our videotaped Simulated Social Interaction Test (SSIT), at pretreatment, posttreatment, and at a 2-year follow-up. Descriptions of both the SRI and the SSIT are presented in Chapter 11. Patients were asked to complete the SRI twice, once indicating the degree of anxiety they would experience in each of the 105 social situations described (SRI anxiety measure) and a second time recording the level of social skill that they would display in coping with each of the situations (SRI skill measure). The SSIT is a role-play test consisting of eight simulated social situations, seven of which parallel the seven factors represented in the SRI.

Although the 2-year follow-up data had been collected at the time this chapter was written, it had not yet been evaluated; therefore, only pre- and posttest data will be discussed. After all posttreatment data had been collected, pre- and posttest videotapes of the subjects' SSIT interactions were randomly presented to two experimentally blind raters who independently rated each patient on each scene for anxiety (SSIT anxiety) and social skills (SSIT skill). The procedures involved in SSIT ratings are described in Chapter 11. Interrater reliability was in the .90 range for both social skills and anxiety. To determine whether there were significant pretreatment differences among the groups on the dependent measures, analyses of variance were performed on pretreatment data. These revealed no significant differences.

The major findings of the study showed that from pre- to posttest the social skills group improved markedly on the SSIT skill measure whereas there was no change in the control group. Results on the SSIT anxiety measure paralleled those on the skill measure. No differences were obtained on the SRI.

The results of Study I suggested that our social skills treatment program was effective in improving our patients' social competence as measured by the SSIT. The lack of improvement for patients assigned to the control group suggested that the improved performance for social skills group patients was likely not due to a practice effect from repeated measurement on our SSIT. Although these results were encouraging, more controlled research needed to be done before we could be more confident about the effectiveness of our treatment program.

STUDY II

Our second experiment (Monti, Fink, Norman, Curran, Hayes, & Caldwell, 1979) was designed to address the question of whether the effectiveness of our program was simply attributable to the information provided in our skills training manual or was due to the information provided in our manual plus the specific components of the treatment protocol (e.g., modeling, reinforcement, feedback, coaching, etc.). This question was prompted by the increased popularity and use of many self-help manuals and texts that purport to facilitate the development of assertiveness and social competence. Our clinical intuition was that such untested manuals and self-help texts might prove useless to some of their audience—particularly to many of the skill-deficient psychiatric patients whom we observed reading such material. The design of the study included three groups: social skills training, bibliotherapy, and an assessment-only control. The study included specific measures to test for the generalization of treatment effects as well as a 10-month follow-up.

The subject pool for this study consisted of 50 male and female psychiatric inpatients or day hospital patients of Butler Hospital (Providence, Rhode Island), who, in the opinion of their primary psychiatrist, had social skills deficits. The exclusionary criteria included organic brain syndrome, thought disorder, illiterateness, or inability to follow instructions. All patients gave informed consent. The study was run in two cohorts, which were replications of each other. In each cohort four patients did not complete pretreatment assessment, leaving 42 patients. In each cohort each of 21 patients was randomly assigned to one of the three groups. Additional attrition during treatment and posttest assessment resulted in a final number of 10 for each group. Patients who completed treatment and assessment did not differ from those who were lost to attrition according to the results of t-tests that were performed on pretreatment data. The three groups of subjects were roughly equivalent in age (range 18–56 years, mean 36 years), educational level (range 7–16 years, mean 12 years), diagnostic category (7 psychotics, 23 neurotics), and patient status (19 inpatients, 11 day hospital patients). There were an equal number of males and females in each group.

Patients assigned to the social skills training group participated in hourly sessions that were conducted by male and female cotherapists, five times per week for 2 consecutive weeks. The therapists were clinical psychology interns who had completed all other training and course work for the PhD. Both therapists were experienced in conducting social skills training groups with a variety of populations. Group sessions were based on our 10-chapter treatment manual. Each chapter was the focus of a particular session. Treatment was conducted as described earlier.

Patients assigned to the bibliotherapy group received each chapter of our manual plus its respective homework assignment daily in 10 installments. Chapters were distributed to patients individually and homework was collected by a research assistant on each of 10 mornings. If the patient reported that he or she had not read a chapter or had not done the assignment on a particular day, the research assistant requested that he or she do so and returned at the end of the day to collect the material. All patients completed most of the homework assignments. Patients assigned to the assessment-only control group participated in the normal hospital routine for the 2-week treatment period.

All patients were administered the Rathus Assertiveness Schedule (Rathus, 1973), and each individually participated in an eight-situation role-play test at pretreatment, posttreatment, and at follow-up. The eight situations of the role-play test were very similar to those that make up the SSIT. Four of the situations for the role-play test were incorporated into the treatment sessions (trained scenes). The remaining four situations were not presented during treatment (untrained scenes). This was done to test for generalization effects. The role-play test took place in an audiovisual studio and the procedure was similar to that described in Chapter 11. After follow-up data had been collected, all videotapes were rated according to the procedures outlined in Chapter 11. Interrater reliability was .70 for social skill and .68 for anxiety. At follow-up patients also participated in an *in vivo* generalization task designed after that described in Curran, Little, and Gilbert (1978). This involved a waiting room situation during which the patients' social behavior was unobtrusively evaluated by two confederates who were blind to patients' group membership. In addition, all patients were evaluated on the Clinical Outcome Criteria Scale (as described in Strauss & Carpenter, 1972) by a psychiatrist who was also blind to group membership. This scale includes items such as quality and number of social relationships, employment history, job satisfaction, and ability to meet one's needs. Data were obtained for the 10-month interval from posttreatment to follow-up assessment.

To determine whether there were significant pretreatment differences among the treatment groups on any of the dependent measures, analyses of variance were performed on the pretreatment data. Although these revealed no significant differences, some of the differences approached significance and for this reason analyses of covariance, using prescores as the covariate, were performed on the data.

The results of this study at posttest indicated that patients in the social skills group significantly improved their self-reported assertiveness, as measured by the Rathus Assertiveness Schedule, when compared to patients in the bibliotherapy group. Further, social skills group patients performed significantly better than control group patients on our role-play test of social skill. Due to attrition, follow-up measures were not included in the overall statistical analysis of our data. To determine if the six patients in each group who returned at follow-up differed on the basis of their pre- and posttest data from those who did not return, additional analyses of variance were performed. These analyses revealed no significant differences, suggesting that the patients who returned for follow-up did not systematically differ, according to our measures, from those who did not return. Results of the available follow-up data suggested that both self-report and behavioral improvements were maintained.

To assess the effects of generalization of our social skills treatment's effectiveness, an analysis was made of patients' scores on the Clinical Outcome Criteria Scale. An analysis of variance revealed a highly significant group effect and follow-up analyses showed that the social skills group patients appeared significantly better adjusted than both bibliotherapy and control group patients who did not differ from each other. This finding is especially noteworthy since the Clinical Outcome Criteria Scale was given 10 months after treatment ended and it is a global measure that assesses a wide range of functioning, such as employment status, family situation, and number of acquaintances. To further assess the effects of generalization, an analysis was made of patients' skill performance on trained versus untrained scenes at posttest. Although significant overall trial and group effects were found, the analysis did not show any main or interaction effects due to training, suggesting that the superior performance demonstrated by social skills training group patients at posttest was not restricted to those scenes on which they received practice in treatment. As a final measure of generalization, measures taken during the *in vivo* generalization task were analyzed. Although patients in the social skills training group consistently performed more skillfully than patients in either of the other two groups, statistical analysis revealed no significant differences between the three groups.

In general, the results of Study II indicate the effectiveness of our social skills group treatment for the clinical population tested. Both self-report and behavioral measures of social skill indicated that patients who received social skills training improved at posttest and these changes seemed to be maintained at follow-up. Bibliotherapy did not prove to be effective for our socially deficient patients. The most exciting finding of this study concerns our results regarding the generalization of our treatment's effectiveness. Results on the Clinical Outcome Criteria Scale are particularly noteworthy, since they suggested that social skills training group patients were significantly more healthy 10 months after treatment when compared to other patients tested. Such long-term generalized treatment effects are indeed satisfying.

STUDY III

The third study (Monti, Curran, Corriveau, DeLancey, & Hagerman, 1980) conducted in our treatment-outcome research program was designed to provide a more stringent test of our social skills treatment package. Although both Study I and Study II provided empirical support for the effectiveness of our social skills group treatment package as compared to typical hospital treatment, no well-controlled clinical study including follow-up had compared social skills group treatment with another similar type of group treatment. The need for controlled comparisons of behavioral treatment with other types of psychiatric treatments has been clearly identified by Paul (1969), who suggests that such comparisons may provide reasonable control for variables such as therapist and group interaction effects. Another major purpose of this study was to address the issue of incremental effectiveness. That is, the study was designed to address the question of how much improvement beyond that already gained in a very active treatment program can systematic social skills training offer a diagnostically mixed group of socially deficient psychiatric patients. Data relevant to such questions are essential in order to demonstrate the clinical significance of social skills training.

In this study we compared the effectiveness of our social skills treatment package to the effectiveness of a sensitivity training group treatment package in the context of an active day hospital program. Sensitivity training was chosen as the comparison treatment for several reasons. First, sensitivity training consists of a clearly identified set of procedures that can be systematically offered in a group setting. Second, sensitivity training is commonly conducted in clinical settings, such as the day hospital where this study was run. Third, both treatments share the common goal of more effective interpersonal communication. Although sensitivity training and social skills training may share this common goal, these treatments are derived from clearly different theoretical underpinnings. Sensitivity training emphasizes feelings and perceptions, whereas skills training emphasizes behavioral change through learning, which is facilitated by a variety of procedures such as feedback, reinforcement, and rehearsal. This study did not include a typical hospital treatment control group since the inclusion of this group in Studies I and II suggested that such treatment had essentially no effect as measured by our typical dependent measures. In addition, the ongoing program of the day hospital unit on which this study was run precluded assigning subjects to a no-treatment group since the patient census was small, the patients knew each other, and such differential treatment would not have been accepted by the patient community.

The subjects were 56 male psychiatric inpatients or day hospital patients of the Providence VA Medical Center who had been referred by their primary therapist for social skills training. Since our day hospital unit has a reputation for treating patients with social skills problems, nearly all day hospital admissions during a 5-month period were offered treatment in this study. Exclusionary criteria included organic brain syndrome, thought disorder, or inability to follow instructions. All patients gave informed consent.

In order to secure an adequate sample of patients, the study was run in four cohorts that were replications of each other. In each cohort each of 14 patients was randomly assigned to one of the two treatment groups, following pretreatment assessment. Although 28 patients were assigned to each treatment group, five in each group were lost to attrition, resulting in the final number of 23 per group. Patients who completed treatment did not differ from those who were lost to attrition according to results of t-tests that were performed on pretreatment data. The resulting treatment groups were roughly equivalent in age (range 24–58 years, mean 40 years), education level (range 6–18 years, mean 11 years), diagnostic category (16 psychotics, 30 neurotics), and patient status (6 inpatients, 40 day hospital patients).

All treatment for both the skills training groups and sensitivity training groups was conducted by male and female cotherapists who assumed equivalent leadership roles in each treatment. Two pairs of cotherapists, each of which included a master's level day hospital staff member experienced in conducting sensitivity training sessions as well as a behaviorally oriented clinical psychology intern, provided all treatment. All four therapists participated in several hours of training lessons conducted by the authors prior to beginning the study. Since the procedure was replicated in order to increase the number in each condition, each therapist was crossed-over to the opposite experimental condition for his or her second group. Thus, therapist orientation and sex were counterbalanced across treatment groups.

Social skills training groups and sensitivity training groups met during the same 60-minute period, 4 days per week for 5 consecutive weeks. Patients assigned to the skills training group participated in sessions that were based on our 10-chapter treatment manual. Each chapter was discussed for two sessions and treatment was conducted as described earlier in this chapter. Sensitivity training group patients participated in sensitivity training sessions, which largely consisted of patients and therapists following a packaged sensitivity training program presented on an audiotape that detailed numerous sensitivity training exercises. Patients and therapists first listened to a given section of the audiotape, discussed it, and then followed through with the particular exercises. Different segments of the Planned Experiences for Effective Relating (PEER) audiotape (Berzon, Reisel, & Davis, 1969) were presented during each group session. A therapists' training manual was used for training the sensitivity group therapists. This manual essentially consisted of a detailed outline of the content of the PEER audiotape. The manual also served as the therapists' training outline for the sensitivity group. An important aspect of this study was that all patients participated in all ongoing clinical treatment offered at the day hospital while they were subjects in this study. This included activities such as community meetings, occupational therapy, individual psychotherapy, family therapy, and so forth. Thus, as mentioned previously, the question of incremental effectiveness was addressed.

Assessment consisted of patients completing the Rathus Assertiveness Schedule (Rathus, 1973), the Personal Orientation Inventory (POI) (Shostrom, 1966), and the Social Reaction Inventory (SRI) at pretreatment, posttreatment, and at a 6-month follow-up. Patients also participated in our SSIT at each assessment period. The POI was administered in addition to our usual assessment battery because it is supposedly sensitive to changes in personal growth, a construct which we were attempting to influence through our sensitivity training. All patients were asked to complete the SRI and to participate in the SSIT as described in Chapter 11. Patients' performance on the SSIT was evaluated as described in Chapter 11. Interrater reliability for this study was .85 for social skill and .75 for anxiety.

In order to determine whether there were significant pretreatment differences among the treatment groups on any of the dependent measures, analyses of variance were performed on all pretreatment data. No significant differences were found. To assess between group posttest and follow-up differences on the SRI and SSIT, multivariate analyses of covariance were performed using prescores as the covariates. Roy's maximum root criterion was used as a significance test of the results of these analyses (Harris, 1975).

Pretest, posttest, and follow-up group mean scores on the SSIT anxiety measure suggested that the social skills training group subjects were less anxious from pre- to posttest and from pretest to follow-up, whereas the sensitivity group subjects appeared more anxious at posttest and unchanged from pretest at follow-up. Results of statistical analyses showed a significant difference between groups at posttest and at follow-up. Pretest, posttest, and follow-up group mean scores on the SSIT skill measure suggested that the social skills training group improved from pre- to posttest and from pretest to follow-up, whereas the sensitivity group appeared slightly worse at posttest and somewhat improved at follow-up. Results of statistical analyses again showed significant differences between groups at posttest and follow-up. For both SSIT anxiety and skill measures at posttest and follow-up, the linear combination of scenes, corrected for pretested scores, showed more improvement for the skills group than for the sensitivity group.

Pretest, posttest, and follow-up group mean scores on the SRI anxiety measure suggested that the social skills training group appeared less anxious from pre- to posttest and from pretest to follow up. The sensitivity training group showed some improvement from pre- to posttest and still more improvement from pretest to follow-up. Results of statistical analyses showed a significant difference between groups at posttest and follow-up. Analogous group mean scores on the SRI skill measure suggested that the social skills training group improved from pre- to posttest and from pretest to follow-up and the sensitivity group showed similar though somewhat less improvement. Statistical analyses again showed a significant difference between groups at posttest and follow-up. The linear combination of situations, corrected for pretest scores, for both SRI anxiety and skill measures at posttest and follow-up showed more improvement for the skills group than for the sensitivity group.

Results on the Rathus Assertiveness Schedule were consistent with those from other dependent measures. Analysis of covariance performed on these data showed a significant difference between groups at posttest, with the corrected mean of the social skills training group higher than that of the sensitivity training group. No difference was found at follow-up. Finally, results on the POI showed a very slight improvement for both groups at posttest and essentially no change from pretest at follow-up assessment. No differences were significant.

The results of Study III strongly support the effectiveness of social skills group treatment for our patients. Performance of the patients in the social skills training group significantly improved as compared to that of patients in the sensitivity training group at posttest on our observational measures of social skill and social anxiety, and these differences were maintained at a 6-month follow-up period. Similar and equally significant results were found on our self-report measures of social skill and social anxiety. The absence of differences between treatment groups on the POI suggests that neither treatment differentially affected our patients' perceptions of their personal growth.

Study III extends our previous work and has stronger implications in that significant change occurred even when our social skills treatment package was compared to another substantial group treatment package. This experiment thus controlled for potential unspecified group interaction variables, therapist variables, setting variables, and so on. Another feature of Study III that contributes to the clinical significance of the findings is that the treatments were compared in the context of an otherwise very active treatment regime. Thus, this study also demonstrated the incremental effectiveness of offering our social skills treatment package to patients in a day hospital setting.

STUDY IV

The major purpose of the next study conducted in our clinic (DeLancey, 1979) was to test the effects of covert reinforcement as a potential social skills training procedure. Covert reinforcement consisted of patients imagining themselves behaving in a socially appropriate manner and subsequently being reinforced for doing so. It was reasoned that if covert reinforcement proved to be an effective social skills training procedure, it could be economically added to our existing treatment package with the potential of further promoting maintenance and generalization of behavior. The study involved four treatment groups: social skills training plus covert reinforcement, covert reinforcement, social skills training, and a nondirective therapy control. Study IV differed from those previously described in this chapter in several important aspects. First, this study was an analogue study in that only four treatment sessions were offered. Second, only a small portion of our typical treatment program was employed, namely, lessons on the expression and reception of criticism. Third, treatment was given individually rather than in group sessions. Fourth, the assessment instruments employed were somewhat different than those used in the previous studies reported in this chapter.

Subjects were 56 male and female psychiatric inpatients or outpatients in treatment in several different hospitals located in the greater Providence area. Hospitals were counterbalanced across treatment conditions. After giving informed consent and completing pretreatment assessment, patients were assigned to the four treatment groups. Due to the heterogeneity of the population, stratified random assignment to groups on the basis of subjective pretreatment measures, hospital, and sex was employed. The resulting groups were roughly equivalent in age (range 16–65 years, mean 35 years), diagnostic category (28 psychotics, 15 neurotics, 13 characterological disorders), and sex (40 males and 16 females).

All treatment was given in four individual sessions by four therapists, two men and two women, all of whom were graduate students in psychology. Therapists were counterbalanced across treatment groups. They were all given extensive training prior to beginning treatment and all treatment was closely supervised by the author throughout the study. Patients in the social skills training group received skills training on two dimensions of social behavior, namely, the expression and reception of criticism. Social skills training consisted of instruction, role playing, modeling, rehearsal, feedback, and homework assignments. Approximately 15 relevant social situations were presented in treatment. Three or four situations were presented during each session. In addition, patients were given a written outline of the content of each treatment session. Patients in the covert reinforcement group were given a rationale as to how reinforcing certain imagined situations could positively affect their problematic interpersonal relationships. Next, they were given two trials of a covert rehearsal of a social response and a covert reinforcement. On the first trial, the therapist verbally described while the patient imagined the social response and provided his or her own reinforcement. On the second trial, the entire sequence was prompted by the therapist. The situations used in covert rehearsal were identical to those used in the social skills training group. During session one, patients imagined three situations, practicing each situation twice.

On three subsequent treatment sessions, patients practiced four situations during each session. Patients were assigned five situations to perform as homework assignments for each session. Social skills and covert reinforcement sessions each lasted 25 minutes. Patients assigned to the social skills treatment plus covert reinforcement group received both treatments as described above. Patients assigned to the nondirective therapy control group individually met with therapists and discussed interpersonal relationship problems. The therapists responded in a nondirective manner. The combination treatment group and the control group each met for 50-minute sessions.

Assessment consisted of patients completing the Rathus Assertiveness Schedule and a subset of the SRI (namely, factors 1, 3, and 6, which were summed to provide one score) at pretreatment, posttreatment, and follow-up. The subset of the SRI that was administered specifically dealt with giving and receiving criticism. Patients also participated in a role-play test at each assessment. In the role-play test patients were asked to respond to social situations on a prerecorded audiotape. Half of the situations involved a male and half involved a female confederate. Patients were instructed to imagine and act as if they actually were in the situations described and to respond at the end of a prerecorded message. The patient's verbal response was recorded on a second audiotape recorder. Order of the situations was randomized. After follow-up data had been collected, all audiotapes were randomly presented to three experimentally blind raters who independently rated each patient on each situation for anxiety and social skill. Ratings were made on 11-point Likert scales. Interrater reliabilities for skill and anxiety were .92 and .89, respectively.

To determine whether there were significant pretreatment differences among the treatment groups on any of the dependent measures, analyses of variance were performed on the pretreatment data. No significant differences were found. Pretest, posttest, and follow-up group mean scores for the judges' ratings of social skill showed that patients in the social skills treatment group performed better from pre- to posttest and from posttest to follow-up than did patients in any other group. Results of repeated measures analyses of variance and appropriate follow-up tests indicated that the social skills treatment group had significantly better performance at posttest and follow-up than groups that did not receive social skills training. Pretest, postttest, and follow-up group mean scores for rated anxiety showed that all patients, regardless of treatment groups, performed with less anxiety across time. Results of statistical analyses indicated that the decrease in anxiety across time was significant.

Pretest, posttest, and follow-up group mean scores for the three-factor SRI skill measure showed improvement across time. This effect was significant according to a repeated measures analysis of variance. Further analyses revealed that the combined treatment group improved patients' SRI skill scores more than did other treatments. Pretest, post-test, and follow-up group mean scores for the SRI anxiety measure showed no differences between the groups and no improvement over time. Repeated measures analyses of variance on the Rathus Assertiveness Schedule scores revealed a main effect for time of testing and further tests indicated that this effect was localized in the combined treatment group and in the covert reinforcement alone group.

The results of this analogue study once again support the effectiveness of social skills training for the patient population studied. Social skills training was more effective than both the covert reinforcement group and the nondirective therapy control group as measured by improved performance on the behavioral role-play test. Furthermore, this improvement was maintained at follow-up. The addition of covert reinforcement to social skills training did not further enhance the effectiveness of social skills training as measured in the role-play test. No treatment effects were found on either our behavioral measures of anxiety or on our self-report measure of anxiety.

In light of the results of previous studies described in this chapter, the absence of any treatment effect for anxiety was unexpected. Two obvious explanations may account for these results. First, anxiety may not have been influenced because of limited treatment. In this study only four sessions were offered as compared to our usual 15 or 20 sessions. A second possibility is that our measure of anxiety in this study was not as sensitive as that in other studies of our treatment-outcome research program. Due to logistical problems, we employed audiotaped role-play situations in this study. A videotaped measure has been employed in all of our previous work. Since many indicators of anxiety are nonverbal (e.g., knees trembling, posture, body movements, etc.) it may well be that the audiotape measure simply was not adequately sensitive in the present study.

Since we were somewhat disappointed with the results of adding a cognitive component in the present study, yet remain convinced of the potential for more cognitive interventions with our patient population, we are presently conducting a study in our clinic that will compare a more complete cognitive therapy package to our standard skills training approach. We have been encouraged by our initial clinical impressions of the effectiveness of our cognitive intervention.

CONCLUSIONS

In general, the results of our social skills group treatment program have been encouraging. Studies I, II, and III systematically demonstrate the effectiveness of our group treatment protocol in improving the social skills of our psychiatric patients. Each successive study was a more stringent test of our treatment program than the previous study. Study I showed that our protocol was more effective than outpatient treatment typically received at the mental hygiene clinic of the Providence VA Medical Center. Study II showed that the group format plus all of the training components (e.g., modeling, rehearsal, etc.) was superior to both an assessment-only control as well as a bibliotherapy group. Study III showed that our group format plus our treatment components were more effective than another substantive group treatment package. Study III was the most conservative test of our treatment in that this study controlled for possible unspecified therapist variables, group interaction variables, and so forth. Although the results of Study IV are not directly comparable to the other studies due to methodological differences, the general findings of this study also support the efficacy of social skills training with psychiatric patients. All treatment results have been clearly demonstrated on our behavioral measures of social skills. Consistently positive results have been obtained across a variety of patient populations.

One of the major thrusts of our research program has been in assessing the durability of changes that have been brought about as a result of our social skills treatment. We have demonstrated maintenance of behavior change at both 6- and 10-month follow-up intervals. We are presently analyzing data from a 2-year follow-up of our first treatment-outcome study. Although our follow-up results are not surprising given that other studies have demonstrated maintenance at follow-up assessments (e.g., Field & Test, 1975; Goldsmith & McFall, 1975), they are important in two respects. First, our follow-up data have been collected at one of the longest follow-up intervals reported in the treatment-outcome literature. Second, we have provided comparison follow-up data for appropriate control group patients in three of our studies. In the absence of such control group data, (which is typically not reported in treatment-outcome studies), it is difficult to assess the meaning of experimental treatment group data. We believe that our data provide support for the durability of our treatment's effects as measured by our dependent measures.

A paramount issue in the social skills training literature has been in demonstrating that the effects of social skills training generalize. Although many studies have demonstrated change on specific behavioral components that have been trained and then tested on measures that are somewhat similar to training situations, considerably less evidence is available from more conservative tests of generalization. For example, most studies have not demonstrated generalization as measured by improved performance in situations dissimilar to those trained (e.g., Gutride, Goldstein, & Hunter, 1973; Jaffee & Carlson, 1976). Furthermore, studies have demonstrated generalization on some measures but not on others (e.g., Falloon, Lindley, McDonald, & Marks, 1977; Marzillier, Lambert, & Kellett, 1976). For our skills training program we have demonstrated generalization from trained to untrained scenes; shown appropriate trends on our *in vivo* measures of generalization; and shown significant improvement at follow-up on real-life functional dimensions such as job status, number of acquaintances, and so forth. The fact that the results of the Clinical Outcome Criteria Scale showed that patients who received our treatment were judged to be significantly more healthy 10 months after treatment than patients receiving other treatments is of clinical importance.

Intuitively, we attribute our positive treatment results to our special emphasis on promoting the generalization of social competence. Generalization is specifically programmed through several different techniques. The primary avenue through which we attempt to promote generalization is through the extensive use of extrasession homework assignments as described earlier in this chapter. These are an essential part of every session of our treatment groups. Although the use of homework assignments is not unique to our program, comparison of this component to its counterpart in other published treatment-outcome studies suggests that we place a greater emphasis on homework than do some programs. Another aspect of our program that is designed to facilitate generalization is the incorporation of a patient's specific skill deficient problem areas into the content of his or her treatment. For example, if during a treatment session that deals with giving criticism a patient acknowledges that he or she has difficulty criticizing an unreasonable roommate, then criticism directed at this roommate will be a focus of this session for this patient. This procedure serves to tailor our program, within the general limits of our protocol, to the special needs of our patients. The obvious purpose is to make our program as relevant as possible to the needs of each and every patient. Although the link between relevancy of behaviors taught and generalization of treatment effects has not been empirically demonstrated, we feel that the more relevant the treatment, the greater the likelihood of learning and thus the greater the likelihood of generalization. Recent efforts being made by Wallace, Liberman, and their colleagues (see Chapters 1 and 2) to identify more relevant information to incorporate into their treatment package certainly seem to be a step in the right direction.

A final aspect of our program that we believe positively influences both generalization and maintenance of behavior change is the intensity and frequency of our treatment. A perusal of the literature indicates that our program offers more treatment than many other programs designed for diagnostically mixed groups of patients. Our typical group meets for 20 sessions. Other protocols call for many fewer sessions. For example, Falloon et al. (1977) offered 12 hours of treatment and Jaffee and Carlson (1976) offered 6 hours of treatment. Although even our 20-hour protocol is quite modest in comparison to Liberman's suggestion (see Chapter 1) that several months of treatment may be necessary, it should be emphasized that our work has been done with a mixed group of patients, relatively few of whom are schizophrenic, whereas his suggestions are clearly aimed at a well-diagnosed schizophrenic population. Nevertheless, we are considering expanding and intensifying our treatment protocol.

Although we are reasonably satisfied with the results of our treatment program, we feel that there is room for improvement. We are especially interested in tailoring our treatment for particular patient groups. With the advent of DSM-III (1980) and more reliable and valid diagnostic practices, we feel that more systematic work should be focused on fitting treatment protocols to patients with specific diagnoses. Such matching procedures should include guidelines as to what the optimal treatment and number of treatment sessions might be for specific behavioral disorders. Although we realize that there must always be room for accommodating to the particular needs of a particular patient, we feel that only when assessment and group treatment strategies are brought more into focus with each other can we expect optimal return from our clinical interventions.

REFERENCES

Berzon, B., Reisel, J., & Davis, D. P. PEER: An audiotape program for self-directed small groups. *Journal of Humanistic Psychology*, 1969, *9*, 71–86.

Curran, J. P., Corriveau, D. P., Monti, P. M., & Hagerman, S. Self-report measurement of social skill and social anxiety in a psychiatric population. *Behavior Modification*, 1980, *4*, 493–512.

Curran, J. P., Little, L. M., & Gilbert, F. S. Reactivity of males of differing heterosexual social anxiety to female approach and non-approach cue conditions. *Behavior Therapy*, 1978, *9*, 961.

DeLancey, A. *The effects of covert reinforcement and social skill training with psychiatric patients.* Unpublished doctoral dissertation, Boston College, 1979.

Diagnostic and statistical manual of mental disorders (3rd ed.) (DSM-III). Washington, D.C.: American Psychiatric Association, 1980.

Falloon, I. R., Lindley, P., McDonald, R., & Marks, I. M. Social skills training of outpatient groups: A controlled study of rehearsal and homework. *British Journal of Psychiatry*, 1977, *131*, 599–609.

Field, G. D., & Test, M. A. Group assertive training for severely disturbed patients. *Journal of Behavior Therapy and Experimental Psychiatry*, 1975, *6*, 129–134.

Goldsmith, J. B., & McFall, R. M. Development and evaluation of an interpersonal skill-training program for psychiatric inpatients. *Journal of Abnormal Psychology*, 1975, *84*, 51–58.

Gutride, M. E., Goldstein, A. P., & Hunter, G. F. The use of modeling and role-playing to increase social interaction among asocial psychiatric patients. *Journal of Consulting and Clinical Psychology*, 1973, *40*, 408–415.

Harris, R. J. *A primer of multivariate statistics.* New York: Academic Press, 1975.

Jaffe, P. G., & Carlson, P. M. Relative efficacy of modeling and instructions in eliciting social behavior from chronic psychiatric patients. *Journal of Consulting and Clinical Psychology*, 1976, *44*, 200–207.

Laska, E. M. The multi-state information system. In J. L. Crawford, D. W. Morgan, & D. T. Ginturco (Eds.), *Progress in mental health information systems: Computer applications.* Cambridge, Mass.: Ballinger, 1974.

Marzillier, J. S., Lambert, C., & Kellett, J. A controlled evaluation of systematic desensitization and social skills training for socially inadequate psychiatric patients. *Behaviour Research and Therapy*, 1976, *14*, 225–238.

Monti, P. M., Curran, J. P., Corriveau, D. P., DeLancey, A., & Hagerman, S. Effects of social skills training groups and sensitivity training groups with psychiatric patients. *Journal of Consulting and Clinical Psychology*, 1980, *48* (2), 241–248.

Monti, P. M., Fink, E., Norman, W., Curran, J. P., Hayes, S., & Caldwell, A. The effect of social skills training groups and social skills bibliotherapy with psychiatric patients. *Journal of Consulting and Clinical Psychology*, 1979, *47*, 189–191.

Paul, G. L. Behavior modification research: Design and tactics. In C. M. Franks (Ed.), *Behavior therapy: Appraisal and status.* New York: McGraw-Hill, 1969.

Rathus, S. A. A 30-item schedule for assessing assertive behavior. *Behavior Therapy*, 1973, *4*, 398–406.

Richardson, F. C., & Tasto, D. L. Development and factor analysis of a social anxiety inventory. *Behavior Therapy*, 1976, *7*, 453–462.

Shostrom, E. L. *Manual: Personal Orientation Inventory.* San Diego: Educational & Industrial Testing Service, 1966.

Strauss, J., & Carpenter, W. The prediction of outcome in schizophrenia: I. Characteristics of outcome. *Archives of General Psychiatry*, 1972, *27*, 739–746.

7

COMMUNICATION SKILLS TRAINING FOR MARRIED COUPLES

NEIL S. JACOBSON

"What we have here is a failure to communicate." This famous line, uttered by Paul Newman in the film *Cool-Hand Luke*, is an apt summary for our society's view of why marriages fail. Breakdowns in communication are implicated as a cause of marital dysfunction in virtually every major theoretical model of marital distress. Therefore it is not surprising that communication training comprises the core of a variety of marital therapy regimens, despite differences in theoretical underpinnings. Behavior therapy is no exception to this trend. Although communication training is not the only intervention strategy in the repertoire of the behavioral marital therapist, it has played a major role in most widely disseminated programs (Jacobson & Margolin, 1979; Margolin & Weiss, 1978; O'Leary & Turkewitz, 1978; Weiss & Birchler, 1978).

This chapter provides an overview of communication training programs for married couples, emphasizing those that have evolved from a behavioral perspective. In the first section, a review of the research literature on the role of communication deficits in marital conflict is provided. Then the basic strategies for communication training are presented. A third section surveys a variety of communication skills that couples are taught, along with rationales for teaching these skills. Finally, a brief review of the outcome literature will be undertaken, literature that investigates the effectiveness of communication training both in isolation and when combined with other techniques.

Neil S. Jacobson. Department of Psychology, University of Washington, Seattle, Washington.

THE ROLE OF COMMUNICATION DEFICITS IN MARITAL CONFLICT

Until the 1970s, the view that communication deficits were a major source of marital conflict was popular, although the supporting evidence was largely anecdotal or based on research plagued by methodological problems. Gottman (1979) has recently reviewed this early literature. It is clear from his review that the centrality of communication in theoretical conceptions of effective marital functioning has been taken for granted ever since experts began to speculate on the reasons for marital disruption. This largely single-minded focus on communication has tended to preclude the careful scrutiny of other variables that may be equally or more important in determining the success of a marriage. Couples spend a substantial proportion of their time, both together and apart, engaging in activities other than direct interaction. But it is direct interaction that has been, and continues to be, the focus of most theoretical speculation. This trend has been perpetuated in recent years by behavioral researchers. Thus, in the literature that I will be reviewing, the reader should remember that there has been very little work done on the relative importance of communication to a successful marriage.

OBSERVATIONAL RESEARCH

By far the most common strategy for studying marital communication has been to observe couples engaged in structured interaction in laboratory settings. These studies have typically focused on discriminating between distressed and nondistressed couples in terms of their communication styles.

The pioneering work in this area was conducted by Robert L. Weiss and his associates (Birchler, Weiss, & Vincent, 1975; Vincent, Friedman, Nugent, & Messerly, 1979; Vincent, Weiss, & Birchler, 1975). In these studies, couples were instructed to interact in two types of tasks: one was a conflict resolution task, where spouses attempted to agree on the solutions to hypothetical marital conflict situations; the second task was a casual conversation. Trained observers coded the behaviors of both spouses, using the Marital Interaction Coding System (Hops, Wills, Patterson, & Weiss, 1971). Interactional behaviors were first given one of 30 behavioral codes, and then summarized into one of six summary codes (positive verbal behavior, positive nonverbal behavior, negative verbal behavior, negative nonverbal behavior, problem-solving behavior, and neutral problem description). It is important to note that these summary codes were not empirically derived, but represented the experimenters' beliefs regarding what constituted positive and negative communication.

The studies demonstrated that distressed couples engaged in a significantly greater frequency of negative behaviors than did nondistressed couples on both the conflict resolution task and in casual conversation. Positive behaviors were significantly more common in the repertoires of nondistressed couples during the conflict resolution, but there were no differences between distressed and nondistressed couples during casual conversation. These differences did not reflect general communication deficiencies in distressed spouses, since they were not manifested in interactions with opposite-sex strangers. Thus, the observed differences were relationship specific.

Gottman (1979) has reported a number of studies that both replicated and extended the findings on communication discrepancies between distressed and nondistressed couples. Gottman used his own coding system, in which each behavioral unit was given a verbal code (based on speech content) and a nonverbal code (based on affect, which was inferred from vocal, facial, and kinesic cues). There were a number of variables that discriminated distressed from nondistressed couples during conflict resolution tasks. Interestingly, verbal behavior was a much less powerful discriminator than nonverbal behavior. In fact, very few differences were uncovered when verbal behavior was observed in isolation. The most striking verbal difference was that the ratio of agreements to agreements plus disagreements was significantly higher for nondistressed couples. Most of the striking discrepancies occurred on the nonverbal, or affect, dimension. Distressed couples exhibited negative affect significantly more often, and neutral affect significantly less often, than did nondistressed couples.

In addition to discriminating between distressed and nondistressed couples on the cumulative frequencies of various behaviors, Gottman (1979) conducted sequential analyses of the interaction sequences. A number of interesting findings emerged. First, distressed couples exhibited negative reciprocity; that is, the probability of one spouse responding with negative affect following a partner's negative affect was significantly greater than the unconditional probability of negative affect. No such pattern was discernible for nondistressed couples. This means that distressed couples tended to produce chains of negative behaviors; one negative tended to prompt another. Nondistressed couples, on the other hand, tended to intersperse their negative behaviors in such a way that such chains were less likely. Second, when discussing conflict areas in their relationship, nondistressed couples produced validation loops at the beginning of their discussion. One partner would state the problem, and this would be followed by either an agreement or some other supportive remark by the partner. The function of these validation loops was to lend the appearance of one partner attempting to understand the other's concerns. No such patterns were evident in the interaction patterns of distressed couples. Instead, distressed couples began their discussion with sequences labeled by Gottman (1979) as "cross-complaining" sequences, in which partners would simply alternate complaints, with no attempt on the part of either spouse to validate the other's remarks. Third, although both distressed and nondistressed couples would spend some time arguing during the middle phase of the discussion, nondistressed couples would end up with an agreement or contract, whereas distressed couples were less likely to reach resolution.

Both Gottman's research and the research by Weiss and his associates demonstrate that when distressed couples talk to each other, particularly when they are in conflict, they exhibit an inordinately high rate of behaviors that others see as negative. Gottman has further demonstrated that there are systematic differences in the strategies used by distressed couples to deal with conflict. The fact that there are specific interactional correlates of marital distress, and the fact that these correlates do correspond to our intuitive conceptions of positive and negative behavior, suggest that marital conflict is associated with communication deficiencies, and in particular deficiencies in interactional strategies for dealing with conflict.

However, all of the research reviewed thus far relies on judgments by the investigators as to what constitutes positive and negative communication. What about the spouses themselves? Gottman, Notarius, Markman, Bank, Yoppi, and Rubin (1976) conducted a study in which spouses were asked to rate their communication as well as their partners' communication. Each time one of them spoke, the spouse rated the intent of his or her own remark on a 5-point scale ranging from "superpositive" to "supernegative." The partner was also asked to rate each remark delivered to him or her in terms of its impact, using the same 5-point scale. Distressed couples did report impact ratings that were significantly less positive than those of their nondistressed counterparts. However, intent ratings failed to discriminate between the two groups. In other words, distressed spouses perceived the other's remarks as significantly less positive than did nondistressed spouses, but they reported that their own remarks were intended to be as positive as those reported by nondistressed spouses. This discrepancy between intent and impact suggested to the authors that a communication deficit explanation of marital conflict was appropriate. It seemed that distressed couples were well intentioned, but their remarks were likely to be misperceived as negative. Although this explanation is plausible, it is unfortunately confounded by the equally plausible interpretation that social desirability factors account for the intent–impact discrepancy in distressed couples. It is not socially desirable to admit to intending negative communication, and it could be that distressed spouses were not owning up to their negative intentions. Nevertheless, this study does provide evidence that, even when spouses themselves are the judges of the quality of communication, distressed and nondistressed couples can be differentiated on the dimension of positiveness.

Although marital distress seems to be correlated with certain communication deficiencies, it is unclear from the findings reported thus far whether or not there is a causal relationship between negative communication and marital distress. Markman (1979) completed the only study to date that suggests that such a causal relationship exists. He asked a sample of couples planning to marry to participate in a longitudinal study. Among other things, these couples engaged in a communication task similar to that reported by Gottman, Notarius, Markman, Bank, Yoppi, and Rubin (1976). The couples were then followed for 2½ years. The question was, to what extent could marital satisfaction 2½ years later be predicted by the quality of communication prior to marriage? The results confirmed the prediction that communication quality was related to subsequent marital satisfaction. For example, the overall positiveness of impact ratings was significantly ($r = .61$) related to subsequent scores on a self-report questionnaire measuring marital satisfaction. Thus, at least one study has established that the quality of communication as assessed by the spouses themselves before marriage is predictive of subsequent marital satisfaction. The results of this study, combined with the cross-sectional studies, provide compelling evidence that, at the very least, there are deficiencies in communication associated with marital distress. Distressed couples seem to exhibit some general characteristics that allow them to be reliably discriminated from nondistressed couples, and these differences have been specified to the point that particular impairments in their ability to talk to each other about conflict can be identified. Distressed spouses themselves confirm these findings by reporting that their communication is less positive than that reported by nondistressed spouses.

SPOUSE OBSERVATIONS IN THE HOME

As I mentioned earlier, studies of marital communication in the laboratory have not shed much light on the relative importance of communication versus other dimensions of marital behavior in contributing to marital satisfaction. Married couples spend a small proportion of their time engaged in direct interaction, and it is reasonable to suppose that other variables play important roles in determining the quality of their marriage: they engage in shared activities, they make love and engage in other physically affectionate behaviors, and they engage in a variety of instrumental tasks. How central is communication to a satisfying marital relationship, relative to these other events?

In our laboratories at the University of Iowa, and now at the University of Washington, we have been trying to identify the effective reinforcers and punishers in both distressed and nondistressed marital relationships. Spouses are used as observers. The standard procedure, first developed by Wills, Weiss, and Patterson (1974), involves having spouses complete a lengthy behavioral checklist each evening, along with subjective, global marital satisfaction ratings. The checklist, a modified version of the Spouse Observation Checklist (Weiss & Perry, 1979), consists of over 350 items, which can be divided into subcategories tapping the various dimensions of married life. In our research the items are grouped into four categories: shared activities; physical contact; communication and direct interaction; and instrumental tasks. Each subgroup can in turn be divided into pleasing and displeasing behaviors. We have assumed that, by correlating each of the subcategories with global daily satisfaction ratings (DSR), it is possible to identify classes of behavior that are most critical for a particular couple in determing the quality of a marriage.

In a study already completed (Jacobson, Waldron, & Moore, 1980), distressed and nondistressed couples were compared. For distressed couples, the response class that best predicted DSR was negative communication and interaction, which was inversely correlated with daily satisfaction ($r = -.40$). Thus, on those days when spouses reported relatively high frequencies of displeasing communication, they were least satisfied with their relationships. For nondistressed couples, negative communication was not predictive of DSR, but positive communication was directly related to DSR. Thus, for these couples, on days when communication was positive, marital satisfaction was at its peak.

For wives, their partners' positive communication was the single best predictor of their daily satisfaction, whereas for husbands, shared activities was the most predictive. In terms of overall frequencies, nondistressed couples recorded a significantly greater number of communicative acts, and significantly fewer displeasing communications, than did distressed couples (Jacobson & Moore, in press). These data confirm the observational studies and underscore the destructive impact of negative communication in distressed couples. More than any other class of behavior, negative communication detracts from marital satisfaction in distressed couples. It seems as if distressed couples rely on communication more than any other means to punish one another. It should be noted that these differences between distressed and nondistressed couples cannot be reduced to differences in the frequency of negative communication, since the correlations between behavior and DSR were computed after the behavioral scores were standardized, partialing out base rate differences.

To conclude, there is some basis in the experimental literature on marital exchange for focusing on communication training as a treatment strategy. Although the research has not established communication deficiencies as the primary cause of marital conflict, such deficiencies are at least a by-product of marital distress. And, since our own research suggests that communication problems exacerbate marital conflict in distressed couples, it seems reasonable to attempt to correct these deficiencies as a way of turning the relationship around. In the next section, strategies designed to correct faulty marital communication will be described.

COMMUNICATION TRAINING

What follows is a review of treatment procedures designed to correct dysfunctional communication in married couples. The review will be selective and will focus in some depth on procedures used in my own laboratories. Elsewhere, I have distinguished between general communication training and training that is specifically designed to help couples resolve conflicts more effectively. This distinction can be attributed to Weiss's emphasis on modality checking (Weiss & Birchler, 1978; Weiss, Hops, & Patterson, 1973). At times the task facing couples is one of providing empathy, support, and understanding. These skills are really quite different from the more task-oriented skills needed to bring about behavior change. Both sets of skills will be emphasized in the upcoming review. But, whatever the skills, there are certain treatment strategies that are useful and have been used in a variety of social skills training programs. These will be described first.

INTERVENTION STRATEGIES

Like any behavior therapy training program designed to increase interpersonal competence, marital therapy adopts the assumption that there are certain instructional components that will maximize the likelihood that the new skills will be acquired, maintained, and generalized to the natural environment. Behavioral communication training is explicitly didactic and instigative. It relies both on in-session practice and homework assignments. Let us now examine the specific instructional components, along with the rationales for each.

Instructions

Since behavioral communication is didactic, at the core of every treatment program lies a set of systematic instructions for communicating more effectively. Usually, these instructions are presented verbally with the aid of treatment manuals (cf. Gottman, Markman, Notarius, & Gonso, 1976; Jacobson & Margolin, 1979). Often, these instructions involve modeling. Modeling is a very useful way to present instruction to couples for a number of reasons (cf. Eisler & Hersen, 1973; Jacobson, 1977b; Jacobson & Margolin, 1979); in addition to all of the general instructional aids modeling provides, it helps cut through power struggles by presenting couples with a face-saving way to change their behavior. By simply imitating the therapist, spouses can attribute their more positive, collaborative behavior to emulation of the therapist. Although ultimately collaborative behavior is essential to the production of lasting changes in the relationship, imitation of the therapist can often suffice as a temporary expedient.

Marital therapists must guard against one major disadvantage of modeling; imitation is often considerably easier than producing the desired behavioral sequences on one's own, and therefore successful imitation can serve to cover up deficient learning. In order to guard against this problem, modeling should be faded as treatment progresses and spouses should gradually assume more and more of the responsibility for the production of desirable behaviors on their own. Moreover, debriefing processes can be structured into the modeling procedures to make sure that spouses are processing the events that they are observing. For example, spouses can be asked how the modeled performance differs from their own, a question that forces them to reflect on what they have been observing and grasp the essential basis for distinguishing between their own behavior and the behavior of the model.

It is also important that the therapist model behaviors for both spouses, in order to guard against alliances with only one. It is not unusual for spouses to become competitive during communication training, and to try to take advantage of modeling by forcing an alliance with the therapist against the spouse whose behavior is being corrected. In addition to equalizing the amount of corrective modeling for both partners, the therapist can minimize the likelihood of such alliances by cutting off efforts of one spouse to criticize the spouse whose behavior is being corrected.

Feedback

The therapist must provide immediate, regular, and consistent feedback to spouses regarding their communication. This feedback can be provided verbally, or by means of audio- or videotapes. The relative advantages and disadvantages of the two types of feedback have been discussed elsewhere (Jacobson, 1977b; Jacobson & Margolin, 1979), and will not be repeated here. But it is important that the feedback be discrete, specific, and stated in neutral, nonjudgmental language. It is also important that spouses receive positive feedback for positive communication rather than simply corrective feedback for negative communication.

Behavior Rehearsal

Through practicing the behaviors modeled and suggested by the therapist, couples have the opportunity to attain a degree of mastery impossible without such practice. Practice also provides the therapist with feedback. Without such feedback, there is no way of knowing the extent to which the instruction and feedback have been understood. With the addition of behavior rehearsal the learning process can be thought of as analogous to a shaping procedure, where the practiced performance, followed by feedback and further instructions, gradually comes to resemble the behavior that the therapist is desiring to produce.

Strategies for Fostering Generalization

Since the goals of communication training are not simply to produce desirable communication in the therapist's office, specific steps must be undertaken to ensure that desirable communication is transferred to the home. Homework assignments, where skills taught during therapy sessions are repeated and extended, are an essential component of the generalization process. At first, homework assignments are structured to be as similar to the therapy sessions as possible, including the same prompts used to elicit desirable behavior in the treatment sessions. Couples record their practice sessions on audiocassettes, as a way of extending the therapist's influence into the home. Gradually, the prompts are faded so as to promote increased self-regulation. A second strategy for fostering generalization includes gradual fading of therapy sessions, with more and more of the responsibility for effective communication simultaneously transferred to the couple. For example, therapy sesisons that were once held weekly may be reduced to biweekly sessions, with the couple encouraged to meet on their own during the intervening week at a prearranged time. This meeting can be characterized as a "state of the relationship" session. These sessions are gradually to become substitutes for meetings with the therapist. The policy is to provide spouses with the skills they need to become their own therapists subsequent to the termination of therapy.

Finally, the treatment sessions themselves are structured in such a way that generalization is fostered. As in previous examples, spouses are frequently asked to reflect on and discuss what they have learned, and to apply their newly acquired communication skills to new situations. At the end of every session they will be asked to summarize what they have learned about good communication during the past hour. As much as possible, spouses are urged to take an active role in the learning process, and to learn principles rather than simply respond correctly to therapist prompts.

The summary of interaction strategies has been brief (see also Jacobson & Margolin, 1979). Basically, couples are taught communication skills using the same strategies used to teach interpersonal skills to individuals. The process is a highly structured, didactic one, with the therapist directing and prompting change, and then gradually receding so that the spouses can develop the capacity for functioning on their own.

It is reasonable to ask whether all of this is really necessary. Despite our predilection for behavior rehearsal and systematic feedback, there has been surprisingly little research conducted on the relative contribution of these fairly elaborate skill training intervention strategies. Recently, however, we completed a study that seems to vindicate our insistence on the use of those procedures (Jacobson & Anderson, 1980). Couples seeking a marital enrichment experience were randomly assigned to one of five treatment groups: a waiting list control group, a group receiving the instructional treatment without either feedback or behavior rehearsal; a group receiving instructions plus feedback but no behavior rehearsal; a group receiving instructions plus behavior rehearsal but no feedback; and a complete treatment group receiving instructions, feedback, and behavior rehearsal. The treatment package consisted of instructions involving training in problem-solving skills, which will be described in detail later in this chapter. Acquisition of the communications skills was assessed through observations of marital interaction before and after therapy. Frequency counts of positive problem-solving behavior, as well as global ratings of problem-solving effectiveness, were included as criteria for improvement. On both measures, couples receiving the complete treatment manifested more improvement than any other condition. In fact, this was the only condition that showed significant, consistent improvement relative to the control group. Thus, it seems that both feedback and behavior rehearsal are essential, at least for the acquisition of problem-solving skills. Their effects seem to be synergistic rather than additive since neither feedback nor behavior rehearsal, when used in isolation from the other, lead to significant improvement.

Now that I have presented an overview of the intervention strategies, the following sections will elaborate on the content of behavioral communication training programs, that is, the skills that couples are actually taught.

GENERAL COMMUNICATION TRAINING

It is difficult to generalize about the kinds of skills couples are taught in communication training programs, since to some extent communication deficits are as numerous and variegated as the number of distressed couples. But there do seem to be some general deficiencies that occur often enough to warrant discussion. All of the skills to be discussed in this section can be thought of as the "soft" skills, to distinguish them from the more task-oriented problem-solving skills designed to bring about behavior change. They can be thought of as ways to promote closeness and intimacy, rather than interactions to alter the status quo.

Listening Skills

Both paraphrasing and reflecting have been emphasized by many proponents of communication training (Gottman, Markman, Notarius, & Gonso, 1976; Guerney, 1977; Jacobson & Margolin, 1979; O'Leary & Turkewitz, 1978; Weiss & Birchler, 1978). These are both ways that one spouse can communicate to another that they are interested in what the other person is saying, that they understand, and that they support the other person. There are many situations in married life where one spouse simply wants to talk, and needs the understanding that can only be provided by active listening. These are uncommon skills in a marital relationship. A more common response is to give advice, or to simply listen in silence. But it is very reinforcing to have another person's undivided attention, and often the feedback that one is understood is more important than even potentially valuable advice. Paraphrasing and reflecting are also useful in helping couples learn to track the behavior of one another more accurately.

Paraphrasing simply requires that the listener summarize what the speaker has said. Reflecting adds an inference about the emotional state underlying the speaker's remark. One major caution in the use of reflecting is that, by asking listeners to draw inferences regarding the feelings implicit in the speaker's remark, couples are being advised to mind read. This tactic can be controlling and manipulative, especially if delivered in an accusatory tone and accompanied by negative affect. For example, a listener can defend against a criticism by emphasizing an alleged feeling that is not really to the point, and thereby avoid having to deal directly with the criticism:

HUSBAND: Honey, you forgot to enter this check and the next one bounced.
WIFE: You sound angry.

Reflecting can also be unsupportive and insensitive, as in the following example where a reflection is used to contradict the speaker's own explanation of her behavior:

WIFE: I don't want to have sex tonight; I'm tired.

HUSBAND: What I hear you saying is that you don't feel close to me tonight, probably because I was flirting with Jane at the party last night.

Validation

Validation refers to a particular type of listener response, one that was common in the nondistressed couples studied by Gottman (1979). A validating response is one that affirms that the speaker's remark is legitimate and understandable. All listener responses should be validating. Jacobson and Margolin (1979) illustrate how even an outrageous suggestion on the part of the speaker can be validated:

WIFE: Steve, the baby-sitter of ours is really doing a lousy job. She keeps forgetting to change Karin's diaper, last night she fell asleep with the stove on, and two weeks ago she didn't even show up. I've been thinking about this, and I've decided what we should do. I think we should knock her off—kill her.

HUSBAND: I understand that you're upset at the baby-sitter and frustrated by our inability to change her. Your frustration is real and legitimate. I think, however, that your solution is not the best way to deal with the problem, and we should explore some alternatives.

The husband here, although disagreeing with his wife, explicitly affirms the legitimacy of her feelings. Since the distinctions between paraphrases, reflections, and validations are often subtle, extreme examples such as the above are often useful. If one can validate a proposal to kill the baby-sitter, one can validate almost anything.

Validation can be particularly useful when the speaker is emotionally upset. Often, spouses who are upset want to know that they are accepted and loved even while upset, and that their feelings are understandable. Couples often have difficulties in such situations, because the listener feels compelled to provide a prescription, and since that is often impossible, the outcome is frustrating for both participants. The speaker fails to obtain needed support, and the listener feels like a failure. Training in validation skills can greatly enhance the ability of marital partners to cope with such situations.

Feeling Talk

It is not uncommon for one spouse to complain that the partner is unwilling to disclose personal feelings. Direct training aimed at promoting feeling expression can be helpful in adding feeling expression to the unexpressive partner's repertoire. Jacobson and Margolin (1979) conceptualized feeling expression as a skill consisting of four phases: noticing feelings as they occur, and being able to associate them with particular situations; having these feelings serve as discriminative stimuli for disclosing those feelings later to the partner; being able to recall those feelings retrospectively to make disclosure possible; and ensuring that feeling expression is reinforced by the partner.

As a strategy for helping spouses learn to recognize feelings and associate them with events as they occur, self-monitoring is recommended. Checklists of various possible feelings are also used (e.g., anger, amusement, disgust) so that the process of labeling feelings is facilitated. Recall is facilitated naturally when spouses continuously track and record the relationship between events and feelings. Cues placed in the home environment can help spouses in remembering to discuss these feelings with their spouses. Finally, careful attention must be given to the interpersonal consequences of feeling expression. The expresser will be quickly extinguished by belittling comments from the partner, criticisms or judgments about the appropriateness of the feelings, or ignoring the disclosure altogether.

Frequently, spouses object to the artificial or structured nature of feeling talk exercises. They express understandable concern about the wisdom of fostering spontaneous feeling expression through contrived, forced procedures. But, as we usually explain when such objections are voiced, labeling, recognizing, and disclosing feelings constitute skills that will not become habitual until they are well learned.

Negative Feeling Expression

Although distressed spouses usually come into therapy with a great deal to complain about, they are often at a loss as to how to share this information with the partner in a way that avoids making matters worse. The destructive consequences of either keeping angry feelings private, or expressing them in a way that alienates the partner are well known to marital therapists. If angry feelings are verbalized at all, they are often augmented by threats, demands, and put-downs. Distressed couples also tend to be vague regarding the antecedents of their anger, so that valuable information is lost, and the probability of eradicating the situation is low. As a result of these deficiencies in anger expression, the recipient tends to either cross-complain (Gottman, 1979), or in other ways respond defensively so that the impact of the disclosure is destructive rather than constructive.

But anger disclosure need not be destructive in its impact. In training couples to express anger more productively, we encourage them to restrict their disclosures to simple feeling–cause statements, including nothing more than a statement of the feeling and a specification of the behavioral cause of the feeling. "I am angry at you for coming home late" exemplifies the simple feeling–cause statement. Threats ("If you come home late again I will leave you"), demands ("I insist that you stop coming home late"), and put-downs ("You are inconsiderate") are prohibited.

Feeling–cause statements have no unnecessary material to deflect the discussion. The basis for the feeling is specific and clearly communicated. The recipient has little basis for cross-complaining or in other ways responding defensively. The most common response is to accommodate to the other's expressed feeling.

Positive Expressions

Statements of affection and caring tend to drop out of couples' interactional repertoires with time. Yet these positive feeling expressions often remain powerfully reinforcing for both partners. Often, statements such as "I love you" are avoided not because the feelings are absent but because it is assumed that there is no need to express them. It is erroneously assumed that the partner is already aware of these feelings. Even when this is true, many spouses find it reinforcing to hear those feelings expressed. In some cases, positive feeling expressions are inhibited by deficiencies in the expresser's repertoire, or by embarrassment about expressing love to the partner. Behavioral rehearsal can be a useful way to enhance one's repertoire in these instances. Suggestions from the receiver are encouraged, since he or she usually knows what is most reinforcing.

By specifically focusing on active listening, validation, feeling talk, and negative and positive feeling expression, I do not mean to imply that these are the primary skills that distressed couples lack. Rather, these are examples of the more common emphasis in communication training with distressed couples. In the next section, the focus will be on the more task-oriented training procedures that focus on enhancing couples' ability to negotiate behavior change in their relationship, when behavior change is necessary.

PROBLEM-SOLVING TRAINING

Problem-solving training is focused on the acquisition of conflict resolution skills. Although such procedures were developed prior to the publication of Gottman's (1979) findings (cf. Jacobson & Margolin, 1979; Patterson & Hops, 1972; Weiss, 1978; Weiss *et al.*, 1973), Gottman's research vindicates our belief that distressed couples are markedly deficient in their capacity for dealing effectively with conflict. Training in problem-solving skills is a very important component of behavioral marital therapy, not only because it provides needed instruction in strategies for dealing effectively with conflict, but also because, despite the process focus of problem-solving training, content issues are also addressed, since couples solve presenting problems as they acquire the new skills. Problem-solving training, in its ideal form, is also preventive, since the skills are designed to be applied in the future, subsequent to the termination of therapy, when new problems arise.

In this section, some general aspects of problem-solving training will be delineated, followed by a brief summary of the guidelines that couples are asked to follow when they talk to each other about conflicts.

Problem Solving as Specialized Communication

Couples are asked to conceptualize problem-solving behavior as specialized communication, unlike any other. Every effort is made to place problem-solving interaction under the stimulus control of rules, so as to maximize the likelihood that old, maladaptive behavior patterns will not interfere with effective conflict resolution. To start with, couples are instructed to hold their problem-solving sessions at certain preordained times, and to avoid attempting behavior change at other times. The scheduling of problem-solving sessions at specified, regular times is an attempt to counteract destructive attempts to deal with conflict "at the scene of the crime." Emotional distance, which is greatly facilitated by a temporal lag between the occurrence of a conflict and an attempt at resolution, is necessary in order for the couples to collaborate in an attempt to improve their relationship. Usually, problem-solving sessions are conducted in the evening, after the children have either retired or are at some safe distance. The telephone should be either unplugged or ignored when it rings.

Coping with Couples' Resistance to Problem Solving

As even a cursory perusal of the problem-solving manual will indicate (cf. Jacobson & Margolin, 1979), effective problem solving requires collaborative behavior. It requires that all marital conflict areas are viewed as common problems that negatively affect the relationship, and that the resolution of each problem is in the interest of both partners, despite the potentially costly nature of a particular change agreement for one or both individuals. For example, one wife wanted to discuss her husband's tendency to procrastinate when it came to completing projects around the house. In order to solve this problem successfully and in a collaborative manner, the benefits to the relationship had to be viewed as primary by the husband, in order to override his desire to continue his role as a procrastinator. This tendency to view problem solving as a cooperative venture is often diametrically opposed to distressed couples' typical strategies for dealing with conflict. The typical strategies often involve competitive power struggles where each person is attempting to get as much from the other as possible, while giving as little as possible. Or the goal of the discussion may not be resolution at all, but may involve simply the expressing of angry feelings, or, in the worst of cases, the motive may be one of revenge, and the goal may be focused on hurting the partner. Couples must be shifted from a competitive to a collaborative set (Jacobson, 1977b), and this requires no small degree of clinical skill. To produce collaborative behavior, the therapist must, first of all, insist upon it. When couples exhibit tendencies toward destructive, competitive behavior during problem-solving sessions, the therapist must interrupt to remind them of the rules, and enforce behaviors that are consistent with a collaborative set. When spouses protest that collaborative behavior is discrepant with their current feelings, it is often appropriate to request such behavior anyway. If the appropriate behaviors can be prompted, the beneficial consequences to the relationship are usually sufficient to convince couples that future collaboration is in their best interests. In other words, collaborative behavior can be encouraged without waiting for a change in feelings that are consistent with such behavior. If the therapist can produce a commitment to collaborate, whatever reservations the couple have, a process is set in motion that usually produces feelings that are consistent with that behavior.

The therapist who is desirous of producing collaborative problem-solving behavior would be ill advised to stifle couples' tendencies toward arguing or fighting. The goal is not to eliminate arguing and fighting, but rather to establish problem solving as a viable alternative to be used at times, when the goal is constructive behavior change. The task consists of demonstrating to couples that, although arguing may be cathartic and in other ways reinforcing, it is not viable as the sole response to conflict. When spouses depart from the rules of problem solving, and begin to behave competitively and abusively toward one another, the therapist might interrupt them with the following: "You are not collaborating. Have you decided that you don't want to problem-solve?" If they have decided that they prefer to fight, the therapist will allow them to do so, but they will be asked to move to a different part of the room, and the therapist will withdraw from his or her normally active role, by immersing himself or herself in work, or simply by turning away. What is important here is not that the couple always problem-solve, but that when they fight instead of opting to problem-solve, they realize what they are doing, and are made aware of the consequences of their choice. When the differences between the two approaches to resolving conflict are understood in this way, few couples opt to continue fighting.

Another strategy for fostering collaborative problem solving is to delay the onset of training until the couple has already derived some benefit from therapy. Since problem solving is a demanding task, and since it requires collaboration, its chances of succeeding are greatly enhanced if some progress has already been made. Behavioral marital therapy is multifaceted, and there exists a number of intervention strategies that minimize the demands made on couples (cf. Jacobson & Margolin, 1979). Typically, problem-solving training will not be the initial intervention strategy employed.

Problem Definition versus Problem Solution

Problem-solving training involves instruction in highly structured, specialized modes of communication. A problem-solving session is divided into two major components. The first component is a problem definition phase, where the task is to arrive at a mutual understanding of the problem, as experienced by the spouse responsible for the agenda. The skills that are required during this phase include pinpointing, feeling expression, and active listening skills. Until the problem has been adequately identified, a discussion of possible solutions is prohibited. The solution phase is radically different from the definition phase, and begins as soon as the definition has been arrived at. The exclusive focus during the solution phase is on producing an agreement that will eliminate the problem. Usually, but not always, this agreement will involve some sort of behavior change on the part of one or both partners. During this phase, any return to behaviors appropriate to the definition phase is prohibited.

The division of a problem-solving session into two distinct phases anticipates many of the difficulties that plague couples who are attempting to resolve relationship conflicts. Relatively distinct skills are required in the two phases. The definition phase requires that couples adhere to some general communication skills that foster clear communication. Our experience has been that couples often discuss conflict areas with differing conceptions of what the problem is, because their communication has been unclear. Reaching a viable agreement under such conditions is highly unlikely. It is equally problematic to include in the discussion of various solutions behaviors that are better suited for the definition phase. Couples often become fixated on describing problems, and never move with any determination toward making the necessary changes that would remedy the situation. Problem-solving training is explicitly directed toward change; this emphasis is underscored by the devotion of the second phase to producing a viable change agreement.

Let us now examine more specifically the guidelines for each of the phases of a problem-solving session.

Guidelines for Defining Problems

The procedure for defining problems is notable both for its guidelines and for those behaviors that are contraindicated. Assuming that, for any given problem-solving session, there is one spouse who has a complaint, and the other who is the receiver of the complaint, consider the goals for each spouse. The spouse who has the complaint wants to communicate to the partner precisely what is bothering him or her. He or she wants to communicate the complaint in such a way that the partner will remain collaborative and engaged in the task. Thus, specificity is important, along with whatever cues are necessary to minimize the likelihood that the partner will become alienated or defensive. The receiver's task, as defined by the problem-solving guidelines, is to listen carefully to what the communicator is saying, ask questions to clarify the nature of the problem, and make sure that he or she understands what the problem is, and that the understanding is demonstrated to the partner.

The most common pitfall to the efficient formulation and definition of a problem is the tendency for couples to compete during this phase. Gottman (1979) has labeled this phenomenon "cross-complaining." One variant of the phenomenon is for the listener to respond to a complaint with a complaint of his or her own. Below is an example:

HUSBAND: I am upset with you for being inconsistent in your methods of disciplining the children.

WIFE: Well, I'm upset with you for never playing with the children.

Another common variant is to either deny ("I do discipline the children consistently"), defend ("It is good to be inconsistent with children"), or in other ways invalidate the complaint ("I can't help being inconsistent with the children"). Once a debate regarding the legitimacy of a problem begins, it is very difficult to terminate. The issue becomes the rightness or wrongness of the complaint. We circumvent this problem by changing the issue to the following: What is it that X is upset about? We define the receiver's task as twofold: understanding the complainer's defined problem, and acknowledging that concern. It is simply not an issue whether or not the complainer is right. Rightness or justifiability is neither assumed nor denied; it is simply removed from consideration. It is not part of the task of defining problems. The receiver is assured that an avoidance of the issues of blame or responsibility does not imply an admission of guilt; rather, such questions are simply not part of the task of problem definition. By defining away these common tendencies to defend and deny responsibility, we allow couples to get beyond this severe obstacle to effective problem solving. Receivers initially feel stifled by this constraint, but they are assured that they will have an opportunity to address these concerns at a later point in the session. By postponing this defensive behavior to a later stage of the discussion, the probability of its occurrence is greatly reduced, provided that the complainer has not prompted it.

The complainer has an important impact on the receiver's likelihood of responding defensively. There is much that the complainer can do to reduce this tendency, and many of the guidelines for the receiver's behavior are designed to facilitate this end. First, by defining the complaint in specific behavioral terms, the receiver is less likely to perceive it as a global attack. Second, by placing the complaint in a context that emphasizes positive aspects of the relationship as well, the receiver is more likely to put the complaint in perspective. For example, complaints are to be prefaced by some positive statements about the relationship, such as, "I appreciate the effort you've been making to share affection and express positive feelings. The only thing I feel like we still need to work on is being honest with one another about when we're angry, and expressing the anger directly." Third, the complainer is urged to admit to his or her role in perpetuating the problem. Since most relationship conflict areas are interactional, definitions that include the roles of both partners are usually more complete. But beyond this, spouses who are the objects of complaints from the partner are much more likely to be receptive when the complainer admits to some sort of complicity in the occurrence or maintenance of the problem.

To summarize this discussion for problem definitions, following is a list of the guidelines: (1) begin with something positive; (2) be specific; (3) express your feelings; (4) admit to your role in the problem; (5) be brief.

Problem Solutions

Once the problem is defined, the discussion is focused on arriving at a workable solution to the problem. The culmination of this discussion is a written change agreement, which specifies the behavior changes of each partner that will best eliminate the problem. The skills involved in this phase of the problem-solving session include brainstorming, negotiation skills, and the skills involved in formulating workable agreements. The specific tasks involved are the following: (1) generating alternative solutions; (2) discussing the pros and cons of each alternative; (3) integrating the desirable alternatives into a specific contract or agreement; (4) recording the agreement in writing; and (5) testing the agreement through implementation.

Brainstorming is used to generate a list of potential solutions (D'Zurilla & Goldfried, 1971; Jacobson & Margolin, 1979). This technique involves the generation of a long list of alternatives; in fact, a premium is put on quantity, whereas quality is temporarily disregarded. Couples are urged to avoid censoring any ideas, even if they seem patently absurd. When couples first begin brainstorming, the therapist often participates in the generation of alternatives, including a few obviously absurd solutions, so that the spouses quickly learn that the goal of brainstorming is quantity, not quality. Brainstorming is immensely valuable for a number of reasons. For one thing, its structure forces partners to maintain a solution focus, rather than returning to definitional concerns. In addition, the technique liberates couples from their tendency to inhibit ideas before they are verbalized. The deemphasis on quality, and the prohibition on censorship, fosters a creative approach to conflict resolution. Out of this large quantity of uncensored proposals, a quality solution is more likely to emerge.

An additional rule of brainstorming is that spouses are prohibited from commenting on the quality of the solutions that are suggested. Thus, the exercise consists exclusively of the production of a list of proposals, one following the other.

Once the couple has exhausted their repertoire of ideas, the next phase of the problem-solving session encourages them to peruse the list and eliminate only those items that are patently absurd. Then, each proposal is considered individually. First, the positive consequences of each are considered, then the negative consequences are considered. On the basis of this discussion, an agreement is formulated, and recorded in writing. The agreement is specific, and includes exactly what behaviors on the part of each spouse are to be changed, when the behavior changes are to occur, and the conditions under which the behavior changes are to occur. A written agreement is used to obviate the need to rely on memory. Written agreements also tend to produce a more desirable degree of specificity. Finally, there is some symbolic value to having agreements recorded in writing; they serve as public commitments to implementing changes that are directed toward improving the relationship.

In the process of negotiating agreements to reduce marital conflict, two principles are emphasized. They are the principles of mutuality and compromise. Taken in tandem, these principles are designed to perpetuate the collaborative set until the agreement has been attained and successfully implemented. "Mutality" means that most effective change agreements involve change on the part of both partners. "Compromise" refers to the expectation that each spouse be willing to sacrifice for the sake of the relationship. Often, the compromise entails that each spouse settle for less than what he or she would ideally desire in the best of all possible worlds. But also, hopefully, the agreement exceeds the threshold of acceptability for each spouse.

Implementing and Renegotiating Agreements

Contracts should not be viewed as static entities, but rather as hypothesized strategies for conflict resolutions. All contracts are tenative until their effectiveness has been demonstrated. While the couple is in therapy, a portion of each session is spent evaluating agreements that were reached in previous weeks. If either spouse becomes dissatisfied with the specifics of a particular agreement, this agreement is renegotiated.

Problem Solving Subsequent to the Termination of Therapy

Problem-solving training is structured so that spouses gradually assume increasing responsibility for their handling of conflict situations. It is hoped that problem solving will become a permanent part of the couple's repertoire. Toward this end, the learning process includes homework assignments during which couples hold their own therapy sessions. These sessions gradually replace regular meetings with the therapist. The content of these sessions includes an evaluation of past contracts, a renegotiation of past agreements that for some reason are now proving to be unsatisfactory, and a problem-solving session if new problems need to be discussed.

To Provide Consequences, or Not to Provide Consequences

In closing this section on problem-solving training, the use of contingencies in contracts with spouses should be mentioned. Historically, authors have recommended that contracts between married persons include the specification of consequences for either complying or not complying with its terms (Stuart, 1969; Weiss, Birchler, & Vincent, 1974). The rationale for the inclusion of contingencies is discussed in these papers, as well as in Jacobson and Margolin (1979). We have generally abandoned the use of explicit contingencies in couples' written change agreements. Our reasons for doing so follow (cf. Jacobson, 1978b; Jacobson & Margolin, 1979).

First, specified consequences are unnecessary. The stimuli that are chosen as the reinforcers for behavior changes in a contingency contract are often quite arbitrary, and virtually always selected because the spouses identify them as pleasant, rather than because their reinforcing properties have been demonstrated. Usually, these specified consequences compete with other more natural consequences in the environment, which collectively support or retard the behavior change process. As I have suggested elsewhere (Jacobson 1978b), the effective reinforcers in a marital relationship are exceedingly complex, and difficult to provide on demand. The potency of the types of consequences specified in contingency contracts often pales in comparison to other environmental events occurring as a contract is implemented. For example, as one spouse changes behavior in a desirable direction, the other's appreciation, as expressed verbally or nonverbally, usually has powerful reinforcing consequences. Moreover, as many behavior changes are implemented simultaneously, and both spouses are attempting to accommodate each other, each partner's behavior change tends to reinforce the other's in a series of implicit quid pro quos. To the extent that these favorable conditions are occurring, behavior changes are naturally reinforced, and specified consequences are unnecessary. To the extent that these favorable conditions are absent, the specified consequences are unlikely to have much of an effect.

Second, specified consequences may be self-defeating. It is our (largely untested) belief that the reinforcing impact of most important relationship behavior depends on the attributions the receiver makes as to the meaning of the giver's action. For example, imagine a hypothetical wife entering her home and being greeted by a smiling husband, who hugs her and says, "I missed you." The reinforcing impact of that series of behaviors will depend, at least in part, on her attribution regarding the meaning of his actions. If her inference is "He loves me," the impact is likely to be positive. If, however, she tells herself that "He is being nice to me so that I'll have sex with him later," or, "He wants me to call his mother," she is likely to feel manipulated rather than reinforced. Attributions that are internal, that is, those that interpret apparently loving behavior as a spontaneous expression of loving feelings, are usually reinforcing; however, a readily available external attribution may neutralize the effect of such behavior. By definition, any reinforcer that is applied as a consequence of fulfilling a contractual obligation carries with it a readily available external attribution: "He is doing this for me because the contract compels him to do so." Therefore, specification in a contract may reduce or neutralize reinforcing power.

Third, immediate contingency control may perpetuate the problems that brought them into therapy. Research by Gottman (1979) and Jacobson et al. (1980) suggests that distressed couples may utilize immediate contingencies in controlling the behavior of one another to a greater degree than nondistressed couples. Jacobson and Moore (in press) have suggested that control via immediate contingencies, whether positive or negative, may be a characteristic of dysfunctional relationships (Gottman, Notarius, Markman, Bank, Yoppi, & Rubin, 1976; Gurman & Knudson, 1978). Marital happiness may be characterized by high rates of noncontingent positive behavior; if so, it is the very absence of such discrete contingencies, and not just the base rate differences in positive behavior, that distinguishes distressed couples from nondistressed couples. Insofar as this distinction between distressed and nondistressed couples is accurate, contingency contracts encourage couples to continue their dysfunctional patterns.

Of course, the utility of contingency contracts is utlimately an empirical question. Our concerns are really speculations and remain untested. But currently, I have largely abandoned the use of contingency contracts, and substituted written change agreements without the specification of consequences for change.

RESEARCH ON THE EFFECTIVENESS OF
BEHAVIORAL COMMUNICATION TRAINING

Detailed reviews of the literature on the effectiveness of communication training, and marital therapy in general, have been published elsewhere (Gurman & Kniskern, 1978; Jacobson, 1978c, 1979a). Here I will confine my efforts to a brief summary.

In our laboratories, a series of studies have been conducted that support the efficacy of behavioral marital therapy (BMT) (Jacobson, 1977a, 1978a, 1979b; Jacobson & Anderson, 1980). Two studies have found behavioral marital therapy to produce significant positive changes relative to waiting list control groups on both observational and self-report measures (Jacobson, 1977a, 1978a); follow-ups of a 6-month (Jacobson, 1978a) and a 1-year (Jacobson, 1977a) duration suggested that these changes were persistent. One of the studies included a very credible placebo control group, and found that BMT was significantly more effective than the placebo condition. However, these studies evaluated a treatment package consisting of both problem-solving training (PST) and other procedures, and therefore the effectiveness of problem-solving training per se cannot be evaluated. The only study in our laboratories that attempted to examine PST in isolation involved a series of single-subject experiments (Jacobson, 1979b). Six severely distressed couples received PST after an instructional control treatment. In four of the six cases, PST proved to be effective in producing desired changes in the relationship. These changes persisted through follow-ups of various durations.

In addition to other studies, evaluating multifaceted BMT treatment packages (e.g., Harrell & Guerney, 1976; Liberman, Levine, Wheeler, Sanders, & Wallace, 1976), Gottman (1979) evaluated a communication training workshop for couples. In one study, group communication training was compared to a bibliotherapy control, and although both conditions produced some positive changes, they did not differ from one another. In a second study, couples received a similar treatment package presented in a 2-day intensive workshop. Significant improvement in marital satisfaction was demonstrated, compared to couples in a waiting list control condition.

O'Leary and Turkewitz (1978) reported a study comparing communication training (CT) to a behavior exchange (BE) condition (cf. Jacobson & Margolin, 1979). The results of this study are somewhat equivocal, but the most interesting finding was an age $\times$ treatment interaction, such that CT was effective for older couples only, and BE was effective for younger couples only.

Finally, Margolin and Weiss (1978) evaluated an approach to communication training that is highly innovative and does away with some of the systematic instructional components that we have outlined in this chapter. Their approach basically involves shaping helpful communication using feedback provided by the spouses themselves. Using undergraduate students as therapists, spouses provided feedback to one another each time the receiver felt that the partner had emitted a helpful communication. The sender of the message also rated his or her own communications in a similar manner. After being exposed to this shaping procedure, couples were assessed on a number of behavioral and self-report measures. A cognitive–behavioral treatment condition included a cognitive restructuring component, in which couples were reminded that negative communication reflected a skill deficit, and should not be interpreted as reflecting either negative intentions or motivational deficiencies. In addition, the cognitive–behavioral condition included an avoidance conditioning component, in that partners had to agree on the helpfulness of their communicative acts in order to avoid the sounding of an aversive buzzer. Both the cognitive–behavioral condition and the behavioral condition were compared to a nondirective control condition. Although all three conditions were equally effective in reducing the frequency of negative behavior, only the communication-shaping procedures were effective in increasing positive behavior and overall marital satisfaction. On some measures, the cognitive–behavioral condition was the most effective treatment of all. This is a promising treatment both from the standpoint of efficiency (only two treatment sessions were required) and in its use of professional manpower, since undergraduates were utilized.

Clearly, although there is some evidence supporting the effectiveness of PST and behavioral communication training, there has been an insufficient amount of data from which to draw any firm conclusions. Many important practical and theoretical issues remained unexplored. The O'Leary and Turkewitz (1978) study reminds us that, like any treatment, communication training may be differentially effective for certain kinds of couples. The relative effectiveness of group therapy versus individual conjoint therapy is another important clinical comparison that needs to be addressed. Finally, given the potential importance of communication deficits in producing marital conflict, such training may be useful as a preventive measure. Markman and Floyd (1980) have begun a research program to explore the preventive implications of behavioral communication training.

SUMMARY AND CONCLUSIONS

There is still a great deal to be learned about the role of communication in producing marital conflict, as well as the efficacy of currently available treatment packages for teaching couples the skills they need in order to communicate more effectively. Behavioral research that either analyzes or attempts to alter marital communication patterns is proliferating furiously, and the progress in the last 10 years has been notable. Although we must remain cautious and tentative in our appraisal of this current literature, on the basis of what we know, we are on the right track: Communication deficits appear to be central to marital conflict, and communication training may be the treatment of choice for reducing marital conflict.

REFERENCES

Birchler, G. R., Weiss, R. L., & Vincent, J. P. A multimethod analysis of social reinforcement exchange between maritally distressed and nondistressed spouse and stranger dyads. *Journal of Personality and Social Psychology*, 1975, *31*, 349–360.

D'Zurilla, T. J., & Goldfried, M. R. Problem solving and behavior modification. *Journal of Abnormal Psychology*, 1971, *78*, 107–126.

Eisler, R. M., & Hersen, M. Behavioral techniques in family-oriented crisis intervention. *Archives of General Psychiatry*, 1973, *28*, 111–115.

Gottman, J. M. *Marital interaction: Experimental investigations*. New York: Academic Press, 1979.

Gottman, J., Markman, H., Notarius, C., & Gonso, J. *A couple's guide to communication*. Champaign, Ill.: Research Press, 1976.

Gottman, J., Notarius, C., Markman, H., Bank, S., Yoppi, B., & Rubin, M. E. Behavior exchange theory and marital decision making. *Journal of Personality and Social Psychology*, 1976, *34*, 14–23.

Guerney, B. *Relationship enhancement*. San Francisco: Jossey-Bass, 1977.

Gurman, A. S., & Kniskern, D. P. Research on marital and family therapy: Progress, perspective, and prospect. In S. L. Garfield & A. E. Bergin (Eds.), *Handbook of psychotherapy and behavior change: An empirical analysis* (2nd ed.). New York: Wiley, 1978.

Gurman, A. S., & Knudson, R. M. Behavioral marriage therapy: I. A psychodynamic systems analysis and critique. *Family Process*, 1978, *17*, 121–138.

Harrell, J., & Guerney, B. Training married couples in conflict negotiation skills. In D. H. L. Olson (Ed.), *Treating relationships*. Lake Mills, Iowa: Graphic Press, 1976.

Hops, H., Wills, T. A., Patterson, G. R., & Weiss, R. L. *Marital Interaction Coding System*. Eugene: University of Oregon, Oregon Research Institute, 1971. (Order from ASIS/NAPS, c/o Microfiche Publications, 305 East 46th Street, New York, N.Y. 10017.)

Jacobson, N. S. Problem solving and contingency contracting in the treatment of marital discord. *Journal of Consulting and Clinical Psychology*, 1977, *45*, 92–100. (a)

Jacobson, N. S. Training couples to solve their marital problems: A behavioral approach to relationship discord. Part II: Intervention strategies. *International Journal of Family Counseling*, 1977, *5*(2), 20–28. (b)

Jacobson, N. S. Specific and nonspecific factors in the effectiveness of a behavioral approach to the treatment of marital discord. *Journal of Consulting and Clinical Psychology*, 1978, *46*, 442–452. (a)

Jacobson, N. S. A stimulus control model of change in behavioral marital therapy: Implications for contingency contracting. *Journal of Marriage and Family Counseling*, 1978, *4*, 29–35. (b)

Jacobson, N. S. A review of the research on the effectiveness of marital therapy. In T. J. Paolino & B. S. McCrady (Eds.), *Marriage and marital therapy: Psychoanalytic, behavioral, and systems theory perspectives*. New York: Brunner/Mazel, 1978. (c)

Jacobson, N. S. Behavioral treatment for marital discord: A critical appraisal. In M. Hersen, R. M. Eisler, & P. M. Miller (Eds.), *Progress in behavior modification*. New York: Academic Press, 1979. (a)

Jacobson, N. S. Increasing positive behavior in severely distressed adult relationships. *Behavior Therapy*, 1979, *10*, 311–326. (b)

Jacobson, N. S., & Anderson, E. A. The effects of behavior rehearsal and feedback on the acquisition of problem solving skills in distressed and nondistressed couples. *Behaviour Research and Therapy*, 1980, *18*, 25–36.

Jacobson, N. S., & Margolin, G. *Marital therapy: Strategies based on social learning and behavior exchange principles*. New York: Brunner/Mazel, 1979.

Jacobson, N. S., & Moore, D. Behavior exchange theory of marriage: Reconnaissance and reconsideration. In J. P. Vincent (Ed.), *Advances in family intervention, assessment, and theory*. Greenwich, Conn.: TAI Press, in press.

Jacobson, N. S., Waldron, H., & Moore, D. Toward a behavioral profile of marital distress. *Journal of Consulting and Clinical Psychology*, 1980, *48*, 696–703.

Liberman, R. P., Levine, J., Wheeler, E., Sanders, N., & Wallace, C. Experimental evaluation of marital group therapy: Behavioral vs. interaction–insight formats. *Acta Psychiatrica Scandinavica*, 1976, *Supplement.*

Margolin, G., & Weiss, R. L. A comparative evaluation of therapeutic components associated with behavioral marital treatment. *Journal of Consulting and Clinical Psychology*, 1978, *46*, 1476–1486.

Markman, H. J. Application of a behavioral model of marriage in predicting relationship satisfaction of couples planning marriage. *Journal of Consulting and Clinical Psychology*, 1979, *47*, 743–749.

Markman, H. J., & Floyd, F. Possibilities for the prevention of marital discord: A behavioral perspective. *The American Journal of Family Therapy*, 1980, *8*, 29–48.

O'Leary, K. D., & Turkewitz, H. The treatment of marital disorders from a behavioral perspective. In T. J. Paolino & B. S. McCrady (Eds.), *Marriage and marital therapy: Psychoanalytic, behavioral, and systems theory perspectives.* New York: Brunner/Mazel, 1978.

Patterson, G. R., & Hops, H. Coercion, a game for two: Intervention techniques for marital conflict. In R. E. Ulrich & P. Mountjoy (Eds.), *The experimental analysis of social behavior.* New York: Appleton, 1972.

Stuart, R. B. Operant–interpersonal treatment for marital discord. *Journal of Consulting and Clinical Psychology*, 1969, *33*, 675–682.

Vincent, J. P., Friedman, L. L., Nugent, J., & Messerly, L. Demand characteristics in observations of marital interaction. *Journal of Consulting and Clinical Psychology*, 1979, *47*, 557–566.

Vincent, J. P., Weiss, R. L., & Birchler, G. R. A behavioral analysis of problem-solving in distressed and nondistressed married and stranger dyads. *Behavior Therapy*, 1975, *6*, 475–487.

Weiss, R. L. The conceptualization of marriage from a behavioral perspective. In T. J. Paolino & B. S. McCrady (Eds.), *Marriage and marital therapy: Psychoanalytic, behavioral, and systems theory perspectives.* New York: Brunner/Mazel, 1978.

Weiss, R. L., & Birchler, G. R. Adults with marital dysfunction. In M. Hersen & A. S. Bellack (Eds.), *Behavior therapy in the psychiatric setting.* Baltimore: Williams & Wilkins, 1978.

Weiss, R. L., Birchler, G. R., & Vincent, J. P. Contractual models for negotiation training in marital dyads. *Journal of Marriage and the Family*, 1974, *36*, 321–331.

Weiss, R. L., Hops, H., & Patterson, G. R. A framework for conceptualizing marital conflict, technology for altering it, some data for evaluating it. In L. A. Hamerlynck, L. C. Handy, & E. J. Mash (Eds.), *Behavior change: Methodology, concepts, and practice.* Champaign, Ill.: Research Press, 1973.

Weiss, R. L., & Perry, B. A. *Assessment and treatment of marital dysfunction.* Eugene: Oregon Marital Studies Program, 1979. (Available from Robert L. Weiss, Department of Psychology, University of Oregon, Eugene, Ore. 97403.)

Wills, T. A., Weiss, R. L., & Patterson, G. R. A behavioral analysis of the determinants of marital satisfaction. *Journal of Consulting and Clinical Psychology*, 1974, *42*, 802–811.

8

ASSERTION TRAINING FOR WOMEN

MARIAN L. MACDONALD

The title of this chapter will probably not seem unusual to those who read it. But it very probably should, for there is a striking and revealing contrast between this title and the titles of treatment topic papers usually seen in journals and texts. Consider, for example, the following recent entries: "Analysis of Stimulus Control Treatment of Sleep-Onset Insomnia" (Zwart & Lisman, 1979), "Self-Monitoring and Reactivity in the Modification of Cigarette Smoking" (Abrams & Wilson, 1979), "Self-Desensitization and Meditation in the Reduction of Public Speaking Anxiety" (Kirsch & Henry, 1979), "Imagery Elaboration and Self-Efficacy in the Covert Modeling Treatment of Unassertive Behavior" (Kazdin, 1979), and "Self-Monitoring of Mood versus Activity by Depressed Clients" (Harmon, Nelson, & Hayes, 1980). In each of these examples, of course, there is a treatment technique or set of techniques paired with a clinical behavior problem. In this chapter title, however, which is substantively identical to other titles on the same topic (e.g., *The New Assertive Woman*, Bloom, Coburn, & Pearlman, 1975; *Self-Assertion for Women*, Butler, 1976; "Assertion Training for Women," Linehan & Egan, 1979; *Assertive Training for Women*, Osborn & Harris, 1975), there is a treatment technique or set of techniques paired with a defined population. The implication of the acceptance of this pairing is clear: being a woman somehow qualifies an individual as necessarily being a legitimate candidate for a therapeutic intervention and, moreover, a candidate for whom the particular therapeutic intervention, here assertion training, is somehow especially appropriate.

Marian L. MacDonald. Department of Psychology, University of Massachusetts, Amherst, Massachusetts.

To underscore the unusualness of this position, namely, assuming that membership in a certain demographic category somehow qualifies one as an appropriate candidate for a particular therapeutic intervention, consider the following fictitious but analogous titles: "Stimulus-Control Treatment for Residents of Los Angeles"; "Self-Monitoring and Reactivity for Individuals with Brown Hair"; "Self-Desensitization and Meditation for Persons Shorter than Five Feet"; "Imagery Elaboration and Self-Efficacy Training in the Covert Modeling Treatment of Persons Who Register as Democrats"; and "Self-Monitoring of Mood versus Activity for Civil Service Employees." The fact that "Assertion Training for Women" does not seem unusual as a title, then, is itself unusual—and it reflects the assumptions about womanhood upon which behavior therapy, and contemporary American society in turn, currently are operating. An analysis of assertion training for women requires an examination of these assumptions.

ASSERTION AND THE FEMALE SEX ROLE

Historically, female and male sex roles have been conceptualized as distinct from one another in several important ways. Most often these roles have been conceptualized as consisting of mutually exclusive sets of characteristics differentially distributed between persons of each biological sex; individuals displaying characteristics typically displayed by the opposite biological sex would, as Berzins (1975) has noted, at best be assumed to have sex-role confusion or ambivalence, and at worse be assumed to have disquieting deviations in sexual behavior, extending to bisexuality, homosexuality, or more general maladjustment. For both sexes, sex-typed behavior, it is now generally recognized, is encouraged powerfully from an early age and throughout one's life; cross-sex-typed behavior is punished just as powerfully (Schaffer, 1980).

More recently, researchers have questioned the assumption that femininity and masculinity are mutually exclusive and have instead posited that feminine and masculine characteristics are independent, so that a given individual of either gender may be high or low on characteristics modally associated with either or both sex roles (Bem, 1974). Most recently, individuals endorsing above-median levels of characteristics typically associated with both feminine and masculine sex roles have been termed "androgynous" (Bem, 1974, 1977; Kelly & Worell, 1977; Worell, 1978). It should be noted, however, that both the older, mutually exclusive model of sex roles and the newer, independent (androgynous) model of sex roles rest on the assumption that there are modal feminine and masculine characteristics. The difference between the two models is found in their different assumptions about the nature of the relationship between feminine and masculine sex-typed behaviors rather than about the existence of sex roles; on the latter point, both models agree that sex roles, and sex-typed behaviors, do in fact exist.

Most formulations of the differences between the feminine and masculine sex roles have utilized some variant of an expressive–instrumental dimension (Johnson, 1963; Kaplan & Sedney, 1980; Kelly & Worell, 1977). Parsons and Bales (1955), for example, suggested that the cultural definition of masculinity reflects a cognitive instrumentality and goal-directedness, while femininity is culturally defined by expressive, supportive, and affective responses. Bakan (1966) characterized masculinity as involving a concern for oneself and one's own goals and femininity as a concern for oneself in relation to others. Sex roles, and therefore socially desirable characteristics, for males, then, have been noted to include a constellation of patterns involving instrumentality, independence, task-directedness, cognitive orientation, and appropriate assertion, while sex roles, and therefore socially desirable characteristics, for females include a constellation of patterns involving supportiveness, dependence, expressiveness, affectivity, and acting with concern for others (Kelly & Worell, 1977). These patterns describe those qualities that form society's sex-typed standards of desirable behavior for men and women (Bem, 1974), or behaviors that are expected and rewarded if performed by men and women, respectively (Spence, Helmreich, & Stapp, 1975).

As a rule, assertiveness as a behavior characteristic has been valued when performed by males and taught as a socially appropriate behavior for males to display (Bem, 1974; Frodi, Macauley, & Thorne, 1977; Heilbrun, 1976; Spence et al., 1975). Females, on the other hand, have been expected and socially encouraged to subjugate their own desires and rights in a given situation to the desires and rights of others present (Bem, 1974; Costrich, Feinstein, Kidder, Marecek, & Pascale, 1975; Schaffer, 1980).

The notion of androgyny, originally introduced to challenge the assumption that female sex-typed characteristics and male sex-typed characteristics were necessarily mutually exclusive, has often been suggested as an indication that the rigidity in sex-role typing is disintegrating (Dworkin, 1974); the assertion has been made that androgynous persons, whether female or male, would have a broader array of effective behavioral options at their disposal and would therefore be able to be more flexible and consequently more effective over a wider range of situations (Bem, 1974, 1975; Bem & Lenny, 1976; Kelly, O'Brien, Hosford, & Kinsinger, 1976). In reviewing the research on androgyny, however, Kelly & Worell (1977) note:

> The general (but not without exception) finding has been that androgynous and masculine-typed persons perform well and "look best" and frequently do not differ significantly from one another on characteristics for which sex-role categories are compared. In contrast, feminine-typed and undifferentiated subjects (when the latter group is designated) tend to cluster together and "look worse" relative to the other two groups, especially in self-esteem and life history data. Even on some tasks designed to evoke stereotypically feminine expressiveness and affectivity, feminine-typed persons do not perform well (Bem, 1975; Bem, Martyna, & Watson, 1976). This raises the possibility that feminine-typed expressive behaviors are less socially effective for an individual than masculine-typed behaviors, and they simply do not lead to positive outcomes as frequently. *If this hypothesis of differential social utility value is correct, it would indicate that while androgynous persons possess approximately equal numbers of masculine and feminine characteristics, it may be principally the masculine-typed behaviors (assertiveness, instrumentality, dominance, etc.) that have greater potential for leading to social reinforcements in our society.* (p. 1113, italics added)

The data suggest, then, that the inclusion of androgyny as a sex-role alternative has not altered the fact that it is the traditionally masculine characteristics of assertiveness and concern for oneself and one's own rights and goals, rather than the traditionally feminine characteristics of expressiveness and concern for oneself in relation to others, that are socially valued as more desirable and societally rewarded as most effective (cf. Kaplan & Sedney, 1980; Rosenkrantz, Vogel, Bee, Broverman, & Broverman, 1968). The tentative result is that introducing the notion of androgyny, rather than blurring the distinctions between the traditional sex roles, has stimulated research suggesting that what has been held as the traditional male sex role is more functional for members of both sexes than is what has traditionally been held as the female sex role.

It would appear that the growing interest in assertion training for women during the past decade, an interest reflected both in professionals' increased attention to the issue and women's more frequent, specific requests for assertion training (Linehan & Egan, 1979), rests on an acceptance of the apparent social reality that behaving unassertively, that is, in the stereotypically feminine manner, is not in a woman's best interest. The appeal of assertion training for women, then, rests on several interlocking assumptions: (1) that women have been trained to conform to what is essentially a dysfunctional role; (2) that as a consequence of this training, women are typically less assertive than are men, and (3) that it would be in women's best interest to replace certain significant portions of what has traditionally been identified as their appropriate sex role with responses traditionally associated with masculinity (cf. Kelly & Worell, 1977).

These assumptions, generally held to legitimize the utility of assertion training for women (Linehan & Egan, 1979), also underlie studies on sex typing. Sex-role research, which has typically regarded assertion as a characteristic of the masculine sex role, generally contends that there is a difference between the actual assertion levels of women and men. This contention, while widely held, appears to be largely a derivative of a generalized belief that sex differences do exist on a variety of dimensions (Unger, 1979), which is a popular, but not empirically unequivocal, position (Maccoby & Jacklin, 1974). Before examining and presenting data on the relative levels of women's and men's assertion, it is important to note some qualifications. Historically, psychologists, like members of society at large, have tended to assume sex differences before the fact (Unger, 1979); in the past, these assumed differences have often been studied in biased contexts so that disconfirmations were not likely, and with the result that issues have become quickly politicized (Shields, 1975). As early as 1910, Wooley, reviewing the literature on what was then known as the psychology of sex, commented: "There is perhaps no field aspiring to be scientific where flagrant personal bias, logic martyred in the cause of supporting a prejudice, unfounded assertions, and even sentimental rot and drivel, have run riot to such an extent as here" (p. 340).

More recently, Unger (1979) has argued convincingly that even the most contemporary research in the area of neuropsychology, which might be regarded as the most potentially objectifiable area of psychology, is saturated with interpretations based on the assumptions that sex differences exist, are somehow important, and invariably indicate that women are basically inferior when compared to men.

Since the "assertion training for women" movement rests on these very assumptions, namely, that there are sex differences between women's and men's levels of assertion, that levels of assertion are critically influential in determining one's degree of social reward, and that women's assertion levels are inferior to those exhibited by men, the area must be examined skeptically. Questions must be asked and answered with considerable caution, and the answers derived must be interpreted with awareness of the biases that have permeated past work on differences between the sexes.

COMPARISONS BETWEEN WOMEN'S AND MEN'S LEVELS OF ASSERTION

Comparing women's and men's levels of assertion requires defining the behavior variable on which comparisons will be made. Although there is no general agreement on what specific behavioral referents are implied by the term (Linehan & Egan, 1979; MacDonald, 1978, in press-a), there is consensus that assertion is an interpersonal behavior that is socially defined and whose form varies as a function of its situational context. A major question underlying many of the alternative definitions offered, especially recently, is whether assertion should be restricted in meaning to include only those behaviors that serve to maintain one's rights, or whether the meaning of the term should be broadened to include rights-maintenance behaviors as well as behaviors expressive of such positive feelings as praise, appreciation, and affection (Hollandsworth & Wall, 1977).

The recent interest in expanding the meaning of assertion is very probably resulting from the field's increasing recognition that social skills, or interpersonal behavior, is a vastly varied and critically significant arena of psychological import (Phillips, 1978) and consequent interest in broadening the meaning of the term "assertion," which has been the only specific social skills category generally recognized and researched (Redd, Porterfield, & Andersen, 1979), to include additional clearly important social behavior categories such as expressing praise, appreciation, and respect. To broaden the meaning of assertion so extensively, however, Salter (1977) has argued, would stretch the concept so much as to render it linguistically nonsensical:

> To define assertion as including warm, friendly feelings is linguistically incorrect. It's like defining "fat" to include its antonym—i.e., *fat* is everybody who is thin, as well as everybody who is overweight. If we were to interview

at random a hundred adults who are not psychologists, and if we were to ask them "What does 'assertion' mean?" they would give us a correct dictionary definition. (p. 34)

It is perhaps recognition of this dilemma that has led proponents of the broader conception to distinguish between rights-maintenance and positive-affect-expressive behaviors and label them negative and positive assertion, respectively (see Hollandsworth & Wall, 1977).

There is a second disadvantage to broadening the meaning of assertion so extensively: to do so would very probably inadvertently suppress the identification and study of other equally important and conceptually independent categories of prosocial skills (MacDonald & Cohen, 1981). For these two reasons, then, namely to avoid broadening the meaning of the term "assertion" to such an extent as to render it linguistically nonsensical, and to avoid inadvertently discouraging the study of other, independent social skills, the term assertion should probably be restricted in meaning to refer to those behaviors that the term was largely intended originally to imply: behaviors that serve to maintain one's rights (Alberti & Emmons, 1978; Lange & Jakubowski, 1976; Lazarus, 1973; MacDonald, 1978; McFall & Marston, 1970; Wolpe & Lazarus, 1966).

Assertion as behavior that serves to maintain one's rights, then, is the behavior in question. As the definition implies, this conception of the term is a functional one; as is the case with all behavior (Ullmann & Krasner, 1965, 1975), assertion does not occur and cannot be evaluated in an environmental vacuum. The question of whether there are differences between women's and men's levels of assertion involves not only whether there are differences in the topographics of modal responses that might be emitted in identical situations, but also whether there are differences in the environmental contexts, either antecedent or consequent, which surround responses that might be topographically identical but emitted by members of different sexes.

Throughout the literature on sex differences, these two questions, of whether differences exist within the individuals or whether differences exist within other persons with whom the individuals interact, have often been confused (Unger, 1979), but they are two very different questions, and they have two very different sets of implications that follow from their answers. The first question, in this context, asks whether women and men who are confronted with the same rights-infringement situation respond differently to it, and this is the question that has most frequently been addressed. The second question includes the consideration of sex not as an individual difference but as a stimulus variable. In part it asks whether women and men who are confronted with identical situations, and who respond in topographically identical ways, meet with different environmental responses to their behavior. But with recognition of the fact that assertion is a behavior that exists in a surrounding environmental medium, which is the entire thrust of the literature highlighting assertion's situational specificity (cf. Galassi & Galassi, 1977; Gambrill & Richey, 1975; Hersen, Eisler, & Miller, 1973, 1974; MacDonald, 1974, 1975), it is clear that considering sex as a stimulus variable raises questions not only about the consequents, but also about the antecedents, of assertive behavior. Just as there may be differences in the environmental response to the same assertive behavior depending on whether the assertion is emitted by a woman or a man, there may be differences in the nature and/or number of situations that confront women and men with rights infringements.

The issues raised by recognizing sex as a stimulus variable, as will become evident, are very important ones to consider. If there are differences in this regard, that is, differences in the nature and/or number of rights-infringement situations confronting women and men or differences in the environmental reactions to identical rights-maintenance behaviors emitted by women and men, the most fundamental issue may not be whether there are or should be differences in women's and men's levels of assertion when confronted with identical situations, but rather whether there are or should be differences in the antecedent and consequent environmental contexts within which women and men function.

The question of whether there are differences in women's and men's levels of assertion, then, is not a simple one; embedded in it are several different questions, each of which must be examined:

    1. Are there differences in the nature and/or number of rights-infringement situations that confront women and men?

    2. Are there differences in how women and men respond to identical situations presenting a rights infringement?

    3. Are there differences in how identical responses emitted by women and men are received, given identical situations presenting a rights infringement?

Data bearing on each of these questions are presented separately in the subsections that follow.

RIGHTS-INFRINGEMENT SITUATIONS:
NATURE AND/OR NUMBER OF DIFFERENCES

The failure of this country to date to ratify the Equal Rights Amendment would seem to be one clear unobtrusive measure suggesting that there may well be differences in the rights that are generally granted to women and men in today's society, differences that would explain Sherman's (1971) finding that more adult women (20%–31%) than men (4%) report recalling conscious desires to belong to the other sex. Data collected in diverse contexts suggest that there are fundamental differences in the environments that confront females and males from birth onward, and that, in general, the differences that exist most often place the rights of females at risk.

Birth data indicate that the likelihood of having a third child is significantly greater in families where the first two children are both girls than it is in families where the first two children are both boys (Pohlman, 1969), and that the length of time between birth of the first child and conception of the second is significantly greater when the first child is a boy (Pohlman, 1969). Sexual preference surveys indicate that 66% of all childless young adults have a preference for the sex of their first-born child and that of those couples with a preference, 92% would like to have a boy (Peterson & Peterson, 1973); confronted with the possibility of having only one child, over 80% of the men and over 66% of the women wanted their only child to be male (Hoffman, 1977; Peterson & Peterson, 1973). These data indicate that even before birth, there seems to be a clear and behavior-relevant preference favoring males over females; Schaffer (1980) has interpreted this conclusion, indicated across many replicated studies, as reflecting an "underlying assumption . . . that males are somehow more valuable human beings than females" (p. 16).

If Schaffer's (1980) interpretation of the underlying assumption is correct, there should be evidence indicating that males, held as somehow more valuable human beings than are females, should receive better treatment than do females; that is, they should be accorded more rights and confronted with rights-infringement situations less frequently.

That there may be differences in the range of accorded rights based on sex alone has been suggested by results reported by Bem and Bem (1976), who found that if you ask parents of a newborn male child to

predict what he will be doing 25 years later, they will answer that it is
not possible to make the prediction since he has so many available
options, while if you ask parents of a newborn female child to predict
what she will be doing 25 years later, parents will predict with some
confidence that she will be a wife and mother.

The educational environment, which is a powerful socialization
force, has been described as follows: "One of the first messages communicated to girls and boys at school is that girls are less important"
(Schaffer, 1980, p. 26) than boys or, put differently, have fewer or more
narrowly defined rights. Serbin and O'Leary (1975) found that even
though teachers were not aware that they were treating the sexes
differently, teachers gave more attention to boys than they did girls,
gave girls half as much individual instruction on tasks as they gave boys,
and prompted boys to be creative and independent in their activities
more often than they prompted girls to be so. Weitz (1977) found that
when teachers were asked to name the most creative (and by implication deserving of freedom) children in their classes, they consistently
named more boys than girls, even though no significant differences
between the sexes were demonstrable on tests of creative performance.

Differential treatment, predicated on differences in ascribed sex-
role rights, continue throughout adulthood. Zimmerman and West
(1975), observing females and males interact as couples in a natural
setting, found that men tend to interrupt their partners more than do
women, a result also reported by Bernard (1972). Zimmerman and West
(1975) also found that males tend to use their interruptions to take
control over the topics of conversation. Moreover, 100% of the overlaps
in conversation that occurred when two people talked at once were
initiated by male speakers (Zimmerman & West, 1975).

Studies of nonverbal behavior yield corroborating results. In mixed-
sex couples, women are more likely to be touched than are men (Henley,
1973). Studies of personal space indicate that women tend to have less
territory and take up less personal space than do men, but despite this
difference, the smaller space that women typically have is more frequently violated than is the personal space of men (Frieze & Ramsey,
1976).

Attitude research, even restricted to studies conducted after the
advent of the women's movement, continue to reveal that men are not
willing to permit women to assume supervisory, decision-making, or
leadership roles outside of the family; smaller increases in rights, such
as better jobs and better pay for women, are viewed as acceptable by

men only if those changes do not become threatening to their own positions (Jones, O'C. Chernovetz, & Hansson, 1978; Osmond & Martin, 1975). These attitudes would appear to be consequential: women who do work are paid less and promoted less often (Kanter, 1976) than are men, even when training and performance are held constant (Schaffer, 1980). Moreover, these attitudes would appear to be consequential as early as at the point of entry: women of equal credentials have been accepted less often than have men for graduate school, professional school, and in employment, particularly for high-status jobs (Ekstrom, 1972; Fidell, 1970; Schaffer, 1980).

If it is accepted that the veridical rights of women and men are equivalent, the work reviewed suggests that women are confronted with more rights-infringement situations than are men. Data from the assertion literature are consistent with this hypothesis. In a study of male psychiatric patients, Eisler, Hersen, Miller, and Blanchard (1975) found that subjects were significantly more likely to request that a female change her behavior than a male and significantly more likely to offer spontaneously to perform a favor for another male as opposed to a female. Viewing these data from the partner's rather than the subject's, point of view, then, they suggest that when interacting with men, women are significantly more likely than are men to be confronted with situations requiring assertion on two counts: they are more likely than are men, when performing the same behavior in the same situation, to be asked by men to change unliked behavior, and they are less likely than are men, when performing the same behavior in the same situation, to be offered a spontaneous favor by men. Converging data have been reported from field studies: both males and females are more likely to honk at a female than a male driver who is blocking an interesection (Deaux, 1971; Unger, Raymond, & Levine, 1974); that is, both men and women are more likely to ask women to change their unliked behavior than they are to ask men to change the same unliked behavior.

Although differences in methodology prohibit direct comparisons, data from our laboratory are consistent with the proposition that women are confronted with more rights-infringement situations than are men. As part of two separate research programs to develop role-play assertion measures for female and male college students, we asked college women and men to report situations they had encountered over the past week "where assertion was or would have been the best course of action." The sample reporting instances confronting college men described an average of 4.93 situations per respondent (MacDonald,

Swan, & Itkin, 1979), while the sample reporting instances confronting college women described an average of 7.63 situations per respondent (MacDonald, 1974, 1978).

This review is not intended to be exhaustive. It is intended to suggest the empirical tenability of the propositions that women relative to men are afforded fewer rights and that, assuming legitimately equivalent rights, women relative to men are confronted with more rights-infringement situations.

In large measure, it is the acceptance of these propositions as accurate and unjust that has generated interest in the women's movement (Carden, 1974). At least in part, it is the belief that increasing women's levels of assertion will result in expanded rights for women that has prompted interest in women's assertion training. If this is to be an effective solution to the situation, it must also be the case that women, who are presently oppressed, are less assertive than men and that increased levels of women's assertion meet with positive responses from the environment. The data on these questions do not suggest that women's assertion training will be a sufficient response to things as they stand.

RESPONSES TO RIGHTS INFRINGEMENTS

Are there differences in how women and men respond to identical situations presenting a rights infringement? As has been noted, this question must be asked in the context of knowing that, very probably, the rights-infringement situations confronting females and males in the natural environment are both quantitatively and qualitatively different. Framing questions about comparisons between females' and males' levels of assertion around situations that are identical, then, is in some ways an artificial question, for it asks if there are differences in responses to identical social worlds between people who live in different ones. With recognition of the fact that searching for sex differences in identical circumstances is only a partial question whose answer must be evaluated in a larger context, however, this issue can be addressed.

The fact that assertion has historically been regarded as a valued characteristic for males and an undesirable characteristic for females (Bem, 1974; Heilbrun, 1976; Johnson, 1963; Kelly & Worell, 1977; Spence et al., 1975) would certainly suggest that women should be less assertive than men, given the power of socialization (Schaffer, 1980).

The expectation that the predicted difference is a veridical one is so strong, in fact, that actual differences have rarely been examined (Hollandsworth & Wall, 1977).

When Hollandsworth and Wall (1977) reviewed the assertion literature to explore the question of sex differences, they identified seven studies that provided data from 13 discrete female and male samples on levels of assertion as measured by self-report. Across all seven studies, males self-reported higher levels of assertion than did females (Bates & Zimmerman, 1971; Galassi, DeLo, Galassi & Bastien, 1974; Hollandsworth, 1976; Morgan, 1974; Orenstein, Orenstein, & Carr, 1975). Subjecting T scores for these samples to t-tests, however, indicated that for only four of the 14 comparisons were the differences significant (Galassi et al., 1974; Gay, Hollandsworth, & Galassi, 1975; Morgan, 1974; Orenstein et al., 1975).

To address the question directly, Hollandsworth and Wall (1977) drew Adult Self-Expression Scale (Gay et al., 1975) protocols from existing data files for four samples comprising a total of 702 people (294 males and 408 females). The samples were deliberately heterogeneous, and included adults attending evening courses, university undergraduates, and community college undergraduates. The data analysis consisted of computing separate t-tests for each sample on each of the 48 items from the scale, a self-report measure "specifically designed to encompass a broad range of both interpersonal situations and assertive behavior" (Hollandsworth & Wall, 1977, p. 219). If the t-test for a given item was significant ($p < .05$) for at least two of the four samples tested, a consistent sex difference was concluded.

Of the 48 items, which include questions tapping both negative assertion and what has been termed "positive assertion," 22 failed to yield significant sex differences for any of the four samples, and 14 were found to be significantly different in one sample only. Of the seven items yielding significant sex differences in assertion as lexically defined for two or more samples, males reported themselves as being more assertive on six, representing five different types of situations: saying no to a boss or supervisor, expressing anger to a boss or supervisor, asserting rights to authority figures, asserting rights to a friend, and asking a boss or supervisor for a behavior change; women reported themselves as being more assertive on one, tapping the expression of anger to parents.

On the basis of the results from their literature review, which had indicated that four of 14 comparisons were significant, and their own direct analysis of responses to the Adult Self-Expression Scale, which had indicated consistent sex differences favoring males on six items, Hollandsworth and Wall (1977) concluded that "the results of these two studies suggest that women may be somewhat less assertive than men" (p. 220).

The ratio of derived to examined sex differences invites speculation that the conclusion of veridical differences was based at least as much on the cultural assumption that the expected differences were there to be found as it was on the self-reported sex differences that were observed, a speculation supported by the authors' own later qualification that "to say unequivocally, however, that women are less assertive than men may be a misinterpretation, *since for three-quarters of the samples, these differences were not significant*" (Hollandsworth & Wall, 1977, p. 221, italics added; see Unger, 1979).

Greenwald (1978) and Schroeder and Rakos (1978) have reported data that further complicates the interpretation of the results from Hollandsworth and Wall (1977). Schroeder and Rakos (1978) suggested that as a function of recent changes in attitudes concerning the desirability of assertion for both sexes, it may have become socially desirable for women as well as men to describe themselves as behaving assertively, regardless of whether they actually behave in an assertive manner. They based their suggestion on uncontrolled changes they had observed in their own laboratory over time, noting:

> Between 1975 and 1976, the precentage [sic] of self-referred nonassertive subjects who failed to meet the operational definition of nonassertion on the CRI (Conflict Resolution Inventory; McFall & Lillesand, 1971) increased from 24% to 82%. However, this was not matched by an increase in actual assertive behavior in role-play assessments. The behavioral assessment produced an increase from 12% to only 20% in operationally defined nonassertion. (Schroeder & Rakos, p. 965)

Schroeder and Rakos (1978) reasoned that the recent increases in media exposure to assertion and its merits may have resulted in making assertion a socially valued characteristic to at least report for both sexes, but particularly and more so for women. In support of their reasoning, they found that women reported significantly greater increases in assertion than did men, as well as significantly more media exposure to the merits of behaving assertively.

Greenwald (1978) reported corroborating data, noting that while high-frequency dating females describe themselves as being signifi-
~antly more assertive than do low-frequency dating females, in actual

situations their behavior is more submissive. Other findings support the notion that perceived social desirability may moderate the relationship between self-reported and enacted assertion. Kiecolt & McGrath (1979), comparing individuals who scored high and low on a social desirability scale, found that high scorers rated themselves as significantly more assertive than did low scorers on self-report scales measuring assertion, while in role-play measures of assertion, the assertive content of high social desirability scorers' responses was significantly less than was the assertive content of low social desirability scorers' responses. We have observed converging results in our own laboratory; as part of a study to evaluate the external validities of several laboratory measures of assertion, we found self-reported levels of assertion to be positively correlated with social desirability scale scores in college women (MacDonald, in press-b; MacDonald & Tyson, submitted), while actual assertion in unobtrusive, contrived observational settings was negatively correlated with social desirability scale scores (MacDonald & Tyson, submitted).

It seems, then, that self-reported levels of assertion are particularly vulnerable to the influences of the current perceived appropriateness, or social desirability, of describing oneself as assertive. It seems tenable, then, that self-reported levels of assertion may be influenced more by respondents' perceptions of the appropriateness or social desirability of describing themselves in a certain manner than by respondents' actual behavior in rights-infringement situations.

Frodi et al. (1977) have noted that it is especially dangerous to evaluate whether there are sex differences via self-report on questions where there are strong expectations about whether or not there will be. Illusions about sex differences, which are held by both females and males (Unger, 1979), have been found to influence self-reports more than they do behavior in either laboratory or field settings (Unger, in press). In essence, scores derived from self-ratings, as were those reviewed and analyzed by Hollandsworth and Wall (1977), rest on a data base that is overly influenced by culturally mediated assumptions that essentially determine subjects' responses so that prevailing cultural beliefs, whether holding that there are or are not sex differences, will necessarily be confirmed. It would seem, then, that observed behavior, rather than self-ratings, would provide the most appropriate avenue for exploring the question of whether there are sex differences in levels of assertion to identical rights-infringement situations; it is testimony to the strength of the cultural assumption that there will be differences to note that this approach has almost never been used (cf. Frodi *et al.*, 1977).

There are some data that have been interpreted as indicating that females typically employ nonverbal behaviors associated with low levels of assertion more often than do males: women are silent more often than are men in mixed-sex discussions (Fishman, 1965), women smile more often than do men when conversing (Deaux, 1976), and women are more likely than men to avoid a direct glance (Libby & Haklevitch, 1973). These data, while based on observed behavior rather than self-report, were not collected under circumstances equating the situations confronting the men and women responding, however, so that it is not possible to determine whether the observed differences resulted from differences between the sexes or differences between the situations confronting the sexes (see Unger, 1979).

In one of the few published studies exploring sex differences in actual responses to an identical rights-infringement situation, Harris (1974) observed the reactions of females and males standing in a line to a male who cut in front of them. She found that an equal number of females and males made verbal statements expressing displeasure to the offender (Harris, 1974), a result indicating no difference in levels of assertion (Tyson & MacDonald, submitted).

To explore this question further, Pamela Tyson and I recruited 88 volunteers from the psychology department's subject pool at the University of Massachusetts. Half of the sample was female, and half of the sample was male. The experimental task was a role-play one; subjects were asked to record the responses they would have if they were actually encountering each of 20 situations as they heard them.

The presented situations were selected to tap several different types of rights-infringement situations known from previous work (MacDonald, 1978; MacDonald *et al.*, 1979) to be confronted by both females and males. Two of the types of situations—namely, ones in which a peer is making an unreasonable demand or request, and ones in which a peer is being inconsiderate—have been found to be the most salient components of rights-infringement situations, and so each of these types was represented by six items. The remaining types of situations have been found to be less salient, and so each was probed by only one or two items.

The design was intended to explore, then, not the general question of whether there were sex differences in levels of assertion to identical rights-infringement situations, but rather whether there were sex differences in levels of assertion to specific types of identical rights-infringement situations. Moreover, with half of the items presented to each sex, the presented offender was a female and with half of the items presented to each sex, the presented offender was a male, so that the question of whether offender sex differences influenced or interacted with subject sex levels of assertion could be explored.

Illustrative situations sampling or probing each type of situation are as follows:

> You and a girl [or guy] you are jointly doing a class project with are standing by Tobin Hall. The two of you need to get in touch with six people in connection with your project. She [or he] is in a hurry to get home so, as a quick way to organize things, the girl [or guy] says, "Hey, why don't you call those people this afternoon?" (Situations in which a peer is making an unreasonable demand or request)

> You're sitting in your psych class before it starts. Some girl [or guy] next to you asks if she [or he] can copy the notes from last class, and you hand her [or him] your notebook. The professor comes in, greets you all, and starts to lecture. The girl [or guy] is still copying your notes. (Situations in which a peer is being inconsiderate)

> Your professor has just handed your last test back, one you studied really hard for. As you open it up, you see that you got an A, and you hear the girl [or guy] next to you mutter, "I wonder what you did to get that?" (Situations in which a peer is questioning the person's competence)

> You're sitting in your room thinking about how to finish all you have to do. Suddenly the phone rings, you pick it up, and all you hear is the sound of heavy breathing. (Situations in which someone is being sexually intrusive)

> You're eating out with one of the guys [or girls] you've been dating and another couple. While you're eating, the other couple suggests that you should all go to see a new movie at the mall after dinner; it's a movie you'd really like to see. Without consulting you, the guy [or girl] you're with says, "No thanks. We just want to go back and watch tv." (Dating situation in which the partner is being inconsiderate)

> Your psychology teaching assistant said she'd [or he'd] help you during her [or his] office hours today. Her [or his] office hours are supposed to start at 10 o'clock. It's now 10:30, and you've been waiting half an hour. You see her [or him] coming; as she [or he] gets to where you are, she [or he] says, "Couldn't find a parking spot. Sorry." (Situations in which an authority figure is making an unreasonable demand or request)

> You're working hard to finish a tough exam. Time is short, and you are trying to remember something you forgot. Out of nowhere, the professor taps your shoulder; as she [or he] does so, she [or he] says, "Keep your eyes on your own paper; I won't have cheating in my class." (Situations in which an authority figure is being inconsiderate)

Subject responses to the situations were coded as falling into one of several (intertype range, 7–9) different levels of assertion on the basis of criteria established and available in previous work (see MacDonald, 1974, 1978; MacDonald, *et al.*, 1979). Each response was coded independently by two trained coders. Average intercoder agreement, calculated by dividing the number of agreements by the number of coded responses, was .95 (interitem range, 1.00–.86). With situation types represented by two or more items, data were analyzed using a three-factor analysis of variance (subject sex × offender sex × situation), with repeated measures on the situation factor. With situation types probed by only one item (i.e., situations where someone is being sexually intrusive; dating situations where one's partner is being inconsiderate), which were also situations where the offender sex was not manipulated, data were analyzed using t-tests for independent means.

The results of these analyses were as follows. For situations in which a peer was making an unreasonable demand or request, the F-ratios for the sex of subject main effect, sex of offender main effect, and sex of subject by sex of offender interaction were all nonsignificant ($F(1,84) = 3.92$, 1.42, and 2.62, respectively). For situations in which the peer had questioned the individual's competence, the F-ratios for the sex of subject main effect, sex of offender main effect, and sex of subject by sex of offender interaction were all nonsignificant ($F(1,84) = 1.28$, .00, and .59, respectively). For the sexual intrusion item, the t-ratio exploring sex of subject differences was nonsignificant ($t(42) = .02$). For the item in which the dating partner was being inconsiderate, the t-ration exploring sex of subject differences was nonsignificant ($t(42) = .39$). For situations in which an authority figure was making an unreasonable demand or request, the F-ratios for the sex of subject main effect, the sex of offender main effect, and the sex of subject by sex of offender interaction were all nonsignificant ($F(1,84) = .45$, .00, and 1.17, respectively). For situations in which an authority figure was being inconsiderate, the F-ratios for the sex of subject main effect and sex of subject by sex of offender interaction were both nonsignificant ($F(1,24) = .10$ and .00, respectively), although both females and males did tend to show greater levels of assertion when the inconsiderate authority was male as opposed to female ($F = 4.40$, $p < .05$; $\bar{x}$ (male authority) = 3.79, $\bar{x}$(female authority) = 3.25).

In sum, these data failed to support the hypothesis that there are sex differences in levels of observed assertion. Clearly, the failure to find differences cannot confirm the null hypothesis. But it can be interpreted to reaffirm the well-established tradition in psychological research that the null hypothesis must be assumed without unbiased data to the contrary.

RECEIVED RESPONSES, IDENTICAL SITUATIONS

Are there differences in how identical responses emitted by women and men are received, given identical situations presenting a rights infringement? Perhaps not surprisingly, this question, which considers sex of asserter as a stimulus variable (see Unger, 1979), has rarely been addressed in an unbiased fashion. Hull and Schroeder (1979), Linehan and Siefert (1978), Mullinex and Galassi (1978), and Woolfolk & Dever (1979) have all reported data indicating no differences in perceived appropriateness or social impact (effectiveness) of assertion in identical situations, whether the assertion is performed by females or males. Hess, Bridgwater, Bornstein, and Sweeney (1980) have criticized the procedures of these studies, however, noting that their methodologies were likely to both depress the salience of the asserter's sex and place subjects in the position of essentially describing themselves as sexist, making it unlikely for significant differences to emerge.

Despite these methodological problems, behavior therapists interested in women's assertion training have tended to regard the findings as veridical ones and to conclude that women may not only need to be taught to behave more assertively, but also may need to be taught to regard their concerns over the consequences of behaving more assertively as irrational ones:

> Feminist rhetoric suggests that in most, if not all, instances, women are nonassertive because of a high probability of punishing consequences. We have been unable to uncover any well-controlled empirical studies which directly confirm this contention. . . . Linehan and Siefert (1978) found no effects for sex of the subject when male and female community persons were asked to evaluate the appropriateness of assertion. Interestingly, results suggested that females, but not males, expected the *opposite* sex, as compared to the *same* sex, to be more disapproving of their own potential assertive behavior. These results would suggest that a woman's fear of negative consequences from acting assertively may be a function of her erroneous expectations about male disapproval. (Linehan & Egan, 1979, pp. 253–254)

As Linehan and Egan (1979) also note when qualifying their conclusion, there is an alternative explanation for these data: perhaps "there is a discrepancy between what men *report* as their attitude about assertive behavior in women and their actual response to an assertive woman" (p. 254).

Data that have been collected on actual behavior suggest that this second, rival hypothesis may well be the most plausible one. Hull and Schroeder (1979) compared male and female subjects' reactions to female confederates enacting either assertive, submissive, or aggressive roles. They found that while female subjects responded differently to the female confederates in the several conditions, that is, acquiesced more to female assertive and aggressive behaviors than to the submissive ones, male subjects did not. Eisler *et al.* (1975), investigating male psychiatric inpatients' reactions to assertion situations involving familiar and unfamiliar female and male partners, found their subjects significantly more likely to comply to a request made by a male than a request made by a female. Hess *et al.* (1980) examined the perceived assertion levels of taped female, male, and ambiguous sex voices stating the same response to identical rights-infringement situations; although differences were not significant, female voices were judged as the least assertive. When observing mixed-sex group discussions, Fishman (1975) found that conversation topics introduced by women tend to be dropped in favor of those introduced by men. It would appear from these data, then, that when women behave in a manner that would be perceived as assertive if enacted by a man, their behavior is regarded as nonassertive and is received, particularly by men, as if it were not.

Given that historically assertion has not been viewed as an appropriate component of the female sex role, it would be expected that when women behave in a way which is perceived as assertive, their behavior, like any violation of an ascribed social role (Ullmann & Krasner, 1975), would be negatively sanctioned. And indeed there are data to support the validity of this expectation. Lao, Upchurch, Corwin, and Grossnickle (1975) found that college students attribute low levels of intelligence and low levels of likability to highly assertive women and that women responding with levels of assertion as high as men's were perceived as significantly less intelligent and likable than were their male counterparts. Meyer and Lewis (1976) found that as wives were perceived by their husbands as being more assertive, they were also perceived as more dominant, less loving, and less affectionate.

Corroborating results were reported in a particularly careful study of differential reactions to female and male assertion by Kelly, Kern, Kirkley, Patterson, and Keane (1980). These investigators asked subjects to evaluate one of eight female or male videotaped confederates behaving in either an assertive or unassertive fashion in response to the unreasonable behavior of another person. They found that, while female and male unassertive models were rated comparably, and always more favorably, than assertive models, female assertive models were rated as significantly less friendly, less pleasant, less considerate, less open-minded, less good-natured, less kind, less likable, less thoughtful, and less warm than were the male assertive models enacting the objectively identical behavior. Moreover, assertive females were judged as being less attractive than any other group, while assertive males were judged to be higher than any other group on an ability/achievement factor marked by appropriateness, education, intelligence, and social skill. Kelly *et al.* (1980) summarized their results as suggesting that "this pattern of interaction effects between stimulus model behavior and sex of the model demonstrates that female assertive behavior is consistently evaluated in less favorable terms than the same assertive behavior when exhibited by a male" (p. 14).

Although there is a clear need for field studies addressing this question, there are indications that the negative attitudinal reception women's assertion receives may be mirrored in negative behavioral reactions as well. Haccoun and Lavigueur (1979) found that therapists interviewing female confederates presenting two rights-infringement situations, being mistreated by a desired social partner and being mistreated on a job, responded with significantly fewer empathic statements, significantly fewer statements giving advice, significantly fewer statements expressing supportiveness, and significantly fewer requests for factual information if the woman presented the content with nonverbally communicated anger than they did if the woman presented the same content with nonverbally communicated depression. Consistent with these behavioral differences, therapists rated the angry female as reacting significantly more inappropriately to her problem than they did the depressed one. Young, Beier, Beier, and Barton (1975) found that male aggression toward females increased dramatically in response to unfeminine (i.e., highly assertive) behavior on the women's parts, perhaps as a function of the male's feeling that their masculinity was threatened by women's clear assertion (Babl, 1979). And Meehan and Goldkopf (1979) noted that women who had increased their levels of assertion in response to assertion training reported subsequent deliberate decreases resulting from their husbands' and bosses' punishment of their assertive behavior.

It has been observed that women who become more behaviorally assertive as a function of assertion training also become more anxious

(Kiecolt & McGrath, 1979). Often this anxiety is viewed as resulting from women's irrational expectations about what the consequences of behaving assertively will be (see Linehan & Egan, 1979), but perhaps it would be more appropriate to view the anxiety as realistic (cf. Attowe, 1973). Since there are indications that expectations about the probable effects of assertion influence the likelihood of one's behaving assertively (Eisler, Frederiksen, & Peterson, 1978; Fiedler & Beach, 1978), and since there are data suggesting that women who behave assertively may experience either nonrewarding or punishing consequences, the suggestion that women's assertion training programs should include components designed to alter women's beliefs about the consequences of behaving assertively (see Linehan, Goldfried, & Goldfried, 1979) may need to be reconsidered.

CONCLUSIONS

It should be clear at this point that inquiring about whether there are sex differences in levels of assertion is neither a simple nor a complete question to address. It appears not to be the complexity of the question, however, but rather the strong and shared preconception about the answer that would result if it were asked, that has discouraged its careful study. The behavioral data that there are suggest that there are not differences between women's and men's levels of assertion when sex is treated as an individual difference variable, but that there probably are sex differences in the antecedents and consequents of assertion when sex is treated as a stimulus variable. Continued exploration of these conclusions is clearly warranted; but if research on these issues is to be meaningful, it must be conducted with recognition of preconceived notions and with deliberate choices of methodological strategies that are not biased toward illusorily obvious results.

The meaningful data available at this point suggest that when confronted with identical rights-infringement situations, the behavior of women is objectively as assertive as is the behavior of men. The data also suggest, however, that if the veridical rights of men and women are regarded as equal, women are confronted at least more frequently, and perhaps more fundamentally, with rights-infringement situations. They further suggest that when women defend their rights at a level equivalent to the level exhibited by men, their behavior is more likely than is men's to be either disregarded or negatively sanctioned.

If further laboratory and field research supports the validity of these conclusions, a fundamental redirection will be implied, for it follows from them that it is inappropriate to view assertion training for women as the correct strategy to alleviate women's oppression. The thrust of the available data is that the relatively greater constrictions placed on women's rights result from environmental antecedent and consequent events rather than assertion skill deficiencies in women as a group. To regard the oppression of women as either a result or function of women's assertion deficiencies, then, is an instance of the general theme Ryan (1971) has called blaming the victim. The problem of women's oppression is an institutional, not an individual one; the treatments that will be genuinely effective, then, will be those that are directed toward and have an impact on the environment.

ACKNOWLEDGMENTS

The author wishes to express her appreciation to Pamela Ann Tyson and Alexandra G. Kaplan for their comments on the draft for this chapter.

REFERENCES

Abrams, D. B., & Wilson, G. T. Self-monitoring and reactivity in the modification of cigarette smoking. *Journal of Consulting and Clinical Psychology*, 1979, 47, 243–251.

Alberti, R. E., & Emmons, M. L. *Your perfect right* (3rd ed.). San Luis Obispo, Calif.: Impact, 1978.

Attowe, J. W. Behavior innovation and persistence. *American Psychologist*, 1973, 28, 34–41.

Babl, J. D. Compensatory masculine responding as a function of sex role. *Journal of Consulting and Clinical Psychology*, 1979, 47, 252–257.

Bakan, D. *The duality of human existence.* Chicago: Rand-McNally, 1966.

Bates, H. D., & Zimmerman, S. F. Toward the development of a screening scale for assertive training. *Psychological Reports*, 1971, 28, 99–107.

Bem, S. L. The measurement of psychological androgyny. *Journal of Consulting and Clinical Psychology*, 1974, 47, 155–162.

Bem, S. L. Sex role adaptability: One consequence of psychological androgyny. *Journal of Personality and Social Psychology*, 1975, 31, 634–643.

Bem, S. L. On the utility of alternative procedures for assessing psychological androgyny. *Journal of Consulting and Clinical Psychology*, 1977, 45, 196–205.

Bem, S. L., & Bem, D. Training the woman to know her place: The power of a nonconscious ideology. In S. Cox (Ed.), *Female psychology: The emerging self.* Chicago: SRA, 1976.

Bem, S. L., & Lenny, E. Sex typing and the avoidance of cross-sex behavior. *Journal of Personality and Social Psychology*, 1976, 33, 48–54.

Bem, S. L., Martyna, W., & Watson, C. Sex typing and androgyny: Further explorations of the expressive domain. *Journal of Personality and Social Psychology*, 1976, 34, 1016–1023.

Bernard, J. *The sex game.* New York: Atheneum, 1972.

Berzins, J. N. New perspectives on sex roles and personality dimensions. In R. Bednar (Chair), *Sex roles: Masculine, feminine, androgynous, or none of the above?* Symposium presented at the annual meeting of the American Psychological Association, Chicago, August, 1975.

Bloom, L. Z., Coburn, K., & Pearlman, J. The new assertive woman. New York: Dell, 1975.

Butler, P. E. Self-assertion for women. San Francisco: Canfield Press, 1976.

Carden, M. L. The new feminist movement. New York: Russell Sage Foundation, 1974.

Costrich, N., Feinstein, J., Kidder, L., Marecek, J., & Pascale, L. When stereotypes hurt: Three studies of penalties for sex-role reversals. Journal of Experimental Social Psychology, 1975, 11, 520–530.

Deaux, K. Honking at the intersection: A replication and extension. Journal of Social Psychology, 1971, 84, 159–160.

Deaux, K. The behavior of women and men. Monterey, Calif.: Brooks Cole, 1976.

Dworkin, A. Woman hating. New York: Dutton, 1974.

Eisler, R. M., Frederiksen, L. W., & Peterson, G. L. The relationship of cognitive variables to the expression of assertiveness. Behavior Therapy, 1978, 9, 419–427.

Eisler, R. M., Hersen, M., Miller, P. M., & Blanchard, E. B. Situational determinants of assertive behavior. Journal of Consulting and Clinical Psychology, 1975, 43, 330–340.

Ekstrom, R. Barriers to women's participation in post-secondary education: A review of the literature. In S. Ball & P. Cross (Chair), Barriers to women's continuing education. A symposium presented at the annual meeting of the American Psychological Association, Honolulu, September 1972.

Fidell, L. Empirical validation of sex discrimination in hiring practices in psychology. American Psychologist, 1970, 25, 1094–1097.

Fiedler, D., & Beach, L. R. On the decision to be assertive. Journal of Consulting and Clinical Psychology, 1978, 46, 537–546.

Fishman, P. Study of male–female conversations. Paper presented at the annual meeting of the American Sociological Association, San Francisco, August 1975.

Frieze, I., & Ramsey, S. Nonverbal maintenance of traditional sex roles. Journal of Social Issues, 1976, 32, 133–141.

Frodi, A., Macauley, J., & Thorne, P. R. Are women always less aggressive than men? A review of the experimental literature. Psychological Bulletin, 1977, 84, 634–660.

Galassi, J. P., DeLo, J. S., Galassi, M. D., & Bastien, S. The College Self-Expression Scale: A measure of assertiveness. Behavior Therapy, 1974, 5, 165–171.

Galassi, M. D., & Galassi, J. P. Assert yourself! How to be your own person. New York: Human Sciences Press, 1977.

Gambrill, E. D., & Richey, C. A. An assertion inventory for use in assessment and research. Behavior Therapy, 1975, 6, 550–561.

Gay, M. L., Hollandsworth, J. G., & Galassi, J. P. An assertiveness inventory for adults. Journal of Counseling Psychology, 1975, 22, 340–344.

Greenwald, D. P. Self-reported assessment in high- and low-dating college women. Behavior Therapy, 1978, 9, 297–299.

Haccoun, D. M., & Lavigueur, H. Effects of clinical experience and client emotion on therapists' responses. Journal of Consulting and Clinical Psychology, 1979, 47, 416–418.

Harmon, T. M., Nelson, R. D., & Hayes, S. C. Self-monitoring of mood versus activity by depressed clients. Journal of Consulting and Clinical Psychology, 1980, 48, 30–38.

Harris, M. B. Mediators between frustration and aggression in a field experiment. Journal of Experimental Social Psychology, 1974, 10, 561–571.

Heilbrun, A. B. Measurement of masculine and feminine sex role identities as independent dimensions. Journal of Consulting and Clinical Psychology, 1976, 44, 183–190.

Henley, N. The politics of touch. In P. Brown (Ed.), Radical psychology. New York: Harper, 1973.

Hersen, M., Eisler, R. M., & Miller, P. M. Development of assertive responses: Clinical, measurement, and research considerations. *Behaviour Research and Therapy*, 1973, *11*, 505–521.

Hersen, M., Eisler, R. M., & Miller, P. M. An experimental analysis of generalization in assertive training. *Behaviour Research and Therapy*, 1974, *12*, 295–310.

Hess, E. P., Bridgwater, C. A., Bornstein, P. H., & Sweeney, T. M. Situational determinants in the perception of assertiveness: Gender-related influences. *Behavior Therapy*, 1980, *11*, 49–58.

Hoffman, L. Changes in family roles, socialization, and sex differences. *American Psychologist*, 1977, *32*, 644–657.

Hollandsworth, J. G. Further investigation of the relationship between expressed social fear and assertiveness. *Behaviour Research and Therapy*, 1976, *14*, 85–87.

Hollandsworth, J. G., & Wall, K. E. Sex differences in assertive behavior: An empirical investigation. *Journal of Counseling Psychology*, 1977, *24*, 217–222.

Hull, D. B., & Schroeder, H. E. Some interpersonal effects of assertion, nonassertion, and aggression. *Behavior Therapy*, 1979, *10*, 20–28.

Johnson, M. M. Sex role learning in the nuclear family. *Child Development*, 1963, *34*, 319–333.

Jones, W. H., O'C. Chernovetz, M. E., & Hansson, R. O. The enigma of androgyny: Differential implications for males and females. *Journal of Consulting and Clinical Psychology*, 1978, *46*, 298–313.

Kanter, R. Women in organizations: Sex roles, group dynamics, and change strategies. In A. Sargent (Ed.), *Beyond sex roles*. St. Paul: West Publishing, 1976.

Kaplan, A. G., & Sedney, M. A. *Psychology and sex roles: An androgynous perspective.* Boston: Little, Brown, 1980.

Kazdin, A. E. Imagery elaboration and self-efficacy in the covert modeling treatment of unassertive behavior. *Journal of Consulting and Clinical Psychology*, 1979, *47*, 725–733.

Kelly, J. A., Kern, J. M., Kirkley, B. G., Patterson, J. N., & Keane, T. M. Reactions to assertive versus unassertive behavior: Differential effects for males and females and implications for assertive training. *Behavior Therapy*, 1980, *11*, 670–682.

Kelly, J. A., O'Brien, C. C., Hooford, R., & Kinsinger, E. Sex roles as social skills: A behavioral analysis of "masculinity," "femininity," and "psychological androgyny." Paper presented at the annual meeting of the Association for Advancement of Behavior Therapy, New York, December 1976.

Kelly, J. A., & Worell, J. New formulations of sex roles and androgyny: A critical review. *Journal of Consulting and Clinical Psychology*, 1977, *45*, 1101–1115.

Kiecolt, J., & McGrath, E. Social desirability responding in the measurement of assertive behavior. *Journal of Consulting and Clinical Psychology*, 1979, *47*, 640–642.

Kirsch, I., & Henry, D. Self-desensitization and meditation in the reduction of public speaking anxiety. *Journal of Consulting and Clinical Psychology*, 1979, *47*, 536–541.

Lange, A. J., & Jakubowski, P. *Responsible assertive behavior: Cognitive/behavioral procedures for trainers.* Champaign, Ill.: Research Press, 1976.

Lao, R., Upchurch, W., Corwin, B., & Grossnickle, W. Biased attitudes toward females as indicated by ratings of intelligence and likability. *Psychological Reports*, 1975, *37*, 1315–1320.

Lazarus, A. A. On assertive behavior: A brief note. *Behavior Therapy*, 1973, *4*, 697–699.

Libby, W., & Haklevitch, D. Personality determinants of eye contact and direction of gaze aversion. *Journal of Personality and Social Psychology*, 1973, *27*, 197–206.

Linehan, M., & Egan, J. Assertion training for women. In A. S. Bellack & M. Hersen (Eds.), *Research and practice in social skills training*. New York: Plenum, 1979.

Linehan, M. M., Goldfried, M. R., & Goldfried, A. P. Assertion therapy: Skill training or cognitive restructuring. *Behavior Therapy*, 1979, *10*, 372–388.

Linehan, M. M., & Siefert, R. How appropriate is assertive behavior? Real and perceived sex differences. Unpublished manuscript, University of Washington, 1978.

Maccoby, E. E., & Jacklin, C. N. The psychology of sex differences. Stanford: Stanford University Press, 1974.

MacDonald, M. L. A behavioral assessment methodology applied to the measurement of assertion (Copyrighted doctoral dissertation, University of Illinois at Urbana-Champaign, 1974). Dissertation Abstracts International, 1975, 35, 6101B. (University Microfilms No. 75-11, 819)

MacDonald, M. L. Teaching assertion: A paradigm for therapeutic intervention. Psychotherapy: Theory, Research, and Practice, 1975, 12, 60–67.

MacDonald, M. L. Measuring assertion: A model and method. Behavior Therapy, 1978, 9, 889–899.

MacDonald, M. L. The behaviormetric assessment model: A reconciliation of two traditions. In N. Hirschberg & L. G. Humphreys (Eds.), Multivariate methods in the social sciences: Applications, in press. (a)

MacDonald, M. L. A cross-validation of the College Women's Assertion Sample. Journal of Educational and Psychological Measurement, in press. (b)

MacDonald, M. L. & Cohen, J. B. Trees in the forest: Some components of social skills. Journal of Clinical Psychology, 1981, 37, 342–347.

MacDonald, M. L., Swan, G. E., & Itkin, S. M. The College Men's Assertion Sample. Paper presented at the annual meeting of the Association for the Advancement of Behavior Therapy, San Francisco, December 1979.

MacDonald, M. L., & Tyson, P. A. External validities for several laboratory measures of assertion. Manuscript submitted for publication, 1980.

McFall, R. M., & Lillesand, D. B. Behavior rehearsal with modeling and coaching in assertion training. Journal of Abnormal Psychology, 1971, 77, 313–323.

McFall, R. M., & Marston, A. R. An experimental investigation of behavior rehearsal in assertive training. Journal of Abnormal Psychology, 1970, 76, 295–303.

Meehan, E. F., & Goldkopf, D. A. Multifaceted group training and attitudinal restructuring in modifying assertive behavior for women. Unpublished manuscript, College of Staten Island of the City University of New York, 1979.

Meyer, R., & Lewis, R. New wine from old wineskins: Marital power research. Journal of Comparative Family Studies, 1976, 7, 397–407.

Morgan, W. G. The relationship between expressed social fears and assertiveness and its treatment implications. Behaviour Research and Therapy, 1974, 12, 255–257.

Mullinex, S. D., & Galassi, J. P. Social impact of interpersonal behavior in a work–conflict situation. Paper presented at the annual meeting of the American Psychological Association, Toronto, September 1978.

Orenstein, H., Orenstein, E., & Carr, J. E. Assertiveness and anxiety: A correlational study. Journal of Behavior Therapy and Experimental Psychiatry, 1975, 6, 203–207.

Osborn, S. M., & Harris, G. G. Assertive training for women. Springfield, Ill.: Charles C. Thomas, 1975.

Osmond, M., & Martin, P. Sex and sexism: A comparison of male and female sex-role attitudes. Journal of Marriage and the Family, 1975, 37, 744–758.

Parsons, T., & Bales, R. F. Family, socialization and interaction process. New York: Free Press of Glencoe, 1955.

Peterson, C., & Peterson, J. Preferences for sex of offspring as a measure of change in sex attitudes. Psychology, 1973, 10, 3–5.

Phillips, E. L. The social skills basis of psychopathology: Alternatives to abnormal psychology and psychiatry. New York: Grune & Stratton, 1978.

Pohlman, E. The psychology of birth planning. Cambridge, Mass.: Schenkman, 1969.

Redd, W. H., Porterfield, A. L., & Anderson, B. L. *Behavior modification: Behavioral approaches to human problems.* New York: Random House, 1979.

Rosenkrantz, P. S., Vogel, S. R., Bee, H., Broverman, I. K., & Broverman, D. M. Sex-role stereotypes and self-concepts in college students. *Journal of Consulting and Clinical Psychology,* 1968, *32,* 287–295.

Ryan, W. *Blaming the victim.* New York: Vantage, 1971.

Salter, A. On assertion. In R. E. Alberti (Ed.), *Assertiveness: Innovations, applications, issues.* San Luis Obispo, Calif.: Impact, 1977.

Schaffer, K. F. *Sex-role issues in mental health.* Reading, Mass.: Addison-Wesley, 1980.

Schroeder, H. E., & Rakos, R. F. Effects of history on the measurement of assertion. *Behavior Therapy,* 1978, *9,* 965–966.

Serbin, L., & O'Leary, K. D. How nursery schools teach girls to shut up. *Psychology Today,* 1975, *9,* 56–58.

Sherman, J. *On the psychology of women: A survey of empirical studies.* Springfield, Ill.: Charles C. Thomas, 1971.

Shields, S. A. Functionalism, Darwinism, and the psychology of women. *American Psychologist,* 1975, *30,* 739–754.

Spence, J. T., Helmreich, R., & Stapp, J. Ratings of self and peers on sex-role attributes and their relation to self-esteem and conceptions of masculinity and femininity. *Journal of Personality and Social Psychology,* 1975, *32,* 29–39.

Tyson, P. A., & MacDonald, M. L. *Relevance of item difficulty levels to behavior sample (direct observational) measures.* Manuscript submitted for publication, 1980.

Ullmann, L. P., & Krasner, L. (Eds.). *Case studies in behavior modification.* New York: Holt, 1965.

Ullmann, L. P., & Krasner, L. *A psychological approach to abnormal behavior* (2nd ed.). Englewood Cliffs, N.J.: Prentice-Hall, 1975.

Unger, R. K. Toward a redefinition of sex and gender. *American Psychologist,* 1979, *34,* 1085–1094.

Unger, R. K. Sex as a social reality: Field and laboratory research. *Psychology of Women Quarterly,* in press.

Unger, R. K., Raymond, B. J., & Levine, S. M. Are women a "minority" group? Sometimes! *International Journal of Group Tensions,* 1974, *4,* 71–81.

Weitz, S. *Sex roles.* New York: Oxford University Press, 1977.

Wolpe, J., & Lazarus, A. A. *Behavior therapy techniques: A guide to the treatment of neuroses.* New York: Pergamon, 1966.

Wooley, H. T. Psychological literature: A review of the recent literature on the psychology of sex. *Psychological Bulletin,* 1910, *7,* 335–342.

Woolfolk, R. L., & Dever, S. Perceptions of assertion: An empirical analysis. *Behavior Therapy,* 1979, *10,* 404–411.

Worell, J. Sex roles and psychological well-being: Perspectives on methodology. *Journal of Consulting and Clinical Psychology,* 1978, *46,* 777–791.

Young, D. M., Beier, E. G., Beier, P., & Barton, C. Is chivalry dead? *Journal of Communication,* 1975, *25,* 57–64.

Zimmerman, D. H., & West, C. Sex roles, interruptions and silences in conversation. In B. Thorne & N. Henley (Eds.), *Language and sex: Differences and dominance.* Rowley, Mass.: Newbury House, 1975.

Zwart, C. A., & Lisman, S. A. Analysis of stimulus control treatment of sleep-onset insomnia. *Journal of Consulting and Clinical Psychology,* 1979, *47,* 113–118.

9

THE IDENTIFICATION AND TREATMENT OF CHILDREN WITH PEER-RELATIONSHIP DIFFICULTIES

DORAN C. FRENCH
THOMAS F. TYNE

As children grow older, the peer group takes on an increasingly important role in the socialization process (Hartup, 1970, 1976). There is growing consensus in the child development literature that a variety of social behaviors are learned within the context of the peer culture, and in the absence of these experiences children fail to develop the social skills needed for positive interpersonal relationships. For example, children acquire aggressive behaviors as a result of their exposure to other children (Patterson, Littman, & Bricker, 1967), and learn to regulate their aggressive impulses through experiences with their peers (Hartup & DeWitt, 1974). Sexual socialization also appears to occur predominantly as a result of peer rather than adult tutelege (Hartup, 1976). Furthermore, the development of such social–cognitive skills as role taking and moral judgement are reportedly influenced by one's peer experiences (Hartup, 1979).

Further interest in the importance of peer relationships during early and middle childhood has been spurred by findings that a child's status within the peer group is predictive of later psychological adjustment. It has been reported that the extent to which children get along with and are accepted by their peers is an indicator of adolescent delinquency (Roff, Sells, & Golden, 1972), adult mental health (Cowen, Pederson, Babigian, Izzo, & Trost, 1973), military bad conduct discharges (Roff, 1961), dropping out of high school (Barclay, 1966; Ullman, 1957), and adult suicide (Stengel, 1971). It should be emphasized that these

Doran C. French. Department of Educational Psychology, University of Wisconsin, Madison, Wisconsin.

Thomas F. Tyne. Department of Psychology, University of Rhode Island, Kingston, Rhode Island.

findings are derived from correlational studies, and it is difficult to determine whether poor peer relations cause later adjustment difficulties, or whether peers are simply sensitive to socioemotional disorders in their preliminary states (Hartup, 1979). Given the high correlation between poor peer relations and subsequent maladjustment, it is troubling that somewhere between 5% and 15% of elementary school students experience significant interpersonal relationship problems (Asher & Renshaw, 1981; Glidewell & Swallow, 1969; Gronlund, 1959; Stennett, 1965).

In this chapter, we will focus on the identification and treatment of children with peer-relationship difficulties. In the first part of the chapter we review the assessment methods commonly used to identify these children. This is followed by a discussion of the various types of children experiencing peer-relationship difficulties and the basis for these out-group categorizations. While out-group children are often thought of as a homogeneous group, several types of such children can be delineated (Asher & Hymel, 1981). Some of these children appear to be neglected or ignored by other children, whereas others are actively rejected by their peers (Asher, 1978; Gronlund & Anderson, 1957). While many of these children interact very little with their peers, others interact with great frequency and intensity (Gottman, 1977). Differentiation of the various subgroups of out-group children is important given the possibility that both the intervention strategy of choice, and the outcome of the treatment, differ depending upon the type of child involved.

In the second part of the chapter, we will review the various remedial programs that have been developed for teaching children social skills and increasing peer acceptance. Our primary focus in this section is on categorizing these intervention efforts in terms of the population of out-group children targeted. The existing reviews of children's social skill training programs have offered comprehensive analyses of the methodologies and impact of these programs, but have not addressed the relevance and efficacy of the strategies in terms of the characteristics of the subgroups with which they were used. The emphasis in this review is on the content of the program and the particular skills targeted. The specific intervention techniques employed (i.e., reinforcement of acceptable behavior, problem solving, modeling, role playing) are mentioned, but are not discussed in detail. The rationale for emphasizing content rather than technique is the assumption that the skills taught in these programs should reflect the behavioral deficits or excesses of the treatment group. It follows that a program's content may be more appropriate for one type of out-group child than another.

PROCEDURES USED TO IDENTIFY STUDENTS WITH
PEER-RELATIONSHIP PROBLEMS

The assessment of social competency in adults has typically relied upon self-report data, or on the observation of behavior in naturalistic or analogue situations (Bellack & Hersen, 1977). While observational procedures and teacher judgments have been used to identify certain types of children with peer-relationship difficulties (O'Connor, 1969, 1972), sociometric assessment techniques are the most frequently used identification method (Oden & Asher, 1977). Sociometric procedures require each member of a group to report on their perceptions or feelings about other group members as social companions. Three types of sociometric techniques are typically used in identifying students with peer-relationship difficulties, namely, positive nominations, negative nominations, and/or peer ratings. These procedures, along with behavioral observation and teacher judgments, will be discussed below.

PEER NOMINATIONS

The most commonly used method of assessing children's social competence and the degree to which they are accepted by their peers is peer nominations (Moreno, 1960). There are two types of nomination procedures, positive and negative. In both cases children in a social group (e.g., classroom, summer camp, club, etc.) are asked to specify which of their peers fits a particular criterion. Positive nominations are obtained by asking such questions as "Name your three best friends," or "Whom do you most like to play (or work) with?" Negative nominations are obtained in a similar manner, with the members of a group being asked to specify those children whom they dislike, or with whom they do not like to interact. The number of nominations each child receives is assumed to reflect the child's relative peer status within the group. Positive nominations are assumed to measure social acceptance, or the extent to which a child is valued as a companion. Negative nominations are taken as a measure of peer rejection, and the extent to which the individual is shunned by the peer group.

Despite the apparent simplicity of sociometric nominations, this technique has good psychometric characteristics (Asher & Hymel, 1981). Temporal stability estimates of positive nominations in elementary school populations have been reported to be as high as .84 when assessed over an 8-week period (Busk, Ford, & Schulman, 1973), and .40 when assessed over a 3-year interval (Sells & Roff, 1967). With preschool children stability is lower but still substantial, ranging from .68 (Hartup, Glazer, & Charlsworth, 1967) to .38 (Asher, Singleton, Tinsley, & Hymel, 1979). While test-retest reliabilities of negative nominations are somewhat less than those reported for positive nominations, they are still in the acceptable range (Hartup, 1970). For example, Roff *et al.* (1972) found the stability of negative nominations to be .40 when assessed across a 1-year period, and .34 over a 3-year interval.

The validity of sociometric nominations has been established by comparing students' relative social status with concurrent teacher judgments of overt behavior, and/or observations of peer interactions (Asher & Hymel, 1981; Hartup, 1970). Nominations also have been found to have good predictive validity in several longitudinal mental health studies (Cowen, Dorr, Trost, & Izzo, 1972; Roff *et al.*, 1972).

Several investigators have combined positive and negative nomination scores into a single social status score by subtracting the number of negative nominations from the number of positive nominations (e.g., Roff *et al.*, 1972). However, there are data indicating that positive and negative nominations tap somewhat different aspects of children's social functioning, and should therefore be used independently. Evidence for the relative independence of the two dimensions comes from correlational studies in which low or no significant correlations between positive and negative nominations have been reported (Asher & Hymel, 1981; Gottman, 1977; Hartup *et al.*, 1967; Van Hasselt, Bellack, & Hersen, 1979). Given these correlations, and data indicating that the behavioral correlates of accepted and rejected children differ, it appears that positive and negative nominations tap somewhat different dimensions of peer functioning (Asher & Hymel, 1981). The richness of each procedure may be lost when the two scores are combined.

PEER RATINGS

Peer sociometric ratings differ from nomination techniques both in method and in the type of information they provide. Children are typically presented with a list of their peers and are asked to rate each child along some social or interpersonal dimension. An illustration of this procedure is provided by Tyne and Flynn (1979), who had each child in a class rate every classmate on a 6-point Likert-type social distance scale. This scale was anchored on the positive end by "One of my best friends" and the negative by "Don't like them." A mean sociometric rating was then generated by averaging the scores given to each child.

The test–retest reliabilities of rating scales are usually in the .70 to .80 range, and are generally superior to those of nomination procedures (Oden & Asher, 1977; Thompson & Powell, 1951). Rating scales' higher temporal stability apparently stems from the greater number of peer judgments contributing to each student's sociometric score (Asher & Hymel, 1981).

Although there are high correlations ($r = .68 - .87$) between rating scales and peer nominations (Asher & Hymel, 1981; Justman & Wright-stone, 1961), there are data indicating that the two procedures tap somewhat different aspects of peer functioning (Oden & Asher, 1977). It may be that peer rating scales assess children's overall level of peer acceptance, while positive and negative nominations measure the extent to which the child is someone's best friend or worst enemy (Asher & Hymel, 1981).

TEACHER JUDGMENTS

Teacher judgments are frequently used to identify children experiencing peer-relationship difficulties, and are obtained through the use of nomination, checklist, or rating procedures. Nomination procedures require the teacher to specify the children who fit a particular criterion (e.g., shy or aggressive). With checklists the teacher indicates which descriptors reflect each student's behavior, while with ratings the teacher quantitatively estimates the extent to which a given descriptor is characteristic of each child.

Teacher judgments are one of the most convenient methods for identifying out-group children. Compared to sociometric evaluations this procedure is more attractive to some researchers because the data are easily collected and parental permission is not required. Teacher's exposure to a large and wide range of children, and their access to normative comparisons when making decisions about the atypical nature of a child's behavior, are seen as additional advantages of this procedure. Based on these factors, Janes and Hesselbrock (1977) have suggested that teacher judgments can be used in lieu of sociometric assessments because of the practical and ethical constraints involved in the use of the latter procedure.

However, a number of concerns regarding the use of teacher judgments should be addressed prior to advocating the use of this procedure. Perhaps most problematic is that while there are significant correlations between the data generated by teacher judgments and sociometric procedures (Green, Forehand, Beck, & Vosk, 1979), the magnitude of this overlap is not convincingly large. Tyne and Flynn (in press) found that the agreement between teacher nominations and peer sociometric ratings ranged from 55% for fifth-grade males to 19% for third-grade females. One would hope for higher agreement indices if teacher judgments were to be substituted for peer sociometric procedures. Additional concerns about the use of teacher judgments come from studies indicating that teachers frequently rely on invalid or inappropriate selection criteria (Phillips, 1968), make stereotypic assumptions about maladaptive behavior (Eaton, D'Amico, & Phillips, 1966), and incorporate their own criteria into the referral guidelines (Saunders & Vitro, 1971). Given the shortage of concurrent and predictive data on teacher assessment techniques, mental health professionals should be cautious in employing this identification procedure, and whenever possible use sociometric or observational techniques in conjunction with teacher selection methods.

NATURALISTIC OBSERVATION

Naturalistic observation has frequently been used to identify children with peer-relationship difficulties (Allen, Hart, Buell, Harris, & Wolf, 1964; Furman, Rahe, & Hartup, 1979; O'Connor, 1969, 1972). In most of these studies, researchers have focused primarily on the frequency of peer interactions. Observations of the quality of peer interactions have not typically been used to identify out-group members. Instead, they have been utilized to assess the behavioral characteristics of children who have already been identified as having peer-relationship difficulties.

Frequency of interaction appears to provide a different index of interpersonal functioning than does sociometric procedures; in fact, little relationship has been found between the frequency of children's interaction, and the extent to which they are accepted by their peers (Gottman, 1977; Hymel & Asher, 1977). Many well-liked children apparently interact infrequently with their peers, while many unpopular children interact extensively with others (Gottman, 1977). Researchers have used observational procedures to identify children with low levels of peer involvement, but have not typically used this method to select those actively accepted or rejected by others.

Other assessment methods that are of potential use in assessing peer-relationship problems include interviewing (Ciminero & Drabman, 1977) and self-report (Cowen, Trost, Lorian, Dorr, Izzo, & Isaacson, 1975). These procedures are only beginning to be used with children, and their utility has not yet been fully assessed.

CLASSIFICATION OF CHILDREN EXPERIENCING
PEER-RELATIONSHIP PROBLEMS

Using the previously discussed measures of social competence singularly, or in combination, it is possible to distinguish several subgroups of children who experience peer-interaction difficulties. One type of out-group children has been labeled "isolated," and can be identified purely on the basis of a low frequency of peer contact. A second type, "rejected" children, can be selected using positive and negative peer nominations or peer ratings. The third type is labeled "neglected," and its members are characterized by a low number of positive and negative nominations. Each of these three groups will be discussed below, and the behavioral characteristics of each out-group population will be delineated.

ISOLATED CHILDREN

Several investigators have identified children who exhibit low rates of peer involvement as isolates (O'Connor, 1969, 1972). The label "withdrawn" is also frequently applied to these children, with the implication that isolates are anxious and/or socially unskilled, and that they would like to interact with their peers but are unable to successfully do so (Gottman, 1977).

Intuitively, it would appear as if interaction rates would provide a good method of identifying children with peer-relationship difficulties. However, no criteria for gender or age-specific interaction rates are available for determining pathology, deviance, or the need for intervention. Investigators have therefore been required to establish their own criteria for what constitutes isolation. The criteria selected have varied from study to study, and in some cases the criteria have been set quite liberally. Asher and Renshaw (1981) noted that the percentage of peer contact criteria for identifying isolates has ranged from 5% to 50% in different studies.

In addition, the low relationship between frequency of interactions and other measures of social competence casts further doubt on the utility of classifying children as having peer-relationship difficulties based solely on their low rates of interaction. While it is commonly assumed that isolates are withdrawn, this latter term does not appear to be a particularly appropriate descriptor of this population, as isolates do not appear to be uniformly high on "hovering" (Gottman, 1977), a set of shy, anxious, and fearful behaviors (McGrew, 1972).

Overall, it remains to be demonstrated that isolates experience significant interpersonal problems, or that a low rate of interaction in and of itself constitutes a problem necessitating intervention. At this point, isolates appear to be a relatively heterogeneous group. While some of these children may have significant peer-relationship problems, others may be relatively well adjusted. Thus, it appears that other criteria, in addition to that of low rates of interaction, may be needed to identify those isolates who experience significant interpersonal difficulties.

NEGLECTED VERSUS REJECTED CHILDREN

A distinction can be made between two groups of children who have difficulty interacting with their peers, namely, children who are neglected by others and those who are rejected by their peers (Asher & Hymel, 1981). Identification of these two groups is typically made on the basis of combined results of the positive and negative peer nominations. Neglected children receive few positive nominations, and receive few, if any, negative nominations; as such they are low on both peer acceptance and peer rejection. Rejected children also receive few positive nominations, but are given a large number of negative nominations. They can be termed low on peer acceptance and high on peer rejection. Peer ratings can also be used to identify children who are rejected by their peers, but generally cannot be used to differentiate between rejected and neglected children (Asher & Hymel, 1981).

The utility of distinguishing between these two groups is supported by data indicating that there are personality and behavioral differences between rejected and neglected children. These differences were addressed in a study by Gronlund and Anderson (1957). Rejected and neglected seventh- and eighth-grade students were identified on the basis of positive and negative peer nominations. Additional rating data were obtained through a "Guess Who?" instrument, a technique requiring each student to rate his or her classmates on 18 personality and behavioral dimensions. Clear differences were found in the ratings given to the neglected and rejected children. Neglected children's scores were neither high nor low on the various interpersonal dimensions tapped by the instrument. The authors suggested that the neglected children were the neutral personalities who were overlooked rather than disliked by the classmates. Thus, neglected children appear to lack the endearing attributes promoting peer affiliation. Rejected children, while similar to the neglected children in that they were rarely given positive trait descriptors, were rated quite differently on the negative trait dimensions. Socially rejected boys and girls were described as being untidy, not likable, unattractive, and too talkative. Thus, rejected children, in addition to lacking the attributes that typically lead to acceptance, also possessed characteristics that were negatively perceived by others.

Further support for the utility of distinguishing between the absence of positive attributes and the presence of negative attributes is found in Hartup *et al.* (1967). These authors found a significant relationship between a child's level of positive social acceptance, and the amount of positive reinforcers dispensed to others. However, no relationship was found between peer rejection and the amount of social reinforcement given to others. Peer rejection was closely associated with the presence of aversive behaviors in the child's behavioral repertoire (e.g., noncompliance, interference, derogation, and attack), but not associated with the frequency of positive behavior. Similarly, low sociability is associated with low popularity at all age levels, but is not strongly correlated with peer rejection (Hartup, 1970). Thus, the absence of endearing attributes is related to low peer acceptance, while rejection is marked by the presence of aversive behaviors. Additional support for the suggested relationship between rejection and the presence of aversive behaviors comes from a study by Green, Vosk, Forehand, and Beck (1979). These authors found that rejected children were rated as more hyperactive than their accepted peers. Furthermore, there are data indicating that the aggressive behavior of rejected children is likely to be more socially unacceptable and indirect than the aggressive behavior of nonrejected children (Dunnington, 1957; Hartup, 1970).

The distinction between neglected and rejected children may have clear implications for the design of intervention programs. Programs for neglected children may require the building up of social skills that would enable these children to be more attractive and positively reinforcing social companions. Programs for rejected children may, in addition to the above, require treatment to decrease the level of negative or aversive behaviors and substitute more socially appropriate responses. As of now, there is no clear distinction made between intervention programs available to or appropriate for isolated, neglected, or rejected children. As a first step toward accomplishing this goal, we will attempt next to review the various intervention programs in light of the outgroup populations targeted. This review is separated into three sections, each focusing on the remediation of isolated, neglected, or rejected children's social skills. Decisions regarding the assignment of the available intervention programs to one of the three sections were made by examining the identification criteria used by the researchers. It is hoped that this review will facilitate decisions about the relative efficacy of using the available intervention programs with isolated, neglected, and rejected populations.

TREATMENT OF ISOLATED CHILDREN

Two types of intervention programs have been used to improve the social interactions of isolated children. One type of program has focused on increasing the frequency of an isolate's social interactions either by employing reinforcement procedures, or by involving the isolated child in a social companionship program. The second type of program centers on teaching the child specific social skills. The assumption underlying this latter technique is that improving specific skills leads to an increase in the quantity and quality of the child's peer interactions. These two types of programs are discussed below.

INCREASING THE INTERACTION RATES OF ISOLATED CHILDREN

The initial intervention efforts with isolated children utilized reinforcement techniques to increase the rates of peer interaction. Allen *et al.* (1964) found that the frequency of an isolate's social exchanges could be increased by having the teachers offer contingent praise and attention whenever the child physically approached or verbally engaged another child. Similarly, in two single-case studies (Buell, Stoddard, Harris, & Baer, 1968; Hart, Reynolds, Baer, Brawley, & Harris, 1968), it was found that the frequency of the isolates' peer contacts could be increased by reinforcing appropriate interactions with contingent teacher praise.

Other researchers have found that reinforcement procedures could be used to increase the attractiveness of the isolated child as a social companion. In one investigation, Kirby and Toler (1970) found that the frequency of an isolated child's interactions could be increased by having the child dispense candy to classmates. The authors suggested that this manipulation led to the isolate taking on reinforcing properties and serving as a positive discriminative stimulus. Furthermore, it has been found that teacher-contingent reinforcement of an isolate's social interaction leads to an increased frequency of peer-initiated social contacts with the child (Strain & Timm, 1974). The authors suggested that the isolates' classmates were vicariously reinforced when they observed the target child being rewarded for social initiations. This, in turn, increased the frequency of peer-initiated social contacts, and provided the isolate with additional opportunities to interact and be reinforced for initiating and responding to peer interactions (Strain, Shores, & Kerr, 1976).

Others (Walker & Hops, 1973) have increased the social interaction rates of isolated children by reinforcing the isolates and their classmates for the initiation of social exchanges. The goal of this technique is to create conditions that promote positive and reinforcing peer interactions, thereby facilitating the maintenance of these interactions in the absence of experimenter-imposed contingencies (Baer & Wolf, 1970).

It has also been demonstrated that social interaction rates can be increased by environmental restructuring or peer-companionship treatments. Probably the best example of this type of intervention strategy was that employed by Furman et al. (1979). These authors paired isolated nursery school children with either a same-age or younger companion for 20 play sessions of 10 minutes. The isolated children in both groups were found to increase their interactions, but those paired with a younger child showed the greatest increase. It was suggested that exposure to a younger child provided the isolate with an opportunity to initiate and direct social activities, experiences apparently missing in the course of their normal social interactions.

TRAINING ISOLATED CHILDREN IN SOCIAL SKILLS

Several investigators have attempted to decrease the social withdrawal of isolates by teaching them certain social skills that are assumed to be necessary for successful peer interactions. The skills include motoric behaviors (eye contact, physical approach, smiling), verbal responses (initiating conversation, regulating loudness of speech, making requests, expressing feelings, etc.), and interpersonal cognitive skills (making self-statements, understanding others' viewpoints). These skills have been taught through the use of modeling, coaching, and/or reinforcement techniques.

Considerable interest in the use of symbolic modeling has been stimulated by O'Connor's (1969) findings. O'Connor worked with children identified by their teachers as being withdrawn, and observed to interact with their peers less than 15% of the time. O'Connor found that after viewing a training film, the isolates increased their level of peer involvement to that of nonisolated classmates. The film depicted 11 episodes in which a child actor entered a group activity and was positively received by the other children. The film was accompanied by a narration in which the ongoing activity was described, the subjects were instructed in the most effective ways to interact, and the positive consequences of the successful interaction were highlighted (Asher & Renshaw, 1981).

Other investigators have generally reported that the O'Connor film is effective in increasing the peer-interaction rates of socially isolated children. These increases have been found immediately after viewing the film (Evers-Pasquale & Sherman, 1975), and following a 4- to 6-week interval (Evers & Schwarz, 1973; Jakibchuk & Smeriglio, 1976; O'Connor, 1972). An exception to the reported efficacy of symbolic modeling was raised by Gottman (1977), who failed to find any change in two isolates' interaction rates when assessed 7 weeks after viewing the film. Given the absence of immediate posttest measures, it is uncertain whether the film was ineffective or whether the effects were not maintained across the 7-week time span (Asher & Renshaw, 1981).

Keller and Carlson (1974) demonstrated that symbolic modeling procedures could also be used to teach isolates such specific skills as social initiation, smiling, laughing, token taking, and physical contact. Preschoolers identified by their teachers as having low frequencies of peer interaction were shown videotapes illustrating the above social skills. The frequency of the isolates' peer contacts was found to increase following treatment, with the majority of these gains stemming from increases in the children's social initiation, smiling, and laughing behaviors.

Ross, Ross, and Evans (1971) demonstrated the effectiveness of a live modeling program in teaching an isolated child specific social skills. These authors found that having a 6-year-old observe and rehearse a live adult's social approach, initiation, and interaction behaviors led to an increase in the frequency of the child's peer interactions. The gains occurred in both the training and nontraining setting, and were still apparent 2 months after treatment.

While symbolic modeling procedures have generally been shown to be effective in modifying social withdrawal, others have investigated the efficacy of treatment packages that utilize symbolic modeling in conjunction with other intervention techniques. In these programs, a variety of methods, including role playing, coaching, rehearsal, and reinforcement have been used to teach isolates specific social skills. In the majority of these studies, no attempt was made to discern which component of the package was responsible for any treatment gains.

Weinrott, Corson, and Wilcheskey (1979) had isolates view a film that depicted various social behaviors, and then role-play the targeted skills. Subjects were then reinforced for exhibiting these skills in the classroom. It was found that the 25 isolates increased the frequency of their peer contacts to a level comparable with that of the nonisolated children at the conclusion of the treatment, and at a 2-week follow-up.

An intervention program employing coaching, behavior rehearsal, and feedback was used to increase the eye contact, loudness of speech, and verbal requests of four unassertive and withdrawn children (Bornstein, Bellack, & Hersen, 1977). These children rehearsed and modeled the target behaviors in a laboratory setting, and were evaluated on an analogue role-play task. Substantial improvement on the target behaviors was demonstrated at posttesting, and was still apparent 4 weeks after termination of the treatment program. Unfortunately, no data were collected on the generalization of these improvements to the classroom. The generalization issue was subsequently addressed by Beck, Forehand, Wells, and Quante (1978), who used the Bornstein *et al.* (1977) package with two elementary school isolates. While increases in eye contact, smiling, and verbal interactions were obtained in the analogue setting, these gains did not generalize to the classroom setting, nor did they lead to a change in the child's sociometric status within the classroom. Combs and Lahey (1979) also employed a treatment package to improve the social skills of three children identified by their teachers as having low levels of peer involvement. The children were exposed to two hour-long self-instruction and modeling sessions where they practiced various social interaction skills (eye contact, maintenance of physical proximity, verbal initiation, and verbal responding). The frequency of these behaviors increased in the training setting, but these gains did not generalize to the classroom until they were directly reinforced by the teacher. While it has been demonstrated that it is possible to increase the level of isolates' specific social skills (Beck *et al.*, 1978; Bornstein *et al.*, 1977; Combs & Lahey, 1979), generalization from a training setting to the natural environment remains problematic. Further research is needed to determine how the generalization of these skills to the nontreatment environment can be enhanced, and to discern which component of the treatment package accounts for the gains in treat- and nontreatment settings.

Peer tutoring has also been successfully employed in teaching isolates specific social skills (Butler & Lahey, 1978). Two preschool children were trained in the use of eye contact and reinforcement, and were then used as therapists to teach their isolate peers how to use these skills in their play with others. Posttest and follow-up data indicated that the three target children increased the frequency of their verbal and physical praise, and their verbal responsiveness to peer-initiated verbalizations.

Champagne and Tyne (1980) used a self-monitoring procedure to teach specific social skills to children identified as isolates by their teachers, and observed to have the lowest rates of interaction in the class. Three of the six isolates were taught to record the occurrence of their peer-initiated and responded–reciprocated social interactions. The other three children were instructed to observe and record these same interactions along with the consequence (positive, neutral, or negative) of the interaction. While both procedures produced comparable increases in the frequency of the isolates' initiated and responded peer contacts in the classroom, the group that recorded the consequences of their interactions demonstrated greater generalizability to a nontreatment setting (recess–play period) and maintained these gains over a longer time period. Peer sociometric nominations from the Peer Evaluation Inventory (Pekarik, Prinz, Liebert, Weintraub, & Neale, 1976) indicated that the likability ratings for the isolates in both treatment conditions increased, while their withdrawal ratings decreased. The observational and sociometric data indicate that self-monitoring procedures may prove to be a viable and easily implemented technique for increasing isolates' interactive behaviors.

In reviewing the studies attempting to increase the frequency of isolates' social interaction, it appears as if a variety of intervention techniques have been successful. It has been demonstrated that reinforcing children for peer contact, and pairing isolates with same-age and younger social companions leads to increases in their rates of social interaction. Other researchers have shown that the frequency of peer contacts can be increased by teaching initiation of contact, smiling, and positive reinforcement of others.

An important issue that was discussed earlier in this chapter is the question of whether or not social isolation in and of itself constitutes a significant problem requiring remediation. It should be noted that in only one study did the intervention lead to increases in both rates of interaction and sociometric status (Champagne & Tyne, 1980). In the remaining investigations, the authors reported data only on the frequency of peer interactions or more specific social behaviors. While the quantity of isolates' social behaviors before and after treatment may be of technical interest, the extent to which low levels of social interactions reflect socioemotional difficulties needs to be established. Future researchers should direct themselves toward investigating questions about the deviance and pathology of social isolation, the behaviors contributing to these interpersonal difficiencies, and the methods effective in enhancing isolates' interactive competencies.

TREATMENT OF NEGLECTED CHILDREN

Our review of the literature uncovered only one treatment program for increasing the social skills and social acceptance of neglected children— that is, those who are identified as being neither accepted nor rejected in sociometric evaluations (Whitehill, Hersen, & Bellack, 1980). Several programs, however, have attempted to improve the social adjustment of children who are low on peer acceptance. The identifying criterion employed in these latter studies was that of receiving the fewest positive nominations on a sociometric instrument. A problem in utilizing low acceptance as the selection criterion is that this is a defining characteristic of both neglected and rejected populations. Therefore, it is uncertain whether the targeted treatment groups in these studies consisted of neglected, rejected, or both neglected and rejected children. Despite these concerns, these studies will be reviewed in this section. The rationale for doing so is that low peer acceptance is the primary defining characteristic of the neglected population. In order to avoid confusion, subjects identified only on the basis of low peer acceptance will be labeled unaccepted, whereas those identified on the basis of both low acceptance and low rejection will be labeled neglected.

The initial studies attempting to improve the peer acceptance of unaccepted children focused on relatively nonspecific social skills (Bonney, 1971; Hansen, Zani, & Niland, 1969; Kranzler, Mayer, Dyer, & Munger, 1966; Mayer, Kranzler, & Mathes, 1967). These programs did not develop particular intervention strategies, but relied instead on counseling or teacher reinforcement to remediate the idiosyncratic deficiencies of those receiving the fewest positive sociometric nominations. Unfortunately the authors provided little information on the content of the counseling or reinforcement techniques, except that Rogerian and Skinnerian principles were employed in the respective treatment conditions. Nor was there any discussion of which appropriate interpersonal skills were targeted in the counseling or reinforcement conditions. It was reported that counselor-led groups were an effective means of improving the sociometric status of unaccepted elementary school students when accepted peers or "stars" were included in the counseling group as models (Hansen et al., 1969). Counseling students in groups composed solely of unaccepted students appeared to improve social acceptance, but only when counseling was paired with teacher reinforcement of acceptable behavior (Kranzler et al., 1966; Mayer et al., 1967). Mixed results were obtained in the studies where teacher reinforcement alone was used to improve the status of the low-accepted children (Bonney, 1971; Kranzler et al., 1966; Mayer et al., 1967). These findings should be interpreted with caution. Selecting students who were "interested in getting along better with their peers," using only one or two counselors, and having the counselors also serve as consultants to the teachers in the classroom reinforcement condition, are factors to be considered when viewing and interpreting these results.

A more specific treatment program for improving the skills of nonaccepted children was developed by Gottman, Gonso, and Schuler (1976). Subjects in this study were two female third-grade children who received the lowest number of "best friend" sociometric nominations. No measures of peer rejection were employed, and consequently, it cannot be determined whether these children were rejected or neglected. The specific skills targeted in the treatment program included referential communication skills, the distribution and reception of verbal reinforcement, and friendship-making skills. These skills were presented and practiced in a variety of ways, including symbolic modeling, coaching, rehearsal, and role playing. Posttest results indicated that the subjects received more "work with" and "play with" sociometric nominations, but did not increase their number of "best friend" nominations. Observational data indicated that the frequency of the students' interactions did not change throughout the study; however, the subjects did distribute their interactions over a larger number of students.

In only one study (Whitehill et al., 1980) were both low-acceptance and low-rejection sociometric data incorporated into the selection criteria. Consequently, this study is the only one in this section that in fact treated a neglected population. Children who scored lowest on positive and negative sociometric nominations and a roster and rating instrument, were deficient in three or more conversational skills, were rated by teachers as experiencing difficulties in group activities, and spent a disproportionately large amount of time alone during free play were the subjects of the study.

The training program focused on improving the conversational skills (the use of informative statements, open-ended questions, and requests to share activities) of the four 8- to 10-year-old subjects. The subjects participated in nine training sessions, during which they received instruction, observed models, and obtained feedback on their performance on the three targeted conversational skills. Multiple baseline data indicated that all four students improved on the targeted conversational skills in both the training and classroom settings and that these gains were apparent at the 4- and 8-week follow-up. While the observational data indicated successful treatment effects, teacher ratings and sociometric data revealed no improvement in the students' interpersonal acceptance. Although the searchers were successful in demonstrating improvement in the targeted social skills, it does not appear that the improved conversational skills were of sufficient consequence to improve these children's social acceptance.

Overall, the programs attempting to improve the specific social skills of low-accepted or neglected students have not demonstrated convincing treatment effects. In only one study (Whitehill et al., 1980) were significant increases in observed social skills reported. Yet, the treatment package did not lead to a concomitant increase in peer acceptance, suggesting that the remediation of conversational skills may not be a propitious means of enhancing neglected children's peer relationships. The other studies in this section suffer from other difficulties. As previously mentioned, it is not clear if the groups targeted in the other studies consisted of neglected or rejected children. Furthermore, while several of these studies reported significant treatment gains (Bonney, 1971; Hansen et al., 1969; Kranzler et al., 1966; Mayer et al., 1967), the vagueness of the intervention strategies restricts statements about the relative efficacy of counseling and teacher reinforcement in improving social status. In contrast, Gottman et al. (1976) specified the behaviors targeted in their program and offered a framework for why these skills were related to out-group membership (Gottman, Gonso, & Rasmussen, 1975). However, the complexity of the intervention program also precludes a determination of which components of the treatment package accounted for the increases in improved scores in the "work" and "play with" sociometric dimensions.

TREATMENT OF REJECTED CHILDREN

Comparatively few intervention programs have been developed for improving the social functioning of rejected children. Although this group appears to be the most seriously impaired, and have the most deficient social skill repertoire (Rutter, 1975), researchers have not given this group the attention it warrants. Three of the five studies in this section used both positive and negative sociometric ratings in the selection process (Hymel & Asher, 1977; Oden & Asher, 1977; Tyne & Flynn, 1979). The other two projects relied on teacher ratings to identify the treatment groups (Cowen et al., 1973; Shure, 1979), a technique that, as previously mentioned, has methodological limitations. It can be inferred that those treated in these two studies were groups composed primarily of rejectees, although it appears as if a few nonrejected isolates were also included in the sample. In three of the studies reported in this section, the experimenters worked directly with the children on developing specific interpersonal skills (Hymel & Asher, 1977; Oden & Asher, 1977; Shure & Spivack, 1975). In the two remaining programs, classroom teachers (Tyne & Flynn, 1979) or nonprofessional volunteers (Cowen et al., 1975) served as the service delivery agents.

Oden and Asher (1977) identified third- and fourth-grade children who received the lowest scores on a "work with" and "play with" sociometric rating scale. These rejected children were then assigned to one of three conditions. Subjects in the coaching treatment were given instruction in partricipation, cooperation, communication, and validating and supporting others. Following instruction, children in the coaching condition practiced these skills with a nonrejected peer. Subjects in a peer-pairing condition interacted with the same nonrejected peer, but were not provided with any instruction. Subjects in a no-treatment condition played solitary games in the company of the nonrejected peer but did not interact with the child. No posttest differences were found for any of the groups on behavioral measures of task orientation or participation, peer cooperation, support, or rejection. There were no gains in the scores received by the rejected students on the "work with" or "best friend" sociometric scales. However, subjects in the coaching condition received more "play with" nominations than did those in the peer-pairing or no-treatment conditions. These gains were still intact 1 year later. The authors suggested that while the coaching treatment was effective in increasing the general acceptance of the rejected subjects, it apparently did not provide the students with sufficient social skills to enter into a "best friend" relationship.

In a related study using the same identification criteria with third-through fifth-graders, Hymel and Asher (1977) compared the effects of the Oden and Asher coaching program with a more individualized coaching program and a peer-pairing treatment. Individualized coaching focused on the same four skill concepts as the coaching program but tailored the instruction and peer rehearsal to the individual student's social skill deficiencies. The rejected students in the peer-pairing condition engaged in play sessions similar to those the students in the other conditions participated in, but received no coaching. In order to make statements about the targeted subjects' relative treatment gains, data were also collected on a group of nonrejected students. Observational data indicated no differences between any of the rejected students and their nonrejected classmates before or after treatment, nor were any differences reported on the "best friend," "work with," or "play with" sociometric scores.

Hymel and Asher's inability to replicate Oden and Asher's (1977) results on the "play with" dimension were surprising in that the individualized treatment package was expected to be more effective than the standard intervention procedure, but this was not the case. Another factor that should be considered is that neither the Oden and Asher nor the Hymel and Asher studies found any treatment effects on the behavioral observation measures. Therefore, it was not demonstrated in either study that the children manifested any improvement in their social skill performance as a consequence of the intervention program. Furthermore, the inclusion of several components in the intervention package makes it difficult to discern which part of the treatment accounted for the gains in the Oden and Asher study.

Shure and Spivack (1975) also employed a specific and well-defined intervention program to improve the interpersonal problem-solving skills of out-group children. Subjects were teacher-identified impulsive children. Upon examination of the selection criteria it appears these children were rejectees, but that a small number of inhibited or withdrawn children were also included in the treatment group. Based on their previous investigations of the correlates and characteristics of socially adjusted and maladjusted children, and the relationship between these interpersonal difficulties and social problem solving, Shure and Spivack developed an Interpersonal Cognitive Problem-Solving (ICPS) curriculum. The ICPS treatment package consists of 35 activities designed to teach children to be sensitive to social dilemmas, to use causal and consequential thinking, and to approach problem situations and generate alternative solutions. This training program was presented to all members of the preschool classroom, and can therefore be considered both a preventive and ameliorative intervention technique. It was found that the preschool and kindergarten children involved in the ICPS program improved their scores on the Preschool Interpersonal Problem-Solving Test (PIPS; Shure & Spivack, 1974). The targeted children showed more gains than their nontargeted peers on both the PIPS and on the teachers' ratings of classroom behavior. These gains were still apparent 1 and 2 years later, and were found to generalize to a nontreatment setting. It should be emphasized, however, that using teacher judgments instead of sociometric data makes it difficult to determine the characteristics of the targeted children. The lack of observational data also limits statements about the pre- and posttreatment behaviors of these children, and whether their improved problem solving affected their peer interactions. While Shure and Spivack do offer strong arguments for the use of social problem-solving programs with at-risk populations in general, there is little discussion of the use of these strategies with rejected children. Furthermore it remains to be demonstrated that problem-solving deficiencies are salient factors contributing to peer rejection.

The remaining two studies in this section have used less specific intervention strategies to improve the social skills and peer acceptance of rejected students. Another difference between these and the three previously discussed programs is that the experimenters in these two studies did not work directly with the children, but served as consultants. In Tyne and Flynn (1979) suggestions were offered to teachers on improving the classroom environment and developing acceptable peer interactions, while Cowen *et al.* (1975) employed nonprofessional aides to work with the out-group children on improving their interpersonal skills.

The population of the Tyne and Flynn study were third-, fourth-, and fifth-graders who received the lowest positive peer ratings, and the highest negative ratings on a sociometric scale. The teachers of these rejected children in the consultation condition were provided with several strategies of potential use in ameliorating social rejection. These strategies emphasized the importance of a positive self-concept, causal-critical thinking, general friendship skills, academic performance, nonaggressive interactions, physical appearance, and initiating and maintaining positive peer interactions. Rejected children in a second condition were identified to another group of teachers, but the teachers were not provided with intervention suggestions. At the conclusion of the 3-month program, sociometric ratings were again collected, and it was found that the students in the consultation condition increased in peer acceptance, while those in the identification-only group declined in status. The methodology of this study precludes a determination of which particular strategies or teacher behaviors were responsible for the treatment gains, but it is clear that the consultation procedure, and not the identification of socially rejected children, was responsible for the increase in peer acceptance.

Another service-oriented program intended to improve the socioemotional adjustment of out-group children is the Rochester Primary Mental Health Project (Cowen, Gardner, & Zax, 1967; Cowen *et al.*, 1975). The treatment group was composed of students rated by their teachers as having classroom adjustment difficulties, and who received the lowest scores on both a psychological self-report inventory and a peer nomination scale. This group consisted primarily of rejected students, although it appears that some isolates were included. The targeted primary-grade students were assigned to nonprofessional aides who worked individually or in small groups with the students for 30–45 minutes a week. The content of the sessions included discussions of recent problems, the child's feelings about these incidents, and explorations of solutions to these difficulties. The program stressed the communication of acceptance and support in these sessions, and consultation with classroom teachers on various aspects of classroom climate and the children's interpersonal functioning.

Based on results from peer nominations, teacher ratings, and psychological inventories, it was concluded that the program was effective in improving the targeted students' classroom behaviors and peer acceptance (Cowen *et al.*, 1972, 1975). However, there are indications that the program may have been more beneficial for the isolates than for the rejectees (Lorion, Cowen, & Caldwell, 1974). The authors suggested that the companionship program may have had greater impact on the isolates because the aides were selected primarily for their warmth and nurturance, and not for psychotherapeutic skills. Furthermore, it appears as if the rejected students had more serious interpersonal relationship problems, and greater deficiencies in their social skill repertoires than did the isolates. As in the Tyne and Flynn (1979) study, it is difficult to determine which intervention methods used by Cowen *et al.* (1975) contributed to the treatment gains. Although the volunteer aides did undergo an extensive training program, there is little discussion of the actual content of the treatment and consultation sessions. Like other studies reviewed in this section, Cowen and his colleagues do not offer a strong conceptual basis for the intervention program. The justification for these programs appears to be more intuitively than empirically derived, with little discussion supporting the use of these strategies in preference to other techniques.

While four of the five studies reviewed in this section were reportedly successful in improving rejectees' interpersonal skills or peer acceptance, it is difficult to make an overall judgment about their relative effectiveness. This difficulty is attributable to several factors. First of all is the nonspecific selection criteria in two of the studies (Cowen *et al.*, 1975; Shure & Spivack, 1975), and the attendant problems of teachers accurately identifying rejected students (Tyne & Flynn, in press). A second problem is the breadth of the intervention methods used in each of the studies, making it difficult to discern which facets of the programs account for treatment gains. This problem is particularly apparent in the Tyne and Flynn (1979) and Cowen *et al.* (1975) projects, as a range of nonspecific strategies were implemented by teachers and aides. Without more elaborate methodologies, one can only state that "something" done by the treatment agents accounted for the gains. Improvements in the intervention strategies for rejected children are dependent upon the delineation of the particular social skill deficits of this group, and the development of techniques to train children in these skill areas. Furthermore, an issue that has not yet been addressed is whether rejected children exhibit behavioral excesses as well as behavioral deficits (Hartup et al., 1967). Perhaps programs should focus on reducing the frequency and intensity of aversive behaviors in addition to developing a positive social skill repertoire.

CONCLUSIONS

In this section several issues emanating from the discussions in the previous sections are highlighted. The emphasis here parallels the general goal and purpose of the paper—that is, to review the programs attempting to improve the social skills of various types of out-group children. This discussion focuses on (1) procedures used to identify out-group children; (2) the type of remediation program employed; and (3) the relative effectiveness of the various intervention programs.

IDENTIFICATION

The differentiation of the various types of out-group or at-risk children is dependent upon the identification procedure(s) employed. Two problems become apparent when reviewing several of the studies focusing on neglected and rejected children. The first problem entails the use of teacher judgments as the sole selection criterion. The second issue involves the failure to employ both positive and negative sociometric procedures when identifying neglected and rejected populations.

While teacher judgments are an efficient and pragmatically useful selection technique, it appears that teachers are only moderately successful in differentiating various types of out-group children. Thus, it would be advantageous for investigators to employ sociometric and perhaps observational techniques in addition to teacher identification measures. By offering teachers specific guidelines on the behaviors characteristic of the particular targeted group, it may be possible to refine this identification procedure. These advances would be dependent upon obtaining more information on the characteristics of isolated, neglected, and rejected children.

A further concern in the identification of out-group children involves the failure of many researchers to collect both positive and negative sociometric data. Without both types of data, either in the form of nominations or ratings, it is very difficult to distinguish between neglected and rejected children. The use of positive nominations alone provides information on a child's level of acceptance, but precludes statements about peer neglect or rejection. Greater attention to subject selection and description will enhance the development of more refined categorization systems, and facilitate comparisons of treatment groups across studies.

THE INTERVENTION PROGRAM

The second area to be discussed is the content of the intervention program. Given the lack of information on the social skill repertoires of isolated, neglected, and rejected children, investigators have relied on clinical intuition or information derived from studies of socially deficient adults to determine treatment strategies. In theory, treatment should focus on the amelioration of the social skill deficits of the target population. In addition, researchers need to examine the interpersonal behaviors of these out-group members' socially competent peers prior to formulating a program's content and strategies. For example, Gottman (1977) notes that "despite the fact that most intervention programs teach isolated children how to gain entry into a peer group, these programs are not based upon the knowledge of how nonisolated children at a specific developmental level gain entry" (p. 71).

An ancillary concern is the specificity or generality of the social treatment program (Asher, 1978). When a child is taught a broad or nonspecific skill, she or he is required to extrapolate from the general concept underlying this skill, and derive a particular behavior to be performed in a given situation. For example, in Shure and Spivack (1975), the child is taught interpersonal problem-solving strategies, and is expected to utilize these skills in subsequent interpersonal exchanges. An alternative approach is to teach a specific skill (e.g., initiation of conversation), and have the child formulate a general concept about this skill or set of behaviors. This, in turn, is assumed to facilitate generalization of the target response to novel situations (Asher, 1978). There is little information available on the relative efficacy of either approach.

The final issue related to the content of treatment programs is the technique by which social skills are taught. Some skills and concepts may be taught more effectively by one method than another. For example, some skills may be best developed through the use of teacher or peer reinforcement, while others may benefit from being introduced through the use of coaching, modeling, or role playing. Also worth considering is whether the targeted behavior should be taught in an analogue or natural setting, and which procedures are most likely to insure maintenance and generalization of the treatment gains.

THE EFFECTIVENESS OR OUTCOME OF THE INTERVENTION PROGRAM

The final and probably most important concern in this area is the relative effectiveness of the various intervention programs with different out-group populations. While direct comparisons of treatment success with these groups have not been attempted, it appears as if researchers have had considerably more success intervening with isolates than with either neglected or rejected children. One possible explanation for this is that the deviance and pathology of neglected and rejected children may be greater than that of isolates. It should be noted in this regard that isolation in and of itself has not been demonstrated to be a significant interpersonal problem.

An additional concern is the definition of what constitutes a successful intervention program with isolates versus a successful program with neglected and rejected children. Since isolation is defined purely on the basis of a low frequency of peer interactions, treatment success is measured simply by an increase in the frequency of peer contacts. On the other hand, being neglected or rejected is determined by one's social or sociometric status (i.e., other group members' perceptions of the child). One's social status, however, appears to be a function of numerous characteristics, some of which are changeable (e.g., sociability, cooperation, etc.) and some of which are less alterable (e.g., physical attractiveness, socioeconomic status) (Asher, Gottman, & Oden, 1977; Hartup, 1970). Given the multifaceted nature of social status constructs, it is not surprising that researchers have been more successful in ameliorating isolation than rejection–neglect. Furthermore, a change in the frequency of interaction can be accomplished simply by altering the target child's overt behavior. Social status changes, however, necessitate changing the target child's behavior such that other children's perceptions of that child will be modified.

Despite the relative difficulty of producing measurable change with rejected and neglected children, continued research on the development and evaluation of intervention programs for these at-risk groups is warranted. While researchers have been successful in treating isolate populations, the necessity of intervening with these children needs to be more clearly established.

REFERENCES

Allen, K. E., Hart, B., Buell, J. S., Harris, F. R., & Wolf, M. M. Effects of social reinforcement of isolated behavior of a nursery school child. *Child Development*, 1964, *35*, 511–518.

Asher, S. R. Children's peer relations. In M. E. Lamb (Ed.), *Social and personality development*. New York: Holt, Rinehart & Winston, 1978.

Asher, S. R., Gottman, J. M., & Oden, S. L. Children's friendships in school settings. In E. M. Hetherington & R. D. Parke (Eds.), *Contemporary readings in child psychology*. New York: McGraw-Hill, 1977.

Asher, S., & Hymel, S. Children's social competence in peer relations: Sociometric and behavioral assessment. In J. D. Wine & M. D. Smye (Eds.), *Social competence*. New York: Guilford Press, 1981.

Asher, S. R., & Renshaw, P. D. Children without friends: Social knowledge and social skill training. In S. R. Asher & J. M. Gottman (Eds.), *The development of children's friendships*. New York: Cambridge University Press, 1981.

Asher, S. R., Singleton, L. C., Tinsley, B. R., & Hymel, S. A reliable sociometric measure for preschool children. *Developmental Psychology*, 1979, *15*, 443–444.

Baer, D. M., & Wolf, M. M. Recent examples of behavior modification in preschool settings. In C. Neuringer & J. L. Michael (Eds.), *Behavior modification in clinical psychology*. New York: Appleton-Century-Crofts, 1970.

Barclay, J. R. Sociometric choices and teacher ratings as predictors of school dropouts. *Journal of School Psychology*, 1966, *4*, 40–44.

Beck, S., Forehand, R., Wells, K. C., & Quante, A. *Social skills training with children: An examination of generalization from analogue to natural setting*. Unpublished manuscript. University of Georgia, 1978.

Bellack, A. S., & Hersen, M. *Behavior modification: An introductory text*. Baltimore: Williams & Wilkins, 1977.

Bonney, M. E. Assessment of efforts to aid socially isolated elementary school pupils. *Journal of Educational Research*, 1971, *64*, 359–364.

Bornstein, M. B., Bellack, A. S., & Hersen, M. Social skills training for unassertive children: A multiple baseline analysis. *Journal of Applied Behavior Analysis*, 1977, *10*, 183–195.

Buell, J., Stoddard, P., Harris, F. R., & Baer, D. M. Collateral social development accompanying reinforcement of outdoor play in a preschool child. *Journal of Applied Behavior Analysis*, 1968, *1*, 167–173.

Busk, P. L., Ford, R. C., & Schulman, J. L. Stability of sociometric response in classrooms. *Journal of Genetic Psychology*, 1973, *123*, 69–84.

Butler, C., & Lahey, B. B. *Use of peer therapists to increase appropriate interaction in socially deficient preschool children in a natural setting*. Unpublished manuscript, University of Georgia, 1978.

Champagne, G., & Tyne, T. F. *The relative effectiveness of self-monitoring on children's social isolation*. Manuscript submitted for publication, 1980.

Ciminero, A. R., & Drabman, R. S. Current developments in the behavioral assessment of children. In B. B. Lahey & A. E. Kazdin (Eds.), *Advances in clinical child psychology* (Vol. 1). New York: Plenum, 1977.

Combs, M. L., & Lahey, B. B. Evaluation of a cognitive skills training program for young children: Lack of generalized effects. *Behavior Modification*, 1979.

Cowen, E. L., Dorr, D., Trost, M. A., & Izzo, L. D. A follow-up study of maladapting school children seen by nonprofessionals. *Journal of Consulting and Clinical Psychology,* 1972, *36,* 235–238.

Cowen, E. L., Gardner, E. A., & Zax, M. *Emergent approaches to mental health problems.* New York: Appleton-Century-Crofts, 1967.

Cowen, E. L., Pederson, A., Babigian, H., Izzo, L. D., & Trost, M. A. Long-term follow-up of early detected vulnerable children. *Journal of Consulting and Clinical Psychology,* 1973, *41,* 438–446.

Cowen, E. L., Trost, M. A., Lorian, R. P., Dorr, D., Izzo, L. D., & Isaacson, R. V. *New ways in school mental health.* New York: Human Sciences Press, 1975.

Dunnington, M. J. Behavioral differences of sociometric status groups in a nursery school. *Child Development,* 1957, *28,* 103–111.

Eaton, M. T., D'Amico, L. A., & Phillips, B. M. Problem behaviors in school. *Journal of Educational Psychology,* 1966, *47,* 350–357.

Evers, W., & Schwarz, J. Modifying social withdrawal in preschoolers: The effects of filmed modeling and teacher praise. *Journal of Abnormal Child Psychology,* 1973, *1,* 248–256.

Evers-Pasquale, W., & Sherman, M. The reward value of peers: A variable influencing the efficacy of filmed modeling in modifying social interaction in preschoolers. *Journal of Abnormal Child Psychology,* 1975, *3,* 179–189.

Furman, W., Rahe, D. F., & Hartup, W. W. Rehabilitation of socially withdrawn preschool children through mixed-age and same-age socialization. *Child Development,* 1979, *50,* 915–922.

Glidewell, J., & Swallow, C. *The prevalence of maladjustment in the elementary schools: A report for the Joint Committee on the Mental Health of Children.* Chicago: University of Chicago Press, 1969.

Gottman, J. The effects of a modeling film on social isolation in preschool children: A methodological investigation. *Journal of Abnormal Child Psychology,* 1977, *5,* 69–78.

Gottman, J., Gonso, J., & Rasmussen, B. Social interaction, social competence and friendship in children. *Child Development,* 1975, *46,* 709–718.

Gottman, J., Gonso, J., & Schuler, P. Teaching social skills to isolated children. *Journal of Abnormal Child Psychology,* 1976, *4,* 179–197.

Green, K. D., Forehand, R., Beck, S. J., & Vosk, B. *An assessment of the relationship among measures of children's social competence.* Unpublished manuscript, University of Georgia, 1979.

Green, K. D., Vosk, B., Forehand, R., & Beck, S. *An examination of differences among sociometrically identified accepted, rejected, and neglected children.* Unpublished manuscript, University of Georgia, 1979.

Gronlund, N. E. *Sociometry in the classroom.* New York: Harper, 1959.

Gronlund, N. E., & Anderson, C. Personality characteristics of socially neglected and socially rejected junior high school pupils. *Educational Administration and Supervision,* 1957, *43,* 329–338.

Hansen, N. C., Zani, L. D., & Niland, T. M. Model reinforcement in group counseling with elementary school children. *Journal of Personnel and Guidance,* 1969, *47,* 741–744.

Hart, B. M., Reynolds, N. J., Baer, D., Brawley, E. R., & Harris, F. R. Effects of contingent and noncontingent social reinforcement on the cooperative play of a preschool child. *Journal of Applied Behavior Analysis,* 1968, *1,* 73–78.

Hartup, W. W. Peer interaction and social organization. In P. H. Mussen (Ed.), *Carmichael's manual of child psychology.* New York: Wiley, 1970.

Hartup, W. W. Peer interaction and the behavioral development of the individual child. In E. Schopler & R. J. Reichler (Eds.), *Psychopathology and child development.* New York: Plenum, 1976.

Hartup, W. W. Peer relations and the growth of social competence. In M. W. Kent & J. E. Rolf (Eds.), *Primary prevention of psychopathology* (Vol. 3): *Social competence in children.* Hanover, N.H.: University Press of New England, 1979.

Hartup, W. W., & DeWitt, J. *Determinants and origins of aggression.* New York: Mouton, 1974.

Hartup, W. W., Glazer, J. A., & Charlsworth, R. Peer reinforcement and sociometric status. *Child Development,* 1967, *38,* 1017–1024.

Hymel, S., & Asher, S. R. *Assessment and training of isolated children's social skills.* Paper presented at the biennial meeting of the Society for Research in Child Development, New Orleans, 1977.

Jakibchuk, L., & Smeriglio, V. L. The influence of symbolic modeling on the social behavior of preschool children with low levels of social responsiveness. *Child Development,* 1976, *47,* 838–841.

Janes, C., & Hesselbrock, V. Problem children's adult adjustment predicted from teachers' ratings. *American Journal of Orthopsychiatry,* 1977, *48,* 300–309.

Justman, J., & Wrightstone, J. W. A comparison of the three methods of measuring pupil status in the classroom. *Educational and Psychological Measurement,* 1961, *11,* 364.

Keller, M., & Carlson, P. The use of symbolic modeling to promote social skills in preschool children with low levels of social responsiveness. *Child Development,* 1974, *45,* 912–919.

Kirby, F. D., & Toler, H. C. Modification of preschool isolate behavior: A case study. *Journal of Applied Behavior Analysis,* 1970, *3,* 309–314.

Kranzler, G. D., Mayer, G. R., Dyer, C. O., & Munger, P. F. Counseling with elementary school children: An experimental study. *Personnel and Guidance Journal,* 1966, *44,* 944–949.

Lorion, R. P., Cowen, E. L., & Caldwell, R. A. Problem types of children referred to a school-based mental health program: Identification and outcome. *Journal of Consulting and Clinical Psychology,* 1974, *42,* 491–496.

Mayer, C. R., Kranzler, G. D., & Mathes, W. A. Elementary school counseling and peer relations. *Personnel and Guidance Journal,* 1967, *46,* 360–365.

McGrew, W. C. *An ethological study of children's behavior.* New York: Academic Press, 1972.

Moreno, J. L. *The sociometry reader.* Glencoe, Ill.: Free Press, 1960.

O'Connor, R. D. Modification of social withdrawal through symbolic modeling. *Journal of Applied Behavior Analysis,* 1969, *2,* 15–22.

O'Connor, R. D. Relative efficacy of modeling, shaping, and the combined procedures for modification of social withdrawal. *Journal of Applied Behavior Analysis,* 1972, *79,* 327–334.

Oden, S. L., & Asher, S. R. Coaching children in social skills for friendship making. *Child Development,* 1977, *48,* 495–506.

Patterson, G. R., Littman, R. A., & Bricker, W. Assertive behavior in children: A step toward a theory of aggression. *Monographs of the Society for Research in Child Development,* 1967, *32* (Whole No. 113).

Pekarik, E. G., Prinz, R. I., Liebert, D. E., Weintraub, S., & Neale, J. M. The pupil evaluation inventory. A sociometric technique for assessing children's social behavior. *Journal of Abnormal Child Psychology,* 1976, *4,* 83–97.

Phillips, B. The diagnostic intervention class and the teacher–psychologist–specialist: Models for the school psychology services network? *Psychology in the Schools,* 1968, *5,* 135–139.

Roff, M. Childhood social interactions and young adult bad conduct. *Journal of Abnormal and Social Psychology,* 1961, *63,* 333–337.

Roff, M., Sells, S. B., & Golden, M. M. *Social adjustment and personality development in children.* Minneapolis: University of Minnesota Press, 1972.

Ross, D., Ross, S., & Evans, T. A. The modification of extreme social withdrawal by modification with guided practice. *Journal of Behavior Therapy and Experimental Psychiatry,* 1971, *2,* 273–279.

Rutter, M. *Helping troubled children.* Harmonds Worth: Penguin Books, 1975.

Saunders, B., & Vitro, F. Examiner expectancy bias as a function of the referral process. *Psychology in the Schools,* 1971, *8,* 168–171.

Sells, S. B., & Roff, M. *Peer acceptance–rejection and personality and personality development* (Final Report, Project No. OES-0417). Washington, D.C.: U.S. Department of Health, Education and Welfare, 1967.

Shure, M. B. Training children to solve interpersonal problems. In R. F. Muñoz, L. R. Snowden, & J. B. Kelly (Eds.), *Social and psychological research in community settings.* San Francisco: Jossey-Bass, 1979.

Shure, M. B., & Spivack, G. *Social adjustment of young children: A cognitive approach to solving real life problems.* San Francisco: Jossey-Bass, 1974.

Shure, M. B., & Spivack, G. *A mental health program for preschool and kindergarten children, and a mental health program for mothers of young children: An interpersonal problem-solving approach toward social adjustment* (A comprehensive report of research and training, No. MH-20372). Washington, D.C.: National Institute of Mental Health, 1975.

Stengel, E. *Suicide and attempted suicide.* New York: Penguin, 1971.

Stennett, R. G. Emotional handicaps in the elementary years: Phase or disease. *American Journal of Orthopsychiatry,* 1965, *35,* 444–449.

Strain, P. S., Shores, R. E., & Kerr, M. M. An experimental analysis of "spillover" effects on the social interaction of behaviorally handicapped preschool children. *Journal of Applied Behavior Analysis,* 1976, *9,* 31–40.

Strain, P. S., & Timm, M. A. An experimental analysis of social interaction between a behaviorally disordered child and her classroom peers. *Journal of Applied Behavior Analysis,* 1974, *7,* 583–590.

Thompson, G. G., & Powell, M. An investigation of the rating-scale approach to the measurement of social status. *Educational and Psychological Measurement,* 1951, *11,* 440–455.

Tyne, T. F., & Flynn, J. T. The remediation of elementary school children's low social status through a teacher-centered consultation program. *Journal of School Psychology,* 1979, *17,* 244–254.

Tyne, T. F., & Flynn, J. T. A comparison of teacher nominations and peer evaluations in the identification of socioemotional at-risk students. *Exceptional Children,* in press.

Ullmann, C. A. Teachers, peers, and tests as predictors of adjustment. *Journal of Educational Psychology,* 1957, *48,* 257–267.

Van Hasselt, B., Bellack, A. S., & Hersen, M. *The relationship between behavioral assessment and sociometric status of children.* Paper presented at the 13th annual meeting of the Association for the Advancement of Behavior Therapy, San Francisco, December 1979.

Walker, H. M., & Hops, H. The use of group and individual reinforcement contingencies in the modification of social withdrawal. In L. A. Hamerlynck, L. C. Handy, & E. J. Mash (Eds.), *Behavior change: Methodology, concepts, and practice.* Champaign, Ill.: Research Press, 1973.

Weinrott, M. R., Corson, J. A., & Wilcheskey, M. Teacher-mediated treatment of social withdrawal. *Behavior Therapy,* 1979, *10,* 281–294.

Whitehill, M. B., Hersen, M., & Bellack, A. S. A conversation skills training program for socially isolated children: An analysis of generalization. *Behaviour Research and Therapy,* 1980, *18,* 217–225.

III

SOCIAL SKILLS ASSESSMENT

While the approaches taken by Curran and the Congers toward the assessment of social skills in their respective chapters appear at first glance to be disparate, they are in effect complementary. Each of these investigators is interested in the assessment of social skills for different purposes. Curran (Chapter 11) is interested in developing a social skills measure that could be used to sample a subject's behavior in a variety of fairly standardized settings on repeated occasions in order to measure changes in social competency that might occur as a result of a social skills training program. Curran opts to utilize trained judges' global ratings of a subject's social skills performance in simulated social situations. It is then necessary for Curran to demonstrate (1) the adequacy of his sampling of social situations to a universe of all possible social situations, (2) that the trained judges' ratings possess integrity and reliability, and (3) that the ratings based on the simulated social situations are related to the subjects' behavior in the naturalistic environment. The advantage of Curran's molar-rating assessment strategy is that it can be used in a variety of situations; however, it has a low information yield. That is, molar ratings indicate the subjects' overall level of social competency or incompetency, but do not provide any information on how the subject actually behaves in a situation.

The Congers' objective in Chapter 10 is to delimit the components of competence in heterosocial situations. Using a behavior-analytic strategy, the Congers had undergraduates generate problematic heterosocial situations, and had peers generate cues that they felt differentiated competent and incompetent males in these situations, then examined whether various cues were related to actual behavior and to overall global ratings of competency. The information yield from this microanalytic approach is high; consequently such an approach is an extremely important step for both assessment and treatment. As was previously mentioned, most of the content of our social skills training program is based on clinical intuition with no empirical justification.

309

Employing a microanalytic strategy such as this can be used to empirically determine the content of our training programs. The disadvantage of this approach, as the Congers mention, is that the cues generated may be context-bound and somewhat idiosyncratically based. That is, the components derived may not typify other interactees not included in the original sample and may not be useful for describing subjects interacting in other situational contexts. The assessment strategies employed by both Curran and the Congers each have their place in the assessment of social skills. As in any assessment endeavor, the methods employed are dependent upon the nature of the assessment question.

Boice (Chapter 12), in viewing the assessment of social skills from the perspective of a human ethologist, encourages social skills researchers to employ naturalistic observational techniques such as time-sampling and pattern analysis. He believes that social skills assessment is becoming ethology-oriented, with an increasing emphasis on both frequent observations in less artificial settings and employment of behavioral indicators. He feels that ethology, with its history of careful observation and exacting description, has much to offer social skills assessment. In addition to urging the use of direct behavioral measures, he states that more complex measures need to be employed in order to get at important parameters such as the timing of responses, syndromy of responses, and predictable patterns of responses. More complex measures are needed in order for us to learn the rules of social interaction. The author presents counterarguments to those who object to naturalistic observation because of its cost, reactivity, and ethical problems, while also admitting that it is difficult and painstaking.

Boice proposes several ideas taken from the field of ethology that he feels may be transferable to the field of social skills. He sees some potential in viewing social skills in terms of the principle of sexual selection and presents some data from the social skills literature consistent with his assumption. As an ethologist, Boice believes that some social behaviors are less modifiable than others, and not all behaviors can be considered equivalent in their situational specificity. He proposes the construct of impassivity as a traitlike quality of individuals that generalizes reliably across social situations. As an ethologist, he stresses the importance of nonverbal behaviors and emotions. He also feels that skills ought to be conceptualized as abilities and not as dispositions. Another construct that plays a central role in ethological research and that Boice feels could be transferred to the field of social skills is the construct of "environmental fits." Boice thinks that social scientists have often ignored in their assessments the relationships between person variables and environmental variables. Ethologists, because of their commitment to functional analyses and patient observation of behaviors in a natural context, are accustomed to assessing environmental fits and consequently have much to offer the assessment of social skills. The ideas proposed by Boice are provocative and should stimulate research in the area of social skills.

10

COMPONENTS OF
HETEROSOCIAL COMPETENCE

JUDITH C. CONGER
ANTHONY J. CONGER

INTRODUCTION

"Social interaction is the very stuff of human life. The individuals of all societies move through life in terms of a continuous series of social interactions" (Goldschmidt, 1972, p. 59). The focus on social exchanges and their impact on the individual's behavior have long held a theoretically prominent position in psychology (Carson, 1969; Raush, 1965; Sullivan, 1953; Swensen, 1973; Thibaut & Kelley, 1959); however, until recent years this position has been largely secondary to more individually focused theories of an intrapsychic or traitlike nature. According to McKeynolds (1979), it is only in the last 10 to 15 years that the "Lewinian truism" that behavior is a joint function of both the person and situational determinants has had any significant impact on empirical research. Indeed, a social skills model with its emphasis on reciprocal social exchanges fits very nicely with the interactionist position.

Aside from the theoretical amenities such a position provides, the importance of social behavior has been documented in the clinical realm as well. Long before behaviorists discovered social skills, Zigler and his colleagues documented the effects of social deficits in a series of research projects relating social competence measures to psychiatric disorders, the process–reactive dimension of schizophrenia, psychiatric prognosis, and alcoholism (Levine & Zigler, 1973; Phillips & Zigler, 1961, 1964; Zigler & Levine, 1973; Zigler & Phillips, 1960, 1961, 1962). Basically, Zigler argued that the better the patient's level of social competency, the greater his chance for successful posthospital adjust-

Judith C. Conger and Anthony J. Conger. Department of Psychological Sciences, Purdue University, West Lafayette, Indiana.

ment. The importance of adequate social adjustment also has been documented by others. For example, Roff (1970) notes that peer dislike as a child is a good predictor of adult maladjustment, and Cowen, Pederson, Babigian, Izzo, and Trost (1973) found that peer sociometrics predicted membership on a psychiatric register 11 years later—better than intelligence, achievement, personality, or teacher rating measures.

The impact of all of this has been continuing extensive research in the assessment and identification of what constitutes social skillfulness as well as the treatment of social deficits, as witnessed by other chapters herein by Curran, Brown, Liberman, Trower, Wallace, and others.

WHAT IS SOCIAL COMPETENCE?

As individuals we probably have no difficulty in judging social competence, but the problem of defining social competence is indeed vexing. Currently there is no single definition around which we rally, and available conceptualizations neither specify the requisite behaviors for competence nor the situational contexts in which those behaviors occur (Curran, 1977; Trower, Bryant, & Argyle, 1978). The evaluation of social competence is made difficult because it is inevitably tied to sociocultural norms, not to mention other personal characteristics such as sex and age. Some definitions of social competence attempt to avoid such norms while others specifically include normative social appropriateness (Combs & Slaby, 1977). At the present time we seem to be confronted with a complex behavioral phenomenon, which, although undefined, is thought to play a major role in psychopathology, even in the form of carry-over effects from childhood (cf. Combs & Slaby, 1977). Undaunted by the absence of specific definitions or criteria we have developed instruments that purport to select and measure people on "it"; indeed, we have treatment programs for people who do not have "it," and still that mysterious "it" eludes specification.

We cannot claim to have resolved this dilemma, but we would like to offer our attempts in this regard. At its most global or megaconstruct level, we consider social competence to be the degree to which a person is successful in interactions or transactions taking place in the social sphere (i.e., any setting involving other persons), regardless of the specific setting, demands, goals, or participants. Included in this arena of social exchanges are an endless variety of activities ranging from saying hello, through the purchase of a bus ticket, or returning an unwanted purchase, to holding an intimate conversation with a significant other. Not only do the settings and participants vary in these exchanges, so do the goals and demands. Some interactions are, in fact, marked by essentially nonsocial goals (e.g., purchasing a meal), while others are marked by essentially social goals (e.g., an intimate conversation with a friend). In the former example, the vendor is a means for obtaining a nonsocial goal and if replaced by a vending machine the event would no longer take place in a social arena. This is not to say that this type of exchange is trivial, because negotiating one's environment is critical. Thus, behaviors of this type represent reasonable target behaviors for bringing minimally functioning psychiatric patients into the outside world. By comparison, some exchanges are almost entirely social in nature in that both the means and the end are social. Further complications may be introduced because some exchanges may appear to have social goals but one or more participants may have personal nonsocial goals. For example, one or both members of a heterosexual dyad may engage in a conversation not for the pleasure of conversing with one another but in order to lay the foundation for later sexual gratification. The analysis of interaction in terms of goals seems to be a necessary step for adequately delineating social competence and researchers adopting communication models have typically included goals (e.g., Wallace, Chapter 2, this volume). In a related manner, Trower et al. (1978) depicted social interactions in a potentially fruitful way. They conceptualized interactions in terms of the contingencies and the way in which these relate to the plans (goals) of the participants. Four kinds of social exchanges may be distinguished: (1) reactive contingency, in which each person responds to the last move by the other, as in impromptu social conversation; (2) asymmetrical contingency, in which one person responds to the other but the second follows an individual plan; (3) mutual contingency, in which each person responds to the other but also has an individual plan; and (4) pseudocontingency, in which each person is simply acting out a learned sequence, as in social rituals.

Taking into consideration the global construct of competence, the goals of interactions, and the types of exchanges, heterosocial interactions are viewed as a subset of social interactions marked essentially by social goals transacted in primarily reactive and mutually contingent exchanges. Infrequently, the goals may be nonsocial and the exchanges could be ritualistic or one-sided; however, competence in the heterosocial arena is most likely incompatible with these latter goals or exchanges. In fact, our working definition of "heterosocial competence" may be stated: "heterosocial competence is the degree to which a person is successful in heterosexual interactions that have as their immediate goal the recurrence of similar interactions."

This construal invites a consequence-oriented definition of competence (e.g., maintaining and/or increasing the frequency of participation) and avoids the need to introduce general social appropriateness or universal interaction sequences. In fact, this construal does not specify any of the behaviors required for successful performance, nor the individual situation or context characteristics that may moderate such behaviors. What this construal does allow is a means of specifying criteria for assessing competence and an invitation to discover behaviors leading to competence.

Acting upon this invitation we have evolved through our own and others' research efforts a components approach to assessing and specifying behaviors leading to socially competent performance. The components approach has grown out of inadequacies inherent in global assessment procedures and is being shaped by identifying converging relationships with criterion measures in diverse areas of social validation, peer perception, global ratings, and self-report.

The purposes of this chapter are to provide background information on the need and desirability for adopting a components approach to social competence and to summarize the results of several research projects that provide converging evidence that specific behavioral acts are the basis of social competence. In addition, some attention will be given to future directions for research and theoretical models underlying our research-assessment strategy.

SOURCES OF INFLUENCE

There have been many sources of influence in this research but a few significant figures stand out. First of all, the work of Duncan and Fiske (1977), with its emphasis on rigorous measurement and ecological validity, has been a source of inspiration. We believe that important sources of behavioral influence will be uncovered using this painstaking, laborious, methodical approach. It is from this scientific framework that we hope to discover behavioral components and, more importantly, interactive patterns that will be useful for the treatment of social skills deficits. Additionally, the work of Trower et al. (1978) fits very nicely with much of our thinking. Trower and his colleagues have attempted to organize and integrate theoretical notions and empirical findings from such diverse areas as clinical and social psychology, as well as the communications area, into a cohesive framework. The way in which they have organized various elements such as voices cues (pitch, inflection, and volume) into higher order constructs (such as emotions and feelings and attitudes) or the way in which various behavioral elements are conceptualized as comprising listening or meshing skills is very reminiscent of Vernon's (1950) hierarchical organization of abilities and is consonant with our thinking.

From our perspective the advantages of a hierarchical approach are twofold: (1) from a scientific point of view it enables one to pinpoint basic behavioral elements that are organized into more and more global units and constitute that thing called social competence; (2) if this "periodic table of social elements" were empirically known and organized into higher order constructs such as listening and turn-taking skills, expressing a particular type of emotion, etc., it would enable the clinician to select and focus on relevant and meaningful behaviors for a particular client. To be sure, Trower and his colleagues have attempted to do just that, but the system lacks a solid empirical basis.

Additionally, implicit in the notion of social skills is that social behavior itself can be pragmatically conceptualized as a skill that can be learned by those who lack it. We use the term "pragmatically conceptualized" purposely, since although we believe that much of social behavior is learned, one cannot rule out biological or genetic contributions. However, when one is confronted with a client or patient who has social deficits, the only intervention available is some kind of experiential or training model. Hence, the emphasis on skill.

GLOBAL ASSESSMENT PROCEDURES

Heterosocial competence traditionally has been assessed on separate dimensions of skill and/or anxiety obtained from self-report questionnaires or from global ratings of role-play performances. Although phrases like "behavioral observations" frequently have been used to describe judges' ratings, this is a misnomer, and objective behavioral frequency or duration measures are less common. Similarly, while many studies invoke the term "heterosexual anxiety," few studies use physiological or behavioral recordings to measure anxiety or to validate self-reported or judged anxiety. Indeed, reviews of assessment procedures in the heterosocial competency area typically cite the absence of critical validation studies (Curran, 1977; Hersen & Bellack, 1977).

LIMITATIONS OF TRADITIONAL APPROACHES (RATINGS AND QUESTIONNAIRES)

Our initial ventures into the heterosocial skills arena centered primarily on issues of reliability and validity. This research included investigations of the generalizability of global ratings collected from different sources under a variety of conditions, and studies of concurrent, content, discriminative, and ecological validity. Results of these investigations will be reported briefly since they document inadequacies in the more global approaches to assessment and have laid the foundation for our emphasis on a components approach to assessment. In addition, although several of these studies appear in print elsewhere, our interpretation of their results has changed somewhat in the face of newer information and reconceptualizations of issues.

In 1976 Al Farrell and Jan Wallander undertook research projects designed to investigate the comparability of questionnaires and ratings used to assess heterosocial anxiety and skill. (These projects preceded the formation of our research team. Both projects had an initial conceptual impetus from Jim Curran and additional shaping and direction from A. Conger and Marco Mariotto.) The overall goal of the Farrell study was to compare global ratings obtained under different rating conditions and from different rating sources. The Wallander study had as its purpose the comparison of different subject-selection techniques ranging from questionnaires to role-play assessments.

The overall design of the Farrell study involved self-ratings collected prior to role plays, at the end of each of two role plays, and from videotapes of the role plays. Ratings were also collected from confederates at the end of each role play and from trained judges using videotapes of the role plays. This design thus incorporated different situations (role-play types), different sources or modes (self vs. judge), and different methods (live vs. videotape). The use of generalizability theory (Cronbach, Gleser, Nanda, & Rajaratnam, 1972) to analyze data allowed for a simultaneous, comprehensive evaluation of the comparability of ratings of skill or anxiety relative to the measurement conditions.

The results of this project were presented with a slightly pessimistic interpretation (Farrell, Mariotto, Conger, Curran, & Wallander, 1979). Briefly, the results indicated that while ratings were reasonably consistent across role-play types or across judges within a method, persons were rank-ordered very inconsistently across modes or sources (i.e., self vs. judge or confederate). The major conclusion reached was that a small number of trained judges could provide global ratings that could be combined into a moderately good (i.e., reliable) measure of heterosocial skill or anxiety. Unfortunately such a measure would not be highly comparable to self-reported skill or anxiety. Most important was the realization that by using global ratings, systems of assessing skill and anxiety were being adopted that focused on either an *affective appraisal* of performance (i.e., how skilled or anxious subjects reported they felt) or on an *appearance appraisal* of performance (i.e., how skilled or anxious subjects looked to the trained judges or confederates). A particular problem in the latter case is not that ratings of apparent skill are made; rather, the problem is, What does the training procedure teach the judges to look at and at what do they look in addition? Farrell's confederates and judges had been provided with some examples of behavioral indicators of anxiety (e.g., trembling voice, speech dysfluencies, body position, or posture) and of skill (e.g., giving compliments, using the confederate's name), but were allowed to combine these indicators into overall impressions as they saw fit.

Farrell et al. (1979) also noted that ratings of social skill and anxiety were highly correlated. A variety of studies (e.g., Christensen, Arkowitz, & Anderson, 1975; MacDonald, Lindquist, Kramer, McGrath, & Rhyne, 1975; Twentyman & McFall, 1975) used both attributes but did not report between attribute relationships. The question of whether anxiety and skill ratings are sufficiently distinct to warrant their being used as separate measures was not addressed until recently. Thus, even though anxiety and skill are often considered as different constructs or aspects of heterosocial competence, judgments based on appearance appraisals may be insufficiently distinct to claim divergent validity.

The relationship between judgments of social skill and anxiety was investigated by analyzing ratings from five different sets of judges trained by three different researchers (Conger, Wallander, Ward, & Farrell, 1979). In one study, ratings of 79 subjects made by two confederates immediately after each role play and by two judges from videotape recordings were reanalyzed. A second study used videotapes of 45 subjects rated by six judges, and a third study used 32 of those 45 subjects and included some judges rating only one attribute (anxiety or skill), while others rated both. The ratings were analyzed using generalizability theory modified to study among attribute relationships (Conger, 1981). The results of all three studies converged on a single conclusion: there was no evidence of differential measurement of the two attributes. The ratings showed either that anxiety and skill were almost perfectly correlated (when corrected for unreliability), or that different judges agreed no more with one another on a single attribute than they agreed when one rated skill and the other rated (lack of) anxiety. In the analysis of judges who rated only one dimension, it was found that their ratings were at least as highly correlated as those of judges who rated both attributes.

One discrepant type of information does exist to warrant some claim of independence. Several studies (Glasgow & Arkowitz, 1975; Greenwald, 1977; Wessberg, Mariotto, Conger, Farrell, & Conger, 1979), in addition to our own analyses, have found differential changes in mean levels of anxiety versus skill between groups or across experimental conditions or settings. For example, Greenwald (1977) reported a difference between high and low socially competent females for rated skill but not for rated anxiety, while we found (Wessberg et al., 1979) that subjects apparently decreased in skill but not in anxiety when the situation changed from a role play to a waiting period. Although questions of illusory impact or judge-set peculiarities could be raised to account for differential changes in mean level, despite the nearly perfect association within a setting, it may be the case that the behaviors or context events are themselves changing enough to influence rated skill level but not rated anxiety level. One way to resolve this paradox of high dependence within settings, but not across settings, is to measure components of behavior and determine whether the level of behavioral components related to skill, for example, change while the level of behavioral components related to anxiety do not. This issue is addressed further in a study of components reported below.

An investigation of a variety of self-report instruments used for subject selection and treatment-outcome evaluation was run concurrently with the study of ratings (Farrell et al., 1979). This study (Wallander, Conger, Mariotto, Curran, & Farrell, 1980) compared four commonly used paper and pencil questionnaires designed to assess dating experience or social anxiety. Included were the Social Avoidance and Distress Scale (SAD) developed by Watson and Friend (1969), the Situation Questionnaire (SQ) from Rehm and Marston (1968), the Survey of

Heterosexual Interactions (SHI) from Twentyman and McFall (1975), and the Social Activity Questionnaire (SAQ) of Christensen and Arkowitz (1974). All four questionnaires included items about how anxious or uncomfortable a subject felt in social situations and the SHI and SAQ both included items about dating frequency and experience.

The major findings were that intercorrelations among the four scales were moderate (in the .50 to .60 range); however, principal components analyses and analyses of pairwise-selection agreements indicated major problems. First, the principal components analyses indicated that the battery was multidimensional rather than unidimensional. The extracted dimensions were interpreted as being associated with both differences in content and in method variance. Specifically, content differences were associated with the attitudinal or affective aspects versus dating experience aspects. Dating experience items further broke into several dimensions as a function of item-response format (open-ended vs. class interval) and content (number of dates vs. number of girls dated). Secondly, despite moderate correlations among the selection instruments the selection agreement analysis revealed that virtually independent subject samples were selected by different instruments. Of the four selection procedures only the SHI appeared to be identifying extreme quartile groups somewhat comparable with those identified by other procedures.

The results brought into contrast two different approaches to identifying social competence or incompetence: self-reported discomfort versus dating experiences. The SAQ assessment procedure is a basically consequence-oriented measure emphasizing the number of dates a subject has had. As such it corresponds more closely to our construal of heterosocial competence than does the SHI, SQ, or SAD. Unfortunately, the dating experiences information appeared to be somewhat method-contaminated and would not appear to be a valid procedure for assessing competence. Dating experience also seems too delimited to warrant its use as a sole criterion for heterosocial competence, a point cogently raised by Curran (1977). On the other hand, the SHI emerged as a central measure in that it alone was related to all other criterion measures. Finally, in a concurrent validity study, Wallander (1977) related ratings of anxiety and skill to the various self-report measures. The result of this analysis was that role-play assessments were about as meaningfully related to the other instruments as the other instruments were to themselves; that is, there was only a moderate relationship.

Taken together the above studies indicated that global assessment procedures were somewhat unsatisfactory measures of heterosocial competence. A general conclusion was that measures differing in method manifest the most divergence even when they purport to measure the same thing, while measures sharing a method tend to lack divergence even when they measure purportedly different attributes. From this we concluded that research on heterosexual social problem behaviors based on different measurement instruments is not a homogeneous enterprise. The research indicated a lack of convergence of the measurement instruments on a unitary problem behavior or behavior construct and this lack most likely stems from the strategies used to develop the measures and the absence of consensually agreed-upon criteria. We concluded that there was a major need to specify more completely an empirically determined set of behavioral indicators related to heterosocial skill and anxiety and more specific guidelines for combining these indicators into heuristic composite measures of skill and anxiety.

ROLE-PLAY ANALYSES AND ECOLOGICAL VALIDITY

Many investigators in the skills area have used role-playing procedures as a means of assessing behavior. Although most researchers would argue that direct observation in the actual situation should yield the best sample of behavior, reality constraints, as well as ethics, generally preclude this. Role playing thus inevitably represents a compromise in that attempts are made to simulate reality with the assumption that an individual's behavior will be highly similar across the two situations. Simulation methods are certainly not new to psychology (McReynolds & DeVoge, 1978) and McFall (1977) attributed their rediscovery to the corresponding interest in behavioral approaches to treatment. McFall also noted that the development and validation of simulation assessment measures have lagged behind the development of behavioral treatment techniques.

Although role playing has been used extensively to assess social skills and anxiety, there is quite a bit of variability in the procedure in terms of the goals, format, length, modality, and measures employed (Bellack, 1979). Additionally, there has been a somewhat arbitrary distinction made between role-play tests and the "as if" type of naturalistic interaction (Bellack, 1979); however, both types of interactions are simulated and a naturalistic interaction is presumed on a logical basis to be more realistic than a highly contrived role-play test. The scenarios for these procedures have been selected, by and large, on the basis of face validity and seem limited only by the ingenuity of the investigator. However, because a situation seems more realistic is no guarantee of external validity, and further validational evidence needs to be gathered as to the validity and utility of various types of role-play procedures.

The validity issue is a complex one and the question, Validity for what purpose? should be kept in mind. As previously mentioned, a concurrent validity of role-play assessments as they relate to self-report devices was addressed by Wallander (1977). He found that role-play assessments were about as meaningfully related to the self-report instruments as the self-report instruments were to one another. This moderate relationship between role-play performance and self-report information has been demonstrated in a variety of other studies as well (cf. Hersen & Bellack, 1977). None of these results, however, related to the more critical issue of whether performance in role plays was like performance in naturalistic settings. The specific demands inherent in a role play as well as the obtrusiveness inherent in being studied could invalidate their use in obtaining representative performance.

Requests for demonstrating ecological validity had been made repeatedly (e.g., Curran, 1977; Hersen & Bellack, 1977; Twentyman & McFall, 1975). The few studies attempting to relate role-play behaviors to naturalistic behavior yielded inconsistent results (Bellack, Hersen, & Lamparski, 1979; Christensen & Arkowitz, 1974; Christensen et al., 1975; Greenwald, 1977; Twentyman & McFall, 1975).

To evaluate the ecological validity of extended role plays we compared performance in role plays to performance in waiting periods (Wessberg et al., 1979). This study had 45 males interact with confederates (trained to be minimally responsive) in a series of interactions: an initial role play for 4 minutes, a 3-minute waiting period ostensibly necessary because of scheduling problems, a second 4-minute role play with different content, and a final 3-minute waiting period (again due to "scheduling difficulties"). One role play and one waiting period were done with one confederate, and the other role play and waiting period used a different confederate. Ratings of skill and anxiety were made by the subjects after the role plays but not after the waiting periods; however, the main dependent measure was based on trained judges' ratings of videotapes of all the interactions.

Overall, the results indicated that performance in the role-play periods correlated well with performance in the waiting periods ($r = .68$ for anxiety and $r = .62$ for skill) but the subjects were rated as more skillful in the role plays than in the waiting periods. Taken at this level, role plays appeared to be a reasonable method for simulating more naturalistic interactions; but due to the inherent limitations of this study a claim of ecological validity for role plays cannot be made. Furthermore, when judges' ratings of performance regardless of the type of interaction were related to dating frequency, as measured by the SAQ (Christensen & Arkowitz, 1974), it was found that skill ratings did not significantly differentiate dating frequency groups but anxiety ratings did. Substantive interpretations of this result were further complicated by the fact that self-reported ratings of role-play skill differed across dating frequency groups but their anxiety ratings did not. These relationships between role-play assessments and dating frequency are important to consider as an additional source of validity in that dating frequency is, at face value, a direct, albeit complex, measure of social competence. These results therefore feed into the equivocality of using judges' ratings in role plays as a measure of ecologically valid social competence.

The equivocality of using role plays was subsequently underscored in research on the relationship between components of assertive behavior on the Behavioral Assertiveness Test—Revised (BAT-R) and behavior measured in interviews and treatment group sessions (Bellack, Hersen, & Turner, 1978). Although components of the BAT-R predicted judges' global ratings of assertiveness for the BAT-R, they did not relate to performance in the two distinct criterion situations. In a later study, Bellack et al. (1979) assessed the relationship between brief role plays and an extended naturalistic interaction. They found a moderate relationship for females but not for males. Lest it be assumed that females are more consistent than males, the study by Farrell et al. (1979) used only males and employed brief role plays and an extended interaction. Those results indicated that performance was not influenced by role-play type to any great extent!

The final answer awaits us, but an important proviso governing the validity of role plays was offered by McReynolds and DeVoge: "The greater the similarity between the behavioral situation from which one is predicting a person's behavior and the behavioral situation to which the tester is predicting that person's behavior, the greater will be the accuracy of prediction, other things being equal" (McReynolds & De-Voge, 1978, p. 237). This statement includes two critical points: situational similarity and the equivalence of other assessment conditions. The inconsistencies between performance in role plays and naturalistic settings should be viewed with these problems in mind. Thus the negative findings for the BAT-R may well be due to the social context differing from that of the extended interactions: that is, low situational similarity. And, while the Farrell comparison of brief problem-oriented role plays versus an extended interaction superficially contains different contexts, the use of the same minimally responsive confederates in both may have established equivalently strong situational demands to make the role plays sufficiently similar. In the same way, the use of minimally responsive confederates in the role play and waiting periods used by Wessberg et al. (1979) created similar contexts, but behaviors called for in these situations may differ from those involved in more naturalistic dating situations.

The above discussion of role plays is offered for several reasons. One reason is to restate the need to consider the representativeness of the role-play interactions relative to real-life situations involved in heterosocial interactions. In this regard, role plays should be developed to cover the range of situations normally encountered in real life, but except for McFall (1977), little has been done on this problem. Another reason is to account for discrepancies among the various assessment procedures; namely, they are related to different external behaviors. Thus a failure to find substantial relationships between initial conversational interactions (like those used by Wessberg et al., 1979) and dating frequency measures should not be surprising when one considers that dating frequency is a substantially more complex phenomenon. A third reason was only alluded to in the previous discussion and that is the problem of the constraints imposed by the confederates' behavior. Different researchers have trained confederates to behave in quite different ways. Farrell et al. (1979), using a training procedure inherited from Curran, had subjects interact with two minimally responsive and at times abrasive confederates in an attempt to make performance maximally difficult. Wessberg et al. (1979) had subjects interact with one minimally responsive but pleasant confederate in an attempt to make performance only moderately difficult. This range of conditions could be extended to include a confederate who is trained to facilitate performance in an attempt to detect those males who cannot perform under the best of circumstances. Thus any consideration of role-play performance relative to real-world performance needs to consider degree of similarity to the real-world situation along the lines of inclusion of relevant situations and contextual demands of those situations.

Although behavioral assessors have shied away from more traditional approaches to assessment, they are now beginning to realize the potential of classical test theory as applied within a behavioral framework (Cone, 1977; Cone & Hawkins, 1977; Linehan, 1980). Role-play assessments provide a case in point: role plays can be construed as being analogous to items on a test with format, number, content, and type of confederate behavior being analogous to item characteristics. Further, the type of behavior the subject emits can be considered in terms of the desired response characteristics. For example, does the procedure require a brief response or an extended one? Is typical, maximal, or minimal performance being sought? If one views role plays within this framework then the relevance of content, predictive and concurrent validity, and reliability becomes obvious.

We have expended some time and effort dealing with the intricacies of role plays because they are an essential part of a components approach. While it is essential that role plays possess content validity and include stimulus characteristics that "pull" for the kind of behavior that is being assessed by global ratings, it is equally true that these conditions hold if one is interested in discovering specific component behaviors. The question we are thus faced with is what should be the nature of role-play interactions in terms of format, content, and type of confederate behavior?

A STEP TOWARD A BEHAVIOR-ANALYTIC ASSESSMENT OF HETEROSOCIAL SKILLS

It seemed critical to us to find out more about the dating behaviors of college-aged males, socially competent or not, in terms of what they did and where they went, and what kinds of problems they encountered. Other studies had been done on dating habits and problems (Klaus, Hersen, & Bellack, 1977); however, they began with structured questionnaires, which a priori limited the content and therefore missed a basic and perhaps critical step. One approach to obtaining the desired information is the behavior-analytic technique advocated by Goldfried and D'Zurilla (1969). This approach was used by them to study social competence and was also employed by Goldsmith and McFall (1975) to construct treatment content and outcome measures for skills training in a psychiatric population. McFall (1977) presents an excellent general discussion of this procedure.

Our behavior-analytic study of heterosocial competence in college-aged males was conducted by Kulich and Conger (1978), who requested subjects from an introductory psychology pool to list the problems they encountered while interacting and to identify the situations that they found to be most problematic. The 740 subjects generated some 2200 responses, which were abstracted and classified into global categories. About 25% of the responses mentioned physical contact problems and an approximately equal number mentioned maintaining a conversation as a major problem. Substantially smaller percentages referred to initiating or terminating interactions and the rest of the responses fell into a variety of miscellaneous categories. The surprising outcome was that the major foci were engaging in conversation or were physical contact-related but were *not* in the area of initiating interactions. Since physical contact was considered outside our scope of interest we were encouraged to pursue the analysis of conversational behaviors.

Information from this study was also used to construct questionnaires to investigate differences between high- and low-frequency daters and among demographic groups on the occurrence of specific problems, how dates were made, what was done on dates, and so forth. These results indicated that high- and low-frequency daters differed only in terms of subjective discomfort and difficulties in physical contact and conversation, but not in terms of how they obtained dates or where they took them.

From these studies it was reasoned that unskilled males were not particularly deficient in behaviors or knowledge about how to make dates or where to take them; rather, they were deficient in conversational skills or in matters related to sexual activities. This latter problem has really not been adequately addressed in the literature and further underscores the need to delineate the goals of the interactions.

The existence of different goals has been further supported by anecdotal data collected from interviews with clinical cases who fall roughly into three groups: (1) males who appear to interact reasonably well with females but have anxieties about sexual encounters; (2) sexually active males unhappy with the social aspects of interacting with females—many of whom do not initiate dates but who luck into them, are fixed up, or who are pursued by females; and (3) a group that has had few social encounters and would like more, but whose members do not even entertain the idea of sex (if they know what it is) or assume it will follow naturally.

Restricting our interest to social goals, the behavior-analytic studies encouraged us to focus on conversational interactions, particularly those involved in initial heterosocial interactions. The role-play content and setting seemed somewhat irrelevant and thus the extended role plays we had been using seemed well suited for exploring conversational skills. What was not directly addressed in the behavior analysis were the behaviors of the other interactant that facilitated or inhibited performance; thus the factor of confederate responsivity was not made explicit.

COMPONENTS OF HETEROSOCIAL COMPETENCE

Social competence, as previously mentioned, is a rather global construct and is normally assessed by global judgments or questionnaires. In everyday person-to-person interactions people undoubtedly operate at a global level of appraisal, but impressions and judgments are based to a certain extent on the behaviors that others emit. Even if we accept the proposition that social behavior is complex in the sense that the whole is greater than the sum of its parts, it is important to recognize that it does not exist independently of its parts. It is these parts or components that we are interested in uncovering as well as the way in which these components might be combined to form the whole. In this regard, Trower (1980) has argued for a components–process distinction, whereby "components" are considered as basic, single-element behaviors and "process" refers to the person's ability to generate skilled behavior according to rules and goals in response to feedback. This conceptualization is capable of encompassing static elemental behaviors as well as the dynamic interactive patterning involved in social functioning.

Our quest for component behaviors (the static elements) was undertaken despite an aura of pessimism generated by previous research. Equivocal relationships between component behaviors and more global criteria of social skill had been reported by others (Curran, 1977). While previous research indicated that high- and low-competency groups (defined by dating frequency or other self-report measures) could be discriminated by global ratings of skill and anxiety, consistent discrimination using specific behaviors had not been found (Arkowitz, Lichtenstein, McGovern, & Hines, 1975; Borkovec, Stone, O'Brien, & Kaloupek, 1974; Glasgow & Arkowitz, 1975; Greenwald, 1977; Twentyman & McFall, 1975).

Curran (1977) has suggested that perhaps we ought to look elsewhere for more complex behaviors in an effort to discover referents of skill. Indeed, Fischetti, Curran, and Wessberg (1977) found that highly skilled males differed in sense of timing from unskilled males, while not differing on selected component behaviors. While we would agree that more complex behaviors (process or interactive behaviors) must be studied, we would also argue that behavioral components are a basic and elemental necessity in detailing a skills repertoire. Thus, it is not a matter of either process or components: both are necessary. Moreover, some research had produced promising results. For example, Barlow, Abel, Blanchard, Briston, and Young (1977), using categories of voice, form of conversation, affect, and motor behavior, found that raters could discriminate adequate from inadequate males in three of the four categories. Further, these groups differed on many of the items comprising the categories, which argues against the notion that simply breadth of category and not specifics were operating. Pilkonis (1977) found that males who were not shy showed shorter latencies to first utterance, spoke more frequently, allowed fewer silences to develop, and broke a larger percentage of silences than males who were shy. Kupke, Hobbs, and Cheney (1979), examining categories of conversational behavior, found that personal attention verbalizations were significantly related to ratings of female attraction. Trower (1980), who was apparently carrying out similar and simultaneous research to our own on a psychiatric population, recently reported that skilled patients spoke, looked, smiled, gestured, and changed posture more than unskilled patients. These studies, coupled with research in other areas where rather simple frequency and/or duration measures have been employed (see Bayes, 1972; Rimé, Bouvy, Leborgne, & Rouillon, 1978; Shrout & Fiske, 1979; Waxer, 1977), suggests that the search for specific behaviors that underlie social competency should not be prematurely abandoned. The question then arises as to why the detailing of components has produced inconsistent results in the skills area. There are several possible reasons for this state of affairs. At a general level, the assessment strategies employed in the delineation of component behaviors may per se have led to the less than optimum results. Because of the lack of well-formulated theoretical models within the heterosocial skill domain, investigators typically have synthetically derived component behaviors from the anxiety literature or communication literature in general, or simply have intuited the relevant skills. A major drawback of such an approach to assessment is that if the assessment system fails to predict socially relevant criteria, it is difficult to pinpoint the source of the problem (Wiggins, 1973). Though the problem is usually a failure of intuition, the specific misjudgment could be in the original appraisal of heterosocial interaction situations, the selection of a particular model of social interaction, or the actual measurement techniques employed. In addition, however, inconsistencies in the reported results could be due to a number of specific factors, including (1) variation in the observational medium (audio, video, or live recordings); (2) variation in the behaviors and their definition; (3) variation in the population investigated; and (4) reliance on self-report devices to form criterion groups (for a more detailed discussion, see Conger & Farrell, 1981).

Our research on discovering components involved in heterosocial competence was predicated on the behavior-analytic finding that conversation maintenance was the major problem among college-aged males and that role plays provided reasonable analogues to more naturalistic interactions. The necessary step seemed to be a detailed investigation of social competence as it was manifested in role-play interactions and at this juncture, two alternative strategies appeared attractive: (1) relating the frequency and duration of potentially important behaviors to global ratings of social competence; and (2) having peers of the interactees specify what they considered to be performance strengths and weaknesses. Since both alternatives could be used to determine specific behavioral acts underlying social competence, both were undertaken using a common set of interactions so that convergence between the results could be investigated.

MICROANALYTIC COMPONENTS

The exploration of specific behavioral differences underlying role-play performances used previously recorded videotapes of college males interacting with trained confederates in role plays and waiting periods. The subjects represented a broad range of heterosocial competency as assessed by self-report devices. The initial criteria measures of role-play performance were obtained from trained judges who made ratings on the appearance of skill and anxiety (details are provided in Wessberg et al., 1979).

Observations were carried out on the following behaviors: gestures, self-manipulations, smiling, head nods, leg movements, subject talk time, confederate talk time, and gaze. We then attempted to relate the behavioral observations to the skill and anxiety ratings via correlational and regression analyses.

The most striking results were the multiple regression analyses, which yielded an R of .66 for anxiety and .90 for skill with talk and gaze

TABLE 10-1. Multiple Correlations with Behaviors as Predictors and Anxiety and Skill Ratings as Criteria

Criterion	Role-play anxiety	Waiting-period anxiety	Role-play skill	Waiting-period skill
Subject talk	$-.55^a$	$-.38$	.83	.50
	$(.014)^b$	(.144)	(.0001)	(.002)
Gaze	$-.42$	0.31	.21	.31
	(.036)	(.152)	(.06)	(.018)
Leg moves	.07	.04	$-.09$	$-.016$
	(.696)	(.806)	(.351)	(.87)
Nods	.02	$-.11$	.07	.07
	(.908)	(.525)	(.45)	(.49)
Smiles	.13	$-.04$	.15	.15
	(.457)	(.83)	(.13)	(.204)
Gestures	.002	.20	.12	.07
	(.991)	(.265)	(.27)	(.49)
Confederate talk	.013	$-.21$	.25	.23
	(.952)	(.299)	(.05)	(.059)
Multiple correlations	.66	.66	.91	.90
	(.057)	(.044)	(.001)	(.001)

[a]Standardized coefficients.
[b]Significance levels.

contributing most heavily to prediction (see Table 10-1)! Although other behaviors had strong simple correlations with skill and anxiety, when all variables were considered simultaneously, these dropped out as major predictors due to the probable redundancy of information. Confederate talk time also emerged as a strong variable correlating with skill ratings, particularly in the waiting periods. Subsequent analyses revealed that confederates tended to talk more with skillful subjects within the waiting period ($F = 8.91$, $p < .001$) than they did within the role-play situation ($F = .886$, $p < .446$) despite our instructions and training. A similar but weaker effect occurred for anxiety ratings. The waiting period was much less structured than the role play and it seems as though skillful subjects had the ability to "pull the confederate out of role" and engage the confederate in conversation.

Simple correlations between the component behaviors and skill and anxiety indicated a consistent trend for behavioral variables to be negatively related to ratings of anxiety and positively related to skill. Subject talk time and gaze were consistently related to both skill and anxiety, although results were stronger for skill regardless of situation (see Table 10-2). Additionally, smiles, gestures, confederate talk time, and

TABLE 10-2. Zero-Order Correlations between Behaviors and Anxiety and Skill Ratings

	Anxiety ratings		Skill ratings	
Criterion	Role play[a]	Waiting period	Role play	Waiting period
Subject talk time	−.49**	−.45**	.78***	.74***
Gaze	−.40*	−.56***	.35**	.70***
Leg moves	−.02	−.03	.18	.07
Nods	−.07	−.14	.04	.08
Smiles	−.03	−.33	.39*	.56***
Gestures	−.17	−.09	.47**	.44*
Confederate talk time	−.00	−.36*	.05	.44*
Self-manipulations[b]	.24	.32	−.08	−.48**

[a] $n = 30$ for role play, $n = 31$ for waiting period.
[b] $n = 22$ for role play, $n = 28$ for waiting period; data lost.
*$p < .05$ for two-tailed test.
**$p < .01$ for two-tailed test.
***$p < .001$ for two-tailed test.

self-manipulations (based on a smaller n due to technical difficulties) correlated significantly with skill ratings in both the role play and waiting period. As was mentioned, these variables "washed out" in the regression analyses due to the probable redundancy of information they provide. Again, skill and anxiety ratings correlated highly with one another ($R = .77$ for role play, $R = .55$ for waiting period), although skill was better predicted than anxiety ($R_S = .90$, $R_A = .66$). Further, component behaviors correlated better with skill in terms of number as well as strength of relationship. These results, as well as previous research, are not promising in terms of the delineation or discrimination between these constructs (Conger, Wallander, Ward, & Farrell, 1979). A picture is emerging that strongly suggests that skill can be better articulated and perhaps anxiety should be relegated to a "private experiential variable" that is not accessible to behavioral observations or ratings. The lack of divergence could be due to the particular population being studied and may be discriminable in psychiatric patients but not in college males. Additional physiological work may shed light on anxiety; however, we are pessimistic as to its separate delineation at this point.

It is probably worth mentioning that simple linear composites of the microbehaviors, subject talk (STT), confederate talk (CTT), and gaze (GZ), correlated quite well with the anxiety and skill ratings, thus substantiating the regression analyses (see Table 10-3). Moreover these composites correlated significantly with both self-ratings of anxiety and skill and with standard self-report inventories (SHI, SAQ), particularly in role-play situations. This tends to lend additional validational support to the selected components.

In summary then, we concluded that behavioral referents of skill could be identified that strongly predicted ratings of skill and anxiety, although skill was better predicted than anxiety. We attributed the success of these results to careful observational procedures and the use of appropriate criteria.

PEER-GENERATED COMPONENTS

An alternative strategy for generating component behaviors, and the approach we utilized, is similar to the informal empirical strategy employed by Barlow *et al.* (1977) with a few major differences. Whereas Barlow *et al.* (1977) utilized a few expert judges from a research team to view informally several socially adequate males and then generate component behaviors, our investigation employed many peer judges who were systematically presented with videotapes of both high- and low-skill males and then asked to generate component behaviors. Thus our study delineated specific social skill behaviors by having potential recipients of interactions (e.g., peers), rather than members of a research team or experts, judge the quality of males' social interactive skills and stipulate what it was that influenced the peer judgments. The purpose of this research was to isolate those behaviors that peers claim to employ in evaluating the heterosocial skill and anxiety of males attempting to initiate a social interaction with females.

The initial peer judgment study was a collaborative effort with Marco Mariotto, Jan Wallander, and David Ward (Conger, Wallander, Mariotto, & Ward, 1980). It used undergraduates (62 males and 73 females) who were volunteers from the same subject pool as the target males, but during a different semester. The videotape segments consisted of the first 3 minutes of an interaction between a male subject and a female confederate and are a subset of the role-play interactions collected by Wessberg *et al.* (1979). The stimulus materials consisted of 12 segments comprised of four high, four middle, and four low socially competent males based on previous ratings by trained judges. Six tapes, two at each competency level, were used in the initial exposure phase. The remaining six tapes were used to establish six different target tape conditions for the cue-generation phase and to obtain component ratings in the cue-estimation phase.

TABLE 10-3. Correlations between Simple Linear Composites of Behaviors and Ratings and Self-Report Devices

| | Judges' ratings[a] | | | | Self-ratings[a] | | Self-report[b] | | |
| | Role play | | Waiting period | | Role play | | | | |
Models	Anxiety[d]	Skill	Anxiety	Skill	SRA	SRSK	SHI	SAQDT	SAQSAT
Role play[c]									
Model I, STT + CTT + GZ	−59***	75***	−47**	69***	−37*	51**	57***	40*	−43*
Model II, STT + CTT	−53**	86***	−32	45**	−36*	46**	41*	34	−29
Waiting period									
Model I, STT + CTT + GZ	−38*	40*	−58***	84***	−22	22	44*	19	−31
Model II, STT + CTT	−31	54**	−53**	85***	−18	24	43*	19	−40

[a]SRA, self-reported anxiety; SRSK, self-reported skill; asked in role plays only.

[b]SHI, Survey of Heterosexual Interactions; SAQDT, Social Anxiety Questionnaire (dating frequency items); SAQSAT, Social Anxiety Questionnaire (satisfaction items).

[c]STT, subject talk time; CTT, confederate talk time; GZ, gaze time.

[d]$n = 30$ for waiting periods, $n = 31$ for role plays.

*$p < .05$ for two-tailed test.

**$p < .01$ for two-tailed test.

***$p < .001$ for two-tailed test.

At the outset all subjects were fully informed about the confederate's role in the videotaped interactions. During the first phase of the experiment, all subjects viewed six interactions and rated how anxious the male appeared, how skillfully he performed, and his physical attractiveness. This phase was used to expose subjects to a common heterogeneous range of performances and to collect naïve ratings for a reliability evaluation and validity comparison to trained judges. With no apparent discontinuity to the subjects, the second phase began by having six different groups rate a new interaction on anxiety, skill, and attractiveness; however, following these ratings the subjects were asked to provide in their own words the specific characteristics and/or behaviors they used to make their judgments. In addition, they were asked to designate each cue as being related either to anxiety, skill, or both. This phase of the study provided cues for developing a classification system and provided global ratings that could be associated with the cues. After a break, the third phase began. All subjects viewed all interactions used in the second phase. As before, they rated anxiety, skill, and attractiveness, but in addition they rated 10 specific components. This phase allowed for modeling peers' global ratings relative to the specific components and for relating peer estimates of components to the actual frequency of occurrence. That is, several of the components the peers rated had been designated as behaviors to be included in a microanalytic study.

The overall experiment was highly successful on all counts. The global ratings provided by peers correlated highly with previously obtained trained judges' ratings, although the untrained peers were slightly less reliable. On this latter point, the mean ratings of about eight naïve peers has a reliability equivalent to the mean of six trained judges. Considering that our normal training procedure takes about 10 hours, while the overall set of 45 ratings in the Wessberg et al. (1979) study required 12 hours, the more efficient method would have been to use untrained judges.

In the second phase the peers generated over 900 cues on which a four-level inclusive hierarchy category structure was imposed. In this category system categories at higher levels subsumed the more specific preceding categories. The hierarchy, categories, and their relationships were based on an intuitive–synthetic method; that is, they made the most sense and related to behaviors and attributes prevalent in nonverbal communications (Knapp, 1972) and kinesics (Birdwhistell, 1970).

The resulting hierarchy had three global first-order categories: non-verbal cues, verbal cues, and general cues. Nonverbal cues were defined on the basis of references to position or body movement. Verbal cues included two major subcategories, speech and voice characteristics and conversation characteristics. Altogether 60 categories were generated, either through the cues being specifically mentioned ($n = 54$) or in order to complete the hierarchical structure at the more global levels ($n = 6$). It should be noted that the verbal and nonverbal categories included 50 of the 60 cue categories and also had the most refined categories.

Subsequent to developing the hierarchy, cues from each subject were categorized by two research assistants. Initial descriptive analyses indicated that verbal cues were used with the highest frequency, particularly cues relating to conversation fluency and structure, speech delivery characteristics, and personal style of the conversationalist. Nonverbal cues relating to gestures and body movements were also frequently mentioned. Cues of topic interest, conversational style and fluency, and physical appearances were commonly associated with skill, while cues of voice quality, calmness, gestures, body position, and movement were related to anxiety. Speech fluency and gaze were the only frequently mentioned cues designated as both anxiety- and skill-related. Detailed results are provided in Conger, Wallander, Mariotto, and Ward (1980).

Despite the clear structure that emerged from the peer-generated cues and the association between this structure and the variables included in component analyses of heterosocial skills research, there remained a question of whether the peers (and researchers) were victims of implicit personality theory illusions. That is, the generation of anxiety or skill cues does not in itself mean that the cues are based on actual behaviors of the males in the videotapes; they could, instead, have been based on prior beliefs about important interaction behaviors. Consequently, to evaluate whether the peer judgments were based on implicit beliefs or actual manifest behaviors, cue and cue-designator frequencies were compared across the three stimulus competency levels and across the two different target males within each competency level. Specifically, it was hypothesized that if the generated cues were a function of the specific male–confederate interactions rather than a function of implicit beliefs, cue frequency would vary across competency levels and across replications within levels. The absence of such differences would call into question the validity of the cues, while the presence of significant differences between replications within levels was considered to be the strongest evidence of cue validity.

In addition, differences between female and male judges were anticipated on the basis of differences in their normal heterosocial interaction roles and on the basis of purportedly greater social acumen and sensitivity on the part of females (cf. Hall, 1978). A female is potentially the more astute judge of male competency because of her normal role as observer and judge of many different males in diverse heterosocial interactions.

The results of the analyses on total number of cues mentioned indicated significant differences between males and females, between competency levels, and a sex by competency level interaction. These effects were almost solely due to females in the high-competency conditions generating more cues than any other group.

Results on the differential use of skill versus anxiety-designated cues showed competency differences, and a sex by competency interaction. Means indicated that females used more skill than anxiety cues for highly competent males and more anxiety than skill cues for low-competent males. Male judges did not differ across stimulus tape conditions. Analyses of variance were also done on the global ratings of anxiety, and skill, and attractiveness in order to determine whether the peers discriminated the anxiety and skill levels of the target males. The results indicated no differences between the sexes, but highly significant differences in ratings existed among the competency levels for anxiety and skill, and smaller but significant differences were also found for attractiveness. These results are particularly interesting in that although sex was an important moderator of cue generation, no sex differences existed in the global ratings. The analyses reported above, it should be noted, used fairly gross measures to ascertain the validity of the category system and no differences were found between tapes within a competency level. An in-depth follow-up analysis was therefore done on the most frequent categories themselves.

In this study by Conger, Wallander, and Conger (1980), analyses were done on the cue categories shown in Table 10-4. The results were highly favorable. Of the 30 categories, 21 showed differences between the two males used at each competency level for either male and female peers or for female peers only. These results yielded strong evidence that the cues the peers provided were indeed a function of what they saw and were not simply due to beliefs about how people behave in

TABLE 10-4. Number of Cues and Attribute Designations for the Most Frequent Individual and Aggregated Categories

Code[a]	Category description	Cues	Attribute designation percentages[b]		
			S	AS	A
Individual categories					
2221	topic interest	25	76		
2230	personal	23	59		
3100	appearance	29	52		
2211	conversation fluency	128	48	43	
3250	personality—other	35	53		
2121	speech fluency	61		50	
1131	gaze	45		56	
2123	voice quality	25			53
3210	anxiety/calmness	64			59
1222	gestures	48			64
1211	body position	27			67
1212	body movement	44			77
Third-level aggregates					
222x	conversation content	58	76		
223x	personal style	77	59		
325x	personality—other	35	53		
310x	appearance	43	52		
221x	conversation structure	154	44	46	
221x	language (speech/voice)	24	44	36	
113x	eyes	46		55	
212x	speech delivery	120		48	
112x	facial expressions	28			50
321x	anxiety/calmness	64			59
122x	arms/hands	59			67
121x	general/overall body	75			73
Second-level aggregates					
31xx	appearance	43	63		
22xx	conversation	319	57		
21xx	speech/voice	154		47	
32xx	personality	139		47	
11xx	head/facial	77		50	
12xx	body	141			71

[a]Category codes are meaningful for aggregating cues to successive levels. For example, cues 2220, 2221, 2222 are combined to yield 222x; cues 221x, 222x, 223x are combined to yield 22xx; and so on.
[b]Attribute designation refers to the association of global labels of skill (S), anxiety (A), or both anxiety and skill (AS) to a cue. Numbers indicate the percentage of respondents using a designator for a particular category; however, percentages of less than 40 have been deleted.

general. But further evidence that peers can pay attention was available from the final phase of the peer study.

CONVERGENCE OF MICROANALYTIC AND PEER COMPONENTS

In phase three of the peer study, subjects were shown all six target interactions, of which they had previously only seen one, and were asked to give global ratings of anxiety, skill, and attractiveness, as well as being asked to estimate, on a 7-point rating scale, the occurrence of 10 component behaviors. These behaviors included head nods, smiles, self-manipulations, gestures, eye blinks, subject talk time, silences, subject gaze time, body fidgeting, and back channel responses. Of course, less technical and more illustrative terms were used to describe these behaviors to the peers. These specific components were selected because they were representative of behaviors frequently investigated in dyadic interactions, and all but the back channel responses had been selected for direct observations by Conger and Farrell (1981) in their study.

The purpose of this phase was to provide further information about peer judgments. In particular, we wondered whether peers could discriminate among targets on the basis of specific behaviors as well as on the basis of global ratings; we were interested in how peer estimates of components related to global ratings, and also how they would relate to actual behavioral differences obtained from frequency counts or durations.

The results of most immediate relevance were the correlations between each of the 10 estimated components and the three global ratings, and between the estimated components and corresponding frequency counts. For global ratings of skill, five components correlated .80 or above. Only three correlations reached this level for anxiety and none reached this level for attractiveness. The critical components for skill were head nods (−.90), gestures (.84), talk duration (.97), silences (−.98), and gaze (.89). The latter three correlated with global anxiety in the opposite direction and to a slightly lesser extent.

The correlations were quite high and would be subject to alternative interpretations of implicit personality or halo were it not for two factors. First of all, head nods is in the opposite direction of what we would predict from an implicit personality viewpoint. Secondly, the absence of strong relationships for smiling, self-manipulations, fidgeting, or back channel responses ruled out halo effects.

The correlation of peer component estimates with the actual behaviors provided further support for their validity. Using data collected by Conger and Farrell on all behaviors except blinks (which they couldn't see) and back channel response (which they didn't study), the peer components were correlated with actual behavioral counts. Peer estimates correlated .80 or above with their measures for six of the eight components. The most striking correlations were .99 for talk duration and .98 for silences. Head nods correlated .85 in the right direction with head nod frequency. The only failures were for gaze and self-manipulations. Conger and Farrell had trouble with missing data for self-manipulations, so we were not concerned about that, but gaze remained a problem. At this time we are not sure whether the failure was due to our not telling the peers where the confederate sat, whether the peers were really subject to illusion, or whether the peers were paying attention to gaze in a way different from that which we intended.

Overall, we were quite pleased with the peers. They provided us with a set of cues that made sense and appeared valid. They also demonstrated that they could pay attention to specific components of behavior—something that other researchers have had trouble doing with trained observers. On the other hand, we were also troubled. The very specificity with which cues were associated with stimulus tapes indicated limitations in the generality of the hierarchy. That is, the hierarchy may not include behaviors that would typify other male interactees not included in our sample. Of course the general structure might be robust, but only the frequencies would vary. At another level of self-criticism, the hierarchy is probably context-bound and may be most useful for describing males interacting with moderately responsive confederates. There were few if any opportunities for the males to demonstrate listening skills, or turn-taking behaviors and so on. But these are problems arising from the use of such highly restrained role-play interactions. Perhaps the most important outcome of this line of investigation is the demonstration that peers cannot only provide valid global judgments (compared to trained judges) but they can also stipulate target-relevant component behaviors and can also accurately estimate relative frequencies of the occurrence of critical components. In the heterosocial competency area we have come to believe that peer judgments can provide useful information along two lines. First, to the extent that entrance into a social interaction is governed by direct

impressions or group-mediated impressions (i.e., rumors), peer judgments should be predictive of heterosocial competence. Second, in lieu
of more direct consequence-oriented assessments, peer judgments
might serve as an indirect measure of consequence; that is, the consequence of skill may be measured by the impact on judgments of significant others (Kazdin, 1977).

In summary, these studies provided us with the following information. Peers provided overall ratings of skill and anxiety that were highly
correlated with those of our trained judges: the peers, particularly
females, provided specific interaction behaviors to justify their ratings
and because of the one-to-one association of cues with stimulus tapes
there is no reason to doubt their validity; the peers, with reasonable
validity, rated the frequency of occurrence of specific behaviors and
these ratings related to their global ratings. These findings, interestingly enough, stand in marked contradiction to previous attempts to
relate specific component behaviors (e.g., eye contact, talk time, etc.) to
global judgments of skill and anxiety or to other assessment devices. We
also realize that cue specificity is problematic. Thus, if the peers are
reacting to fairly idiosyncratic behaviors, a rather large array of components might be involved. The implication of this would be that persons could be socially incompetent in a variety of specific ways and
target-behavior checklists might need to be rather extensive. In addition, despite our earlier assertion that role plays were ecologically valid
(Wessberg et al., 1979) we had not realized the possible contextual
demand introduced by the confederate. What was found in the earlier
study was that role plays with minimally responsive confederates were
reasonably well related to naturalistic interactions with minimally responsive females (confederates). Fortunately, the world is not replete
with minimally responsive members of the opposite sex, but this suggests that the role plays need to be expanded to cover a larger variety of
confederate behaviors (as has recently been attempted by Trower,
1980).

Some questions that emerged as a function of the microanalytic
research led us to reevaluate our procedures. First of all, if confederate
talk time correlated with skill ratings, to what extent did the confederate influence the rating? What impact does her behavior have on the
subject and what are our grounds for stipulating the ways in which a
confederate should behave? The role of confederates is not well standardized (let alone evaluated) across investigators. For example, Curran
instructs his confederates to behave in a minimally responsive fashion

(e.g., Farrell *et al.*, 1979), while we strive for moderate responsivity. What impact does this have on the assessment procedure in terms of the subject's behavior and subsequent selection of populations? Secondly, and perhaps more importantly, the use of confederates may constrict or restrict the interactions in such a way as to bias the emission of relevant component behaviors by subjects. How then can we ever detect ongoing social interactive processes in a situation where the participants are not behaving in a truly reciprocal fashion?

In an attempt to answer some of the questions we are pursuing the following lines of research: (1) we are currently involved in a study (Moisan-Thomas & Conger, 1980) where level of confederate responsivity is being manipulated in terms of its impact on social skill ratings; and (2) we have collected videotapes of naturalistic dyadic interactions (no confederate) and are seeking replication of previous components (talk and gaze) as well as attempting to look at more processlike behaviors such as turn taking, and so forth. Additionally, we are exploring such variables as "social sensitivity" and its relationship to social skills (Firth & Conger, 1980).

DISCUSSION

WHAT IS NEEDED?

As Trower (1980) has pointed out, after a period of euphoric expectations, we are entering into a period of healthy skepticism and critical self-evaluation. Much of the previous work in the social skills area has not provided us with the kind of knowledge that is necessary to provide relevant treatment targets and criteria for assessment. Much of the work we have presented is directed at uncovering skill components that provide the basic elemental substance of the skills repertoire. We believe that we have reasonably good convergent validation stemming from two quite different studies that simple linear combinations of acts (talk and gaze) are meaningfully related to global judgments of skill by trained or untrained raters. Further, these behaviors relate to a variety of self-report measures. Moreover, Trower's (1980) results from a distinctly different population provide confirmation for speech and gaze as being highly contributory to judgments of skill. He also found smiling and gesturing to be less important components, as we did. Components are only part of the story, however, and future research needs to uncover process or interactive behaviors (timing, sequencing, turn taking). Components and processes operate in a presumably integrated fashion in a skilled individual and we need knowledge of what those relevant components and processes are and how they are organized.

There are other issues that need to be addressed as well. The first concerns the establishment of functional rather than correlational evidence relating components to global judgments. If talk and gaze (as well as other variables) provide the basis for global ratings as correlational analyses indicate, then the manipulation of those variables should alter global judgments of skill. For example, Rose and Tryon (1979) systematically varied voice loudness, latency, speech content, gestures, and inflection and found that each of these variables substantially altered judgments of assertiveness. Similar research is needed in the social skills area.

Second, assuming the best of all possible worlds where one has adequate knowledge of components and processes, what is the most effective strategy as regards the practicalities of clinical assessment? We would speculate that the complexity of an assessment procedure is inversely related to its utility. While objective counts of behaviors and social interactive variables are highly desirable and necessary from a scientific viewpoint, complex observational schema are clinically impractical. However, it is possible that the results of observational research can provide an empirical basis as well as validational criteria for the development of more useful instruments such as rating scales. One of the major problems with rating scales is that they are susceptible to sources of bias and subjectivity on the part of the rater. This may stem in part from the globality of the construct being rated as well as from poorly defined points on the scale. However, we have reason to believe that ratings of relatively well-defined behaviors with clearly defined scalar points yield highly reliable and valid information. Jan Wallander, in carrying out his dissertation research, has compared ratings on the amount of talk, gaze, and so forth, with actual objective counts. He has found very good correspondence between these measures. Ultimately, Wallander is interested in developing a Behaviorally Anchored Rating Scale (BARS), which would have a sound empirical basis but which would have high practical utility. If we are to make good use of empirical findings, we must incorporate them into our assessment procedures in a cost-effective way.

Last, but not least, is the issue of what the focus of therapy should be: specific as opposed to more global behaviors? To a large extent, this depends on the nature of the deficits. A client with massive skill component deficits must acquire basic elements before process deficits such as synchrony, sequencing, and others are taught. On the other hand, as Trower (1980) has noted, it is quite possible for a patient to have no component deficits but to fail in timing or in other process-related skills. Further, there are maladaptive cognitions that include erroneous beliefs, expectations, negative self-evaluations, and so forth, which must be considered. Trower (1980) would include these in his model, under skill–process deficits, while others (Curran, 1979) would prefer not to include cognitive variables within a definitional construct of social skills. Nevertheless, maladaptive cognitions might be the sole focus of some therapeutic endeavors, while being inconsequential in others. What is needed, however, is a comprehensive system of assessment that would enable the clinician to hone in on the relevant performance deficits at the appropriate level as well as to assess the degree to which cognitions are a "cause" or "consequence" of social dysfunctioning.

Further, there is not necessarily a one-to-one correspondence between the unit of behavior selected for modification and the type of intervention. That is, discrete behaviors do not necessarily imply interventions that are solely response-focused in a strict operant fashion. Simple instructions, modeling, and so forth, may be more effective and efficient ways of transmitting information than focal shaping; however, what the most effective means are for promoting behavior change remains an empirical question.

ACKNOWLEDGMENTS

The concepts and research discussed in this chapter have resulted from the collaboration of many people. In particular, Marco Mariotto deserves substantial credit as the third principal investigator directing our research team and Al Farrell and Jan Wallander, graduate students, have been indispensable associates for virtually all of the projects. In addition, Judy Dygdon, Betsy Firth, Susan Keane, Ron Kulich, P. C. Moisan-Thomas, Meg Monroe, Joyce Vogel, David Ward, and Harold Wessberg have unselfishly contributed their ideas, skills, and time to various projects. Finally, we would like to thank the numerous undergraduates who have performed as confederates, judges, technicians, research assistants, and clerks.

REFERENCES

Arkowitz, H., Lichtenstein, E., McGovern, K., & Hines, P. The behavioral assessment of social competence in males. *Behavior Therapy*, 1975, *6*, 3–13.
Barlow, D. H., Abel, G. G., Blanchard, E. B., Briston, A. R., & Young, L. D. A heterosocial skills behavior checklist for males. *Behavior Therapy*, 1977, *8*, 229–239.

Bayes, M. A. Behavioral cues of interpersonal warmth. *Journal of Consulting and Clinical Psychology*, 1972, *39*, 333–339.

Bellack, A. S. A critical appraisal of strategies for assessing social skill. *Behavioral Assessment*, 1979, *1*, 157–176.

Bellack, A. S., Hersen, M., & Lamparski, D. Role play tests for assessing social skills: Are they valid? Are they useful? *Journal of Consulting and Clinical Psychology*, 1979, *47*, 335–342.

Bellack, A. S., Hersen, M., & Turner, S. M. Role playing tests for assessing social skills: Are they valid? *Behavior Therapy*, 1978, *9*, 448–461.

Birdwhistell, R. L. *Kinesics and context*. Philadelphia: University of Pennsylvania Press, 1970.

Borkovec, T. D., Stone, N., O'Brien, G., & Kaloupek, D. G. Evaluation of a clinically relevant target behavior for analogue outcome research. *Behavior Therapy*, 1974, *5*, 513–515.

Carson, R. C. *Interaction concepts of personality*. Chicago: Aldine, 1969.

Christensen, A., & Arkowitz, H. Preliminary report on practice dating and feedback as treatment for college dating problems. *Journal of Counseling Psychology*, 1974, *21*, 92–96.

Christensen, A., Arkowitz, H., & Anderson, J. Practice dating as treatment for college dating inhibitions. *Behaviour Research and Therapy*, 1975, *13*, 321–331.

Combs, M., & Slaby, D. Social skills training in children. In B. Lahey & A. Kazdin (Eds.), *Advances in clinical child psychology*. New York: Plenum Press, 1977.

Cone, J. D. The relevance of reliability and validity for behavioral assessment. *Behavior Therapy*, 1977, *8*, 411 426.

Cone, J. D., & Hawkins, R. P. Current status and future directions in behavioral assessment. In J. D. Cone & R. P. Hawkins (Eds.), *Behavioral assessment: New directions in clinical psychology*. New York: Brunner/Mazel, 1977.

Conger, A. J. A comparison of multi-attribute generalizability strategies. *Education and Psychological Measurement*, 1981, *41*, 121–130.

Conger, A. J., Wallander, J. L., & Conger, J. C. *They do pay attention: Further validation of peer-generated cues*. Unpublished manuscript, Purdue University, 1980.

Conger, A. J., Wallander, J. L., Mariotto, M. J., & Ward, D. Peer judgments of heterosexual-social anxiety and skill: What do they pay attention to anyhow? *Behavioral Assessment*, 1980, *2*, 243–259.

Conger, A. J., Wallander J. L., Ward, D., & Farrell, A. *Ratings of heterosocial skill and anxiety: 1 + 1 = 1*. Unpublished manuscript, 1979.

Conger, J. C., & Farrell, A. D. Behavioral components of heterosocial skills. *Behaviour Research and Therapy*, 1981, *12*, 41–55.

Cowen, E. L., Pederson, A., Babigian, H., Izzo, L. D., & Trost, M. A. Longterm follow-up of early detected vulnerable children. *Journal of Consulting and Clinical Psychology*, 1973, *41*, 438–446.

Cronbach, L. J., Gleser, G. C., Nanda, H., & Rajaratnam, N. *The dependability of behavioral measurements: Theory of generalizability for scores and profiles*. New York: Wiley, 1972.

Curran, J. P. Skills training as an approach to the treatment of heterosexual–social anxiety: A review. *Psychological Bulletin*, 1977, *84*, 140–157.

Curran, J. P. Pandora's box reopened? The assessment of social skills. *Journal of Behavioral Assessment*, 1979, *1*, 55–69.

Duncan, S., & Fiske, D. W. *Face-to-face interaction: Research, methods, and theory*. Hillsdale, N.J.: Erlbaum, 1977.

Farrell, A. D., Mariotto, M. J., Conger, A. J., Curran, J. P., & Wallander, J. L. Self- and judges' ratings of heterosexual–social anxiety and skill: A generalizability study. *Journal of Consulting and Clinical Psychology*, 1979, *47*, 164–175.

Firth, B., & Conger, J. C. *Social sensitivity and its relationship to social skills.* Unpublished manuscript, Purdue University, 1980.

Fischetti, M., Curran, J. P., & Wessberg, H. W. Sense of timing: A skill deficit in heterosexual-socially anxious males. *Behavioral Modification,* 1977, *1,* 179–194.

Glasgow, R., & Arkowitz, H. The behavioral assessment of male and female social competence in dyadic heterosexual interactions. *Behavior Therapy,* 1975, *6,* 488–498.

Goldfried, M. R., & D'Zurilla, T. J. A behavioral-analytic model for assessing competence. In C. D. Spielberger (Ed.), *Current topics in clinical and community psychology.* New York: Academic Press, 1969.

Goldschmidt, W. An ethnography of encounters: A methodology for the inquiry into the relation between the individual and society. *Current Anthropology,* 1972, *13,* 59–78.

Goldsmith, J. B., & McFall, R. M. Development and evaluation of an interpersonal skill-training program for psychiatric inpatients. *Journal of Abnormal Psychology,* 1975, *84,* 51–58.

Greenwald, D. P. The behavioral assessment of differences in social skill and social anxiety in female college students. *Behavior Therapy,* 1977, *8,* 925–937.

Hall, J. A. Gender effects in decoding nonverbal cues. *Psychological Bulletin,* 1978, *85,* 845–857.

Hersen, M., & Bellack, A. S. Assessment of social skill. In A. R. Ciminero, K. S. Calhoun, & H. E. Adams (Eds.), *Handbook of behavioral assessment.* New York: Wiley, 1977.

Kazdin, A. E. Assessing the clinical applied importance of behavior change through social validation. *Behavior Modification,* 1977, *1,* 427–452.

Klaus, D., Hersen, M., & Bellack, A. S. Survey of dating habits of male and female college students: A necessary precursor to measurement and modification. *Journal of Clinical Psychology,* 1977, *33,* 369–375.

Knapp, M. L. *Nonverbal communication in human interaction.* New York: Holt, Rinehart & Winston, 1972.

Kulich, R., & Conger, J. *A step toward a behavior analytic assessment of heterosocial skills.* Paper presented at the meeting of the Association for the Advancement of Behavior Therapy, Chicago, 1978.

Kupke, T. E., Hobbs, S. A., & Cheney, T. H. Selection of heterosocial skills: 1. Criterion-related validity. *Behavior Therapy,* 1979, *10,* 327–335.

Levine, J., & Zigler, E. The essential-reactive distinction in alcoholism: A developmental approach. *Journal of Abnormal Psychology,* 1973, *81,* 242–249.

Linehan, M. M. Content validity: Its relevance to behavioral assessment. *Behavioral Assessment,* 1980, *2,* 147–159.

MacDonald, M. L., Lindquist, C. U., Kramer, J. A., McGrath, R. A., & Rhyne, L. L. Social skills training: The effects of behavior rehearsal in groups on dating skills. *Journal of Counseling Psychology,* 1975, *22,* 224–230.

McFall, R. M. Analogue methods in behavioral assessment: Issues and prospects. In J. D. Cone & R. P. Hawkins (Eds.), *Behavioral assessment.* New York: Brunner/Mazel, 1977.

McReynolds, P. The case for interactional assessment. *Behavioral Assessment,* 1979, *1,* 237–247.

McReynolds, P., & DeVoge, S. Use of improvisational techniques in assessment. In P. McReynolds (Ed.), *Advances in psychological assessment.* San Francisco: Jossey-Bass, 1978.

Moisan-Thomas, P. C., & Conger, J. C. *The effect of confederate responsivity on ratings of skill and anxiety.* Unpublished manuscript, Purdue University, 1980.

Phillips, L., & Zigler, E. Social competence: The action-thought parameter and vicariousness in normal and pathological behaviors. *Journal of Abnormal and Social Psychology,* 1961, *63,* 137–146.

Phillips, L., & Zigler, E. Role-orientation, the action–thought dimension, and outcome in psychiatric disorders. *Journal of Abnormal and Social Psychology*, 1964, 68, 381–389.

Pilkonis, P. A. The behavioral consequences of shyness. *Journal of Personality*, 1977, 45, 596–611.

Raush, H. L. Interaction sequences. *Journal of Personality and Social Psychology*, 1965, 2, 487–499.

Rehm, L. P., & Marston, A. R. Reduction of social anxiety through modification of self-reinforcement: An instigation therapy technique. *Journal of Consulting and Clinical Psychology*, 1968, 32, 565–574.

Rimé, B., Bouvy, H., Leborgne, B., & Rouillon, F. Psychopathy and nonverbal behavior in an interpersonal situation. *Journal of Abnormal Psychology*, 1978, 87, 636–643.

Roff, M. Some life history factors in relation to various types of adult maladjustment. In M. Roff & D. Ricks (Eds.), *Life history research in psychopathology*. Minneapolis: University of Minnesota Press, 1970.

Rose, Y. J., & Tryon, W. W. Judgments of assertive behavior as a function of speech loudness, latency, content, gestures, inflection and sex. *Behavior Modification*, 1979, 3, 112–123.

Shrout, D. E., & Fiske, D. W. *Impressions and nonverbal behaviors: Effects of target and sex*. Manuscript submitted for publication, 1979.

Sullivan, H. S. *The interpersonal theory of psychiatry*. New York: Norton, 1953.

Swensen, C. H. *Introduction to interpersonal relations*. Glenview, Ill.: Scott, Foresman, 1973.

Thibaut, J. W., & Kelley, H. H. *The social psychology of groups*. New York: Wiley, 1959.

Trower, P. Situational analysis of the components and processes of behavior of socially skilled and unskilled patients. *Journal of Consulting and Clinical Psychology*, 1980, 48, 327–339.

Trower, P., Bryant, B., & Argyle, M. *Social skills and mental health*. London: Methuen, 1978.

Twentyman, C., & McFall, R. M. Behavioral training of social skills in shy males. *Journal of Consulting and Clinical Psychology*, 1975, 43, 384–395.

Vernon, P. E. *The structure of human abilities*. London: Methuen, 1950.

Wallander, J. L. *An evaluation of selection instruments in the heterosexual–social anxiety paradigm*. Unpublished masters thesis, Purdue University, 1977.

Wallander, J., Conger, A., Mariotto, M., Curran, J., & Farrell, A. Comparability of selection instruments in studies of heterosexual–social problem behaviors. *Behavior Therapy*, 1980, 11, 548–560.

Watson, D., & Friend, R. Measurement of social-evaluative anxiety. *Journal of Consulting and Clinical Psychology*, 1969, 33, 448–457.

Waxer, P. Nonverbal cues for anxiety: An examination of emotional leakage. *Journal of Abnormal Psychology*, 1977, 86, 306–314.

Wessberg, H. W., Mariotto, M. J., Conger, A. J., Farrell, A. D., & Conger, J. C. The ecological validity of role plays for assessing heterosocial anxiety and skill of male college students. *Journal of Consulting and Clinical Psychology*, 1979, 47, 525–535.

Wiggins, J. S. *Personality and prediction: Principles of personality assessment*. Reading, Penn.: Addison-Wesley, 1973.

Zigler, E., & Levine, L. Premorbid adjustment and paranoid–non-paranoid status in schizophrenia. *Journal of Abnormal Psychology*, 1973, 82, 189–199.

Zigler, E., & Phillips, L. Social effectiveness and symptomatic behaviors. *Journal of Abnormal and Social Psychology*, 1960, 61, 231–238.

Zigler, E., & Phillips, L. Social competence and outcome in psychiatric disorder. *Journal of Abnormal and Social Psychology*, 1961, 63, 264–271.

Zigler, E., & Phillips, L. Social competence and the process–reactive distinction in psychopathology. *Journal of Abnormal and Social Psychology*, 1962, 65, 215–222.

11

A PROCEDURE FOR THE ASSESSMENT
OF SOCIAL SKILLS:
THE SIMULATED SOCIAL
INTERACTION TEST

JAMES P. CURRAN

INTRODUCTION

In this chapter, I will describe the social skills assessment protocol that
we developed and have been using over the last several years at the
Behavior Training Clinic at the Veterans Administration (VA) Medical
Center in Providence. Our primary measure, the Simulated Social Interaction Test (SSIT) consists of trained judges' ratings of subjects'
social skills levels after observation of their performances in brief simulated social situations that have been previously recorded on videotape.
Three critical decisions were involved in the development of the SSIT:
(1) the use of simulations as opposed to other observational settings;
(2) the use of a series of brief interactions as opposed to more extended
interactions; and (3) the use of molar ratings as opposed to more
molecular ratings. We wish to emphasize that we do not regard our
choices as "correct" nor our assessment strategy as the "right" way to
measure social skills. Rather, we believe that there are numerous ways
to measure social skills, some of which are better suited for different
purposes. Our decisions were prompted more by the practical considerations involved in applied clinical research than any other factor.
The rationale behind our decision will be presented in this chapter.

James P. Curran. Veterans Administration Medical Center/Brown University Medical
School, Providence, Rhode Island.

We chose simulations as an observational setting because it served best our needs (i.e., the evaluation of a social skills training program in treatment-outcome studies). Our purpose called for a setting in which repeated observations could be made in a fairly standard control manner. Although in one sense it was preferable to have trained judges make social skills ratings based on numerous observations of the subjects' behavior in the natural environment, we opted for simulations because of the logistical, control, and ethical difficulties often involved in naturalistic observations. In addition to the logistical, control, and ethical problems involved in employing trained judges in naturalistic situations, such observations may produce relatively low yield. That is, the judges may observe a subject in a natural environment for 4 hours, during which time the subject does not encounter any particular problematic social situation and, consequently, the judges do not have a good "reading" on how the subject performs in problematic social situations.

As an alternative to trained judges' observations in naturalistic settings, we have employed naive judges (i.e., significant others such as parents and spouses) in several studies. These individuals have obviously had many opportunities to observe the subjects in many types of social situations in the natural environment. However, the employment of untrained significant others also has major liabilities. It is unclear whether these significant others understand the construct to be rated and the integrity of their ratings can be questioned. In addition, because each of these judges is rating a different subject, there is a lack of comparability in the rating process. In several studies, we have also employed untrained judges who are familiar with all the subjects and have had a fair sample of their behavior in a somewhat naturalistic environment (e.g., nurses' ratings of social skills after 5 days of observation on an inpatient unit). However, as in the case of simulated social interactions, it is reasonable to question the representativeness of a subject's behavior on an inpatient psychiatric unit to behavior in the natural environment.

Again, we wish to emphasize that all of the observational settings and rating procedures used possess some deficiencies. However, if convergence among the various assessment strategies can be demonstrated, some confidence may be placed in these ratings. We have concentrated on simulated social interactions because of their relatively high yield per investment. However, it should be kept in mind that no one type of rating procedure can serve as the ultimate criterion because of deficiencies in each rating strategy.

In this chapter, we will discuss the rationale behind our choices of the simulated situations that comprise the SSIT and examine the adequacy of the sampling of these situations. We will examine the validity of our judges' ratings of social skills based on the SSIT, first by a contrasted group strategy and then through convergent validity with other types of ratings. We will describe the training of our judges, the integrity of their ratings, and how their ratings correspond to the ratings employed by other investigators in the area of social skills. Finally, suggestions for future research will be made.

SAMPLING ADEQUACY OF SSIT

We felt it desirable to sample a broad range of situations for our SSIT simulations because of the situational specificity involved in social performance. That is, some individuals may perform skillfully in one type of situation but not in other types of situations. What we needed was some manner of categorizing problematic social situations. Our search for different types of problematic social situations led us to the work of Richardson and Tasto (1976). Richardson and Tasto developed the Social Anxiety Inventory, an instrument they hoped would permit the identification of the most common types of social situations that would elicit anxiety reactions. Items for the Social Anxiety Inventory were generated by requesting researchers and clinicians to submit descriptions of situations commonly encountered in the treatment of social and interpersonal anxiety, especially items from desensitization hierarchies. Over 90 separate hierarchies were submitted. Other items were generated from social anxiety and fear survey scales, from the social anxiety literature, from traditional personality theories, and from the authors' clinical experiences. A prototype scale was constructed that contained 166 items chosen to represent a wide variety of social situations or interpersonal events. Richardson and Tasto (1976) administered this scale to 155 male and 240 female undergraduates. Subjects were asked to rate themselves on a 5-point Likert scale with respect to the level of anxiety they experienced in those situations described in the inventory. Item scores were intercorrelated, and a principal components analysis with a varimax rotation were used to analyze the matrix. The authors felt that seven factors emerged cleanly from the rotated matrix. Richardson and Tasto labeled these situational factors as (1) disapproval or criticism, (2) social assertiveness and visibility, (3) confrontation and anger expression, (4) heterosexual contact, (5) intimacy and inter-personal warmth, (6) conflict with or rejection by parents, and (7) interpersonal loss.

On an intuitive basis, these factors appear to describe quite discrete types of social situations, and we reasoned they may prove useful in the measurement of social skills. In our first study (Curran, Corriveau, Monti, & Hagerman, 1980), we attempted to replicate Richardson and Tasto's situational factors with our patient population, but this time for the measurement of social skills. We employed a revised version of Richardson and Tasto's (1976) Social Anxiety Inventory. The original version of the Social Anxiety Inventory consisted of 166 items, while the revised scale consisted of 105 items. Sixty-five items on this revised scale were items from the original scale that had been demonstrated to have high loadings on one of the seven factors. An additional 40 items were constructed by Richardson and Tasto in an attempt to tap four of the original factors that had relatively few items loading on them in their study. We administered this scale to 195 psychiatric outpatients at our VA Medical Center. Subjects were asked to rate on a 5-point Likert scale how skillful they thought they were in each of the situations described by the items. Like Richardson and Tasto, we used a principal components analysis to reduce our intercorrelation matrix and used a varimax rotation to rotate seven factors. Although the first factor accounted for a sizable proportion of the variance, specific factors were also indicated. While we were not able to replicate Richardson and Tasto's seven factors as cleanly as we had hoped, there was sufficient overlap in our findings to convince us that these seven factors were a good example of different types of problematic social situations.

Parenthetically, the seven factors reported by Richardson and Tasto (1976) appear quite similar to a list of problematic interpersonal situations developed by Goldsmith and McFall (1975) employing a to-tally different development strategy. Goldsmith and McFall employed a behavior-analytic approach to delineate the types of social situations that psychiatric outpatients found problematic. Sixteen psychiatric pa-tients who had previously expressed difficulties encountering social situations were seen for 1-hour individual interviews. They were asked to give specific examples of difficult interpersonal situations they had experienced. The authors found extensive intersubject redundancy in reporting with virtually no new situation described over the last several interviews. Situational contents most frequently reported were dating, making friends, having job interviews, relating to authorities, relating to service personnel, and interacting with people perceived as more intelligent or more attractive. During social interactions, patients most frequently reported the following critical moments: initiating or terminating interactions, making personal disclosures, handling conversational silences, responding to rejection, and being assertive.

The overlap between the situations generated by the psychiatric patients in Goldsmith and McFall's study (1975) and the situational factors derived in Richardson and Tasto (1976) and our own work (Curran, Corriveau, Monti, & Hagerman, 1980) reinforced our belief that these situations represented a broad range of types of social situations. We felt that this scale, relabeled the Social Reaction Inventory (SRI), might be a useful self-report inventory with which to assess our subject's subjective opinion of their social performance in different types of situations. More importantly, however, we felt that the situational factors could serve as the basis for our construction of simulations for the SSIT, which would adequately represent a broad range of social situations encountered in the naturalistic environment. We constructed brief simulated social interactions to represent each of the seven factors derived by Richardson and Tasto (1976). In addition, an eighth simulated interaction was developed (a situation in which an individual is being praised and complimented) because this type of situation did not appear to be tapped by the factors developed by Richardson and Tasto and because many of our patients reported feeling awkward in responding to such situations. Our SSIT situations consist of a narrator who describes the social situation to the subject and a confederate who delivers a prompt. In fact, two confederates are employed—a male and a female confederate who each interact in four of the scenes. Several practice situations are given prior to the eight simulated situations comprising the SSIT to acclimate each subject to the procedures. Table 11-1 contains both the narration and the confederates' prompts for each of our eight SSIT interactions.

We decided to use eight brief social interactions rather than fewer more extended social interactions after a great deal of agonizing. Since we felt it imperative to assess our subjects in a broad range of social situations, and since we felt that assessing our subjects in eight extended interactions would be too prohibitive because of the enormous time it would take to rate these extended interactions, we opted for the brief interactions. In these brief interactions, we sacrifice the give and take of normal interactions and so perhaps miss out on important components of social skills such as in the timing and placement of a

TABLE 11-1. SSIT Items

1. Disapproval or criticism

NARRATOR: You are at work, and one of your bosses has just finished inspecting one of the jobs that you have completed. He says to you—
CONFEDERATE: That's a pretty sloppy job. I think you could have done better.

2. Social assertiveness or visibility

NARRATOR: Let's suppose you respond to an ad in the newspaper and go for a job interview. As the interview goes on, the interviewer says—
CONFEDERATE: What makes you think that you're a good person for the job?

3. Confrontation and anger expression

NARRATOR: For the past two weeks you have been saving your money to go out to dinner. Now you are at the restaurant with some friends. You order a very rare steak. The waitress brings a steak to the table that is so well done it is burnt and tastes awful. After you have a few bites, the waitress comes over and says—
CONFEDERATE: Are you enjoying your steak?

4. Heterosexual contact

NARRATOR: You are at a party, and you notice a woman has been watching you all evening. Later, she walks up to you and says—
CONFEDERATE: Hi, my name is Jean.

5. Interpersonal warmth

NARRATOR: You are seated in a very quiet restaurant with your date. She has been looking depressed all evening. You ask her what's wrong, and she says—
CONFEDERATE: I'm really down. Everything seems to be turning our badly.

6. Conflict with or rejection by parent or relative

NARRATOR: One of your close relatives has come to visit you. Although you enjoy him, tonight he is dominating the conversation and is very critical and rejecting of you. At one point in the conversation, your relative says—
CONFEDERATE: The way you are running your life is a disgrace.

7. Interpersonal loss

NARRATOR: You have had an argument with a close friend. She says to you—
CONFEDERATE: I don't want to talk about it anymore. I'm leaving.

8. Receiving compliments

NARRATOR: You just helped one of your neighbors move several large pieces of furniture. He is very grateful for your help. He says to you—
CONFEDERATE: Thanks a million. Not many people would have given me a hand. You're a really good friend.

---

response (Curran & Mariotto, 1980); however, we do increase some experimental control since it is much easier to standardize a confederate who issues only one prompt than it is to standardize a confederate in a 5-minute interaction. Interestingly enough, in two of our earlier studies (Curran, Monti, Corriveau, Hay, Hagerman, Zwick, & Farrell, 1980; Monti, Curran, Corriveau, DeLancey, & Hagerman, 1980), we actually compromised and had the confederates issue two prompts, the second after the subject's first reply. We later abandoned this procedure because we found it impossible to generate a second programmed response that could fit all possible replies that subjects could make to the first prompt.

We (Curran, Monti, Corriveau, Hay, Hagerman, Zwick, & Farrell, 1980; Farrell, Zwick, Curran, & Monti, 1980) tested the adequacy of our sampling of these eight SSIT situations with three different samples of subjects. The three samples of subjects were exclusively male and consisted of 88 psychiatric outpatients, 52 psychiatric inpatients or day hospital patients, and 43 National Guardsmen. All samples were treated in an identical fashion. After each SSIT interaction, the subjects themselves made a self-rating on 11-point Likert-type scales evaluating their own social effectiveness and experienced degree of anxiety in each situation. Videotapes of the SSIT simulations were made and later presented to trained judges (two judges in the case of the outpatients and four judges for the other two samples) for their rating of social skills and social anxiety on 11-point Likert-type scales.

In these studies, we made use of generalizability coefficients (Cronbach, Gleser, Nanda, & Rajaratnam, 1972) to assess the adequacy of our sampling of SSIT situations. Generalizability coefficients are a general form of an intraclass correlation coefficient and are defined as the square correlation between an observed score attained from a particular set of observations and the universe score, which represents the mean that would be obtained by sampling an infinite number of observations within the defined universe of generalization. For these samples, two sets of generalizability coefficients were calculated: unit sample and full sample (Mariotto & Paul, 1975). Unit-sampling coefficients are based on sampling one condition (e.g., any one simulated interaction) from each facet in the studies' design. Full-sample coefficients are based on all conditions of each facet sampled in the study (e.g., four judges' rating of all eight simulated interactions). Table 11-2 contains the unit- and full-sample generalizability coefficients for the anxiety and skills ratings for the facets in each study, judges, items, and methods (subjects' self-ratings and judges' ratings).

The full-sample coefficients for the skills ratings based on all eight simulated situations ranged from .76 to .87, indicating adequate representation to the universe of all possible similar role plays. The unit-sample generalizability coefficients based on sampling any one simulated interaction ranged from .24 to .40, indicating low generalizability to the universe of all possible similar simulated interactions. In other words, a subject's performance on one of the simulated interactions is

TABLE 11-2. Generalizability Coefficients for Ratings of Anxiety and Social Skills

Universe of generalizability	Anxiety			Social skills		
	Outpatients	National Guardsmen	Inpatients	Outpatients	National Guardsmen	Inpatients
	Judges' ratings					
Judges	.70 (.94)	.66 (.96)	.73 (.97)	.74 (.94)	.72 (.96)	.81 (.98)
Items	.52 (.92)	.54 (.94)	.68 (.97)	.25 (.76)	.24 (.76)	.40 (.87)
Judges and items	.50 (.90)	.50 (.93)	.63 (.95)	.24 (.75)	.23 (.75)	.39 (.86)
	Judges' and self-ratings					
Methods	.41 (.62)	.39 (.58)	.37 (.57)	.41 (.61)	.42 (.59)	.33 (.46)

Note. Unit-sample generalizability coefficients (i.e., based on sampling one condition of each facet) are presented without parentheses; full-sample generalizability coefficients based on the number of conditions of each sample actually sampled are presented in parentheses (i.e., two judges and eight items for the outpatient sample, four judges and eight items for the other two samples).

not very representative of his performance to the universe of all possible simulated interactions (attesting to the situational specificity of performance). However, the ratings from the eight simulated situations are reasonable estimates of a universe score that would be based upon the addition of an infinite number of similar simulated situations.

Two other aspects of Table 11-2 should be noted. First of all, the full-sample coefficients for the judges' ratings of anxiety and skill to the universe of all possible judges were in the middle to upper 90s, indicating excellent generalizability to the universe of similarly trained judges. Second, the relationship established between the judges' ratings and the subjects' self-ratings demonstrated only low to moderate convergence across samples. This lack of convergence was hypothesized (Farrell *et al.*, 1980) to be due to differences in content in the methods employed and confusion on the part of subjects regarding the attributes rated.

VALIDITY: CONTRASTED GROUPS

Satisfied that the above studies demonstrated the sampling adequacy of the situations composing the SSIT, we then attempted to obtain validity data. Our first study (Curran, Wessberg, Monti, Corriveau, & Coyne, 1980) involved a known group or contrasted group strategy. The contrasted group strategy consists of selecting groups presumed to differ on the focal dimension (i.e., social competency) of interest. The groups selected in this study were two of the groups used in the above discussed sampling studies, that is, a combined day hospital and inpatient group and a group of National Guardsmen. Sixty National Guardsmen and 81 patients participated in at least one phase of the study.

The National Guardsmen were chosen as the contrasted group because they share many characteristics with our VA patient population (e.g., age, military experience, etc.). It was assumed that the major difference between these groups would be incidence of psychiatric disturbances. It was also assumed that because psychiatric disorders appear to be associated with social competency (Zigler & Phillips, 1961) that the National Guardsmen would be rated as more socially competent on the SSIT than the psychiatric patients.

In addition to providing data with respect to the validity of our SSIT, we envisioned that the data from this study could also be used as a criterion reference (Kazdin, 1977). That is, previous outcome studies have indicated that social skills training programs lead to statistically significant increases in the social skills level of the treated patients; however, there are few data that would indicate whether these significant increases are clinically important. One procedure for evaluating the clinical significance of any treatment program is to compare the performance of treated subjects to a normal population.

All subjects in this study were treated in an identical manner. All subjects completed two self-report inventories (the Social Performance Survey Schedule and the Social Inventory) and two 11-point rating scales for overall skill and anxiety. The Social Performance Survey Schedule (SPSS) was developed by Lowe and Cautela (1978) as a measure of social skills. The SPSS, which can be completed by the subjects themselves and/or significant others, consists of 100 items describing various behaviors. Fifty of the items describe positive social behaviors and 50 describe negative behaviors. The respondent is asked to indicate how frequently the subject emits such behaviors. The Social Inventory was constructed for this study and consists of 28 items involving the frequency and quality of social activities, satisfaction with work, the quality of social relationships and family relationships, and so forth. Subjects also made self-ratings of skill and anxiety after each of the eight SSIT interactions.

Each of the subjects' performances on the SSIT was videotaped and later presented to four trained judges to be rated for social skills and social anxiety. Judges were blind to the group affiliation of the subjects, and every effort was made to conceal characteristics that might indicate group affiliation. That is, the National Guardsmen were tested in civilian clothes and the same backdrop was used for all the testing. The videotapes were presented to the judges in a random fashion with respect to group affiliation. Cronbach's alpha reliability for the four judges was .98 for both the skills rating and for the anxiety ratings.

Table 11-3 contains the means of the judges' skill and anxiety ratings, the mean SPSS skills score, and the subjects' self-ratings of their overall skill and anxiety and their mean skill and anxiety ratings taken after each of the eight SSIT scenes. The results indicated that the judges perceived the National Guardsmen as significantly more skillful and less anxious on the SSIT role plays than the patients. The National Guardsmen also attained significantly higher scores on the SPSS. The patients rated themselves overall as more anxious and less skilled than the National Guardsmen, and reported significantly more anxiety during the SSIT. Only four of the 28 items on the Social Inventory demonstrated group differences. The psychiatric patients indicated less satisfaction with

TABLE 11-3. Means and p Values for Contrasted-Groups Study

| Measures | Group means | | t^a | df^b | p |
	National Guardsmen	Psychiatric patients			
SSIT skill (judges)	5.60	5.08	2.46	107	<.01
SSIT anxiety (judges)	6.21	6.82	−2.64	107	<.01
SPSS (self)	3.79	3.50	4.70	131	<.01
Overall skill (self)	7.04	5.27	5.41	130	<.01
Overall anxiety (self)	3.18	6.26	−7.95	129	<.01
SSIT skill (self)	5.70	5.87	− .50	127	<.05
SSIT anxiety (self)	3.57	4.52	−2.81	127	<.01

[a]t-tests were one-tailed tests with the prediction being that the National Guardsmen would be more skilled and less anxious.
[b]Degrees of freedom vary because not all the subjects completed every phase of the study.

their jobs, families, and lives in general and reported fewer contacts with family members than did the National Guardsmen.

The results from this initial validity study were encouraging, especially since it employed a rather "weak" contrasted group. That is, the groups were not selected on the basis of known social competency level but rather on the known presence or absence of a labeled psychiatric disorder. While psychiatric disorder and social competency have been demonstrated to be related, the absence of a psychiatric disorder does not ensure a high level of social competency and vice versa.

VALIDITY: CONVERGENT RATINGS

In our next study (Wessberg, Curran, Monti, Corriveau, Coyne, & Dziadosz, in press) we were also concerned with obtaining validity data for the SSIT, but this time a convergent strategy was employed. That is, skills ratings of psychiatric patients (obtained from our trained judges based on SSIT interactions) were compared to ratings made by other observers in other settings. The other rating sources consisted of the patients themselves, five nurses on an inpatient unit, two trained raters who observed the subjects on the ward while they were eating a noon meal, a research assistant who recruited and escorted these subjects to the Behavior Training Clinic, and two senior members of the Behavior Training Clinic, who conducted a structured social history interview.

Each of these rating sources appeared to us to be reasonable sources from which to obtain skills ratings and, in fact, these sources resemble many of the strategies employed in the literature. However, each source has associated with it certain disadvantages. Subjects' self-ratings quite obviously can be based on numerous observations, but the subjects may not understand the attribute to be rated and may be biased in reporting. The use of untrained judges (in this study, the nurses) in a nonlaboratory setting may increase the social validity of the ratings (see Conger & Conger, Chapter 10, this volume), but problems exist with respect to lack of control over the behaviors observed by the different judges. The use of trained judges who observe all their subjects during a similar event (e.g., a noon meal) increases control, but the representativeness of the subject's behavior during this event to his behavior in a natural environment can be questioned. Finally, the use of trained judges who conduct a structured social history interview has the advantage of a longitudinal data base, but it is dependent upon the selective reporting and memory of both the subjects and judges. Other deficiencies exist in each of these data sources but will not be discussed here in order to save space. We reasoned that some moderate convergence of these other rating sources with our SSIT ratings would provide evidence for the validity of the SSIT. Only moderate relationships between the other rating sources and the SSIT were predicted because of the obvious deficiencies in each source (including our trained judges' SSIT ratings) and because of the decided lack of comparability of settings for the observational sources.

The rating sequence was as follows. A research assistant approached a potential subject on his first day on the inpatient unit in order to obtain his informed consent. Three days after the patient was admitted to the unit the nurses made their ratings based on their observations of the patient's behavior on the inpatient unit. Trained judges were stationed in the dining room on the inpatient unit during the lunch meal on the 3rd day and rated each subject (only one subject on any given day) based on their observations. Following lunch, a research assistant escorted each subject to the Behavior Training Clinic. Upon arrival at the clinic, a structured interview designed to assess the subject's developmental social history was conducted by two senior research associates. After the interview, subjects were asked to participate in the eight SSIT role plays. The SSIT interactions were videotaped and rated by four trained judges at a later date. The training and rating process of these judges was similar to those employed in our previous studies. A more detailed description of the training and rating process will be presented in a later section. Subsequent to the SSIT interactions, the subjects were asked to complete a number of other self-report measures of skills. When the subjects finished completing the self-report scales, the research assistant escorted the patient back to the inpatient unit and then rated the patient.

All the judges (including the patients themselves) rated the subjects on an 11-point Likert-type scale for overall skills level. All the judges except the SSIT judges also rated the subjects on an abbreviated version of the Social Performance Survey Schedule (Wessberg, Curran, Monti, Corriveau, Coyne, & Dziadosz, in press). Mean interrater reliability coefficients and alpha coefficients for both the global skills ratings and the SPSS ratings for each category of judges containing more than one rater are contained in Table 11-4.

The Pearson r's and alpha coefficients for the SSIT judges were high. The alpha coefficients for the other judges were in an acceptable range although the Pearson reliabilities were low. The low interrater reliability obtained by the nurses is not surprising since they were untrained judges who observed the subjects in different situations (e.g., two of the nurses were on the evening shift and three of the nurses on the day shift). The moderate and somewhat disappointing reliability obtained for the ward raters may have been due to the fact that the noon meal often turned out to be a poor situation in which to observe the patients' social skills levels. Ward raters often complained that many of the patients were more interested in eating food quickly and leaving than in interacting socially; consequently, the meal proved to be a poor

TABLE 11-4. Mean Pearson r and Alpha Values for Judges in Inpatient Convergent Validity Study

Rating scales	Nurses		Ward raters		Interviewers		Video judges	
	r	α	r	α	r	α	r	α
Global skill	.51**	.80	.64**	.78	.62**	.76	.94**	.98
SPSS skill	.47**	.83	.73**	.83	.76**	.86		

**$p < .01$.

sample of social interactive behavior. The relatively low reliability obtained for the interviewers was also disappointing. Both these interviewers were senior members of our research team and had often exhibited high reliability in rating the social competency level of patients in SSIT interactions. The reason for their poor reliability might have been due to two interrelated factors: stimulus overload and selective memory. That is, each of these interviews lasted approximately 30 minutes and was not recorded. Consequently, the interviewers had to depend upon their memory of the interview in order to make their ratings. Stimulus overload may produce poor reliabilities, especially if the stimulus material cannot be adequately retrieved.

Table 11-5 contains the correlations between the SSIT judges' global skills ratings and each of the other judges' global skills ratings as well as the correlations between the SSIT judges' global skills ratings and the other judges' SPSS ratings. As can be seen in Table 11-5, the SSIT judges' overall skills ratings were significantly related to each of the other sets of judges' (except the ward raters) global skills ratings and their SPSS ratings. While these coefficients are in a low to moderate range, several potential mitigating factors should be kept in mind. First of all, no rating source (including the SSIT judges) should be regarded as the ultimate criterion. In fact, the major problem in social skills assessment is that there exists no ultimate external criterion on which to validate our assessment strategies. The assessment of social skills is essentially a "bootstrap" approach wherein we constantly try to improve assessment strategies on a multifaceted front. Secondly, the observational settings on which these ratings were based varied tremendously on many dimensions. For example, the nurses observed the patients for 3 consecutive days in an inpatient unit, while the inter-

TABLE 11-5. Correlations between SSIT Judges' Global Ratings and Other Rating Sources' Global and SPSS Ratings in Inpatient Convergent Validity Study

SSIT judges	Subjects	Nurses	Ward raters	Interviewers	Research assistants
Global skill	.27*	.53**	.16	.53**	.34*
SPSS skill	.58**	.45**	.23	.53**	.35**

Note. Coefficients across rating sources have been corrected (Guilford, 1954) for the unreliability found between judges within a particular rating source.
* $p < .05$.
** $p < .01$.

viewers made their ratings on the basis of a structured interview. Since we know that behavior varies in different situational contexts, then some inconsistency must be expected. In general, while the magnitude of the obtained correlations were moderate at best, it is still comforting to note that judges' ratings from the SSIT interactions are related to other rating sources utilizing other rating strategies.

SUMMARY OF VALIDITY EVIDENCE

The data from the unit sample G coefficients obtained in our sampling studies indicated that the judges perceived the subjects interacting differentially across the eight SSIT situations. This differential performance makes theoretical sense given the situational specificity of behavior. However, the full-sample G coefficients indicated that our eight SSIT simulations are quite representative of the universe of all possible similarly formated simulated interactions differing in content. Consequently, it would appear that the number of situations used in the SSIT is sufficient in order to obtain adequate generalizability.

The judges perceived differences in skills competency levels between normals and psychiatric patients on the SSIT even though the normals were not selected to be especially socially competent. In addition, judges' ratings of patients' performance on the SSIT were related to other judges' ratings based on different observational settings. Social skills ratings of patients based on the SSIT were significantly related to judges' ratings based on a structured interview with the patient, hospital treatment personnel ratings based on their observation of patients in hospital units, a research assistant's ratings from observation of the subject in a variety of situations, and finally to the subject's own self-ratings. Because our primary dependent measure consists of an overall global rating that is highly dependent upon the complex inferential processes of the judges, the rationale behind this strategy, the training of the judges, and the characteristics of these judges' ratings will be explained in detail in the next section of this chapter.

RATIONALE FOR JUDGES' GLOBAL RATINGS

Our decision to rely on just one overall global rating of social competency as opposed to rating a series of discrete behaviors (e.g., eye contact) was made after some deliberation. Our principal reason for not choosing more discrete molecular units to rate was simply because it was unclear to us what the components of social skills are and how they should be differentially weighed in evaluating overall social competency. Molecular unit recordings often ignore important parameters such as the timing and sequencing of behaviors (Fischetti, Curran, & Wessberg, 1977). It is also quite likely that the component behaviors that compose social skills and the contribution that each component makes with respect to overall social competency vary across many dimensions, including settings. In addition, molecular unit recording requires a good deal of effort in both isolating the units that are relevant, and actual recording of those units by trained raters. Certainly, molecular recordings require more effort than making one overall global judgment. In this sense, a molar judgment is more flexible because it is less time-consuming, and therefore, can be made more easily over a variety of settings.

The major advantage of molecular unit recording over molar unit recording is that it can be operationalized with greater precision, and consequently, should require less inference on the part of the observers. Consequently, molecular unit recordings very often have high reliability. However, as we have seen in the studies previously mentioned, it is possible to obtain high reliabilities for molar judgments if the judges are properly trained. In the studies mentioned in the previous section, very often the obtained reliabilities for overall judgment of social competency were in the 90s. The choice of the "proper" unit of recording (molar vs. molecular) should be determined on an empirical basis. That is, the proper unit is the one that has the highest degree of criterion relevance. As Wiggins (1973) has noted, "The relationship between unit size and criterion relevance cannot be stated dogmatically. Narrowly defined behavioral attributes run the risk of a high degree of specificity, which may preclude the possibility of generalizability to criterion behaviors. On the other hand, units that are too global in nature may yield only vacuous statements that are true of everyone or of no one" (p. 325).

Our use of an overall global judgment should not be regarded as a rejection of the more molecular approach. On the contrary, we feel that it is extremely important for us to evaluate components of social skills and to determine their relative importance in any criterion situation. Our use of an overall global judgment should merely be interpreted as our acknowledgment that we have not yet empirically determined the components of social skills for our criterion situation. We applaud the efforts made by Conger and Conger (see Chapter 10, this volume) to determine the components of social skills for their dating assessment situation. The irony of the search for components is that the isolation of these components may be more important for treatment than it is for the assessment of social skills. That is, it is extremely important for therapists to know what the components are so they can better teach these components in a social skills training program.

At present, our research program is still highly dependent upon the inferential processes of our judges in arriving at an overall rating of social skills. Our judges are our final arbitrators with respect to this overall judgment. For example, even though a subject is making good eye contact, appropriate speech volume, talks about the proper length of time, and so forth, if the judges feel that the verbal statements are inappropriate they may let this last component override the skillfulness of the other components and assign the subject a low social skills rating. Although the overall judgment is still highly dependent on the inferential processes of our judges, our judges are not without guidelines. In fact, as we shall soon see, we give our judges a number of different guidelines for each type of SSIT interaction.

JUDGES' TRAINING

The judges are trained in the following fashion. First, the judges view a training tape on which a senior member of the research team explains the construct of social skills and gives potential indicators, both verbal (e.g., giving a compliment) and nonverbal (e.g., eye contact). It is continually emphasized that although potential skills components are specified during training, the judges are still to depend upon their overall impression and not merely sum the indicators provided in training. It is also stressed that although an individual subject may possess a vast number of these components, it is still possible that the lack of one of these components may completely override the other components and result in a poor social skills rating.

The training tape also contains a series of bogus subjects (research assistants) who portray a wide range of skills levels. After each of these bogus-subject role plays, the tape is stopped and the judges are asked to provide a skills rating. After the judges announce their ratings the tape is restarted and a criterion rating is provided on the tape so that the judges can compare their own ratings for calibration purposes. The criterion ratings were obtained in the following fashion. Six senior members of the Behavior Training Clinic research team had previously rated these bogus subjects. If five of the six senior judges' ratings are within 1 point of each other on an 11-point scale, then the average of these ratings (rounded off to the nearest whole number) serves as a criterion. Besides giving the judge trainees an actual numerical value for the skills rating, the instructional tape also explains the rationale for the criterion rating. For example, if the bogus subject gave a skillful response to the scene in which a job supervisor criticizes the employee's performance, the statements on the tape might resemble something like this: "We felt this person deserved a 10 because he looked his supervisor in the eye when he responded, admitted that the job was not up to his usual standards, explained why his performance was not up to par, asked for suggestions of ways he could improve his performance when faced with a deadline, and proposed a solution for his sub-par work."

After viewing this approximately 1-hour tape, the judge trainees then spend approximately 12 hours rating practice tapes. The practice tapes consists of real subjects from other studies utilizing the same eight SSIT situations. Criterion ratings established in the described manner have been derived for a segment of these practice subjects. After each of the practice subjects simulate interaction, the tape is stopped and the judges make their ratings on an 11-point scale. Raters are generally trained in groups and after viewing each role play they announce their ratings. Feedback is also provided on a random ratio schedule (approximately one out of four) with respect to the criterion ratings. In no cases are the judge trainees' ratings ever changed. However, in cases where major discrepancies in scores occur, these differences are discussed and the judges are asked to provide a rationale for their rating. As mentioned previously, judges are usually trained for approximately 12 hours over several days. Judges are allowed to make formal ratings of experimental tapes only if during the latter stages of their training their degree of agreement with the criterion rating exceeds a correlation of .80 or better.

During the rating of the experimental tapes, a member of the research team proctors the rating sessions. After each judgment, the raters announce their ratings. Again, criterion ratings obtained in the above described manner are provided on a variable ratio schedule. In no case does the proctor allow the judges to change their ratings after hearing the criterion rating. We provide criterion feedback on a variable ratio schedule in order to diminish problems of criterion drift. Previous investigators (O'Leary & Kent, 1973) have demonstrated that it is possible for raters to obtain high interrater reliability but still be drifting away from the criterion established during training. Since the criterion drift phenomenon has been established for even more molecular unit recordings than those used in rating a global construct such as social skills, and since raters very often need to rate tapes over several weeks or months, we felt it necessary to periodically check on agreement with criterion. This procedure successfully recalibrates our judges. In one rating analogue study (Curran, Beck, Corriveau, & Monti, 1980) we demonstrated that such a procedure significantly increases judges' accuracy to criterion when compared to a condition in which the judges received no feedback.

As a result of the training procedures, our judges generally have been found to have high interrater reliability and good agreement with criterion. In fact, in many of our studies, interrater reliabilities have been established in the 90s (e.g., Wessberg, Coyne, Curran, Monti, & Corriveau, in press). In the generalizability studies (Farrell et al., 1980) described earlier, full-sample G coefficients for judges ranged in the 90s for all three samples, indicating excellent generalizability to the universe of similarly trained judges. In addition, Farrell et al. (1980) found no differences in mean-level rating between judges. Not only were the judges rank ordering the subjects similarly, but they also showed very high agreement in the level of ratings assigned. Farrell et al. (1980) also found the judges' ratings of anxiety and social skills were only moderately related, thus appearing to have good discriminate validity. A judge's ability to discriminate between anxiety and skills has been called into question by other investigators (Conger, Wallander, Ward, & Farrell, 1979). In a series of studies to be described below, we manipulated a number of factors in order to determine whether such manipulations would affect our judges' ratings.

JUDGES' INTEGRITY

In most of the studies we have conducted, we have presented the videotaped performances of our subjects to our trained raters in a sequential fashion (i.e., all scenes for one subject followed by all scenes for another subject). We were concerned that this procedure led to our judges perceiving artificial consistency in responding across scenes because of carry-over effects. An alternate procedure (though more time-consuming) would be to present the first scene for all subjects followed by the second scene, and so forth. In a rating analogue study (Corriveau, Vespucci, Curran, Monti, Wessberg, & Coyne, in press) we examined whether these two methods of presentation would differentially affect the judges' perceived reliability of a subjects' skills level across the different scenes. A second variable manipulated in the study involved the training of the judges. Three different training conditions were employed. In one condition, the judges were instructed to expect differential performance of a subject across scenes and were given a few practice scenes demonstrating such variability. Another group of judges was just informed that they should expect differential performance and another group of judges was given no such instructions. The results indicated the order of presentation of videotapes had little effect on perceived variability. However, the training manipulation did have an effect, with the group that received both instructions and practice in perceived variability showing more variance in their ratings.

Wessberg, Coyne, Curran, Monti, and Corriveau (in press) examined the stability of our judges' ratings over time. This study is relevant to the question of whether judges change their criterion over time. The question of the empirical stability of these judges is also important in a sense because the stability affects our expectations regarding upper limits of interrater reliability coefficients. Because the correlation of any measure to another measure (in this case two judges) is limited by the correlation of each measure to itself (Ferguson, 1971, p. 371), the intrarater reliability of each rater is an important consideration in an assessment. The stability of judges was examined not only with respect to their rank ordering but also with respect to their mean-level differences. Interrater reliability addresses the rank ordering of subjects, the stability of which is necessary for accurate judges' ratings within subject groups. Drift involving mean-level changes is important when comparing multiple groups at one time or a single group at two separate times (e.g., pretreatment and posttreatment).

The two judges employed in the study were experienced judges from the Behavior Training Clinic. Training was consistent with the procedures outlined above, and the scenes presented to them were from the SSIT. The original training consisted of approximately 2 hours a day for 4 days. After training, the raters rated 102 psychiatric patients in each of the eight SSIT scenes. The stability of these judges was examined by having them return 6 months after the initial rating to rerate a subset of the original scenes. The judges were not told during the original ratings that they would rerate the same patient later. When contacted with respect to rerating, these raters were openly and accurately informed that they would be taking part in an assessment development study examining their ratings over time. These judges were retrained in a 2-hour session. The judges were then asked to rerate 33 patients on four scenes each, randomly selected from the originals. Their interrater reliability on occasion one for skill was .97 and on occasion two was .96. The intrarater reliability for rater one between the first and second rating was .88 for skill and for the second judge .91 for skill. Mean-level differences were examined by t-test. No significant differences between mean levels on occasions one or two were found for either of the raters. In fact, the means for either rater across occasions were almost identical. Rater one had a mean for skills on occasion one of 6.61 and occasion two, 6.65. Rater two's means for the skill ratings were 6.72 on the two occasions. Results from this study instills confidence that our judges can make long-term dependable ratings with no apparent drift or decay in their ratings.

In another study contained in the same manuscript, Wessberg, Coyne, Curran, Monti, and Corriveau (in press) examined the effects of expectancy on our judges' ratings. Four female undergraduate volunteers who had no previous rating experience were trained in four 2-hour sessions following our usual procedures. The stimulus material that they were to rate consisted of National Guardsmen who were video-taped on the SSIT. The judges were split into two groups based on their schedule compatibility. These groups met separately to rate the stimulus material. The manipulation consisted of informing the raters that one group of subjects they were rating was comprised of socially competent individuals and that the other group consisted of socially incompetent individuals. Each pair of raters rated 36 National Guardsmen on four of the SSIT situations. Half of the stimulus subjects were on one videotape labeled A and the other half on another videotape labeled B. Each group of judges was shown nine subjects from tape A, followed by nine from tape B, then nine from tape A, and finally nine from tape B. One pair of judges was told that the subjects on tape A were the competent subjects and those on tape B were the incompetent, while the second pair of raters was told the opposite. The judges were told that the subjects' competency classification was based on their self-report. They were told that their ratings might not exactly match the subjects but some consistency was expected. At the debriefing, none of the judges reported awareness or suspicion of any deception.

Interjudge pair reliability for the skills ratings for group one judges was .94 and for the second group of judges .93. The effect of the expectancy manipulation was examined by comparing the judges' ratings of competent and incompetent subjects. No significant mean-level differences were found for either pair of judges for their overall skills ratings. For the first pair of judges, their means for the competent and incompetent subjects were 7.05 and 7.02, and for the second pair of judges, their means were 6.77 and 6.32. The results from this study support the contention that judges can be trained to make global ratings of behavior from videotapes in a manner related to demonstrated performance and not be biased by explicit expectations about subject group characteristics.

Another question that occurred to us was although we have demonstrated that our judges can make dependable ratings and match the criterion established by senior members of our research team, would our judges' ratings agree with other judges trained in other experimental laboratories? That is, how comparable are judges' ratings when those judges have been trained by different investigators? Six different laboratories including our own were involved in this study (Curran, Wessberg, Farrell, Monti, Corriveau, & Coyne, 1980). Each laboratory was mailed videotapes containing 38 subjects who appeared in two of our SSIT scenes. All eight scenes were used but we only sent two, chosen at random, for each subject. Investigators involved were all told to train their raters as they normally train them and to have them rate these tapes in their usual manner. (That is, some of the investigators have their judges rate molecular units of behavior such as eye contact, speech latency, etc.) After rating in their usual manner, each investigator was then instructed to have their judges rate each stimulus subject on our global 11-point scale for social skill.

Table 11-6 contains the correlation among laboratories for the social skill ratings. Although all of the correlations were significant, they range from low to moderate. A generalizability coefficient was calculated that indicated moderate generalizability (G coefficient = .62) using the mean rating of four judges based on all SSIT scenes from any one experimental laboratory to the universe of all potential experimental laboratories. The results, while not as satisfying as one would hope, can still be viewed in an optimistic light because of the numerous mitigating factors that worked against establishing strong relationships. For example, none of the other experimental laboratories had previous exposure to the SSIT. It is clear to us from our own experience in training judges that judges get better at rating social skills with repeated practice with the SSIT. It is interesting to note that the interrater

TABLE 11-6. Correlations among Laboratories for SSIT
Skills Ratings

Laboratory	A	B	C	D	E	F
A		.53	.75	.66	.66	.76
B			.48	.62	.59	.66
C				.63	.60	.71
D					.60	.72
E						.69

reliability between judges in the same laboratories in some cases was much lower than that normally reported from such laboratories, which gives credence to the hypothesis that the unfamiliarity of these judges with the SSIT and the rating scales they were asked to use might have adversely affected the judges. Lastly, cultural differences among the judges from the different laboratories may also have had an effect in reducing the agreement across laboratories. Judges reared in England might differ with judges raised in the American Midwest with respect to the judged social appropriateness of a response.

SUMMARY

The results from our studies examining the reliability and validity of our SSIT are encouraging. The eight scenes employed appear to be an adequate sample and have been demonstrated to have good generalizability to a universe of similar brief scenes differing in content. Our training procedures for judges results in high interrater reliability and few mean-level differences between judges. Our procedure for criterion feedback leads to highly accurate ratings to a criterion established by senior members of our research team. It has also been demonstrated that judges' ratings correspond, in general, to the ratings of judges trained by other investigators. Our judges give dependable ratings over time, both with respect to rank ordering and mean levels. It has been demonstrated that our raters can be trained to make global ratings of behavior from videotapes in a manner related to demonstrated performance and not be biased by explicit expectations about subject group characteristics.

Our SSIT has been demonstrated to differentiate a contrasted group of normal and psychiatric patients. Our judges' ratings from the SSIT have been shown to be significantly related to hospital personnel ratings, interviewers' ratings, and self-ratings. Although we feel that our judges' ratings from the SSIT possess good reliability and adequate validity, we are still not content with the information yield from such ratings.

FUTURE DIRECTIONS

Our judges' ratings merely represent an average of how our judges perceive our subjects' social competency across a variety of simulated social situations. As such, they yield important information but not as much information as we would like. To pursue an analogy from baseball, we can tell you who is a .400 hitter and who is a .150 hitter; however, we do not have adequate information on how our ballplayer hits (i.e., a long-ball hitter or a singles hitter) or under what conditions he or she hits the best. We know from one of our studies (Curran, Miller, Zwick, Monti, & Stout, 1980) that psychiatric patients who were judged as socially incompetent were a diversified group of individuals. Some socially incompetent patients were described as being unassertive, while others were described as being overly assertive or aggressive. Some incompetent patients were seen as self-depreciatory, while others appeared to have an overinflated view of their own self-worth. In fact, in attempting to cluster these patients utilizing various cluster analysis programs, no significantly meaningful clusters of unskilled patients were found. Information regarding the nature of the particular deficiencies is obviously important in treating our patients.

One can view the components of social skills in a hierarchical fashion, as suggested by several investigators (Conger, Wallander, Mariotto, & Ward, 1980; Curran & Mariotto, 1980). At the molecular level would be such behaviors as head nods, eye contact, and so forth. These behaviors could be grouped at a more intermediate level under a component (such as facial expression). Bellack and his associates (Bellack, Hersen, & Lamparski, 1979; Bellack, Hersen, & Turner, 1978) have offered evidence that molecular recordings from simulated social interactions may not correspond very well to molecular recordings made in the natural environment, perhaps because as Wiggins (1973) noted, their very specificity precludes their generalizability. We are currently working on developing a series of components at the intermediate level that we hope will be useful in both the assessment and the treatment of patients. It is our hope that these intermediate components of social skills might yield a greater generalizability to the natural environment than the more molecular behaviors and, at the same time, provide us with a more rich data source than our global ratings. We also feel a strong need to develop assessment strategies that can be employed more readily in the natural environment. The procedures for natural-istic recordings suggested by Boice (see Chapter 12, this volume) seem particularly promising and we will try to adapt some of them in our own work.

The assessment of social skills still remains in its infancy but from my reading of the chapters contained in this book a growing sense of maturity is evident. It is firmly hoped that this maturity will bring with it more sophisticated and valid measures of social skills.

REFERENCES

Bellack, A. S., Hersen, M., & Lamparski, D. Role-play tests for assessing social skills: Are they valid? Are they useful? *Journal of Consulting and Clinical Psychology*, 1979, 47, 335–342.

Bellack, A. S., Hersen, M., & Turner, S. M. Role-play tests for assessing social skills: Are they valid? *Behavior Therapy*, 1978, 9, 448–461.

Conger, A. J., Wallander, J., Mariotto, M. J., & Ward, D. Peer judgments of heterosexual-social anxiety and skills: What do they pay attention to anyhow? *Behavioral Assessment*, 1980, 2, 243–360.

Conger, A. J., Wallander, J., Ward, D., & Farrell, A. D. *Ratings of heterosocial anxiety and skill: 1 + 1 = 1.* Unpublished manuscript, Purdue University, West Lafayette, Indiana, 1979.

Corriveau, D. P., Vespucci, R., Curran, J. P., Monti, P. M., Wessberg, H. W., & Coyne, N. A. The effect of various rating training procedures on the perception of social skill and social anxiety. *Behavioral Assessment*, in press.

Cronbach, L. J., Gleser, G. C., Nanda, A., & Rajaratnam, N. *The dependability of behavioral measures.* New York: Wiley, 1972.

Curran, J. P., Beck, J. G., Corriveau, D. P., & Monti, P. M. Recalibration of raters to cri-terion: A methodological note for social skills research. *Behavioral Assessment*, 1980, 2, 261–266.

Curran, J. P., Corriveau, D. P., Monti, P. M., & Hagerman, S. Self-report measurement of social skill and social anxiety in a psychiatric population. *Behavior Modification*, 1980, 4, 493–512.

Curran, J. P., & Mariotto, M. J. A conceptual structure for the assessment of social skills. In M. Hersen, D. Eisler, & P. Miller (Eds.), *Progress in behavior modification*. New York: Academic Press, 1980.

Curran, J. P., Miller, I. W., Zwick, W. R., Monti, P. M., & Stout, R. L. The socially inadequate patient: Incidence rate, demographical and clinical features, hospital and post-hospital functioning. *Journal of Consulting and Clinical Psychology*, 1980, *48*, 375–382.

Curran, J. P., Monti, P. M., Corriveau, D. P., Hay, L. R., Hagerman, S., Zwick, W. R., & Farrell, A. D. The generalizability of a procedure for assessing social skills and social anxiety in a psychiatric population. *Behavioral Assessment*, 1980, *2*, 389–401.

Curran, J. P., Wessberg, H. W., Farrell, A. D., Monti, P. M., Corriveau, D. P., & Coyne, N. A. *Social skills and social anxiety: Are different laboratories measuring the same construct?* Manuscript in preparation, Brown Medical School, Providence, Rhode Island, 1980.

Curran, J. P., Wessberg, H. W., Monti, P. M., Corriveau, D. P., & Coyne, N. A. *Patients versus controls on a social skill/anxiety role-play test.* Paper presented at the 88th annual convention of the American Psychological Convention, Montreal, Quebec, Canada, September 1980.

Farrell, A. D., Zwick, W. R., Curran, J. P., & Monti, P. M. *Generalizability of anxiety and social skills ratings in three populations.* Paper presented at the 88th annual convention of the Clinical Psychological Associaton, Montreal, Quebec, Canada, September 1980.

Ferguson, G. A. *Statistical analysis in psychology and education.* New York: McGraw-Hill, 1971.

Fischetti, M., Curran, J. P., & Wessberg, H. Sense of timing: A skill deficit in heterosexual-socially anxious males. *Behavior Modification*, 1977, *1*, 179–194.

Goldsmith, J. B., & McFall, R. M. Development and evaluation of an inter-personal skill-training program for psychiatric patients. *Journal of Abnormal Psychology*, 1975, *84*, 51–58.

Guilford, J. P. *Psychometric methods.* New York: McGraw-Hill, 1954.

Kazdin, A. E. Assessing the clinical or applied importance of behavior change through social validation. *Behavior Modification*, 1977, *1*, 427–452.

Lowe, M. R., & Cautela, J. R. A self-report measure of social skill. *Behavior Therapy*, 1978, *9*, 535–544.

Mariotto, M. J., & Paul, G. L. Person versus situations in the real-life functioning of chronically institutionalized mental patients. *Journal of Abnormal Psychology*, 1975, *84*, 483–493.

Monti, P. M., Curran, J. P., Corriveau, D. P., DeLancey, A. L., & Hagerman, S. The effects of social skills training groups and sensitivity training groups with psychiatric patients. *Journal of Consulting and Clinical Psychology*, 1980, *48*, 241–248.

O'Leary, K. D., & Kent, R. N. Behavior modification for social action: Research tactics and problems. In L. A. Hamerlynck, L. C. Handy, & E. J. Mash (Eds.), *Behavior change: Methodology, concepts and practice.* Champaign, Ill.: Research Press, 1973.

Richardson, F. C., & Tasto, D. L. Development and factor analysis of a social anxiety inventory. *Behavior Therapy*, 1976, *7*, 453–462.

Wessberg, H. W., Coyne, N. A., Curran, J. P., Monti, P. M., & Corriveau, D. P. Two studies of observers' rating characteristics in social anxiety and skill research. *Behavioral Assessment*, in press.

Wessberg, H. W., Curran, J. P., Monti, P. M., Corriveau, D. P., Coyne, N. A., & Dziadosz, T. Evidence for the external validity of a simulation measure of social skills. *Journal of Behavioral Assessment*, in press.

Wiggins, J. S. *Personality and prediction: Principles of personality assessment.* Reading, Mass.: Addison-Wesley, 1973.

Zigler, E., & Phillips, L. Social competence and outcome in psychiatric disorder. *Journal of Abnormal and Social Psychology*, 1961, *63*, 264–271.

12

AN ETHOLOGICAL PERSPECTIVE
ON SOCIAL SKILLS RESEARCH

ROBERT BOICE

At first glance, the two research areas of ethology and social skills may appear incompatible. One is an old European tradition with a reputation for evolutionary studies of animal posturings. The other is a young American discipline with a commitment to human subjects and behavior modification.

Part of the appearance of disparity owes to the impression that ethologists do little more than observe birds like arctic phalaropes:

> The first response of a female to a visiting male was striking . . . she flew towards him, often uttering her song and, after alighting, faced him in the same flat, threatening posture she adopted when attacking another female. But she never drove her attack home; a foot or two from the male she suddenly stretched her neck and swam away . . . the first response to a bird of the opposite sex is the same as that to one of the same sex, and the posture is a hostile one. (Tinbergen, 1968, pp. 55–56)

In addition to a reminder about the interdependence of sex and aggression, this traditional account of behavior probably reinforces the old belief that ethologists work in a foreign sphere.

Another part of that seeming disparity is the result of traditional emphases in ethology on the evolutionary mechanisms of behavior (Thorpe, 1979). So long as ethologists concentrated on the behavioral taxonomies that distinguished closely related species of ducks, communication with most psychologists was unlikely (Boice, in press).

Robert Boice. Department of Psychology, State University of New York at Albany, Albany, New York.

CONTEMPORARY VERSUS TRADITIONAL ETHOLOGY

Contemporary ethology has far more to offer psychology than the old scenario just presented. The reasons behind that change may be seen in the more general trend of applying animal study techniques to human problems. In some ways, human ethology mirrors the transition from traditional research on animal learning into the applied analysis of behaviors such as social skills (Kazdin, 1978). Moreover, human ethology has been liberalized because its newest proponents come from a variety of disciplines. Whereas traditional training was almost exclusively biological, ethologists are now as likely to have backgrounds in anthropology, sociology, speech communication, psychiatry, and psychology. The result is a much healthier blend of old emphases on social skills (such as courtship signals and self-presentation postures) with new emphases on human behaviors, including cognitions (von Cranach, Foppa, LePenies, & Ploog, 1979). Equally important, the old ethological style of patient, naturalistic observation is retained but without the insistence on evolutionary and genetic explanations. Contemporary ethology is, then, a unique approach to the study of social skills—an area that has, as yet, had too little impact on research in heterosocial skills.

What sort of acquaintance with ethology is necessary to an application of these much older and broader approaches to the study of social skills? Contemporary ethologists do not suppose, as once woud have been the case, that it is de rigueur to be grounded in studies of stickleback fish (Tinbergen, 1951) or familiar with terms like "fixed action patterns." Nor need psychologists, if they wish to glean useful ideas from ethology, feign an interest in heredity, instincts, or nonhumans. What might help, though, in fostering interaction between the two areas is an understanding of why traditions of ethology and psychology grew apart in the first place. Therein lies an insight as to the continuing reluctance of contemporary psychologists and ethologists to collaborate.

SOURCES OF DIVERGENCE

For most of the century of its existence, ethology has been an almost exclusively European effort (Jaynes, 1969; Klopfer & Hailman, 1967). And until its recent Americanization, ethology was just as exclusively tied to evolutionary studies of social behaviors in birds, insects, and fish (Boice, 1980). Ethology began, as did animal psychology, in the Darwinian inspiration to trace the evolution of mentality (e.g., Romanes, 1884). With the advent of objectivism and the law of parsimony, however, mentality was excluded from legitimate study. Thereafter (by the turn of our century), Americans and Europeans continued with Darwinian inspirations, but in strikingly different directions. American psychologists followed the lead of Thorndike in studying learning, mostly in animals and always with laboratory controls. European ethologists followed the example of pioneers such as Lorenz (1935), who concentrated on patterns of social communication, behaviors that lent themselves to naturalistic study.

Ethology grew very slowly compared to American psychology. Delays of growth were in large part insured by the slower development of academic programs in Europe. Delays in recognition, from American psychologists at least, owed to the dogmatic overemphasis on instincts by traditional ethologists. Decades of field research, some of it brilliant, went unappreciated by Americans, who attended instead to ethologists' claims for instincts that appeared without the aid of learning. Even though ethologists eventually moderated their concept of instinct into other labels (e.g., templates) and to include large components of learning (e.g., Hailman, 1969), the whole affair remains a sore point with many psychologists.

The result of that long hiatus in constructive communication is that researchers in the two traditions tend to see the world in curiously different ways. Stated simply, American psychologists conceptualize research in causative terms, European ethologists in functional terms. Americans have traditionally emphasized experiments, controls, and causes of behavior. Where psychologists have strived to control, modify, and improve behavior, ethologists have opted to understand the function of behavior without intrusion or modification (Boice, 1976; Purton, 1978). The essence of these two styles, causative and functional, may be seen in a comparison of the exemplar journals for each tradition: *The Journal of Comparative and Physiological Psychology* is typically psychological in its terse writing, its emphasis on laboratory controls and modifications, and its graphs and statistics. *Behaviour*, the most prestigious journal of ethology, is nearly the polar opposite. Its articles are usually lengthy and descriptive, with more illustrations than graphs, with few inferential statistics, and with emphasis on understanding behavior—not on manipulating or improving it. In current jargon, traditional psychology and ethology might be loosely characterized as right-versus left-brained, respectively.

AMERICANIZATION

American interest in ethology may have been aided by a change in zeitgeist in the 1960s away from strict environmentalism toward nativism (Herrnstein, 1972). The more specific inspiration would not have been predicted (or condoned) by most European ethologists. The surge of interest in biological explanations came from a series of best-selling books beginning with Ardrey's *African Genesis* (1961). Books of popularized ethology, including Morris's *The Naked Ape* (1967) and Wilson's Pulitzer Prize-winning *On Human Nature* (1978), continue to produce converts to ethology. There is irony in this success given the disdain of ethologists for the glib use of facts and generalizations in popularized ethology.

In the midst of popularized ethology, more substantial approaches to ethology became well known to Americans. Jane Goodall's research on chimpanzee social behavior attracted unprecedented respect for field research on primates. Almost simultaneously, specific groups of social scientists began Americanizing ethology. Anthropologists and then social psychologists (e.g., Sommer, 1969) popularized field studies of territoriality and personal space. Interest in the study of facial expression and in other nonverbal behaviors was revived a century after Darwin's (1873) pioneering efforts in the *Expresison of the Emotions in Man and Animals* (see Ekman, 1973).

Now, about a decade after its American beginnings, human ethology is a discipline with its own journals (e.g., *Ethology and Sociobiology*) and professional associations. The most direct applications of ethology to psychology so far are in areas of developmental research (e.g., Freedman, 1974) and of communications (e.g., Mehrabian & Ferris, 1967; Seay & Altekruse, 1979). The closest approximation of an application to social skills research may be seen in the area of psychiatry (Kramer & McKinney, 1979; McGuire & Fairbanks, 1977; Trower, 1980).

In essence, applied ethology emphasizes the direct observation of behavior (Hutt & Hutt, 1970). As a result, human ethology provides unusually good behavioral predictors, for example, of deficits in transmitting and receiving expressive cues (Kramer & McKinney, 1979), of parental acts in delivery rooms and nurseries that presage child abuse (Gray, Cutler, Dean, & Kempe, 1977), and of distinctive behavioral patterns that characterize newly admitted inpatients who improve (Polsky & McGuire, 1979). Add to these a reminder of traditional ethological interests such as the predictable stages in greeting rituals and of concomitant display rules (von Cranach *et al.*, 1979; Ekman, Friesen, & Ellsworth, 1972) and the potential usefulness to skills researchers is more than apparent.

ETHOLOGY APPLIED TO THE RESEARCH AREA OF HETEROSOCIAL SKILLS

Applied properly, ethology is based on a large component of careful observation and of exacting description. The patience and training that must underlie good behavioral recording is best described by an old-fashioned ethologist:

> It takes time for the eye to become accustomed to recognize differences, and once that has occurred the nature of the differences has to be defined in the mind by careful self-interrogation if the matter is to be set down on paper. . . . The fact remains that an observer has to go through a period of conditioning of a most subtle kind. . . . The observer must empty his mind and be receptive only of the deer and the signs of the country. This is quite severe discipline, calling for time and practice. (Darling, 1937, pp. 24–26)

In addition to a stronger commitment to patient, careful observation, psychologists might profit in trying other ethological practices, such as the description of freely occurring behaviors—preferably from an unobtrusive vantage. As Peterson (1979) notes, graduate students in psychology are less adept at describing phenomena than fitting them into analyses of variance.

Other general differences in approach between ethology and psychology owe to the divergence in their traditions. Ethology is not, for example, much affected by the humanities and is, therefore, open to interpretations typically neglected by the social sciences. The assumption, to be revisited anon, that some social behaviors are less modifiable than others, is obvious to an ethologist but not always to a psychologist (von Cranach *et al.*, 1979). Ethologists also, because of their links to naturalists, prefer to sample the full variety of behaviors and contexts as part of the quest to understand function (McGuire & Fairbanks, 1977). The result is a data base that is descriptive and relatively free of theoretical language. And, once again, the ethologist may see things differently than would a psychologist: the former, but probably not the latter, would expect that some behavioral types would generalize across situations better than others. Thus, some sex-role–related behaviors (e.g., readiness to copulate with strangers) would not be expected to be situation-specific, whereas others (e.g., friendliness) would. This assumption is, of course, tantamount to the trait notions that have been vigorously rejected by many psychologists. The point is that one's understanding of social behaviors may broaden in examining their function developmentally and in a wide variety of unmanipulated situations.

RECOGNITION OF THE NEED FOR BEHAVIORAL RESEARCH WITHIN THE SKILLS AREA

The temptation of any evangelist, myself included, who brings new doctrines to a strange territory is to suppose the inhabitants shamelessly ignorant. In fact, some social skills researchers are already pioneering direct behavioral researches that might delight even the most orthodox ethologist. The import of reviewing that trend lies in showing the apparent readiness of skills researchers to incorporate ethological techniques and concepts. As historians love to note, ideas, no matter how sound, will not be heard until the zeitgeist is ripe.

The call for direct behavioral research on social skills is largely the result of methodological concerns. There is, for example, growing consensus that assessment of social skills must be based on more than the self-report measures of subjects (Wallander, Conger, Mariotto, Curran, & Farrell, 1980). Accordingly, Curran (1977) concludes that heterosocial anxieties must be measured to cognitive (i.e., self-report), physiological, and behavioral dimensions. Related concerns for more direct measures of skills include problems with construct validity (Hersen & Bellack, 1976), the lack of criterion samples (Twentyman & McFall, 1975), and the need to assess individual differences in susceptibilities to treatment (Heimberg, Madsen, Montgomery, & McNabb, 1980; Marzillier & Winter, 1978).

Responses to those criticisms of research on heterosocial skills have taken a direction that can be labeled ethological. Some researchers have begun to place greater emphasis on behavioral indicators such as a trembling voice, some on increasing the number of observations (Farrell, Mariotto, Conger, Curran, & Wallander, 1979), and some on increasing the number of observational situations (Kazdin, 1979). Others have tried to make the situation less obviously artifactual by unobtrusively taping the role plays of subjects in skills experiments (Wessberg, Mariotto, Conger, Farrell, & Conger, 1979). One of the most effective attempts, from within traditional skills research paradigms, to provide greater validity for laboratory research is Kupke's. He and his associates (Kupke, Hobbs, & Cheney, 1979; Kupke, Calhoun, & Hobbs, 1979) did prototypical research in which self-talk was shown to correlate negatively with attractiveness ratings by a partner. Kupke not only demonstrated a simple means of providing criterion-related validity but he also showed how to establish experimental validity; subjects trained in showing personal attention to others got significantly higher ratings of attractiveness from partners.

Less conventional approaches to skills research have come even closer to ethological ideals. Conger and Conger (see Chapter 10, this volume) have compiled an extensive behavioral scale for assessing social skills. Twardosz, Schwartz, Fox, and Cunningham (1979) have shown that behavioral measures such as facial expression and physical contact are better indices of affection than are more traditional measures of speech or other social interaction. And, to complete the example, Liberman, Wallace, Vaughn, and Snyder (1979) found a single behavioral measure, the lack of emotion shown by a relative toward a patient at the time of hospitalization, to be the best predictor of schizophrenic relapse.

The most ethologically ideal study in the skills area is also one of the least well publicized. Barlow, Abel, Blanchard, Bristow, and Young (1977) began their unique report with a sequential analysis of hetero social skills. They surmised that behaviors are probably quite differen in each of three stages—the initiations of relationships, the performance of sexual behaviors, and the maintenance of heterosocial relationships. Identification of skills in the first stage was so difficult a process that these researchers went no further.

Barlow et al. (1977) based their checklist on observations of criterion groups who role-played heterosocial encounters. Each group was a consensus sample, one of popular and datable male students, the other a group of convicted sex offenders referred for treatment of inadequate heterosexual skills. Some 17 social behaviors proved to distinguish the adequate from inadequate males. These behaviors were categorized into voice, form of conversation, affect (e.g., appropriate laughter), and masculine versus feminine motor behaviors. Two aspects of this research deserve special emphasis: first, Barlow *et al.* (1977) were unprecedented in actually identifying the behaviors that distinguish adequate from inadequate skills. Prior researchers (e.g., Borkovec, Stone, O'Brien, & Kaloupek, 1974) found that overall ratings, but not specific behaviors, discriminated between groups. Second, Barlow *et al.*'s (1977) identification of behaviors critical to heterosocial success appears to be generalizable to other interpersonal skills and to other social situations.

Only one other study in the social skills area, by Trower (1980), is nearly so ethological. He divided psychiatric patients into skilled and unskilled groups in part based on reports of their social relationships with families and peers. Then, in a role-played test of social skills in speaking, listening, and assertion, Trower found striking differences between the two groups. Unskilled patients were not only deficient in terms of specific components of behaviors (e.g., speaking much less in a first encounter) but also in process skills such as monitoring, timing, and sequencing. Unskilled patients were also markedly deficient in adjusting their social skills to the demands of varying situations. This unresponsiveness to situational demands may be seen as contributing to the heterogeneity (and treatment difficulties) of socially inadequate patients (Curran, Miller, Zwick, Monti, & Stout, 1980).

DIRECT BEHAVIORAL MEASURES AS YET UNDERUTILIZED

Given that skills researchers already recognize the need for direct behavioral research, what can an ethological perspective add? One thing it can add is encouragement; thus far, direct behavioral approaches are rare in skills research. Some leaders of the field continue, with good reason, to question the efficacy of such techniques (e.g., Bellack, 1979). Another thing that ethologists can offer is a proven history of direct behavioral measures that do work well. The solution is in good part a matter of turning toward more complex measures. The insight has already been proposed by skills researchers, including Barlow *et al.* (1977), Kupke et al. (1979) and Trower (1980). Thus far, however, skills researchers have not done much with sequencing and timing analyses of social behavior (cf. Fischetti, Curran, & Wessberg, 1977), the components most emphasized by ethologists.

There is a wealth of material available that shows how to record and analyze the complexities of human social behavior. Much of this ethological material is concerned with social skills. The best general guide to such techniques is Hutt and Hutt's (1970) book, *Direct Observation and Measurement of Behavior*. This monograph begins with an overview of the neglect of observational methods in causative psychology; by Hutt and Hutt's count, fewer than 10% of published studies have relied on direct observation as a principal measure. Indeed, psychologists once took the lead in denigrating direct behavioral observation (e.g., Gellert, 1955).

Hutt and Hutt's system is typically ethological in its dependence on description. This stance is assumed basic to a proper appreciation of behavior patterns, especially as they tend to recur in similar situations. Not only do ethologists pay keen attention to the identification of behavior elements, but they do so with a patient sort of tentativeness. Hutt and Hutt (1970) contrast this to the more commonplace style of investigation: "Too often the investigator has preconceptions of what behavior *ought* to occur, rather than knowledge of what actually occurs, and imposes a spurious orderliness upon his data, either by juxtaposing classes of behavior which are morphologically distinct, or by ignoring large segments of the animal's behavioral repertoire" (p. 29). Moreover, Hutt and Hutt argue, our decisions about types of measurements affect the ways we define and record behaviors.

The actual steps employed in ethological descriptions are too lengthy to detail here, but they include strategies for selecting activity categories, for checking reliability, and for making permanent visual records. Cautions are directed at the evaluation of high- and low-frequency behaviors; some of the latter may provide more useful information than the former. Hutt and Hutt are among several authors (e.g., Knapp, 1978b; McGrew, 1972) who outline sampling and scaling techniques for various social activities. Observational tasks can, for example, be simplified by combining checklists and time-sampling techniques (e.g., Boice & Kraemer, 1977). In this way, data may be quickly summarized in terms of frequencies, durations, and patterns of different activities. Communication of direct behavioral data may also be made more effective with ethological styles of graphing to show, for instance, duration and synchrony of behaviors. The point in attempting to deal with social behavior meaningfully is that it must be seen beyond its simple structures such as frequencies (Altmann, 1974; Peterson, 1979).

Direct observations of behavior are difficult and time-consuming, often forebodingly so to psychologists accustomed to traditional laboratory experiments. Some of the impetus to try these new techniques does arise, however, from the demand for better measures of social skills. Bellack (1979) concludes, for example, that absolute frequencies or quantities are often less important than where and when responses are made. Some of the research in human ethology that could be used as models for studies on social skills is listed here (Knapp, 1978a). Nonverbal behaviors are encoded by recipients in a contextual fashion that includes evaluations of the immediacy (i.e., positiveness), social status, and the activity levels of the sender (Mehrabian, 1972). Moreover, nonverbal signals have a far greater impact than verbal signals for communicating assertiveness and friendship (Argyle, Alkema, & Gilmour, 1972). So it is, for example, that schizophrenics may be seen as too unrewarding to maintain social relationships (Longabaugh, Eldred, Bell, & Sherman, 1966) and as engaging in too little self-presentation behavior (Argyle, 1978).

Another dimension of social skills concerns synchrony. Skilled interactants show a synchrony of speech–body acts so that, for instance, speaker gazes may coincide with grammatical pauses (Condon & Ogston, 1966). This same synchrony is dramatically heightened during courtship (Davis, 1971). Socially skilled people also display a predictable pattern of some six stages of greeting rituals when that interaction is initiated from a distance (Kendon & Ferber, 1973). These stages include a distant salutation (e.g., smile, head toss), a head dip, aversion of gaze just prior to the spoken salutation, and a ritualized form of close salutation (e.g., handshake). Finally, skilled conversants follow predictable rules of gazing. Looking usually occurs while listening; direct gazes rarely last more than a few seconds (Argyle, Ingham, Alkema, & McCallin, 1973; Knapp, 1978a; Trower, 1980).

In even so brief a list as this, a second source of impetus for direct behavioral research is apparent. Not only is the investment in more ethological techniques helpful methodologically, but these more direct observations also suggest new ways of measuring and conceptualizing social skills.

NOVEL PERSPECTIVES

An ethological perspective can do more than simply point out the advantage in considering social rituals as social skills. Because they see things so differently than do most social scientists, ethologists make assumptions about social behaviors that may not have occurred to or that have been dismissed by skills researchers. In the survey that follows, ideas have been chosen for their useful or provocative nature. Some of them may simply be too foreign for immediate acceptance by most psychologists.

Sexual Selection

Ethologists tend to see social behavior in terms of the principle of sexual selection, a Darwinian notion that centers around an observation about gender roles: in most species only a few males impregnate almost all females; whereas many males are not successful with their heterosocial skills, most females are. Females do most of the choosing of mates, presumably because they have a far greater investment in the results of mating than do males (Daly & Wilson, 1978). As a result, the logic continues, predispositions for the heterosexual social skills of females are adaptively different. Males, with their millions of fleeting sperm to dispense among as many females as are receptive, can afford to be undiscriminating. In most species (especially those with sexual dimorphism) males invest little in the relationship after copulation. Females, in contrast, typically invest considerable time, nutrition, and risk of self-injury into their few eggs. So it is, presumably, that human females are generally more coy and discriminating in heterosocial encounters than are males (Wilson, 1978).

Consider some of the ways in which this principle could be related to findings in the social skills area. It might explain why females prefer to enlist for assertiveness training and why males prefer the identical training when it is labeled social skills. Females are, in the ethological view, less concerned about attractiveness than with being able to refuse some suitors. Males, in that same view, wish to make themselves as attractive to as many females as possible. The principle of sexual selection might also explain the general finding that female subjects are more attuned to appropriate social behaviors than are males (e.g., Lowe & Cautela, 1978). Or, to recast another common finding, the principle could explain why women smile more than men in most social interactions. Smiling probably reflects a high level of sociability and a low level of competitiveness (Knapp, 1978a). Females typically do not, accordingly, show heterosexual styles that are seen as aggressive (Rose & Tryon, 1979).

The principle of sexual selection may also illuminate aspects of heterosocial behaviors not yet considered by most skills researchers (Poirer, 1974). Consider, for example, its predictions about differences in the social tension styles of males and females. Men tend to be more at ease with someone they like than with someone they dislike; this is evidenced in the diminished eye contact and the slumping postures they show with the latter (Mehrabian, 1972). Females react almost conversely, putting themselves more at ease with disliked than with liked others. The ethological explanation of this difference is that females must be somewhat reserved in socializing with attractive males. Males, in contrast, need show their reserve only toward people who offer no social gains.

A final example may be the least attractive because it is, as yet, founded only in observations of chimpanzees. Males who are most attractive to females may be characterized in a syndrome of behaviors described as cunning, controlling, punishing, and consoling (van Lawick-Goodall, 1971).

Trait Notions

In an ethological perspective, trait notions would not be so readily dismissed as in psychology. The greater discriminativeness of females in choosing partners for copulation, as we saw earlier, could be one candidate for traitlike tendencies of social behavior. And, once again, because ethologists do not suppose all social behaviors to be equally modifiable or equally generalizable across situations, other skills as reflected in, say, extraversion would not be expected to be traitlike. Stated another way, not all behaviors need be expected equivalent in their situational specificity.

Two somewhat novel conclusions about the skills literature may be drawn from this premise: first, skills researchers may be premature in supposing that anxiety is orthogonal to social skills (e.g., Bellack, 1979). Second, the expectation that skills training will not generalize to new situations (e.g., Eisler, Hersen, Miller, & Blanchard, 1975) is probably too pessimistic. Consider, in the first instance, the possibility that anxiety has not been characterized fairly by self-report inventories as commonly used in skills research. And too, that its absence is not always completely produced by relaxation or desensitization exercises. Ethologists who work with primates, including humans, emphasize a behavioral index of anxiety called impassivity (Stenhouse, 1974). In ethological usage, impassivity is a traitlike quality of individuals that generalizes reliably across social situations. Stated briefly, impassivity is that behavioral quality characteristic of calm emotional reserve of leaders and, to a lesser extent, of other socially skilled individuals. It is by means of this quality that dominant males may be recognized; they show an unemotional response to threats, loud noises, and the like (Boice, in press). Similarly, the most successful chimpanzee mothers can be seen to be generally unemotional and able to calmly punish/console their infants (van Lawick-Goodall, 1971). It might, then, make sense to suppose that impassivity is basic to all effective social skills. The social deficits emphasized by human ethologists (e.g., inappropriate tone, giggling, tense posturings, mistiming of feedback cues) are obviously linked to anxiety. The point is that training in specific skills of communicating impassivity, and not just global training in relaxation, may be necessary to social adequacy.

While most skills researchers might not be amenable to seeing impassivity as a trait that underlies social skills, they might entertain the possibility that ethological approaches could help produce more appropriate generalizability of skills training. Once again, the idea is not unprecedented in the skills literature. Curran (1979) notes that narrowly defined behavioral attributes are almost necessarily limited in generality across situations. It was in the rare instance where skills were defined complexly, as we saw in the Barlow et al. (1979) study, that generality was shown. What can ethologists add to the realization that generalizability may be increased merely by adding more observations and more sophisticated behavioral measures (Farrell et al., 1979)? The answer is more demanding than even the changes advocated by progressive skills researchers who are already beginning to consider assessment in applied (Trower, Bryant, & Argyle, 1978) and natural settings (Kazdin, 1979). Ethologists typically advocate an extensive acquaintance with the subjects and social situations connected with social skills. This approach requires observations in the broadest possible scope of natural activities, a venture in patience not yet attempted by many social scientists (Turner, 1978). The result is a catalog of social behaviors that should include an indication of which skills are most modifiable and which are most appropriately common across situations (McGuire & Fairbanks, 1977). That information could help prepare researchers and clinicians for complexities of training the socially inadequate in the skills and rules of given situations (Trower, 1980).

Skills Notions

A third example of how an ethological vantage could change the think-ing of skills researchers concerns how we conceptualize skills. Etholo-gists, because of their long investment in working with nonverbal communication, are more likely to pay attention to emotional expres-sions than are psychologists. Psychologists, on the other hand, probably emphasize cognitions far more than feelings (Friedman, 1979); so it is that skills researchers usually rely on the self-reports of subjects. While contemporary ethologists do not exclude cognitions from consideration (Mason, 1979), they emphasize the nonverbal components of social communication. The result is that attention is directed away from what people are to what it is that they can do interpersonally (e.g., DiMatteo, 1979). People are, therefore, assessed in terms of abilities. A metaphor for understanding why this approach might work is seen in the differ-ence between personality tests and ability tests. Ability tests have been much more useful as predictors because their component items have intrinsic meaning. Items in most personality tests are, instead, com-monly directed to inferred states and not to behavioral processes.

The emphasis of abilities and actions in social behavior is not, of course, exclusive to ethology. Goffman (1959) is well known for his scheme in which people are viewed as actors whose social abilities may be seen in the effectiveness of the impressions they give off.

Other Novel Approaches

Some of the advantages in an ethological perspective owe to its history of animal studies. Telemetry is one good example. It would probably surprise most ethologists, for instance, to learn that few skills research-ers have used biotelemetry to unobtrusively monitor physiological in-dices of emotionality in subjects. Recent advances in miniaturization have made this tactic as practical with humans as with animals (Blanch-ard, Haynes, Young, & Scott, 1977; Stonehouse, 1979).

Another tradition of ethology that could be transferred with profit is a commitment to training its researchers in observational skills. A basic part of that training is a lengthy exposure to field conditions and experience in cataloging all the social behaviors of a few individuals. Beyond that, training is directed at effective and reliable ways of record-ing and depicting behavior (Boice, in press). The emphasis throughout, as indicated earlier, is on observing with as few preconceptions as possible. One of the most cherished goals of a field ethologist is to sample the full variety of behavior, to identify context-specific relationships in behavior, and to find the functions of behaviors that best characterize a species (McGuire & Fairbanks, 1977). A clear strength of ethology is that its data base is descriptive and relatively free of theoretical language.

Where there is a theoretical bias it is against the prevailing notion in a cognitive psychology that most human behavior is under conscious control (Jaynes, 1977; McGuire & Fairbanks, 1977). In an ethological view, the critical aspects of social communication are expected to be largely unconscious and irrational (Wilson, 1978). Support for this bias may be adduced in a brief example of the signals of courtship readiness (Scheflen, 1965): these are predictable (and generally unconscious) cues of increased muscle tonus, reduced eye bagginess and jowl sag, lessened slouching, and preening behaviors, including hair stroking. Couples actively engaged in exchanging courtship signals also exhibit positional cues that discourage others from entering the conversation; their bodies are positioned so that others cannot easily orient to communicate with either of them.

The same essential courtship behaviors can also be seen as basic to more general social skills. Quasi-courtship signals are used to promote many social relationships but with clear reservations about engaging in sexual behavior (Scheflen, 1965). A therapist, for instance, may respond to a patient's preening with a preen of her or his own—but then follow with a disclaimer such as a yawn. Quasi-courtship signals are not only performed with little conscious awareness; they also provide an interesting example of how subtle social skills deficits may be. Some people are simply deficient in sending or receiving these disclaimers. Scheflin supposes that this area of social communication is uniquely susceptible to misuse and miseducation becaue of its complexities. It is not too surprising, then, that an anxious courter may unintentionally "decourt" by virtue of breaking the synchrony of nodding or by looking at someone else while talking.

The suggestion here is that an ethological perspective could help broaden the approach of skills researchers to many more skills-related behaviors. This expansion would come in part because ethologists are accustomed to making observations in a broad array of naturalistic settings. The broadening could also come from the ethological emphasis on species' typical behavior patterns. These patterns, which need not be

tied to evolutionary considerations, provide a means of assessing appropriate social skills in terms of situational and cultural norms. Some
types of species-typical social skills have already been suggested: courtship patterns are subject to situational, developmental, and cultural
norms such that the predictable sequence of actions may be described as
a courtship dance (Knapp, 1978a). Similarly, greeting rituals follow
prescribed patterns so that skilled interactants do not show signs of
weakness at the outset or an abrupt cut-off upon departure (Eibl-
Eibesfeldt, 1979).

Social skills may also be basic to most forms of effective communication (Knapp, 1978b). Socially appropriate listening skills, for instance,
are a matter of prescribed eye contact, certain postures, synchrony
between listener and speaker, and responsive turn taking (Dittman,
1977). It may be, however, that a socially skilled person does not attend
too carefully to all messages, especially to improprieties (Rosenthal,
1979). A most unique application of a skills approach could be part of the
study of aggression. Humans do engage in surprisingly predictable and
uniform means of achieving rank and dominance (Eibl-Eibesfeldt, 1979).
So too, socially normal individuals use ritualized means of resolving
conflict and for maintaining discipline. There are even somewhat specific rules in human groups regarding who looks at whom (Ellsworth &
Ludwig, 1972; Kendon, 1972); stated simply, the most socially dominant individual is also the focus of the most visual attention (Boice,
1980).

Environmental Fits

Most important of the sorts of novel experiences suggested in an
ethological view is the matter of establishing environmental fits. While
social scientists continue to plead for behavioral assessments based on
the relationship between person and environment (Bem & Funder,
1978; Curran & Mariotto, 1980; McReynolds, 1979), little meaningful
progress has been made. Where skills researchers have developed field
techniques they are limited to instances of, say, training subjects to be
reliable self-recorders (Winett, Neale, & Williams, 1979). Ethologists,
because of their commitment to the functional analyses and patient
observation of behaviors in natural contexts, are accustomed to assessing environmental fits. Recall that ethologists are influenced by old-
fashioned notions of naturalism; conclusions are deferred until thorough
descriptions of the behavioral units are collected across situations

(McGuire & Fairbanks, 1977). Moreover, ethologists are more likely to suppose that social behaviors are the result of past compromises—for both the individual and in cultural evolution. An ethological understanding of the function of a social gesture, then, requires an unhurried study of its multiple determinants.

Failure to carry out this sort of thorough and functional analysis may result in reports where each investigator samples a somewhat separate body of data and where our concept of a social skill is forever changing. The result of studying a social behavior in the settings where it naturally occurs may suggest more generalizable concepts. Done properly, such an examination should reveal patterns toward which people naturally gravitate. Some situations and some events (e.g., sudden disruption of an intimate relationship) might be seen as predictive of depression. Certain kinds of social organizations, in contrast, might be shown to be remarkably consistent across ward situations (Boice & Kraemer, 1977); patients prefer to associate with the staff, whereas the staff members try to isolate themselves (Fairbanks, McGuire, Cole, Sbordone, Silvers, & Richards, 1977). The most useful ethological concepts derived from environmental/behavioral research are as yet unfamiliar to most psychologists. Included in these environmental/behavioral concepts are demonstrations of inhibition (where a stronger stimulus inhibits the action of the weaker), of facilitation (a second stimulus enhances the first), of inaction (as a final response to conflicting stimuli), and of a variety of others, such as displacement and regression (McGuire & Fairbanks, 1977).

CONCLUSIONS

What is it that may keep skills researchers from adopting many of the ideas and concepts presented here? One factor could be lack of communication. Ethologists and psychologists are products of very different traditions; too often, functional and causative researchers assume that members of the opposite camp have nothing to offer. Even when attempts at communication are made, as in the present paper, difficulties may be inevitable.

Many social scientists may stop listening when they hear the word ethology. They might reasonably suppose that the label signals a call for behavioral analysis in terms of genetic or nonhuman dimensions. Even psychologists who listen long enough to discover that contemporary human ethology is not tied to either premise may listen only to a point. The problem is, again, one of background. Consider, first of all, that behaviorism, for all its admirable objectivity, has not been concerned with the sort of descriptive analysis of behavior championed by ethologists. Psychologists are much more comfortable with quantitative counts of operationally defined behaviors (e.g., head nods) than with objective but descriptive accounts. Consider too that psychologists are trained in a causative tradition far removed from patient field research. Causativists often suppose that scientific worth is dependent upon controls, demonstrations of causation and modification, and the prospect of improvement (Boice, 1976). Research done in natural settings without controls and manipulations may appear to be beyond the pale of worthwhile discovery.

Some of the current reservations about field research in skills study help make the point; the seriousness of this hesitancy may be seen in the nature of these arguments. They are carefully reasoned and presented by the most prestigious skills researchers. Curran and Mariotto (1980), while advocating "empirical bootstrapping," nonetheless echo the old beliefs about limitations in field research: naturalistic settings are presumably too expensive, too difficult, and unethical. Bellack (1979) makes a similar argument: naturalistic observation is too costly, it is confounded by the reactivity of people to being observed, and it is circumscribed by the particular sample under scrutiny.

Only one of those reservations, the effort required for field research, has much substance. That, as we shall see shortly, can be turned into a virtue in establishing descriptive catalogs of behavior. The other arguments seem to reflect a lack of familiarity with field research. It is not, in the first place, necessarily more expensive; indeed, field study is typically less expensive than most laboratory research. Investigators need be equipped with little more than checklists, watches, and perhaps tape-recorders. Video-recorders are important to some investigations (e.g., for documentation of ritualized posturings) but should be used sparingly. Cameras attract too much attention and videotapes tend to be left sitting about unscored. Field research is not, in the second place, necessarily confounded by reactivity of subjects. This criticism is more justly applied to laboratory settings where subjects do expect to be watched and probably do act guardedly. Where the field researcher can be seen by subjects, the subjects seem to adapt to that presence quickly, probably because they are in a familiar surround (Hutt & Hutt, 1970). Where the field researcher chooses to observe unobtrusively, his or her presence is, of course, undetected. What, then, about the last criticism, of unethicality? Naturalistic observations need not extend beyond public behaviors. And they need not, in most cases, include permanent records (e.g., videotapes) that could be used to identify subjects. Where video records are made, or where verbal interactions are recorded, prior approval of subjects would be required just as in laboratory experiments. In practice, field research is probably less beset by ethical problems than is its laboratory counterpart.

The real drawback to ethological research is its difficulty. Field study does take more time, the occurrence of significant events often cannot be insured, and it can be uncomfortable for experimenters. Even where skills researchers opt for the sensible compromise of incorporating ethological ideas and laboratory conveniences, the result is still one of added difficulties. Done properly, direct behavioral research in the laboratory is far more demanding than typical skills studies: behavioral units must be carefully defined, agreed upon as functional by trained observers, and then recorded a multitude of times for each pair of subjects. No wonder that few skills researchers have followed the lead of Barlow et al. (1977) in using behavioral measures of criterion groups to establish a checklist for appropriate social skills.

Despite those difficulties, the transition to more complex and time-consuming research on heterosocial skills is already underway. The call for more sophisticated measures of social skills includes demands for assessments of the general appropriateness of behaviors (Bellack, 1979; Curran, 1979; Trower, 1980), for the equation of skills with measurable abilities (Friedman, 1979), and for measurements made in natural environments (Kazdin, 1979). As skills researchers follow those leads they might profit from interactions with ethology, a tradition devoted to the study of social skills for nearly a century.

ACKNOWLEDGMENTS

I am indebted to Richard Heimberg, whose lectures in a course on social skills were the inspiration for this chapter. Three other colleagues contributed—David H. Barlow and Edward B. Blanchard with encouraging comments on an earlier draft, and Peter M. Monti with support and ideas for the final draft.

REFERENCES

Altmann, J. Observational study of behavior: Sampling methods. *Behaviour*, 1974, *49*, 227–267.
Ardrey, R. *African genesis*. New York: Dell, 1961.

Argyle, M. Non-verbal communication and mental disorder. *Psychological Medicine*, 1978, *8*, 551–554.

Argyle, M., Alkema, F., & Gilmour, R. The communication of friendly and hostile attitudes by verbal and non-verbal signals. *European Journal of Social Psychology*, 1972, *1*, 385–402.

Argyle, M., Ingham, F., Alkema, F., & McCallin, M. The different functions of gaze. *Semiotica*, 1973, *7*, 19–32.

Barlow, D. H., Abel, G. G., Blanchard, E. B., Bristow, A. R., & Young, L. D. A heterosocial skills behavior checklist for males. *Behavior Therapy*, 1977, *8*, 229–239.

Bellack, A. S. A critical appraisal of strategies for assessing social skill. *Behavioral Assessment*, 1979, *1*, 157–176.

Bem, D. J., & Funder, D. C. Predicting more of the people more of the time: Assessing the personality of situations. *Psychological Review*, 1978, *85*, 485–501.

Blanchard, E. B., Haynes, M. R., Young, L. D., & Scott, R. W. The use of feedback training and a stimulus control procedure to obtain large magnitude increases in heart rate outside the laboratory. *Biofeedback and Self-Regulation*, 1977, *2*, 81–91.

Boice, R. In the shadow of Darwin. In R. Geen & E. O'Neal (Eds.), *Perspectives on aggression*. New York: Academic Press, 1976.

Boice, R. *Ethological perspectives on human behavior*. New York: Plenum, in press.

Boice, R., & Kraemer, E. B. An ethological study of stereotypies among psychiatric inpatients. *Man–Environment Systems*, 1977, *7*, 42.

Borkovec, T. D., Stone, N., O'Brien, G., & Kaloupek, D. Identification and measurement of a clinically relevant target behavior for analogue outcome research. *Behavior Therapy*, 1974, *5*, 503–513.

Condon, W. S., & Ogston, W. D. Soundfilm analysis of normal and pathological behavior patterns. *Journal of Nervous and Mental Disease*, 1966, *143*, 338–347.

Cranach, M. von, Foppa, K., LePenies, W., & Ploog, D. (Eds.). *Human ethology*. New York: Cambridge University Press, 1979.

Curran, J. P. Skills training as an approach to the treatment of heterosexual–social anxiety: A review. *Psychological Bulletin*, 1977, *84*, 140–157.

Curran, J. P. Pandora's box reopened? The assessment of social skills. *Journal of Behavioral Assessment*, 1979, *1*, 55–71.

Curran, J. P., & Mariotto, M. J. A conceptual structure for the assessment of social skills. In M. Hersen, P. Eisler, & P. Miller (Eds.), *Progress in behavior modification*. New York: Academic Press, 1980.

Curran, J. P., Miller, I. W., Zwick, W. R., Monti, P. M., & Stout, R. L. The socially inadequate patient: Incidence rate, demographic and clinical features, and hospital and posthospital functioning. *Journal of Consulting and Clinical Psychology*, 1980, *48*, 375–382.

Daly, M., & Wilson, M. *Sex, evolution and behavior*. North Scituate, Mass.: Duxbury, 1978.

Darling, F. F. *A herd of red deer*. New York: Oxford University Press, 1937.

Darwin, C. *Expression of the emotions in man and animals*. New York: Appleton, 1873.

Davis, F. *Inside intuition*. New York: McGraw-Hill, 1971.

DiMatteo, M. R. Nonverbal skill and the physician–patient relationship. In R. Rosenthal (Ed.), *Skill in nonverbal communication*. Cambridge, Mass.: Oelgeschlager, Gunn & Hain, 1979.

Dittman, A. T. The role of body movement in communication. In A. W. Siegman & S. Feldstein (Eds.), *Nonverbal behavior and communication*. Potomac, Md.: Erlbaum, 1977.

Eibl-Eibesfeldt, I. Ritual and ritualization from a bciological perspective. In: M. von Cranach, K. Foppa, W. LePenies, & D. Ploog (Eds.), *Human ethology*. New York: Cambridge University Press, 1979.

Eisler, R. M., Hersen, M., Miller, P. M., & Blanchard, E. B. Situational determinants of assertive behaviors. *Journal of Consulting and Clinical Psychology*, 1975, *43*, 330–341.

Ekman, P. *Darwin and facial expression*. New York: Academic Press, 1973.

Ekman, P., Friesen, W. V., & Ellsworth, P. *Emotion in the human face.* New York: Pergamon, 1972.

Ellsworth, P. C., & Ludwig, L. M. Visual behavior in social interaction. *Journal of Communication,* 1972, *22,* 375–403.

Fairbanks, L. A., McGuire, M. T., Cole, S. R., Sbordone, R., Silvers, F. M., & Richards, M. The ethological study of four psychiatric wards: Patient, staff & system behaviors. *Journal of Psychiatric Research,* 1977, *13,* 193–209.

Farrell, A. D., Mariotto, M. J., Conger, A. J., Curran, J. P., & Wallander, J. L. Self-ratings and judges' ratings of heterosexual social anxiety and skills: A generalizability study. *Journal of Consulting and Clinical Psychology,* 1979, *47,* 164–175.

Fischetti, M., Curran, J. P., & Wessberg, H. W. Sense of timing: A skill deficit in hetero-sexual–socially anxious males. *Behavior Modification,* 1977, *1,* 164–173.

Freedman, D. G. *Human infancy: An evolutionary perspective.* Hillsdale, N.J.: Laurence Erlbaum, 1974.

Friedman, H. S. The concept of skill in nonverbal communication: Implications for under-standing social interaction. In R. Rosenthal (Ed.), *Skill in nonverbal communication.* Cambridge, Mass.: Oelgeschlager, Gunn & Hain, 1979.

Gellert, E. Systematic observation: A method in child study. *Harvard Educational Review,* 1955, *25,* 179–195.

Goffman, E. *The presentation of self in everyday life.* Garden City, N.Y.: Doubleday, 1959.

Gray, J. D., Cutler, C. A., Dean, J. G., & Kempe, C. H. Prediction and prevention of child abuse and neglect. *International Journal of Child Abuse and Neglect,* 1977, *1,* 45–58.

Hailman, J. P. How an instinct is learned. *Scientific American,* 1969, *231*(6), 98–106.

Heimberg, R. G., Madsen, C. H., Montgomery, D., & McNabb, C. E. The effects of behav-ioral treatments for heterosocial problems on daily self-monitored and role-played interactions. *Behavior Modification,* 4, 1980.

Herrnstein, R. Nature as nurture: Behaviorism and the instinct doctrine. *Behaviorism,* 1972, *1,* 23–52.

Hersen, M., & Bellack, A. S. Assessment of social skills. In A. R. Ciminero, K. R. Calhoun, & H. E. Adams (Eds.), *Handbook of behavioral assessment.* New York: Wiley, 1976.

Hutt, S. J., & Hutt, C. *Direct observation and measurement of behavior.* Springfield, Ill.: Charles C. Thomas, 1970.

Jaynes, J. The historical origins of ethology and comparative psychology. *Animal Behavior,* 1969, *17,* 601–606.

Jaynes, J. *The origin of consciousness in the breakdown of the bicameral mind.* Boston: Houghton Mifflin, 1977.

Kazdin, A. E. *History of behavior modification.* Baltimore: University Park Press, 1978.

Kazdin, A. E. Situational specificity: The two-edged sword of behavioral assessment. *Behavioral Assessment,* 1979, *1,* 57–75.

Kendon, A. Some functions of gaze-direction in social interaction. *Acta Psychologica,* 1967, *26,* 22–63.

Kendon, A., & Ferber, A. A description of some human greetings. In R. P. Michael & J. H. Crook (Eds.), *Comparative ecology and behavior of primates.* London: Academic Press, 1973.

Klopfer, P. H., & Hailman, J. P. *An introduction to animal behavior.* Englewood Cliffs, N.J.: Prentice-Hall, 1967.

Knapp, M. L. *Nonverbal communication in human interaction.* New York: Holt, Rinehart & Winston, 1978. (a)

Knapp, M. L. *Social intercourse: From greeting to goodbye.* Boston: Allyn & Bacon, 1978. (b)

Kramer, D. A., & McKinney, W. T. The overlapping territories of psychiatry and ethol-ogy. *Journal of Nervous and Mental Disease,* 1979, *108,* 3–22.

Kupke, T. E., Calhoun, K. S., & Hobbs, S. A. Selection of heterosocial skills: II. Experi-mental validity. *Behavior Therapy,* 1979, *10,* 336–346.

Kupke, T. E., Hobbs, S. A., & Cheney, T. H. Selection of heterosocial skills: I. Criterion-related validity. *Behavior Therapy*, 1979, *10*, 327–335.

Lawick-Goodall, J. van. *In the shadow of man.* Boston: Houghton Mifflin, 1971.

Liberman, R. P., Wallace, C. J., Vaughn, C. E., & Snyder, K. L. *Social and family factors in the course of schizophrenia.* Paper presented at the Conference on Psychotherapy of Schizophrenia, Yale University, 1979.

Longabaugh, R., Eldred, S. H., Bell, N. W., & Sherman, L. J. The interactional world of the chronic schizophrenic patient. *Psychiatry*, 1966, *29*, 78–99.

Lorenz, K. Z. Der Kumpan in der Umwelt des Vogels. *Journal of Ornithology*, 1935, *83*, 137–214.

Lowe, M. R., & Cautela, J. R. A self-report of social skill. *Behavior Therapy*, 1978, *9*, 535–544.

Marzillier, J. S., & Winter, K. Success and failure in social skills training: Individual differences. *Behaviour Research and Therapy*, 1978, *16*, 67–84.

Mason, W. A. Maternal attributes and primate cognitive development. In M. von Cranach, K. Foppa, W. LePenies, & D. Ploog (Eds.), *Human ethology.* New York: Cambridge University Press, 1979.

McGrew, W. C. *An ethological study of children's behavior.* New York: Academic Press, 1972.

McGuire, M. T., & Fairbanks, L. A. Ethology: Psychiatry's bridge to behavior. In M. T. McGuire & L. A. Fairbanks (Eds.), *Ethological psychiatry.* New York: Grune & Stratton, 1977.

Mehrabian, A. *Nonverbal communication.* Chicago: Aldine, 1972.

Mehrabian, A., & Ferris, S. R. Inference of attitudes from nonverbal communication in two channels. *Journal of Consulting Psychology*, 1967, *31*, 248–257.

McReynolds, P. The case for interactional assessment. *Behavioral Assessment*, 1979, *1*, 237–247.

Morris, D. *The naked ape.* New York: McGraw-Hill, 1967.

Peterson, G. L. Looking at behavior and seeing as a psychologist. *Personality and Social Psychology Bulletin*, 1979, *5*, 499–503.

Poirer, F. E. Colobine aggression. In R. L. Holloway (Ed.), *Primate aggression.* New York: Academic Press, 1974.

Polsky, R., & McGuire, M. T. An ethological analysis of manic–depressive disorder. *Journal of Nervous and Mental Disease*, 1979, *167*, 56–65.

Purton, A. C. Ethological categories of behaviour and some consequences of their conflation. *Animal Behaviour*, 1978, *26*, 653–670.

Romanes, G. J. *Mental evolution in animals.* London: Kegan, Paul, Trench, 1884.

Rose, Y. J., & Tryon, W. W. Judgments of assertive behavior as a function of speech loudness, latency, content, gestures, inflection, and sex. *Behavior Modification*, 1979, *3*, 112–113.

Rosenthal, R. (Ed.). *Skill in nonverbal communication.* Cambridge, Mass.: Oelgeschlager, Gunn & Hain, 1979.

Scheflen, A. E. Quasi-courtship behavior in psychotherapy. *Psychiatry*, 1965, *28*, 245–257.

Seay, T. A., & Altekruse, M. D. Verbal and nonverbal behavior in judgments of facilitative conditions. *Journal of Counseling Psychology*, 1979, *26*, 108–119.

Sommer, R. *Personal space.* Englewood Cliffs, N.J.: Prentice-Hall, 1969.

Stenhouse, D. *The evolution of intelligence.* New York: Harper & Row, 1974.

Stonehouse, B. (Ed.). *Animal marking.* London: Macmillan, 1979.

Thorpe, W. H. *The origins and rise of ethology.* New York: Praeger, 1979.

Tinbergen, N. *The study of instinct.* New York: Oxford University Press, 1951.

Tinbergen, N. *The curious naturalists.* New York: Anchor, 1968.

Trower, P. Situational analysis of the components and processes of behavior of socially skilled and unskilled patients. *Journal of Consulting and Clinical Psychology*, 1980, *48*, 327–329.

Trower, P., Bryant, B., & Argyle, M. *Social skills and mental health.* London: Methuen, 1978.

Turner, J. L. *Yes I am human: Autobiography of a "retarded" career.* Paper presented at the meeting of the American Anthropological Association, Los Angeles, 1978.

Twardosz, S., Schwartz, S., Fox, J., & Cunningham, J. L. Development and evaluation of a system to measure affectionate behavior. *Behavioral Assessment,* 1979, *1,* 177–179.

Twentyman, C. T., & McFall, R. M. Behavioral training of social skills in shy males. *Journal of Consulting and Clinical Psychology,* 1975, *43,* 384–395.

Wallander, J. L., Conger, A. J., Mariotto, M. J., Curran, J. P., & Farrell, A. D. Comparability of selection instruments in studies of heterosexual–social problem behaviors. *Behavior Therapy,* 1980, *11,* 548–560.

Wessberg, H. W., Mariotto, M. J., Conger, A. J., Farrell, A. D., & Conger, J. Ecological validity of role plays for assessing heterosocial anxiety and skill of male college students. *Journal of Consulting and Clinical Psychology,* 1979, *47,* 525–535.

Wilson, E. O. *On human nature.* Cambridge, Mass.: Harvard University Press, 1978.

Winett, R. A., Neale, M. S., & Williams, K. R. Effective field research procedures: Recruitment of participants and acquisition of reliable, useful data. *Behavioral Assessment,* 1979, *1,* 139–155.

IV

A GENERATIVE MODEL OF
SOCIAL SKILLS

Trower feels that there are a number of major problems with social skills training and research. First of all, there is no clear consensus as to the definition of social skills; hence, they are difficult to train. He feels that the current assessment techniques neglect important parameters such as the patient's own purpose, perceptions, inferences, and evaluations. There is a decided lack of knowledge of social behaviors and norms and a misunderstanding of the structure and function of social discourse, which leads to faulty training objectives. Last, there is an emphasis in social skills training on teaching component skills rather than teaching a generative capability. He feels that because we are using inappropriate paradigms based on a mechanistic model of man that we are asking the wrong questions and are addressing the wrong problems.

Trower prefers models like those proposed by Harré and Secord and by Walter Mischel. In Harré and Secord's model the person is viewed as acting as an agent directing his own behavior. Man is seen as a rational agent who chooses means (behavioral skills, etc.) that will attempt to satisfy his ends (desired rewards). Man is seen as seeking out and processing information and generating, monitoring, and controlling his actions in order to achieve goals. Mischel's model emphasizes variables such as cognitive and behavioral construction competencies, encoding strategies and personal constructs, expectancies involving behavior–outcome and stimulus–outcome relations, subjective values, and self-regulatory systems and plans. Trower proposes a generative model of social skills that includes (1) a monitoring capability of both external and internal events, (2) a performance capability, (3) goals or standards, and (4) cognitive representations and logical functions. Trower feels that his model has implications for both social skills assessment and treatment. He feels that assessment should be aimed at measuring the possession of social knowledge, the ability to produce appropriate plans, and an individual's outcome expectancies and the beliefs that generate them. Training should emphasize the process of generating social skill performance rather than teaching components of social skills. This training should also include the monitoring, logical disputing, and empirical disproving of invalid inferences and negative evaluations, which commonly function to block both the acquisition and generation of social skills.

13

TOWARD A GENERATIVE MODEL
OF SOCIAL SKILLS:
A CRITIQUE AND SYNTHESIS

PETER TROWER

INTRODUCTION

It is inevitable that after a decade or so of enthusiastic development in
social skills training, a number of serious problems should surface and
cause us some heart-searching. But these very problems may be point-
ing us in new directions, and particularly toward a better conceptual
model. They suggest to us that there is something wrong with our
working assumptions and paradigms. Questions and new paradigms
have been raised and offered by a number of eminent psychologists and
philosophers in recent years, but these questions and suggestions have
not yet been sufficiently addressed to social skills and allied training
practices—a puzzling omission in that it is with reference to social
behavior and social learning that they have such pertinence. In this
critique I shall be mainly concerned with the general practice of social
skills training because this is ultimately where the purpose of our
efforts must surely lie. In doing so, however, I shall draw on social skills
theory, research, and methodology. It may be argued that the average
downtown practitioner has little to gain from research; that is, most
self-report measures are said to be of little use in clinical practice—but
this would seem to be a strange state of affairs, and perhaps we had
better assume that research does, or is intended to, influence practice,
and we should try to ensure that we lead, rather than mislead the field.

Peter Trower. Department of Psychology, Hollymoor Hospital, Northfield, Birmingham, England.

With these points in mind, this chapter will be organized as follows. First, some of the current problems in social skills research and practice will be assessed, and an argument made that many of these problems arise directly out of certain paradigms and assumptions commonly held. Second, some new paradigms described in the literature will be reviewed, and a set of definitions based upon these tentatively offered. Third, the notion of generative social skill and its cognitive operations will be developed. Finally, suggestions will be made as to how cognitive therapy may be used as an essential first step in our main therapeutic goal, namely, to facilitate the development of a generative skill capability.

PROBLEMS AND PARADIGMS IN SOCIAL SKILLS TRAINING: A CRITIQUE

THE PROBLEMS

There is an atmosphere of great uncertainty about the assessment of social skills in patients. Unlike many other problem areas, such as phobias and addictions, which can apparently be defined operationally in quantitative terms, social skill problems are far more complex and elusive. There is uncertainty about the definition—a crucial issue since everything else follows from the way we define, and thereby, in a sense, construct the very phenomena we are addressing. As Curran (1979) says, "Unless we reach consensus about the construct we are addressing, we are likely to be building a Tower of Babel" (p. 325).

Are we dealing with social skill response deficits at a molecular level, with impressionistic dimensions at a molar level, with more cognitive failings such as social perceptions and problem-solving skills, or do we take a functional definition in terms of goal achievement, or all of these together plus some others? And behind these questions are more fundamental issues. What is the purpose of training? Who decides on the goals and objectives, on what skills the patient needs, and what the appropriate norms are?

Given the pressing needs of clinical work we do not have the time to wait for rigorous definitions and the orderly assembly of empirical knowledge, yet if we aspire to a scientific understanding, these are important questions. It was hoped that by now we would have a sufficient data base to attempt a descriptive, or better, an explanatory definition, given the extent of the experimental work that has already been done. However, in his appraisal of strategies for assessing social skill, Bellack (1979) states that "the reliability and validity of most social skill assessment procedures are uncertain. It is unclear whether the predominant assessment strategies are adequate, whether specific instruments are sound, or whether the most appropriate aspects of interpersonal functioning are being targeted." Regarding this state of our knowledge, he concludes, "We simply know much less about assessment than we must."

It is undoubtedly time, then, to critically look at our methods of obtaining data and our assumptions that guide the selection of data and our interpretation of it. There are two important sources of information in social skills assessment—the patient's own reports, and his or her behavior as observed by others, including the therapist. The general picture of assessment shows an emphasis on behavior rather than of reports by the person. However, there are some things only the patient can inform us about—his or her goals, his or her evaluation of the problem, and his or her interpretation of events, including his or her own behavior. Despite scepticism about self-reports, these seem empirically to be one of the best data sources about the individual (Mischel, 1968, 1972); this rich source appears to be tapped in the social skills field with many different types of questionnaire. However, this appearance may be more illusory than real. Apart from being flawed by serious psychometric and other inadequacies (Bellack, 1979), there is a yet more fundamental problem: they are not so much self-reports as experimenter-elicited responses, constrained by questions that are designed to test certain assumptions or constructs, occasionally bogus, and that, for the patient, may have little meaning (Curran, 1979, p. 337). I suspect that many of these questionnaires, despite claims to the contrary, still embody, or at least hover dangerously close to, the trait–state assumptions that Mischel (1968) criticized in personality questionnaires, namely, inferring internal dispositions that have enduring and generalized effects on behavior. Assertiveness, social skill, self-expression, or social anxiety scores presumably imply cross-situational consistency of behavior (e.g., "overall skill") and it is an easy step then to invoking dispositional entities that cause this. Summative scores, and other statistical abstractions like factor analysis, tend to encourage this thinking (Vernon, 1964). Taking situation clusters into account again may give an illusion of specificity, but in fact may only amount to narrow traits of the 16 PF kind, rather than broad ones of the Eysenck Personality

Inventory (EPI) kind, or traits invoked only by given situations. What these questionnaires do not tap is the subject's own accounts—his or her interpretations of stimuli, prediction and evaluation of outcomes, and so on, and in this sense are not self-reports. Indeed, the inevitable individual differences in interpretation of test items are treated as error variance and minimized if the questionnaire is well designed.

If these and Bellack's objections to questionnaires hold true, do we need to consider them further in the context of ordinary clinical practice? We believe we should, because they represent attempts to validate and clarify constructs that may be implicitly and widely held and influential in the general approach to assessment, that is, not only in psychometric analysis but in interviewing and behavioral analysis (Meehl, 1960). In other words, trait thinking may be far more pervasive than we would like to admit, and may simply be surfacing under different, more behavioral-sounding names. Let us take a construct that appears to be a respectable, empirical, and specifiable entity—social phobia. It has a good pedigree in simple phobia (e.g., snake phobia), and we try to measure it in the same way—behaviorally, physiologically, and psychologically (by means of a fear thermometer). But are we not often seduced into making the notorious category mistake of inferring a diagnostic entity behind these characteristics, and imbuing it with powers to disrupt or inhibit behavior, using it to explain behavior patterns and so on? We are reminded of Sarbin's case history of the term "anxiety," which began as a metaphor, became a disposition, and finally a mental entity (Sarbin, 1968). Its final reification from a metaphorical description of certain behavior ("like a choking sensation") to an internal cause of the same behavior was hastened by the publication of the Taylor Manifest Anxiety Scale, which was followed by a surge of published experimental inquiries into "the nature of anxiety." While there may be no good reasons why psychologists prefer a trait theory of social phobia, there are at least eminently understandable reasons why they may prefer a trait approach to social skills. As Curran (1979) says, "everyone seems to know what good and bad social skills are but no one can define them adequately." And other explanations, say in terms of operant reinforcement, do not satisfy our intuitive understanding: "If a patient's crazy talk is reinforced in the hospital setting, does that make 'crazy talk' an example of social skill?" (p. 322).

Intuition seems to inform us that there is an implicit consensus— not so far defined—about good and bad social skills and therefore by careful behavioral sampling we shall abstract the essential components and have a universal yardstick against which to measure patients' behavior. The problems inherent in this approach are well known, but must be spelled out. (1) Since the trait is a person variable, the person is presumed to take it with him and be influenced by it across different situations. (2) Only the therapist, by means of his expertise, can supposedly detect the trait, and the patient is only consulted or examined for evidence of the trait at the symptom and sign level, and certainly not for his own explanation of behavior. (3) The therapist either draws upon a test result, or may be doing no more than making a type of personality attribution from intuition when deciding upon molar categories. Neither he nor others may attempt to define the source and structure of his judgments. (4) Ratings are done on scales, which presumably measure the trait's intensity, but tell us nothing about its definition or structure. (5) Each trait or entity is independent insofar as it doesn't depend on any others for its existence or meaning, but is presumed to interact in an external manner (e.g., social skill with social phobia). (6) Situations have been considerably emphasized recently, but presumably traits interact with situations in much the same way as they interact with other traits (e.g., "social skill" with "heterosexual first encounters"). Indeed, as Mischel (1973) argues, situations are also mistakenly treated as independent entities.

The tendency to think dispositionally is a legacy both of a long tradition in clinical psychology—after all, until recent years the main work was to measure such dispositions—and the intrinsic operation (which we share with other human beings) of attributing behavioral causes to personality in others, but to situations in oneself (Jones & Nisbett, 1971).

The argument, then, turns on the status of our constructs, such as assertiveness. They appear to be closely modeled on, and indeed to some extent replace, such personality traits as extraversion, and differ in the extent to which they are given more behavioral-sounding names, and more rigorous attempts are made to operationalize the constructs behaviorally. Such traits will have the status of implicit and intuitive social stereotypes, no doubt widely shared, which are retrieved to fill in for missing information. Thus, when focusing on deficits in the patient (e.g., the occurrence of certain patterns of gaze, facial expression, and so on) it makes sense to us as deficient because of our own tacit knowledge (i.e., norms for behavior appropriate to a particular idealized stereotype, which this particular behavior falls short of). It may be these stereotypes that we tap when we ask naïve (untrained) raters to judge videotaped samples of behavior.

If the above argument is true, how has it escaped notice? The answer may lie in the fact that as official behavioral scientists we adhere to the behavioral doctrine that decrees that cognitive phenomena are epiphenomena, that we must stay closely with the behavioral data, and reject trait constructs not only in our own verbal behavior but in that of the patient. This of course clashes with our intuition, leading us perhaps to repress our awareness of them, and by a quickness of the empirical hand that deceives the mind's eye, institutionalize our cognitive stereotypes in statistically respectable measuring instruments and operationalize them in terms of behavioral components.

As behavioral scientists we spend our best efforts doing the proper scientific task of gathering hard data (behavioral assessment), specifying, for example, the duration and frequency of nonverbal and verbal elements. But as strict behavioral scientists, what informs us that any particular response is deficient or important, since intuition (i.e., tacit knowledge) is no longer legitimate? How are elements to be selected and grouped? Are we to equate a skilled response to anything that is positively reinforced? What we lack, of course, are explicit behavioral baseline norms that are essential to provide assessment criteria and suitable training targets (O'Donnell, 1977), and to evaluate outcome (Kazdin, 1977). Since we can't seem to do without them, what we do is to use our implicit norms surreptitiously without referencing them—note, for example, the paucity of specific reference to norms in outcome studies, pointed out in those few studies that are the exception to the rule (e.g., Goldsmith & McFall, 1975; Hollandsworth & Cooley, 1978). It is highly unlikely that research trainers did not use norms in their training; it is more likely that trainers used them implicitly, intuitively, unsystematically, and unofficially. How else could they proceed with training? ("No, that doesn't feel quite right. Try again with your hands in your pockets. Ah, yes, much better.")

We seem, then, to be caught on the horns of a dilemma—neither the dispositional way nor the behavioral way seems satisfactory. What we may end up doing is not choosing between the two approaches but combining them, behaving officially like behavioral scientists and unofficially like intuitive human beings. We intuitively select our traits (after all, where did they come from before we institutionalized them?), erect them into independent variables or parameters, and then behaviorally analyze them and modify them. What is the effect of this unholy marriage?

Let us consider the perceived importance of global categories (alias traits, constructs, stereotypes, or implicit norms). They have high face validity and seem closely related to the criterion in most studies. Our usual practice has been to take such a molar category as warmth or assertiveness, and, as reported above, to take sample situations in which behavior rated high or low on such a variable are exhibited, and to measure the main molecular elements in terms of mean frequencies and durations, thus (it is hoped) arriving at an operational definition. However, this is a questionable approach. To use an analogy, imagine a linguist who seeks the proportion of nouns, verbs, and so forth in the hope of defining what a sentence is. In practice he will be totally perplexed by such data as 2.3 nouns, 1.8 verbs, or whatever per sentence. Curran (1979) points to the same problem when he is asked whether four 10-second eye glances or three 15-second eye glances are more skillful. In fact, we are worse off than our imaginary linguist, since we do not seem able to partition our molar categories and molecular elements with the precision of sentences, words, and morphemes. Marking out segments of interaction or discourse as we do in role-play tests may not at all coincide with the natural junctures of episodes in conversation (viz., sentences) nor do the discrete behavioral elements that we choose to measure necessarily coincide within an episode of skilled assertiveness (viz., words and morphemes). Moreover, the elements we do identify can hardly aspire to an operational definition of assertiveness (i.e., they are not complete), but at best represent a certain percentage of the complete "package" we aspire to, which is yet to be empirically established. Yet assertive training experiments often appear to be conducted on the basis that we do possess such a complete definition. Even if we are more circumspect and accept that our knowledge is incomplete, we still do not question the validity of global categories or parameters.

Additionally, we have the practice of carving up segments of interaction into what we believe fit or exemplify our categories, and rating and measuring them as independent and discrete units, thus "disembedding" them from their normal context. Recent research shows that units of discourse are embedded in a hierarchical manner in larger units (e.g., strings of exchanges within a transaction), and that smaller units derive their meanings from the larger ones (Coulthard, 1977). For example, we cannot judge the skill of a subject from an isolated segment without knowledge of the higher order categories and personal and cultural (and other) background information (and most importantly without knowing the patient's intentions). It is in this regard that situations are crucial. Situations provide the context—the rules, the roles, and goals—in which episodes and their elements are identified, defined, and understood (Argyle, 1979). A raised hand, for example, may be a part of a greeting, a bid to hold the floor, to speak, or to be excused, a nonverbal emblem, or it may have no social meaning at all. However, taking mean ratings or measures on trait-type disembedded categories and elements across situations effectively destroys the very information we seek (Gergen, 1978). And there are other problems in the experimental assessment situation. Subjects become internally rather than externally focused (i.e., self-conscious), radically altering their behavior (Duval & Wicklund, 1972). Experimental constraints designed to reduce "redundant" variables tend to artificially distort situations and create abnormal behavior that is then attributed to the patient by the rater, rather than the situation itself (Jones & Nisbett, 1971).

There are yet further problems in this marriage of intuitive unofficial trait thinking and behavioral practice pertaining to a rather curious feature of social skills training. Having empirically established only a fragment of skill responses, we proceed to train patients in these fragmentary responses, and somehow expect the patients, at least theoretically, to become skilled. If we are not being absurdly naïve, we are again implicitly attributing competence to the patient, assuming that he or she really knows the rest, and will know what to do with these few elements that we teach him or her, assuming they are relevant. (Otherwise we must believe the patient will simply emit the right responses because "right" equates with reinforced.) Here is another example of doublethink—the one official doctrine, the other intuitive attribution. Failure to question our intuitions allows mistaken attributions of competence to go unnoticed, with unfortunate consequences for training and generalization.

Ironically, the dispositions not only come out of heads, but out of the heads of the experimenters, so that whatever their validity status as truly descriptive of the patient, they are not obtained from the patient but imposed upon him or her. Skepticism of trait and other constructs within the strict behavioral paradigm invites us to ignore the patient's own cognitive constructions, and to treat him or her scientifically as if he or she didn't think. Or, as perhaps Harré and Secord (1972) might more dramatically put it, this skepticism allows us to treat subjects for scientific purposes, as if they were not human beings. In a wider context, and in a different way, Mischel (1973) warns against the same tendency: he points out that a focus on behavior must not obscure the fact that even the definition and selection of a behavior unit for study requires grouping and categorizing. The psychologist includes and excludes events in the units he studies, depending on his interests and objectives. However, the subject also selects and categorizes events into meaningful units, in terms of personal constructs. "Skepticism about the utility of traditional trait constructs regarding the subject's broad dispositions in no way requires one to ignore the subject's constructs about his own and others' characteristics. . . . It would be strange if we tried to define out of existence the personal constructs and other concepts, perceptions and experiences of the individuals whom we are studying" (Mischel, 1973, p. 208).

In summary, it may be argued:

1. There is no clear consensus of what social skill is, which makes it difficult to say what the practice of social skills training is

2. Assessment techniques are not geared to answering the right questions, such as the patient's own purpose, perceptions, inferences, and evaluations

3. There is a lack of knowledge of social behavior and norms and rules, which are by default implicitly supplied by the therapist and may be wrong

4. There is a misunderstanding of the structure and function of social discourse and social situations, giving rise to faulty train ing objectives

5. There is an emphasis on teaching component skills rather than social skills per se (i.e., the generative capability). These problems (I suggest) may well be largely due to the paradigms we employ.

THE PARADIGMS

It is the job of philosophers of science and others to question the presuppositions that lie behind our perceptions and hypotheses, and that thereby go unnoticed. In other words, scientists may fail to solve problems not because they lack empirical knowledge, but because they are asking the wrong questions. If the latter is the case, no amount of investigation will help: the assumptions must be changed. It is the opinion of some authorities that the paradigms that guide research in, for example, social psychology, are indeed mistaken. Given the types of problems in social skills research outlined, it would seem proper to question the paradigms in this area also.

The principles that still guide much work in social skills are to some extent the same as those which Harré and Secord (1972) criticized in the area of social psychology, and Mischel (1968, 1972) criticized in the field of personality. Harré and Secord (1972) and Harré (1977) outline what they term the "old paradigms." The first is the mechanistic model of man, who is seen as a passive organism who responds to the external push and pull of forces exerted by the environment. In the classic stimulus–response view, the organism is subjected to a certain stimulus, and responds in a predictable manner, or, in the stimulus–organism–response view, changes in the organism lead to changes in the responses not directly predictable from the immediate stimulus alone. Such a paradigm may be termed the "billiard ball" model of causality (i.e., the Humean theory of cause, which is essentially that cause is a statistical probabilistic relation between independent events) that is nothing more than the regular sequence of one kind of event, and another that usually follows. The things in which the cause–effect relation occurs play the part only of bearers of this externally applied impetus.

Third, there is logical positivist methodology. This doctrine stressed operationism as a theory of definition, and the principle of verification as a theory of meaning. Propositional assertions were to be reduced to their elementary constituents or logical atoms, which were thought to correspond to absolutely simple observational facts. From these could be built more complex propositions. These paradigms led to the classic experimentation methods that Harré (1977) calls parametric science, in which the experimenter seeks to discover the relations between logically independent entities or variables, which are not internally related:

> The gas law $PV = RT$, relating pressure, volume and temperature, is a relation between parameters such that one can hold constant any one parameter and vary the others, and the property represented by that parameter will remain unaffected by the abstraction. As far as pressure, volume and temperature are concerned, a gas is not a structure of internally related properties. On the other hand an element of an internally related structure ceases to be that element if detached from the structure. In a parametric process the elements interact causally but retain their identity and do not change in type if detached from the structure. . . . In a structured entity the component parts derive their meanings from the other details to which they are internally related. A handshake is not the same action when embedded in a betting routine as when part of a greeting. (pp. 286–287)

Mischel's criticism of trait theory is too well known for us to repeat here, except to say that where Harré and Secord criticize external causal explanations and atomism, Mischel attacks a kind of modern mentalism in which internal variables are inferred to account for behavior. However, both internal (personality) and external (situational) accounts are equally open to the objections of the Harré and Secord critique, the only difference being that the push and pull of forces are inside as well as outside. Dispositional theories are just as parametric as behavioral theories, and indeed some psychologists have combined the two in the form of an interactional model. In this model person parameters interact with situation parameters, and the outcome is a function of this interaction, embodied in the prime parametric statistical tool, analysis of variance. Endler and Edwards (1978) indeed describe the mechanistic model of interaction in just such terms, though they also justifiably argue for its descriptive, rather than explanatory, value.

There are a number of consequences for social skills training that tend to follow from the old paradigms and we shall mention two of the most important. The first point, already referred to, is the disembedding of an item of interaction from its context, believing it to retain its identity and meaning. Thus, a single item such as an unreasonable request, removed from context, forms the stimulus, and the subject's answer, the response, the latter being rated for assertiveness. As Gergen (1978) says, far from exploring the embeddedness of stimuli in their complex spatial and temporal contexts, the experimentalist's aim is to rigorously disembed the stimulus from its surroundings, thereby rendering its meaning obscured or destroyed. What distinguishes social skill from other phenomena is its interactive nature—A's question logically depends upon B's answer (or response) and it is the synchronous relation between A and B's reciprocal exchange that is at the heart of social skill. This is what is obscure or destroyed. In terms of parametric thinking, almost any phenomenon may be labeled as independent and internally homogenous. In assessment it may be a global category or a discrete behavior, and in treatment the same global category or discrete behavior becomes the target of change. In assessment we diagnose social phobia and social skill deficiency at one level, and lack of eye gaze at the other. In training and outcome we target upon the same variables.

The second point is that the patient/subject may, in the parametric model, be regarded as a passive, more or less powerless organism who does not process information and choose actions but who is controlled either by external reinforcing contingencies or internal dispositions, which in turn implies a powerful therapist who assesses the patient's dysfunction on external cues, signs, and responses, who decides upon the appropriate training and dispenses it. In social skills problems this is more serious than in, say, anxiety problems, since the therapist not only decides what the deficit is, but also invariably decides what skills the patient should have to function in the environment. We have already seen the terms in which such dysfunctions are couched—the objective language of parametric and behavioral science, such as anxiety, a social phobia, a skill deficiency that the patient has, a lack of eye gaze, and other specific deficits that he or she exhibits. We can hardly imagine a patient complaining, "I've a terrible social phobia," or "I'm really depressed about my social skills deficit," or "What I really want to do in life is increase my eye-gaze behavior."

Likewise, the therapist decides upon goals, or targets, and homework assignments: "Keep a record of the number of glances each day," or "Maintain two minutes' conversation with three people each day." And as discussed earlier, the therapist's goal (not the patient's) is to train the patient up to a criterion in elements of deficient behavior, thinking these will enable him or her to be assertive. We may even teach the patient perceptual skills—of recognizing certain cues. But what we may fail to do, because we are guided in our own perceptions by mechanistic principles, is to teach the patient how to generate social skills, to which we shortly turn.

NEW PARADIGMS AND DEFINITIONS: A REVIEW

Underlying Mischel's discussion of the common misconceptions of his position is the strong implication that researchers mistakenly believe that they must choose between the extremes of personality dispositional accounts of behavior and situational/conditioning accounts, which imply a personalityless view of man. There is in fact a third way, which is not a combination of these two, as is the mechanistic interactional model, but nonetheless embraces behavioral (learning) and cognitive phenomena without being either mechanistic or mentalistic. Both Harré and Secord (1972) on the one hand, and Mischel (1973) and Bandura (1977) on the other put forward, in different ways (the former more conceptual, the latter more empirical), models that explicate the paradigms that should be considered for social skills. (There are many others whose models have a family resemblance to these: in cognitive psychology and cognitive therapy, in ethnomethodology, in microsociology, and in social psychology.) We shall, for space reasons, limit ourselves to a brief description, first of Harré and Secord's, then of Mischel's approaches, before discussing the new directions intrinsic to both.

HARRÉ AND SECORD'S MODEL

Regularities in human behavior may be explained in one of two ways: (1) the person as object responding to the push and pull of forces, (2) the person acting as an agent directing his or her own behavior. The latter model, as elaborated by a prominent school of modern philosophy, is the one adopted by Harré and Secord. Briefly, this is the long-debated anthropomorphic view of human beings as rational agents, who choose means (behavioral skills, etc.) that will attempt to satisfy their ends (desired rewards). Ends, or goals, are one of the main principles around which behavior is organized. In this model the agent is active rather than passive—he or she seeks out and processes information, and generates, monitors, and controls his or her actions (rather than being impinged upon by stimuli and responding reflexively) in order to achieve goals. The concept of agent (Harré, 1979) entails that a person can represent to himself or herself a wider range of possible actions than can be realized, can realize from these possibilities a course of action, and can abort any particular course of action for another. The actions are generated according to and constrained by rules—both discourse rules and situation rules—that make the actions both intelligible (comprehensive to others) and warrantable (permissible and proper). However, a person not only monitors his or her performance but monitors his or her monitoring (and is capable of self-intervention). This second-order monitoring allows for a continuity of conscious self-awareness and hence awareness of self. The view of people as rational agents, together with the structural science framework, form the basis of Harré and Secord's "The Explanation of Social Behaviour" (1972) (elaborated by Harré, 1979).

Their argument is as follows. As agents we have the power of action. We monitor our actions, but because we also are aware of our monitoring and have the power of speech, we can provide commentaries upon and accounts of our performances, and plan ahead of them as well. The power to plan and give accounts and commentaries is the feature around which the science of psychology must turn. In the anthropomorphic model of human beings we not only have the person as agent but the person as watcher, commentator, and critic as well. It follows from this that the most characteristic form of human behavior is the conscious following of rules and the intentional carrying out of plans. The authors use a number of arguments (e.g., Strawson's arguments on the logically adequate criteria for the ascription of mental predicates; Strawson, 1959), to conclude that it is possible to treat people, for scientific purposes, as if they were human beings. It should be pointed out that Harré and Secord do not claim that people always consciously monitor, or that they are never passive responders to stimuli, but that these exceptions in fact highlight the generative process in most social behavior and in the learning of behavioral sequences.

Harré and Secord assert that if we are to understand the meanings people assign to stimuli in the environment and the rules and conventions they follow in generating and monitoring social behavior, then we must study actual past or present real-life interactions or realistic role-play simulations (see Ginsberg, 1979, for a discussion of the latter) plus the accounts actors give of them. Most of these interactions can be analyzed into episodes, that is, naturally occurring chunks that have identifiable internal structures. Most of these have a beginning and an end, often marked by some ritual, the best known (and studied) being greetings and partings. Sociolinguists and others (e.g., Goffman, 1972) have already established the structure of many social episodes in this way, as we shall later show. Harré and Secord argue that we should study the structure and genesis of formal episodes as models or paramorphs for understanding "enigmatic" or informal episodes. Episodes consist not of response components but of acts and actions—since the emphasis is on things done by rather than to a person—and a sequence of actions complete a recognizable act (such as introducing someone) from which the component actions in turn obtain their meanings. They call this the act/action structure of the episode. Episodes are also bounded by action-guiding rules, some of which will define elements and the meanings and purpose of the episode, others will define the roles of individuals. Formal episodes will have the most explicit set of rules. This analysis is very close to that used by Argyle (1979) in the analysis of situations.

Harré and Secord discuss the principle of checking empirically people's accounts (e.g., by level of consensus). The point emerges here, of course, that social reality is not objective but intersubjective, and that more enigmatic episodes themselves and the accounts given of them are negotiated against the required background of intelligibility and warrantability.

Harré (1977) gives considerable emphasis to cognitive processes, by means of which rule-following action sequences are generated. A person's competence (as opposed to performance) resides in a cognitive "template," which represents a required action sequence. One assumes that to have competence, the capability to perform skilfully, one must have the cognitive representations. Isolated, unskilled individuals may lack these publicly shared representations, and may have idiosyncratic ones, producing behavior that is neither intelligible nor warrantable.

Similar suggestions to those of Harré appear in the theory of scripts put forward (and tested in computer models) by Schank and Abelson (1977). They propose that part of our knowledge is organized around hundreds of stereotypic situations with routine activities (e.g., riding a bus, visiting a dentist, asking for directions, and so on). Through direct or vicarious experience, each person acquires hundreds of such cultural stereotypes. Schank and Abelson (1977) use the term "script" to refer to the memory structure a person has of the stereotype. An example is the restaurant script in Table 13-1. As with other scripts, it has standard roles, props, or objects, conditions for entering the activity, a standard sequence of actions where one action enables or prescribes the next, and some normal results from performing the activity accurately. In a series of experiments and using a methodology we may well emulate in establishing the structure of situations, Bower, Black, and Turner (1979) explored some of the psychological implications of script theory. They found high agreement among subjects not only in generating the "basic action" language of situations ($r = .8$ to $.88$), but also on how to segment the event sequences into constituent scenes or chunks. Such high agreement is essential since participants in a situation must have similar schemata to mutually define and cooperate in the joint activity. "Thus in analyzing the incorporation of strangers into a group (e.g., a party) we will want to say that host, sponsor, and stranger somehow each contain a replica of the structure of the ceremony of incorporation. It is by the transformation of that template into the medium of action that they produce the actual action sequence" (Harré, 1977, p. 289). One way, then, of assessing the intersubjective validity of patients' scripts may be by assessing the degree of concordance with "normals."

The situations used by Bower et al. (1979) were rather structured, so that high agreement might be expected (as it would, for example, of a

TABLE 13-1. Theoretical Restaurant Script

Name:	Restaurant	Props:	Tables	Roles:	Customer
			Menu		Waiter
			Food		Cook
			Bill		Cashier
			Money		Owner
			Tip		
Entry Conditions:		Customer hungry		Results:	Customer has less money
		Customer has money			Owner has more money
					Customer is not hungry

Scene 1: Entering
    Customer enters restaurant
    Customer looks for table
    Customer decides where to sit
    Customer goes to table
    Customer sits down

Scene 2: Ordering
    Customer picks up menu
    Customer looks at menu
    Customer decides on food
    Customer signals waitress
    Waitress comes to table
    Customer orders food
    Waitress goes to cook
    Waitress gives food order to cook
    Cook prepares food

Scene 3: Eating
    Cook gives food to waitress
    Waitress brings food to customer
    Customer eats food

Scene 4: Exiting
    Waitress writes bill
    Waitress goes over to customer
    Waitress gives bill to customer
    Customer gives tip to waitress
    Customer goes to cashier
    Customer gives money to cashier
    Customer leaves restaurant

Note. Adapted from Schank and Abelson (1977).

wedding service). But the model can be applied to ordinary discourse. Ventola (1979) has done such an analysis on the sequences common in casual conversation, namely,

$$G\ Ad\ Id\ Ap\ C\ Lt\ Gb$$

where G = greeting, Ad = address, Id = identification, Ap = approach (direct and indirect), C = centering (topics), Lt = leave taking, and Gb = goodbye.

There are obviously certain important types of social cues that will activate schemata or scripts of the type we have discussed, and there are wide individual differences in the types of cues attended to, but this topic is beyond the scope of the present chapter, and readers are referred to Scherer and Giles (1979).

The structural or ethogenic approach put forward by Harré and Secord has been influential in social psychology in recent years, stimulating changes in approaches that some (Backman, 1979) have described as signs of a paradigmatic revolution in social psychology.

SOCIAL LEARNING THEORY

Mischel (1973) and Bandura (1977) have also developed an alternative model, the (cognitive) social learning theory of social behavior, which is similar in some of its principles—though differently stated—and important in its comprehensiveness. After criticizing trait theories, Mischel (1973) beings his account by showing how an examination of the phenomena of dispositional attribution common among psychologists and lay people alike can lead us to a better conceptualization. "In the present view the study of global traits may ultimately reveal more about the cognitive activity of the trait theorist than about the causes of behavior, but such findings would be of great value in their own right" (p. 264). In the search for person variables, we should look, he suggests, more specifically at what the person constructs in particular conditions rather than inferring what broad traits he or she generally has. Mischel (1973) puts forward five suggestions.

First, through direct and observational learning the individual acquires information about the world and the potential to generate vast repertoires of organized behavior, including among many other things, the social rules and conventions that guide conduct. Some theorists have discussed these acquisitions in terms of the products of information processing and of information integration, others in terms of schemata and cognitive templates. Presumably these schemata or representations of reality are similar to those referred to by Harré and Secord, and would include scripts that guide perception and prescribe action via the selection of component skills. However, while Harré and Secord tend to emphasize situation schemata, Mischel gives emphasis to trait stereotypes or "person schemata" (my terms), and clearly both types operate. Person schemata, whether applied to self or other, also guide both perceptions and behavior. Snyder and Swann (1978) for example, showed how people used social interaction to actively test their hypotheses about other people's personality traits, and Snyder, Tanke, and Berscheid (1977) revealed that people used their stereotypic beliefs about others to guide their behavior toward them (both experiments also revealed how such beliefs also produce self-fulfilling prophecies, to which we will later return). Mischel uses the term "cognitive and behavioral construction competencies" to emphasize that the observer selectively constructs (generates) his renditions of reality, as empirically shown in modeling experiments. Mischel makes useful suggestions about how such competencies can be measured, for example, by using the methods used in achievement testing, emphasizing what the person can do rather than what he or she usually does. It seems that IQ tests may be a good model, where actual tasks are carried out. Research suggests in fact that intellectual and interpersonal competencies may be related, at least conceptually. In short, measuring capability is likely to give a stable and enduring picture.

Mischel's second cognitive variable he terms "encoding strategies and personal constructs." Research shows that a person's selective attention, interpretation, and categorization substantially alters the impact that a stimulus exerts on behavior, and influences what he learns and subsequently can do. In other words, people group and encode the same events and behaviors differently from each other, and information is filtered in a manner that permits it to be integrated with existing schemata, after which it remains available enduringly and exerts further stabilizing effects. The way information is explained and organized depends upon which cognitive schemata are salient (Taylor & Fiske, 1978). Normally, others' behavior is attributed to their dispositions (person-schema-salient), while one's own behavior is explained according to the situation (situation-schema-salient; Jones & Nisbett, 1971). However, when self-focused, one's own behavior is explained according to one's own self-disposition (person-schema-salient; Duval & Wicklund, 1972). A number of authors have shown that knowledge of one's own actions is also organized and represented by cognitive self-schemata (Markus, 1977) that in turn channel the further processing of information about the self and guide subsequent behavior. This raises the idea that socially unskilled behavior would trigger self-focus (Storms & McCaul, 1976) and thereby be interpreted as due to a self-disposition, say, of inadequacy (Trower, 1981). The operation of negative self-beliefs of this kind in selective attention and memory have been investigated in various social problems. Clark and Arkowitz (1975) found that highly anxious men overestimated negative aspects of their performance in conversations with women, and O'Banion and Arkowitz (1977) found that highly anxious women selectively remembered negative information about their performance in conversation with men. Forgus and DeWolfe (1974) found that delusional patients would selectively encode incoming information along dimensions relevant to their delusional themes.

Mischel's third variable moves us on from competence to performance, from what he calls construction capacity and constructs to the construction of behavior. The main variables here are the subject's expectancies about the consequences of different behavioral possibilities. These expectancies or hypotheses guide the person's selection of behaviors from among the enormous number that he or she is capable of constructing within any situation. Although often overlooked by psychologists, subjects can report their expectancies and hence these are available for systematic assessment. One type of expectancy concerns behavior outcome relations, or awareness of the reinforcing contingencies, and leads to choosing and generating actions predicted to produce the best outcome rather than simply emitting an operant that is contingently reinforced. The other type of expectancy concerns stimulus–outcome relations—a cognitive reconceptualization of classical conditioning. The individual learns that certain events (cues, stimuli) predict certain other events or outcomes (rather than simply being a conditioned stimulus). Most social signals have predictive significance in this sense. Mischel (1973) suggests that an adequate study of stimulus–outcome relations would require attention to the idiosyncratic rule system of the individual as well as to the shared sign grammar of the culture and of the transcultural lexicon structure (p. 271). If performance depends on people's expectancies we wil have no way of predicting or understanding the occurrence or nonoccurrence of performance if we fail to ask. This is especially so with patients who will have idiosyncratic and pessimistic outcome expectancies, often resulting from their biased encoding strategies (Beck, 1976). Hence the patient who fails his homework assignment: "I could have told you I couldn't do it—you should have asked."

People act not only on the basis of expectancies, but also on the basis of subjective values, that is, the degree to which they value the outcome. So Mischel (1973) states in his fourth principle that we must also consider the individual's particular stimulus preferences and aversions. These would be stimuli with the power to invoke positive or negative emotional states. Here again Mischel has a number of useful assessment suggestions.

Mischel terms his final variable self-regulatory systems and plans. Persons set performance goals for themselves and react with self-criticism or self-satisfaction to their behavior depending on how well it matches their expectations and criteria (see below). The essence of the self-regulatory system is the subject's adoption of contingency rules that guide his or her behavior in the absence of, and sometimes in spite of, immediate external situational pressures. Self-control is achieved by self-instructions, cognitive transformations and covert rewards for achieving subgoals, by means of plans.

IMPLICATIONS FOR SOCIAL SKILL: A DEFINITION

Let us now return, in the light of this different orientation, to the more practical question of the definition of social skill.

Investigators agree on the importance of defining social skill, but are less agreed about what the definition should contain. Some suggest that only component motor skills should be included, others that it should contain cognitive elements. In the spirit of the structural paradigm I suggest a twofold distinction (Trower, 1980).

First, *social skills* are the actual normative component behaviors or actions—single elements (looks, nods, lexical items, etc.) or identifiable sequences of elements, or acts or scripts (greetings, etc.)—that ordinary people use in social interaction and that are governed by rules. Such components are learned by experience or observation, retained in memory in symbolic form, and subsequently retrieved for use in the construction of episodes, much as words or phrases are retrieved for use in the production of language. The function of a component would depend on any intrinsic meaning (such as a smile or a greeting) and on its meaning in the context of the larger episode.

Second, *social skill* refers to the process of generating skilled behavior, directed to a goal. The social skills model put forward by Argyle and Kendon (1967) was in fact a process model—the individual consciously monitors the immediate situation and his or her behavior and modifies his or her performance in the light of continuous external feedback and internal criteria such as a desired outcome. In the generation of skilled behavior the individual draws on his or her repertoire of components, organizing them into new sequences according to discourse and situation rules and his or her own goals and subgoals, a process that may often involve learning new components or scripts. It seems to us that the main emphasis in the literature has been on social skills (though not quite in the way defined above), and that social skill has been considerably neglected—with certain notable exceptions (e.g., Bellack & Hersen, 1978; Wallace, Nelson, Lukoff, Webster, Rappe, & Ferris, 1978). For this and other reasons we shall focus for the rest of this chapter on generative processes rather than components.

It is important to make one further, superordinate definitional distinction as follows:

> 1. Social competence is the possession of the capability to generate skilled behavior (i.e., the possession of skill and skills), in keeping with the notion of competencies suggested by Mischel and powers suggested by Harré and Secord.
> 2. Social performance is the actual production of skilled behavior in specific situations and requires what Harré and Secord call the enabling conditions and what Mischel calls the appropriate expectancies and subjective values.

THE NOTION OF GENERATIVE SOCIAL SKILL: A SYNTHESIS

We shall now consider in some detail the actual generative process of social skill. The important variables (and arguably a logically necessary part of the definition) are (1) monitoring capability (of both external and internal events); (2) a performance capability (monitored); (3) goals or standards; (4) cognitive representations and logical functions.

Carver (1979) has recently presented an information-processing/ cybernetic model that encompasses the social skills model, and the main variables we have emphasized. It is a humanized version of a feedback-loop theory (Trower, 1979), of which the most explicit is the TOTE (Miller, Galanter, & Pribram, 1960), and consists of a test phase—matching of an input to a standard; an operate phase—attempt to change the existing state of affairs; a second test phase; and finally an exit phase if matching to standard is achieved. Carver (1979) presents the model in the form of a number of propositions, which we take the liberty of adapting and adopting.

Conscious attention (monitoring) may be directed outward to the environment (social cues, etc.) or inward to the self (encompassing proprioceptive feedback, present or past physical behavior, encoded information, attitudes, self-dispositions, etc.).

When attention is directed to the environment, incoming stimulus information is processed, leading to classification of that input in a schema or "recognitory prototype." Such schemata are what we have elsewhere called tacit knowledge and are not themselves the focus of attention but provide the frame or context in which perception can take place. There is some evidence that situations as a whole are represented as schemata (situation schemata or scripts), and persons are also represented in the form of our familiar traits (person schemata).

Carver (1979) suggests that the individual makes a comparison of incoming information with preexisting recognitory schemata (i.e., "recognize" what stimuli mean), and I suggest that situation and person schemata are the two main types. In this way social stimuli appear to inform us what the situation is; personality of the other and so on enable us to make inferences. Social stimuli also help channel the perceptual search for relevant information (relevant, that is, to the schema). One of the main functions of such schemata is to enable the individual to generate behavior in accordance with rules, which brings us to Carver's next point—that the schema used to identify social stimuli invokes in the person a behavioral standard, which is to follow rules and conform to the appropriate role for a situation. These behavioral standards are used in the test phase of the TOTE, and the test itself operates whenever conditions produce self-awareness in the individual.

So far we have dealt with outwardly directed monitoring. What happens when monitoring is directed inward to the self? Apparently much the same thing happens: information is matched against a recognitory schema, in this case a self-schema, and the schema invokes a behavioral standard. For example, people made self-aware wil behave more in accordance with those self-dispositions, self-beliefs, and standards (Pryor, Gibbons, Wicklund, Fazio, & Hood, 1977; Snyder, 1979).

The test phase, then, involves monitoring (internal and external) and comparison with the standard. A standard can have a positive or negative valence—that is, a desired or undesired goal—and will vary in importance, that is, subjective value (Mischel, 1973). Then we move to the operate phase—if there is a discrepancy between standard and performance, this will lead to discrepancy reduction (i.e., increased conformity to the standard) or matching to standard. Testing and operating, or monitoring and matching, form the essence of the normal social skill process—a cycle that continues until the goal is achieved.

Up to this point the process is partially automatic, especially if it involves only the monitoring of scripted behavior (Schneider & Schiffrin, 1977), but if something impedes the matching-to-standard process, behavior is interrupted and an assessment phase or controlled processing (i.e., fully conscious) is evoked. If assessment leads to a favorable outcome expectancy, there is a return to the cycle, but if outcome expectancy is unfavorable this may lead to withdrawal or selection of another behavior (e.g., Fiedler & Beach, 1978). If a person assesses that he or she lacks the necessary skill to carry out the discrepancy reduction, that is, has low efficacy expectations (Bandura, 1977) he or she may withdraw. Additionally, that person will become self-focused. He or she will withdraw earlier in the matching-to-standard sequence when self-focus is high, as will happen as a result of a failure experience. This is because the individual in the self-focusing mode now assesses himself or herself as self-deficient (Fenigstein, 1974), unable to cope, and failing to match self-standards. And as Carver (1979) states, if individuals cannot withdraw, they may be "frozen in the self-assessment phase of the sequence, where they repeatedly reconfront the evidence of their own inadequacy" (p. 1266), and as objects of their own conscious attention may label themselves dispositionally, thus acquiring a negative self-schema. Finally, if a person infers that he or she cannot alter behavior to match the standard, this may lead to negative affect in proportion to the importance of the standard and the magnitude of the discrepancy. Additionally, the negative affect is higher when self-focus is high, and associated with the self when attributed to self-deficiency.

Now the skill process would normally involve a continuous switching from external to internal monitoring, from the incoming feedback with its cue implications for behavior, to internal beliefs and standards, which in turn will guide behavior, the outcome often being a compromise between, or coordination of, situation demands and personal goals. However, there is a body of evidence that skilled individuals tend to be external monitors and situation-oriented, while unskilled individuals tend to be internal monitors and self-oriented, a distinction developed by Snyder and his colleagues (Snyder, 1974; Snyder & Monson, 1975). To speculate, consider two imaginary individuals, one skilled and one unskilled.

The skilled person, being an external monitor, will be a relatively accurate perceiver of those situations and person cues that will guide him or her in appropriate rule-following behavior. He or she will possess situation and person schemata that are intersubjectively valid (i.e., shared by the community), so that his or her inferences from social cues will be valid and subsequent behavior will be intelligible and warrantable (Harré, 1977). Outcome expectancies (inferences) will be empirically based, and have reasonable predictive validity; he or she will have reasonably factual knowledge of his or her capabilities, and the difficulties presented by the situation. This person's self-evaluation of competence (self-efficacy evaluation) will also be empirically based, reflecting past successes and failures, and predicting future successes and failures (self-efficacy expectations).

In comparison, the unskilled person, being an internal monitor, will tend to miss crucially informative situation cues. This person may have social schemata that are not intersubjectively valid but idiosyncratic (e.g., paranoid person schemata), guiding him or her to search for socially inappropriate cues and/or to make inferences from cues that will not be valid, giving rise to subsequent behavior that is negatively received and responded to by others (Beck, 1976). Being an internal monitor, his or her beliefs and self-perceptions will tend to guide his or her perceiving and behaving. Self-standards may be unrealistic and unachievable, ensuring that no matching to standard can be achieved (e.g., the self-standard must be "the best possible"), matching to such a standard may be essential (an absolute demand rather than a relative preference), and achievement must be absolutely perfect (with no single failure) rather than relatively close (Ellis & Grieger, 1977). Being unskilled anyway, the discrepancy between standard and performance thus becomes unbridgeable.

Even for more realistic goals, such a person may have negative outcome expectations that are not empirically based, but derived from isolated instances of failure, the consequent withdrawal ensuring that no firm data base, or competence, is built up. Being thus prone to failure experiences, he or she becomes self-focused, thereby set for attributing failure to self, deriving the inevitable negative self-disposition (Ickes & Layden, 1978). Such self-evaluations will then serve to channel future perceptions (cognitive bolstering) and future performance, which in turn produces negative responses from others (behavioral confirmation), producing a self-perpetuating cycle or self-fulfilling prophecy (Snyder, 1978; Trower, 1981). The extraordinarily pernicious role of negative self-dispositions can thus be seen. Since all dispositions or traits imply a permanent underlying essence or intrinsicness, such characteristics will also apply to a self-attributed trait. In Albert Ellis's terms, any global "self-downing" belief is synonymous with intrinsic worthlessness and so forth, permanent inadequacy, and zero-outcome expectancies.

One of the predictions from these considerations is that skilled external monitors would vary their behavior across different situations, responding to cues, while unskilled internal monitors would be cross-situationally consistent (Moos, 1968), responding to internal beliefs (Snyder & Monson, 1975; Trower, 1980). Trower found that unskilled patients varied their behavior less across various phases of a situation than a skilled group, and there was evidence that the first group was not responding to planted situation cues, especially implicit, nonverbal ones. Unskilled patients did not appear to be obeying situation rules, such as to talk in first encounters. The production of self-fulfilling prophecies via the perceptual and behavioral channeling of negative self-beliefs blocks the social skill generative process, by means of cognitive bolstering and behavioral confirmation effects. This presents a problem for social skills training. At the end of the day the patient will simply report: "I could have told you it wouldn't work—you should have asked." Research elsewhere has shown the power of client expectancies on outcome (Bootzin & Lick, 1979).

Because the process of generating socially skilled behavior has to be by definition closely related to the realities of the social environment, inferences and evaluations must be empirical and rational, and goals must be achievable in the real world. We may say, then, that the essential cognitive processes must include relatively valid inferences from cues, about self and others, and relatively realistic self-standards, so that matching to standard is possible and acceptable—relative (success and failure) rather than absolute (success only) matching to standards. These cognitive processes are in addition to the possession of a repertoire of behavioral component skills. Concentration on teaching component skills or scripts or even rules and roles will not achieve the objective if, for example, the patient is setting impossible standards that guarantee failure and if he or she cannot tolerate failure. Indeed, the patient is unlikely to practice new, imperfect skills (i.e., not do homework) simply because of intolerance of imperfections. Similarly, training will not work if the patient interprets cues wrongly, or if he or she irrationally infers from failed performances to failed identity and withdraws (gives up).

It is to these neglected and fundamental aspects of the generation of socially skilled behavior (and the building up of competencies, scripts, etc.) that rational–emotive therapy (Ellis, 1962; Ellis & Grieger, 1977) and cognitive therapy (Beck, 1976) can be most appropriately and power-fully applied. These procedures are addressed to the very inferences and evaluations so commonly found in socially dysfunctioning patients, and which undoubtedly prevent or deter the acquisition and generation of social skill (Dryden, in press; Trower, 1981; Trower, O'Mahony, & Dryden, in press).

CONCLUSION

In this chapter it has been argued that the problems currently experi-enced in social skills training may be largely generated by a conceptual model that embodies questionable paradigms. By implication, the way ahead is to adopt different paradigms, such as those reviewed earlier, in the hope that these will lead us in new, more fruitful directions.

In conclusion, I suggest three points for further development.

1. Assessment should be aimed at measuring social skill com-petence—the possession of social knowledge, and the ability to produce appropriate plans, and so forth, one methodology being that long-employed in the assessment of intelligence. Further, we should assess individuals' outcome expectancies and the beliefs that generate them.

2. Training should emphasize the process of generating social skill performance rather than (as at present) emphasizing the teaching of the elements of social skills. The theory and method-ology of discourse analysis may well prove useful in this regard (Coulthard, 1977).

3. Training should also include the monitoring, logical disput-ing, and empirical disproving of invalid inferences and negative evaluations, which commonly function to block both the acquisition and generation of social skill. Rational–emotive therapy and cogni-tive therapy presently offer powerful techniques in this direction, and these may well be developed further.

REFERENCES

Argyle, M. Sequences in social behavior as a function of the situation. In G. P. Ginsburg (Ed.), *Emerging strategies in social psychological research*. New York: Wiley, 1979.

Argyle, M., & Kendon, A. The experimental analysis of social performance. In L. Berko-witz (Ed.), *Advances in experimental social psychology*, 1967, 3, 55–98.

Backman, C. W. Epilogue: A new paradigm? In G. P. Ginsburg (Ed.), *Emerging strategies in social psychological research*. New York: Wiley, 1979.

Bandura, A. *Social learning theory*. Englewood Cliffs, N.J.: Prentice-Hall, 1977.

Beck, A. T. *Cognitive therapy and the emotional disorders*. New York: International Universities Press, 1976.

Bellack, A. S. A critical appraisal of strategies for assessing social skill. *Behavioral Assessment*, 1979, *1*, 157–176.

Bellack, A. S., & Hersen, M. Chronic psychiatric patients: Social skills training. In M. Hersen & A. S. Bellack (Eds.), *Behavior therapy in the psychiatric setting*. Baltimore: Williams & Wilkins, 1978.

Bootzin, R. R., & Lick, J. R. Expectancies in therapy research: Interpretive artifact or mediating mechanism? *Journal of Consulting and Clinical Psychology*, 1979, *47*, 852–855.

Bower, G. H., Black, J. B., & Turner, T. J. Scripts in memory for texts. *Cognitive Psychology*, 1979, *11*, 177–220.

Carver, C. S. A cybernetic model of self-attention processes. *Journal of Personality and Social Psychology*, 1979, *37*, 1251–1281.

Clark, J. V., & Arkowitz, H. Social anxiety and self-evaluation of interpersonal performance. *Psychological Reports*, 1975, *36*, 211–221.

Coulthard, M. *An introduction to discourse analysis*. London: Longman, 1977.

Curran, J. P. Social skills: Methodological issues and future directions. In A. S. Bellack & M. Hersen (Eds.), *Research and practice in social skills training*. New York: Plenum Press, 1979.

Dryden, W. Social problems: Cognitive assessment from a rational–emotive perspective. In P. Trower (Ed.), *Cognitive perspectives in social skills training*. Oxford: Pergamon, in press.

Duval, S., & Wicklund, R. A. *A theory of objective self awareness*. New York: Academic Press, 1972.

Ellis, A. *Reason and emotion in psychotherapy*. New York: Lyle Stewart, 1962. (Paperback edition, New York: Citadel Press, 1977.)

Ellis, A., & Grieger, R. (Eds.). *Handbook of rational–emotive therapy*. New York: Springer, 1977.

Endler, N. S., & Edwards, J. Person by treatment interactions in personality research. In L. Pervin & M. Lewis (Eds.), *Perspectives in interactional psychology*. New York: Plenum, 1978.

Fenigstein, A. *Self-consciousness, self-awareness and rejection*. Unpublished doctoral dissertation, University of Texas, 1974.

Fiedler, D., & Beach, L. R. On the decision to be assertive. *Journal of Consulting and Clinical Psychology*, 1978, *46*, 537–546.

Forgus, R. H., & DeWolfe, A. S. Coding of cognitive input in delusional patients. *Journal of Abnormal Psychology*, 1974, *83*, 278–284.

Gergen, K. J. Experimentation in social psychology: A reappraisal. *European Journal of Social Psychology*, 1978, *8*, 507–527.

Ginsberg, G. P. (Ed.). *Emerging strategies in social psychological research*. Chichester: Wiley, 1979.

Goffman, E. *Relations in public: Microstudies of the social order*. Harmondsworth: Penguin, 1972.

Goldsmith, J. B., & McFall, R. M. Development and evaluation of an interpersonal skill-training program for psychiatric patients. *Journal of Abnormal Psychology*, 1975, *84*, 51–58.

Harré, R. The ethogenic approach: Theory and practice. In L. Berkowitz (Ed.), *Advances in experimental social psychology* (Vol. 10). New York: Academic Press, 1977.

Harré, R. *Social being: A theory for social psychology*. Oxford: Blackwell, 1979.

Harré, R., & Secord, P. F. *The explanation of social behaviour*. Oxford: Blackwell, 1972.

Hollandsworth, J. G., & Cooley, M. L. Provoking anger and gaining compliance with assertive versus aggressive responses. *Behavior Therapy*, 1978, *9*, 640–646.

Ickes, W., & Layden, M. A. Attributional styles. In J. H. Harvey, W. Ickes, & R. F. Kidd (Eds.), *New directions in attributional research* (Vol. 2). Hillsdale, N.J.: Erlbaum, 1978.

Jones, E. E., & Nisbett, R. E. *The actor and the observer: Divergent perceptions of the causes of behavior.* Morristown, N.J.: General Learning, 1971.

Kazdin, A. Assessing the clinical or applied importance of behavior change through social validation. *Behavior Modification,* 1977, *1,* 427–452.

Markus, H. Self-schemata and processing information about the self. *Journal of Personality and Social Psychology,* 1977, *35,* 63–78.

Meehl, P. E. The cognitive activity of the clinician. *American Psychologist,* 1960, *15,* 19–27.

Miller, G. A., Galanter, E., & Pribram, K. H. *Plans and the structure of behavior.* New York: Holt, 1960.

Mischel, W. *Personality and assessment.* New York: Wiley, 1968.

Mischel, W. Direct versus indirect personality assessment: Evidence and implications. *Journal of Consulting and Clinical Psychology,* 1972, *38,* 319–324.

Mischel, W. Toward a cognitive social learning reconceptualization of personality. *Psychological Review,* 1973, *80,* 252–283.

Moos, R. H. Situational analysis of a therapeutic community milieu. *Journal of Abnormal Psychology,* 1968, *73,* 49–61.

O'Banion, K., & Arkowitz, H. Social anxiety and selective memory for affective information about the self. *Social Behavior and Personality,* 1977, *5,* 321–328.

O'Donnell, C. R. Behavior modification in community settings. In M. Hersen, R. M. Eisler, & P. M. Miller (Eds.), *Progress in behavior modification* (Vol. 4). New York: Academic Press, 1977.

Pryor, J. B., Gibbons, F. X., Wicklund, R. A., Fazio, R., & Hood, R. Self-focused attention and self-report validity. *Journal of Personality,* 1977, *45,* 513–527.

Sarbin, T. R. Ontology recapitulates philology: The mythic nature of anxiety. *American Psychologist,* 1968, *23,* 411–418.

Schank, R. C., & Abelson, R. P. *Scripts, plans, goals, and understanding.* Hillsdale, N.J.: Erlbaum, 1977.

Scherer, K. R., & Giles, H. (Eds.). *Social markers in speech.* London: Cambridge University Press, 1979.

Schneider, W., & Shiffrin, R. M. Controlled and automatic human information processing: 1. Detection, search and attention. *Psychological Review,* 1977, *84,* 1–66.

Snyder, M. Self-monitoring of expressive behavior. *Journal of Personality and Social Psychology,* 1974, *30,* 526–537.

Snyder, M. Self-monitoring processes. In L. Berkowitz (Ed.), *Advances in experimental social psychology* (Vol. 12). New York: Academic Press, 1979.

Snyder, M., & Monson, T. C. Persons, situations and the control of social behavior. *Journal of Personality and Social Psychology,* 1975, *32,* 637–644.

Snyder, M., & Swann, W. B., Jr. Hypothesis-testing processes in social interaction. *Journal of Personality and Social Psychology,* 1978, *36,* 1202–1212.

Snyder, M., Tanke, E. D., & Berscheid, E. Social perception and interpersonal behavior: On the self-fulfilling nature of social stereotypes. *Journal of Personality and Social Psychology,* 1977, *35,* 656–666.

Storms, M. D., & McCaul, K. D. Attribution processes and the emotional exacerbation of dysfunctional behavior. In J. H. Harvey, W. J. Ickes, & R. F. Kidd (Eds.), *New directions in attribution research* (Vol. 1). Hillsdale, N.J.: Erlbaum, 1976.

Strawson, P. F. *Individuals: An essay in descriptive metaphysics.* London: Methuen University Paperbacks, 1959.

Taylor, S. E., & Fiske, S. T. Salience, attention and attribution: Top of the head phenomena. In L. Berkowitz (Ed.), *Advances in experimental social psychology* (Vol. 11). New York: Academic Press, 1978.

Trower, P. Fundamentals of interpersonal behavior—a social-psychological perspective.

In A. Bellack & M. Hersen (Eds.), *Research and practice in social skills training*. New York: Plenum Press, 1979.

Trower, P. Situational analysis of the components and processes of behavior of socially skilled and unskilled patients. *Journal of Consulting and Clinical Psychology*, 1980, *48*, 327–339.

Trower, P., O'Mahony, J. M., & Dryden, W. Cognitive aspects of social failure: Some implications for social skills training. *British Journal of Guidance and Counselling*, in press.

Trower, P. E. Social skill disorder: Mechanisms of failure. In R. Gilmour & S. Duck (Eds.), *Personal relationships in disorder*. London: Academic Press, 1981.

Ventola, E. The structure of casual conversation. *Journal of Pragmatics*, 1979, *3*, 267–298.

Vernon, P. E. *Personality assessment: A critical survey*. New York: Wiley, 1964.

Wallace, C. J., Nelson, C., Lukoff, D., Webster, C., Rappe, S., & Ferris, C. *Cognitive skills training*. Paper presented at the annual meeting of the Association for the Advancement of Behavior Therapy, Chicago, November 1978.

AUTHOR INDEX

429

SUBJECT INDEX